STRUGGLE IN THE COUNTRYSIDE

International Development Research Center
William J. Siffin, Director
Studies in Development, No. 10

STRUGGLE IN THE COUNTRYSIDE

Politics and Rural Labor
in Chile, 1919-1973

by Brian Loveman

INDIANA UNIVERSITY PRESS
BLOOMINGTON AND LONDON

Published in Canada by Fitzhenry & Whiteside Limited, Don Mills, Ontario

Manufactured in the United States of America

Library of Congress Cataloging in Publication Data

Loveman, Brian.
    Struggle in the countryside.

    (International Development Research Center. Studies in development,
no. 10)
    1. Land tenure—Chile.   2.   Land reform—Chile.   3.   Chile—Rural
conditions.   I.   Title.   II.   Series: Studies in development (Bloomington)
no. 10.
HD505.L68   1975   333.1'0983   74-6521
ISBN 0-253-35565-6   1 2 3 4 5 80 79 78 77 76

CONTENTS

vi : CONTENTS

LIST OF FIGURES

LIST OF TABLES

LIST OF MAPS

FOREWORD

This is a valuable statement about an important topic in a
significant country, a contribution to the store of ordered
knowledge about rural mobilization and land reform in Chile.
This volume also offers insights into larger issues—of Latin
American politics and one type of setting for efforts at rural
transformation.

Chilean politics has roots in a rural past. Key parts of that
past are peasant activism and a complex interplay of government, landowners, and Chilean labor organizations in "managing" and suppressing that activism. The recent decades
have been systematically described and analyzed by R. Kaufman in *The Politics of Land Reform in Chile 1950-1970*.
The work at hand adds almost a third of a century to the
record, along with added evidence of the recent past. It documents a tumultuous politics marked by the repression of
rural labor and the protection of a manorial tenure system.
The use of bureaucratic means in the service of establishmen-
tarian ends is not exactly novel. The vivid details of such an
arrangement have seldom been presented with the authority
found in this book. Students of Chilean government and
history, of Latin American politics, of land reform, and of
urban-rural political relations in so-called developing countries will find this a valuable case study. The emphasis is
upon the complex pattern of a particular political history.
The lessons are left for the reader.

The book is one of a number of *Studies in Development*
produced with the support of Indiana University's International Development Research Center—support made possible by a grant from the Ford Foundation. For the scholar
who wishes to look further into the evidence behind this
study, documentation is available from the Center: *Struggle
in the Countryside: A Documentary Supplement*. The import of the evidence is presented in this book: class and
party alliances were devised and maintained to exploit the

rural work force in the service of political stability, for a time, with effects that ultimately challenged the aims and intentions of the allies.

William J. Siffin, Director
International Development Research Center
Indiana University

PREFATORY NOTE

A common anecdote in Chile has it that as God neared completion of the creation He found that He had a little bit of almost
every ingredient left over—so He created Chile. Continental
Chile is a long narrow strip of land extending from the arid
northern deserts of Tarapacá Province (18°S) to the cold windy
Patagonian plains of Magallanes (56°S). Chile also claims extensive portions of the Antarctic territory (50°W-90°W).[1] With
this 2630-mile stretch that averages 100 miles in width and nowhere exceeds 250 miles from its western boundary at the Pacific Ocean to the eastern frontier of the Andes range, Chile
indeed includes a little bit of everything except tropics.

Northern Chile is one of the driest places in the world and
boasts one of the few weather stations at which no rain has ever
been recorded.[2] Southern Chile is one of the rainiest parts of
South America, "where glaciers descend from snow-covered
mountains to a deeply fiorded coast."[3] Between these two ex-
tremes is middle Chile, the center of population concentration,
economic activity, and national politics. Middle Chile contains
the Chilean central valley, a narrow fertile depression between
the Andes on the east and the coastal mountain range and the
sea on the west.

The variety of Chilean landscapes, topography, and climate
may be illustrated by comparing Chile with the inverted strip of
land running from the desert of Baja California to the Yukon
and Alaska. The Chilean "Great North," or Norte Grande,
which includes the provinces of Tarapacá and Antofagasta, encompasses a desert more barren than the Sahara but rich in copper and nitrates. First the nitrate fields and then the copper
mines have been the principal earners of foreign exchange for
Chile from the late nineteenth century until the present. The
mineral wealth of the northern deserts allowed a relatively small
proportion of Chile's population to produce a relatively large
share of the nation's income in a sparsely settled territory (see
Map 1).

Arica
Pisagua
Iquique
TARARACA
Tocopilla
Calama
Antofagasta
ANTOFAGASTA
Taltal
Chañaral
ATACAMA
Copiapó
Vallenar
Freirina
La Serena
Vicuña
Coquimbo
Ovalle
COQUIMBO
Combarbala
Illapel

● Provincial Capital
○ Departmental Capital

MAP 1   CHILE: THE "NORTE GRANDE" AND "NORTE CHICO"

South of the Norte Grande the provinces of Atacama, Coquimbo, and part of Aconcagua form the "Little North," or
Norte Chico, a gradual transition from the desert to steppes and
the fertile central valley. The central region, or middle Chile, includes part of Aconcagua Province and extends south to Ñuble
Province and the Bío Bío River (see Map 2). Only along the Bío
Bío River at the southernmost part of the valley region does "a
broad flat-floored valley extend all the way to the Pacific."[4]
The streams and rivers that flow from the Andes across the valley run almost at right angles to the sea. These rivers flow over
land that slopes westward from the base of the Andes so gently
that in many areas ordinary gravity canals can be used for irrigation.[5]

The valley has a mediterranean climate with rainfall increasing gradually from the northern transitional desert regions in
Coquimbo to the southern boundary of the region at the Bío
Bío River. The climate and the fertility of the valley's soil provide ideal conditions for intensive truck farming, and for orchards and vineyards in addition to grain crops and livestock.
With the advantage of a harvest season when Europe and North
America enter the winter months, the central valley offers Chile
a potential source of foreign exchange through the export of
high-quality fruits, vegetables, wines, dairy products, and other
specialty crops. Despite this potential for the development of
highly specialized intensive agriculture, throughout Chilean history the central valley has been dominated by a relatively small
number of large estates (*haciendas* or *fundos*) engaged in extensive wheat production and animal husbandry along with vine
cultivation. Into the 1960s only a minority of the haciendas
had moved from traditional patterns of cultivation to more
modern agricultural practices and labor relations.

The industrial center of Concepción and its port, Talcahuano,
serve as the doorway to the "frontier" provinces of Arauco,
Bío Bío, Malleco, and Cautín, south of the Bío Bío River (see
Map 3). This region takes its name from the historical role it
played in the struggle between the Spanish invaders and the
indigenous Indian population. The Bío Bío River marked the
limits of Spanish and then Chilean control well into the nineteenth century. In this region "instead of irrigated fields on
sloping alluvial fans . . . are lands cleared of the forest, bristling

ACONCAGUA
San Felipe
VALPARAÍSO
Valparaíso
Santiago
SANTIAGO
Rancagua
O'HIGGINS
Sn. Fernando
COLCHAGUA
CURICÓ
Curicó
Talca
TALCA
Linares
MAULE
LINARES
Cauquenes
Chillán
ÑUBLE

● Provincial Capital
○ Departmental Capital

MAP 2   CENTRAL CHILE

● Provincial Capital
○ Departmental Capital

MAP 3   CHILE: "LA FRONTERA"

with stumps and littered with the wreckage that accompanies forest clearing the world over."[6] From Arauco to Cautín, the overgrazed, overutilized lands of the Mapuche and "Chilean" smallholders present a vivid red-brown image of eroded soil on the increasingly denuded coastal mountains and on the valley floor. To the east the Andes continue to dominate but are not so high as they are north of the Bío Bío River.

Agriculture in the frontier region depends much less on irrigation than is the case in the central valley of middle Chile. Indeed, while irrigation is a key to agriculture north of the Bío Bío, drainage is a critical concern in the farms in the frontier region and farther south. Cattle, dairy farms, and cereal production predominate in the agriculture of this region while a backward timber industry provides seasonal employment for numerous rural workers.

South of the frontier region the provinces of Valdivia, Osorno, and Llanquihue constitute the Lake Region (see Map 4), a rainy area of hardwood forests. An extension of the frontier region, these provinces experience heavy rainfall. Valdivia receives about three times as much annual rainfall as does Tacoma, Washington (Valdivia 104.8 inches; Tacoma, 40.4 inches). Storminess increases toward the higher latitudes and is greater, latitude for latitude, in Chile than in North America.[7]

Extreme southern continental Chile, from the island of Chiloé to Magallanes, is the sparsely inhabited Canal Region (see Map 5). In Aysén and Magallanes sheep ranching on vast estates is the principal "agricultural" activity. Chiloé is an island of smallholders engaged in potato cultivation, some lumbering, and diversified subsistence agriculture.

Agriculture and the Distribution of Agricultural Property

With some exceptions, notably in the frontier region and in Chiloé, agricultural land in Chile prior to 1964 was highly concentrated in a relatively small number of large estates. In 1962 Marvin Sternberg wrote that the "concentration of landownership in Chile is among the highest in the world."[8] In 1955, 4.4 percent of landholders owned approximately 80.9 percent of the total farm land, 77.7 percent of the agricultural land, 51.5 percent of the arable land, and 43.8 percent of the irrigated land.[9] According to the agricultural census of 1964-65, less

Valdivia

VALDIVIA

La Union
Rio Bueno

Osorno

OSORNO

Rio Negro

Pto. Varas
Pto. Montt

LLANQUIHUE

Maullin
Calbuco

Castro
Achao

CHILOÉ

● Provincial Capital
○ Departmental Capital

MAP 4   CHILE: "THE LAKE REGION"

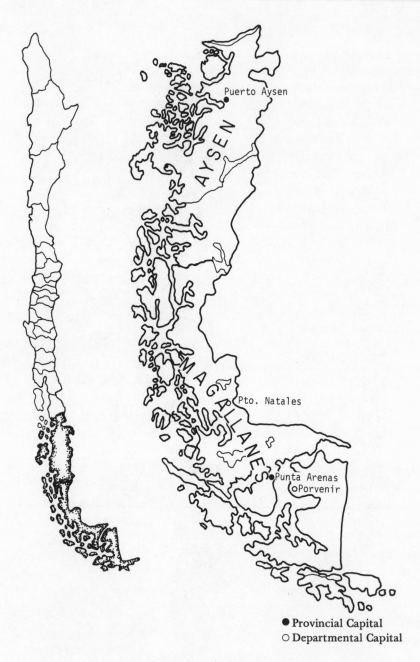

Puerto Aysen

AYSEN

MAGALLANES

Pto. Natales

Punta Arenas
○Porvenir

● Provincial Capital
○ Departmental Capital

MAP 5   CHILE: "LOS CANALES"

than 7,000 farms (out of a total of 253,532) contained approximately 73 percent of all the agricultural land in Chile.[10] The large estates typically underutilized good farm land and left large amounts of irrigated land in natural pastures. From 1945 onward Chilean agricultural production failed to keep pace with domestic population growth, thus becoming a drag on the national economy.

At the other end of the spectrum, some 150,000 farms with less than 10 hectares each (more than half the farms in the country) contained only 2 percent of Chile's agricultural land.[11] This division of the country's farms into a small number of large estates and a large number of subsistence or less-than-subsistence plots is often characterized as the "latifundia-minifundia complex." This pattern dominated the Chilean countryside throughout the nineteenth and twentieth centuries. The political implications of this type of land tenure pattern is a principal theme in the study that follows.

Administrative Divisions

At the time this study was carried out, Chile was divided into twenty-five provinces for purposes of internal administration. Each province was headed by an *intendente* appointed directly by the president of the Republic. The 1925 constitution also provided for provincial assemblies, but these were never constituted. The intendente was the direct representative of the president in each province and, as such, the formal supervisor of all public works and services of the national government.

Each province was in turn divided into departments, the departments into subdelegations, and the subdelegations into districts. The department was headed by a *gobernador* named by the president of the Republic on the recommendation of the intendente of the province. The gobernador could be removed by the intendente with the approval of the president. The gobernador of each department appointed a *subdelegado* as the agent in the subdelegation. He, in turn, named inspectors for each district and could remove them upon prior report to the gobernador that justified such action.

Each subdelegation theoretically corresponded to still another subdivision, the commune. The local administration of each commune was vested in a municipal council elected by the constituents. The council elected a mayor from among its members except in cities of over 100,000, where the mayor could be appointed by the president of the Republic and remunerated for his services. These "local governments" had extremely meager revenues and depended heavily on subsidies from the central government.

ACKNOWLEDGMENTS

The research which made this study possible was financed by the Foreign Area Fellowship Program. In addition to financial support, FAFP's Michael Potashnik provided valuable advice and personal encouragement, for which I am grateful. A Woodrow Wilson Dissertation Fellowship and a fellowship from Indiana University's International Development Research Center supported the writing stage of the project from late 1971 until 1973.

While in Chile I benefited from the stimulation and institutional support of a group of Chilean scholars at ICIRA. Special thanks must go to Enrique Astorga, the national director of ICIRA while I did my research. Enrique supported my efforts to do what many would consider politically sensitive research at a most difficult moment in Chile. Juan Carlos Collarte eased me into an ongoing research project when I arrived in Chile and taught me a great deal about ICIRA and Chilean politics. To him I am especially grateful. I also benefited from discussing my research with Hugh Zelelman, Sergio Gomez, Rafael Baraona, and Cristóbal Kay.

In addition to these Chilean scholars, Almino Affonso, the senior author of the most important study on the rural labor movement in Chile, patiently watched my study develop, made suggestions when they were asked for, answered the numerous questions I posed, and generously allowed me access to the raw data from his own study. His cooperation and encouragement made my stay in Chile that much more productive and enjoyable.

Two American scholars in Chile also provided valuable assistance. Marion Brown of the University of Wisconsin Land Tenure Center not only contributed intellectual stimulation but also made available to me institutional support for much of the field work I did in Chile. This support was even more impressive because it allowed me to do interviewing in fundos and asentamientos where Marion's own research team planned to visit—

before his team carried out its project. This sort of assistance is understandably uncommon. I only hope that someday I can partially repay Marion's generosity.

Without the support of Solon Barraclough this study could not have been carried out. Professor Barraclough is perhaps the foremost expert on Chilean agriculture. As international director of ICIRA he welcomed me upon my arrival in Santiago and from that time on supported my research personally and with the institutional resources at his command. Never once was he too busy to answer my questions, talk to me about my research, or to help me gain access to materials I considered important for the study. Professor Barraclough has also read and commented on most of the chapters of this study. While he doesn't share some of the views expressed herein, his advice and support were invaluable.

The personnel in the Chilean Labor Department and especially in the Labor Archive not only permitted me to do a minute review of the materials in the Archive, but they also assisted me in every possible way, for which I will be forever grateful. Special thanks must go to my friends Maria Saavedra, Clementina Gutiérrez, Manuel Avalos, and Eduardo Mardones. They not only assisted me in my research but also attempted to keep my body warm in the chilly *cueva* where the archival materials were housed. Thanks also must be given to Julian Gonzalorena, who taught me much about the Chilean Labor Department and allowed me to sit in on the sessions of the Junta de Conciliación Agrícola during 1971. Finally, a word of praise for Luz, who patiently cooked eggs for a *gringo* when *las guatitas le hicieron mal.*

As I wrote this study, Professors Alfred Diamant, Iliya Harik, Vincent Ostrom, and James Scobie critically reviewed the manuscript and made suggestions for revision. Philip Sabetti, William Siffin, and Dennis Smith also read and commented on individual chapters. John Hamilton assisted with the preparation of the graphs. Mary Zielinski did a greatly appreciated job of typing the original lengthy manuscript. In addition, the members of the Workshop in Political Theory and Policy Analysis at Indiana University provided valuable intellectual stimulation while I prepared the manuscript.

Marie Mitchell at the International Development Research

Center, Indiana University, provided valuable assistance and support in preparing the material for publication. I would also like to thank Karen Craig for careful, sympathetic editing of the manuscript.

Finally, thanks to Sharon, who edited my prose and put up with my sixteen-hour-a-day love affair with documents in the Chilean Labor Archive.

While I have had much help in carrying out this study, those who provided assistance bear no responsibility for the remaining errors of omission or commission that may still exist in the study.

Unless otherwise indicated, all translations from Spanish to English are my own.

INTRODUCTION

The "land question," or "agrarian question," has been a persistent parameter of Chilean national politics since the end of World War I, taking on increased importance in periods of national political crisis. This was the case in Chile, as in many other political communities, because the system of rural property and rural proprietorship constituted an important element in the existing political order. But in Chile challenges to the system of rural property were also challenges to the very foundations of the Chilean polity—a political system whose highly touted stability and ongoing formal democracy depended for its maintenance upon the dominance of the owners of large rural estates over the rural labor force.

From the time of the Spanish conquest of the territory of Chile, rural proprietorship entailed extensive authority over the rural labor force. The *encomienda* (literally "trust") legalized the exploitation of Indian labor in the mines and in agricultural enterprises by "commending" the care and protection of the Indians in a designated territory to favored Spanish settlers. Usually the encomienda did not vest property rights in land with the conquerors, although sometimes the Indians together with their land passed into the trust of favored Spaniards.[1] Legal title to the land generally remained with the Spanish crown, but because the number of sedentary Indians in Chile was small, the commendation of the native population in a region typically degenerated into de facto control of large tracts of rural property.[2]

Unlike the encomienda, the *merced* ("grant") assigned property rights in rural land to designated conquistadores and later settlers. Introduced into the Spanish American colonies in 1495-1497, the merced played a less important role in Chile during the sixteenth century than did the encomienda.[3] Initially, local governmental officials (the *cabildo*) and the agents of the crown (governors) conceded mercedes to settlers subject to royal confirmation, but the Spanish monarchy soon moved

xxv

to attempt to protect the Indians from the conquerors' rapaciousness by restricting the authority of the cabildo to grant mercedes.

> In Chile the cabildos as well as the governors were characterized by a tendency to hand out lands in a most liberal fashion. . . . Since Chile was a frontier region, at war [with the Indians], the needs of war asserted themselves. The government had to depend upon the settlers [*vecinos*], especially the *encomenderos* [holders of encomienda grants], to sustain the conquest during the sixteenth century.
>
> When granting mercedes the conquerors in Chile did not take into account the needs of the indigenous population. In some cases the merced included Indian settlements themselves; the Indians were then relocated.[4]

During the remainder of the colonial period different types of rural properties were introduced, including the *repartimiento*, *mercedes de estancia, comunidad de pastos,* and *composiciones.* On various occasions the crown also auctioned off land to raise revenues. The different property types entailed varying investitures of authority in individuals to possess, use, and alienate real estate. For example, after a period of conflict and litigation, the estancia came to include the right to pasture animals and to build corrals that enclosed two *cuadras* of land.[5] The right of *demasia* allowed acquisition of property rights (*propiedad*) in vacant lands adjacent to an existing merced.

Despite the variety of property types, the study by Borde and Góngora of the Valley of Puange[6] and the study by Rafael Baraona et al. of the Valley of Putaendo[7] conclude that the great majority of large estates (*haciendas* or *fundos*) that dominated the Chilean rural sector from the seventeenth century onward originated in the mercedes, although some mercedes were made to original holders of encomienda grants. At the beginning of the seventeenth century large amounts of the best agricultural land had already been concentrated in relatively few rural estates.[8]

The large estates served as huge "corrals" for extensive livestock husbandry oriented primarily, but not exclusively, to the domestic market.[9] Near the end of the seventeenth century some landowners turned to wheat production, partially as a response to the demands of the Peruvian market.[10] Because wheat production required more labor than had the extensive livestock operations, the estate owners moved to attract a resident labor force by offering rentals (*préstamos de tierra*). Kay describes the development of the hacienda system in the eighteenth century as follows:

> Due to the new market opportunities, especially for wheat, it was profitable for the landlords to settle as much labor as possible on the estate, particularly by attracting them with tenancies. As the distribution of tenancies did not generally entail any reduction in the land cultivated by the Hacienda Enterprise, it was profitable to settle as many tenants as possible so as to maximize rent income. Tenancies were introduced to such an extent that even former labourers of the Hacienda Enterprise [*peones estables*] were able to secure one, especially during the second half of the 18th century.
>
> The Hacienda System, which during the 17th century had more labourers [peones and slaves] than tenants [*préstamos de tierra*], due to the process of cerealization, increased the number of *arrendatario* tenants to such an extent that they generally outnumbered the labourers of the Hacienda Enterprise.[11]

As population increased within the haciendas the bargaining position of the workers eroded. During the last part of the eighteenth century a commutation of money and kind rents for labor rents began.[12] The gradual replacement of the peon by labor rents has been cited as the origin of the Chilean system of *inquilinaje*, an arrangement whereby resident workers exchange varying amounts of labor for access to productive land and other perquisites.[13] As population continued to increase, the terms of inquilinaje deteriorated to the disadvantage of the rural worker. Toward the end of the eighteenth century the estate owners began to demand a *peón obligado* ("compulsory worker") as part of the tenant's rent. During the nineteenth century the inquilino was required to provide one or more workers to the hacienda for a specified number of days, depending upon the amount of land leased and other perquisites enjoyed.[14] Some inquilinos paid workers to perform their labor services, whereas poorer inquilinos sent members of their families or performed the labor themselves.[15] In this fashion the *hacendado* came to occupy the peak position in the stratified "community" contained within his private rural estate.

By the beginning of the nineteenth century, when independence separated the Spanish colonies from the Spanish crown, the small class of hacendados not only dominated the countryside but constituted a social and political aristocracy with urban residence. Throughout the nineteenth century the ability of the Chilean landed aristocracy to absorb new elements preserved their integrity as a ruling class.[16] The pattern of economic development in Chile was such that the agrarian social structure and, therefore, the base of the *terratenientes* ("landowners") as a class was left largely intact.[17] The hacendados dominated rural Chile and Chilean national politics well into the twentieth century. Property in rural land provided the foundation for national political power, and national political power, in turn, allowed the owners of large estates to protect their rural properties and their political domination of the rural population.

The rural basis of the aristocracy's political power periodically made land reform a prominent national issue after World War I. Repeatedly the hacendados made marginal concessions to middle-class and Marxist political parties, urban interest groups, and labor unions in order to preserve their hold on the countryside. Between 1930 and 1964 competing interests and classes, represented by political parties, workers' organizations, and bureaucratic entrepreneurs, gnawed away at the perquisites and power of the hacendados. To a great extent, however, the underlying stability of the Chilean political system from 1932 until 1964 stemmed from the ability of the hacendados to prevent fundamental transformations in the countryside. They accomplished this through concessions to urban interests in matters involving industrialization and economic policy in exchange for nonintervention of the state in the countryside—except to aid the hacendados and, particularly, to assist them in the repression of rural labor.

But the terms of the "agreement" were rarely explicit. Landowners, urban interests, political parties, and bureaucrats all violated the conditions of the implicit bargain that shaped Chile's political stability. Rural laborers (*campesinos*), never a party to the bargain, recurrently and persistently challenged the existing political order. After 1958 the basis for the stable equilibrium disappeared, and after 1964 the root of the hacendados' power —the existing system of property in rural land—was destroyed. By the end of 1973 the hacienda system itself had been destroyed, and the situation of the rural labor force as well as the political meaning of property in rural land had been radically altered. The leaders of the military coup that ousted President Salvador Allende in September 1973 sought initially to reverse the deposed regime's resolution of the agrarian question, but in so doing immediately recognized the continued significance of the agrarian question in Chilean politics.

Politics and Property in Rural Land

Property in rural land, of course, is but a part of the wider property system that exists in any political community. Historically, however, property in rural land has been a central issue in local, regional, and national politics. Calls for agrarian reform have accompanied every major twentieth-century revolution, including those in the Soviet Union, Mexico, and China. Thus, before entering into discussion of the Chilean case, it is necessary to deal analytically with the political meaning of property in rural land.

Rural land tenure and property systems are interesting from the standpoint of politics[18] insofar as they influence or determine control by some human beings over the behavior of others. This is the meaning of politics in its most elemental sense. Political power is simply the *capability* to influence the behavior of other human beings in intended directions and intensities.[19] Political power may derive from numerous sources. An important source of political power in rural societies is control over natural resources, especially land and water.[20] The importance of land as a source of political power derives in part from its uniqueness as a basis for production and employment. Where there are few or no alternatives to land-based production and occupational opportunity, control over this resource essentially determines the work routine, daily diet, income, and living conditions of the rural population.[21]

Where dependence for the satisfaction of basic human needs is linked to control over land and water resources, these resources become critical political variables. It is not surprising, therefore, that agrarian reform has become a central political issue in one form or another in almost all human communities and nation states.[22]

Land Reform, Agrarian Reform, and the Political Meaning of Property in Rural Land

Land reforms and, more broadly, agrarian reforms, are usually thought of as measures to improve the conditions of small

farmers and rural workers. Indeed, "land reform is often an article of faith. Undeterred by documented evidence of its success
or failure or by doctrinal heresies, it has appeared in nearly
every catechism of social justice prepared for the Third World
in the last quarter century."[23] Yet, there is no intrinsic guarantee that land reform or agrarian reform necessarily improves the
living conditions of rural labor, increases its political power, or
assures better long-term prospects for the agricultural economy.
Land and agrarian reforms include a large range of legal, organizational, and economic alternatives. Many of these alternatives
may make rural labor worse off rather than better off, just as
they may lead to varied outcomes for the agricultural economy
and the larger political community in which they are undertaken.

While writings and discussions of agrarian change often use
the terms "land reform" and "agrarian reform" interchangeably,
in the present book land reform refers to redefinition and redistribution of property in rural land. Agrarian reform, which usually includes land reform, refers to all governmental policies
that alter the political meaning of property in rural land. The
success of governmental agrarian reforms, when success is defined as improvement in the living and working conditions of
the rural population and as an increase in both agricultural production and productivity, depends heavily upon the extent and
quality of mobilization, organization, and technical-managerial
education of the rural labor force. Analytically, it is possible to
distinguish between governmental land and agrarian reforms and
nongovernmental agrarian changes. In practice, however, the implementation (or nonimplementation) of governmental agrarian
programs depends upon the social and economic context, the
balance of forces among contending classes and interest groups
within the polity, and the role of rural labor in the agrarian reform process. For this reason, analysis of agrarian reform must
take into account the nongovernmental influences as well as
the narrower governmental definition of agrarian reform policies and objectives.

An agrarian reform that includes land reform may radically
alter the political meaning of property in rural land without
benefiting rural labor. Depending upon the content and structure of redistribution of proprietary authority and the types of

production units established in the countryside by land reform, agrarian reform may provide effective political power for rural labor or it may increase its subjugation. The outcome in this respect depends upon the relationships established among the new proprietors, between them and urban interests, and upon governmental policy in the countryside.

When the traditional rural proprietor is replaced by or supplemented with new forms of proprietorship, the entrepreneurial function performed by previous proprietors must be carried out by the new proprietors. The linkages of existing proprietors to factor and product markets are not automatically transferred to new proprietary interests. Indeed, traditional sources of agricultural inputs, credit, and technical services as well as customary marketing channels may not be available to workers' enterprises or to recipients of smallholds. Hostility of private capitalists to innovations in proprietary arrangements, which may be seen as a direct threat to their own interests, can be an important obstacle to the operation of new types of rural proprietorship. If favorable substitutes for traditional sources of agricultural inputs, credit, technical assistance, and marketing channels are not available, whether from governments or in the market, deterioration in production may make the new proprietors worse off rather than improve their situation. Similarly, if farm management and marketing skills are not a part of the existing campesino repertoire or are not provided through extension programs, economic ruin may accompany reforms that claim to bring political liberation.

Again, the new proprietors' initial dependence on governmental agencies and governmental policy is evident. If this dependence is not matched by some degree of effective control by the new proprietors over governmental purveyors of goods and services, the dependency of traditional *patrón*-laborer relationships is merely shifted from the private to the governmental sphere. In neither case is there a guarantee of benevolence. In order for new proprietary arrangements to compete with other types of enterprises in a mixed rural economy or to defend their interests vis-à-vis governmental agencies in a system that excludes capitalist enterprise, the development of politico-organizational strength, in addition to farm management and technical skills, is essential. If the new farm operators or their organizations cannot effectively exercise proprietary authority, either governmental bureaus or capitalist entrepreneurs will impose their priorities and authority upon the new proprietors. Where the capitalist alternative is precluded, substitution of bureaucratic oppressors for private oppressors leaves rural labor nonetheless exploited. Only agrarian reform which includes a participatory, relatively autonomous role for rural labor may provide the basis for the political liberation of the rural work force. This liberation cannot be bestowed. Only by developing an independent political capability, based on a reformed legal order and the requisite political determination and organizational strength, can rural labor and other new proprietors maintain the persistent vigilance and efficacy necessary to defend their interests.

Agrarian reform, like any reform, is a political artifact subject to the vicissitudes of the ongoing political process. It can be undone, corrupted, or detoured. Agrarian reform may be part of a rising middle-class effort to displace aristocratic rule, of a revolutionary effort to establish a new utopia, or of a pacification program to construct a social bulwark against communism. The question for rural labor remains the same: What power does it have in determining the terms upon which its labor is sold and used and the manner in which the economic surplus produced in the countryside and the broader political community is distributed? Unless agrarian reform entails the development of relatively autonomous political capability by rural labor, no one will ask the *campesino* his preference in these fundamental political questions. For agrarian reform to benefit rural labor directly, the redefinition and redistribution of property in rural land must provide rural laborers with effective decision-making capability in the rural enterprise and in governmental policymaking that affects the rural sector.

This book focuses on the political processes and social forces that transformed the traditional system of property in rural land in Chile from 1919 until the military coup of 1973. It also examines the redefinition and redistribution of property in rural land and the expanding activist participation of rural labor in Chilean politics. Starting with a framework for the analysis of the political meaning of property in rural land, the book traces the forces which led to the alteration of the rural property system and seeks to evaluate the new meaning of property in rural land which emerged in the agrarian reform programs of the last decade. Throughout, the book emphasizes that, in contrast to conventional wisdom about rural Chile, the transformation of the Chilean countryside between 1919 and 1973 cannot be understood without reference to the long struggle of the campesinos, aided by urban political parties, labor organizations, and the urbanization of the countryside, to wrest control of the rural sector from the hacendados.

LIST OF ABBREVIATIONS

ACR   *Acción Católica Rural* (Catholic Rural Action)

ANOC   *Asociación Nacional de Organizaciones Campesinas* (National Association of Peasant Organizations)

ASICH   *Acción Sindical Chilena* (Chilean Syndical Action)

CIDA   *Comité Interamericano de Desarrollo Agrícola* (Inter-American Committee for Agricultural Development)

CNC   *Confederación Nacional Campesina* (National Peasant Confederation)

CORFO   *Corporación de Fomento de la Produccion* (Chilean Development Corporation; governmental agency)

CORA   *Corporación de la Reforma Agraria* (Chilean Agrarian Reform Corporation; governmental agency)

CTCH   *Confederación de Trabajadores de Chile* (Chilean Confederation of Workers)

CUT   *Central Única de Trabajadores de Chile* (the most important workers central after 1953, uniting the communist and socialist factions of the CTCH, which disappeared)

ECA   *Empresa de Comercio Agricola* (Agricultural Trade Agency; governmental agency)

FAO   Food and Agriculture Organization, United Nations

FCI   *Federación Nacional Campesina e Indígena* (National Federation of Peasants and Indians)

FINTA   *Federación Industrial Nacional de Trabajadores*

Agrícolas (National Industrial Federation of Agricultural Workers)

FOCH   *Federación Obrera de Chile* (Chilean Federation of Workers)

FRAP   *Frente de Acción Popular* (Popular Action Front)

ICIRA   *Instituto de Capacitación e Investigación en Reforma Agraria* (Agrarian Reform Training and Research Institute; joint UN-Chilean governmental agency)

IER   *Instituto de Educación Rural* (Institute for Rural Education)

INDAP   *Instituto de Desarrollo Agropecuario* (Institute for Agricultural Development; governmental agency)

MCI   *Movimiento Campesino Independiente* (Independent Peasant Movement)

OIT (ILO)   *Organización Internacional del Trabajo* (International Labor Organization)

SFF   *Sociedad de Fomento Fabril* (National Manufacturers Society)

SNA   *Sociedad Nacional de Agricultura* (National Agricultural Society)

UCC   *Unión de Campesinos Cristianos* (Christian Peasants Union)

1
The Political Meaning
of Property in Rural Land

1
A Framework for Analysis

The critical relationship between property systems and politics is taken for granted by Marxist and non-Marxist scholars alike. Lenin, in *State and Revolution*, declares that only when there is no difference between members of a society in their relation to the social means of production—that is, no private property in the social means of production—does it become possible to speak of freedom.[1] Milton Friedman, in *Capitalism and Freedom*, argues that, whereas capitalism—a competitive market economy with widespread private property in the means of production—is not a sufficient condition for political freedom, it is a necessary condition.[2] Clearly, these authors have different concepts of freedom, but they both recognize that property systems substantially determine the distribution of authority and power within human communities. Changes in property systems entail fundamental reforms in existing political alignments. Where changes in property systems are drastic we conventionally use the term "revolution."

The "agrarian question"—whether in Chile, the rest of Latin America, in polities with market economies, socialist economies, traditional economies, or admixtures—is integrally linked to the broader relationship between property, property systems, and politics. Indeed, rural proprietorship and political power have been so closely intertwined historically that until World War I landowner control of national and regional governmental institutions was taken for granted in much of Europe as well as in Latin America and other parts of the Third World.

But what do we mean by property in rural land, or property more generally for that matter?[3] Property refers to the legal claims of individuals in relation to objects, resources, and

3

events which governmental or quasi-governmental institutions will enforce. These claims may be defined by tradition or by civil, religious, or customary law. Such enforceable claims allow the proprietor to control the behavior of other persons with respect to the object or events claimed as property. The scope and domain[4] of this authority, or the authorization to control the behavior of other persons privately by virtue of property rights, is the core meaning of private property. Thus, "the term property cannot be defined except by defining all the activities which individuals and the community are at liberty or are required to do or not to do, with reference to the object claimed as property."[5]

In the specific case of property in rural land, M.M. Kelso suggests that

> from the standpoint of human behavior, insofar as the activities of the related parties in a land tenure nexus are concerned with control over one another through control over land, their activities are circumscribed by rights, duties, liberties, and exposures which determine the tenure status of each—which *are* the tenure status of each. Each party possesses through his relationship to landed property certain things he *can* do to another if he so desires, and also certain duties to all other parties, certain things he *cannot* do because they will infringe upon the rights of others.[6]

Property in rural land consists of a bundle of claims of varying scope and domain which are more or less enforceable by resort to the coercive capability of the nation state, local governmental institutions, or private surrogates for police or the armed forces.[7] The structure and content of these claims are simultaneously determinants of the human condition in the countryside and products of the struggle which has been waged at any time between those favored by the distribution of property rights and those excluded or relatively disadvantaged.

With the exception of customary arrangements or traditional patterns of land tenure, the source of property in rural land is statutory law that specifies a bundle of rights and obligations which comprise the legal definition of landownership and proprietorship. The content of this bundle of rights and obligations is subject to great variation. It may convey extensive jurisdictional authority over resident populations, limited jurisdiction, or none at all.[8] Also, it may include authorizations for unlimited land use or for limited and specific land use, or it may restrict land use to nonuse.[9]

Property in rural land, thus, as property generally, conveys decision-making authority. Recognition of this basic relationship makes ownership per se a much less important concept in political analysis than the distribution of proprietary claims in relation to the factors of production and the labor force. It matters much less who is the owner of capital or land, than who has the authority to decide how these resources may, may not, or will be used.

In this sense it is important to conceptualize rural labor legislation as an integral formal aspect of any agrarian system which depends upon wage labor, tenants, sharecroppers, or other non-family labor to cultivate the land. In fact, labor legislation must be considered part of the rural property system itself. Where such legislation exists (minimum wages, health codes, social security, tenancy law, rural unionization provisions), it imposes legal limits on proprietorship which must be considered, from the point of view of the landowner, as impositions on the scope or domain of the authority vested in him as proprietor of rural land. Despite the relative significance of labor legislation for the rural land-tenure system, it is completely ignored in most treatments of land or agrarian reform.[10] As the present study seeks to demonstrate, labor legislation, in particular the organization and activity of rural labor unions or syndicates, tends to restructure decision-making capability with respect to labor and land resources in a fashion that redefines the meaning of proprietorship. Land reform, except in the case of parcelization of existing properties or colonization of unsettled land, implies not only a redistribution of property rights but also the *redefinition of property* in rural land.[11]

The political meaning of property in rural land, then, varies greatly depending upon (1) the particular bundle of legal rights assigned to proprietors, (2) the legal limits on proprietorship as these relate to control over both physical resources and human beings, (3) the disposition and capability of governmental or quasi-governmental institutions and officials to enforce both the prerogatives and limits of proprietorship, and (4) the effective capability of proprietors and rural laborers to force officials to respond to their claims.

Property in rural land does not entail a uniform and invariant bundle of legal and customary claims. Different proprietary arrangements assign proprietors varying substantive claims in regard to physical resources and human beings. The distribution of effective decision-making capability with respect to natural resources and the rural labor force is the defining characteristic of any particular system of rural proprietorship.

Using the term property in this fashion suggests a continuum of proprietary authority and mixes of such authority that range from that of a Hobbesian monarch over a territorial domain to that of a functionally limited short-term usufruct with little, if any, territorial jurisdiction over persons. Extensive proprietary authority in regard to natural resources may or may not be combined with extensive scope and domain of authority over the rural labor force. Very limited proprietary authority in regard to natural resources, as in the case of a contractual concession to exploit a mineral resource, may be combined with extensive scope and domain of authority in relation to the labor force.

In dealing with the scope of landowners' authority over the rural work force, we are concerned with the range of values of interest to the workers that are subject to the authoritative discretion of the rural proprietor. The possible answers to this question may be characterized as a continuum, ranging from a narrowly defined authority over specific work functions to a literally totalitarian "all aspects of the worker's life." The scope of authority is further qualified by the (1) temporal limitations on the exercise of authority, (2) spatial limitations, and (3) functional limitations. Thus, a proprietor might have the authority to order workers to do only certain tasks or to do any work that needs to be done. This authority may apply only at the work site, in any part of the estate including the worker's home, or even outside the estate. The worker may be subject to the proprietor's authority during some specified work hours or for twenty-four hours a day, every day. Each of the three parameters may vary independently so that, theoretically, authority limited to work functions might be exercisable twenty-four hours a day, anywhere, and entail ordering a worker to do whatever task the proprietor desires performed.

The domain of the proprietor's authority refers to his jurisdiction, whatever its scope, over determined persons. The domain may include only the worker himself, or it may include some or all family members. It might also extend to all residents of the estate and even, under some circumstances, to nonestate residents, for example, labor obligations of indigenous communities to landowners in the Andean estates. The scope of authority may vary for different persons within the domain of proprietary authority. Very extensive scope of authority may apply only to limited numbers of workers, whereas less extensive authority is exercised over other estate residents. Over some persons subject to his authority a proprietor may exercise only the limited capability to prevent access to his property. In this sense all nonowners of a piece of real estate are within the domain of authority of a landowner. The scope of this authority is limited to restricting trespassing or property damage.

In short, the meaning of property is varied. There is no substantive essence of the concept. As politico-cultural artifacts, property rights may be redefined and redistributed. To conceptualize property in this fashion is incompatible with Marxist or neo-Marxist propositions such as those formulated by Ernesto Laclau:

> We understand by 'mode of production' an integrated complex of social productive forces and relations linked to a determinate type of ownership of the means of production. From among the ensemble of relations of production, we consider those linked to the ownership of the means of production to be the essential relations, since they determine the forms in which the economic surplus is channeled and the effective degree of the division of labor, the basis in turn of the specific capability of the productive forces for expansion. Their own level and rhythm of growth depends in turn on the destination of the economic surplus. We, therefore, designate as a mode of production the logical and mutually coordinated articulation of: 1. a determinate type of ownership of the means of production; 2. a determinate form of appropriation of the economic surplus; 3. a determinate degree of development of the division of labour; 4. a determinate level of development of the productive forces. This is not merely a descriptive enumeration of isolated 'factors,' but a totality, defined by its mutual interconnections. Within this totality, property in the means of production constitutes the decisive element.[12]

Whether certain types of proprietary authority over the means of production may go together with specific forms of appropriation of the economic surplus, division of labor, and level of development of the productive forces is an empirical question. When property in the means of production is conceptualized in a less holistic fashion, it is not self-evident that ownership of the means of production determines either (1) the form in which the surplus is appropriated, (2) the division of labor, or (3) the level of development of the productive forces. Nor is it self-evident that ownership of the means of production determines how the economic surplus, once appropriated, is allocated or reinvested. Governmental regulation, taxation, and other legal restrictions on proprietary authority may effectively determine the way in which the surplus is appropriated, the direction and magnitude of investment, and the share of the surplus accruing to rural labor. When the constraints of governmental regulation, taxation, subsidies, or tariffs and the potential mobilization and organization of the labor force are introduced, then the relationships between particular property arrangements and the other variables in Laclau's "causal" model become matters for investigation rather than ideological assertion.

In the specific case of landownership it is not clear that forms of appropriating the surplus are necessarily or logically linked to particular kinds of ownership, or that different kinds of property rights might not lead to similar forms of appropriating the economic surplus. Corporate farms, individually owned commercial farms, and collective farms might all appropriate the economic surplus in similar fashions. With respect to the division of labor, or to the manner of employing the factors of capital and labor on the land, there is simply no logical or necessary linkage between the type of ownership and the state of the agricultural art on any particular rural property. Some property systems may tend to elicit uniformly identifiable patterns of production, technology, and labor organization, but, again, this is a question for empirical study, not doctrinal assertion.

Before this kind of relationship can be examined, however, it is necessary to examine what is meant by control over the means of production—to define the substantive content of proprietary authority. Notions like "private property" or "socialist property" provide no basis for examining the relationship between property rights and the other variables that Laclau suggests are linked to ownership of the means of production. Rather, within each land-based rural enterprise the content and internal distribution of proprietary authority must be examined.

The following sections of this chapter present an analytical framework based in part on the concept of property suggested above. The framework centers on the political meaning of property in rural land, which encompasses (1) the prerogatives of individual proprietors, (2) the distribution of the prerogatives of proprietorship, (3) the linkages among rural proprietors, (4) the linkages among rural proprietors, urban interests, and national or regional governmental institutions, (5) the linkages among rural laborers, and (6) the linkages among rural laborers, urban interests, and national or regional governmental institutions.

The Prerogatives of Individual Proprietors

In analyzing any particular land system to determine the political meaning of property it is necessary to ask the following questions about the prerogatives of individual proprietors:

(1) *What can the proprietor legally do with the physical resources over which he claims control or ownership?* What legal discretion does the proprietor have in making decisions about land use, land management, farm management, and the conditions of alienation and transfer of the prerogatives of proprietorship? What are the legal constraints that might exist with respect to appropriation of the economic surplus generated in the exploitation of rural land?

Land use may be subject to incentive systems such as taxation, credits, and subsidies. Externally imposed land use policies may legally designate crop zones, minimum standards of productivity, conditions of forest exploitation, and grazing limits.[13] In other contexts, there may exist no external constraint at all. Likewise, land management decisions, including investment policy, modes of production, and labor-management relations, may be subject to few constraints, to relatively extensive regulation, or to no external constraint whatsoever. In the same fashion, alienation of property rights may be accomplished easily and completely, only in part, or almost not at all—at least legally (for example, the Mexican *ejido*).

The range of possible proprietorships is, therefore, quite large. Whatever the forms of proprietorship—individual, familial, cooperative, corporate, collective, public, or other—the legal rights of proprietors in relation to physical resources that they claim as property depend upon the existing system of property law and the complementary legislation that directly or indirectly regulates use and disposition of those resources.

(2) *Does there exist a legal or customary territorial juris-diction of the proprietor over persons residing within or in proximity to his property?* What is the scope and domain of this jurisdiction? What are the legal and customary obligations of rural labor with respect to rural landowners? An answer to these questions must necessarily include reference to legal and customary relationships among independent smallholders, la-borers, tenants, sharecroppers, and the landowner. Of principal concern are the means available to the different interests at hand of enforcing or securing enforcement of these obligations.

(3) *What legal and customary obligations does the landowner have toward the various strata of the rural labor force?* If the proprietors have no legal or customary obligations toward rural labor, or if these are not enforced, the only limits on the terms of the wage bargain or the tenancy agreement are the current state of the labor market and the minimum income necessary for workers to subsist. On the other hand, labor legislation effectively enforced by governmental regulations or the counterweight of militant rural unions can do much to alter the working conditions of rural labor and to restrict the scope and domain of proprietary authority vis-à-vis the labor force. An answer to this question must, minimally, describe the customary and contractual obligations of rural proprietors toward rural labor, services provided by estate owners in ex-change for labor or money payments, and the conditions of tenancy and sharecropping. Also of importance is the content and administration of labor legislation, as well as the legal or de facto status of rural unions and syndicates. All these potential obligations of landowners are limits on proprietary authority and, thus, a part of the political meaning of property in rural land.

(4) *What exclusive legal and customary prerogatives are exercised by landowners or classes of landowners?* In many historical situations extensive landholdings have been the basis for a very limited electoral franchise. In these circumstances we can speak of extension of the franchise as a devaluation of

property rights in rural land. Likewise, rural property may be the key to access to governmental and private goods and services unavailable to nonproprietors. Credit, technical assistance, marketing assistance, subsidies, export bounties, quality and location of public roads, bridges, and irrigation works—these and many other goods and services may be produced, distributed, and priced on terms favorable to landowners or small classes of landowners.

By focusing on the variety of prerogatives contained in any specific property system, it becomes easier to deal with the evolution of a particular set of property rights—their extension, deterioration, redistribution, or redefinition. Whenever the landowner's legal uses of the land have been restricted, his property rights have been diminished. If customary or legal jurisdiction over persons derived from ownership of land is increased or decreased in scope or domain, then the political meaning of property has changed. Finally, if the legal or customary obligations of landowners toward rural labor are increased, or if rural labor is vested with legal decision-making capability with respect to land and labor resources, then the rights of the original owner are constricted to the extent that those who in the past were nonproprietors acquire proprietary prerogatives.

The Distribution of Property in Rural Land

The political meaning of property in rural land derives not only from the bundle of rights and customary prerogatives of individual proprietors but also from the distribution of proprietorship among individuals in a rural community. In addition to the substantive content of property rights, it is necessary to examine the relative concentration or dispersal of proprietorship with respect both to quantity and quality of property controlled and to the correlates of large versus small proprietorship.

If land is relatively abundant and access rights to it are distributed more or less equally within a community, its usefulness as a means to control the behavior of human beings is not very great. Under such circumstances, *ceteris paribus*, the needs of rural dwellers may be met without submitting to the demands of other landowners. Conditions of employment will tend to be relatively more favorable. Further, any exclusive rights of landowners (for example, suffrage, as suggested above) can be easily acquired by those who consider such rights significant.

In fact, however, land as a physical resource (and especially arable land) is generally quite limited, and property in rural land is not evenly distributed. As property in rural land becomes less evenly distributed, control over land becomes an increasingly important base of political power. It is important to note that this remains the case whether proprietorship resides in private owners (individuals, families, corporations) or in public (governmental) administrators. Transfer of extensive rights of proprietorship to nation states and of their administration to public officials simply shifts political capabilities from private owners to governmental officials. Depending upon the bundle of property rights vested in the public officials, and those reserved to rural labor both as individuals and collectively as class organizations, the transfer from private to public proprietorship may or may not be favorable to the rural labor force. In any case, the question of the extent of concentration of the rights of proprietorship remains crucial: concentration of an extreme sort may place rural labor (as well as most of the rest of the national population) in a situation of great dependence on an oligopoly of private or public landowners.

The political significance of the degree of concentration of ownership of rural land depends on the substantive content of rights entailed in landownership. The more extensive the legal definition of landownership, the more political power is concentrated when property ownership of rural land is concentrated. But even if only the decision to sow or leave fallow remains in the hands of individual owners, a regional monopoly or oligopoly of landownership may allow proprietors discretion to sabotage production, cause unemployment, and produce shortages in basic or industrial farm products. This discretion, divorced from all other usual prerogatives of ownership, is substantial political leverage. For this reason, the distribution of landownership is an essential variable in analyzing the political structure of the countryside.

It is also necessary to examine the distribution of proprietary authority within rural land-based enterprises, apart from the question of ownership. The nature of internal distribution of proprietary authority affects the process and quality of management and investment decisions and the production performance of the rural enterprise. Historically, collective proprietorships face certain types of problems (for example, allocation of labor, production incentives) and are forced to deal with issues (for example, social justice, equity, fairness) that private enterprises deal with exclusively through the wage bargain or the labor contract. Production units which are also territorial-governmental jurisdictions or which deal with the provision of a variety of public goods to the work force, must internalize a number of costs that private enterprise generally ignores. This, in turn, has implications for the appropriate and most efficient distribution of proprietary authority within production units. Different distributions of such authority may produce radically different production and social-welfare outcomes for participants within the concern and for those external to and dependent upon it.

It is important to clarify, however, that distribution of proprietorship does not refer simply to physical exploitation or legal title to land resources, whether by private proprietors or by some type of collective proprietorship. Proprietary authority is not necessarily holistic or coincident with formal definitions of ownership. Since the scope and domain of proprietorship may vary (that is, there may exist different types of rural proprietors with different proprietary authority), it is important not to confuse distribution of land among producers with the distribution of proprietary authority. While landownership may be coterminous with all the rights of proprietorship and sovereignty, the scope and domain of proprietary authority also may vary among proprietors.[14] If so, the distribution of proprietary authority in the rural sector does not coincide with the distribution or number of landowners.

It is quite possible for territorial jurisdictions to exist alongside extensive nonjurisdictional landed estates, small commercial farms, subsistence plots, communal holdings, agricultural cooperatives, and a variety of rental arrangements.[15] Assignments of legal authority that may be made to cooperatives or corporate farms are different from those made to individual or family production units. It is evident that even within the context of a relatively simple mix of landholdings, proprietorship may have a variety of meanings, and the distribution of proprietary authority in the sector does not necessarily coincide with the amount of land "owned" by each type of proprietor—even assuming that proprietary authority within each category is uniform. While distribution of land as a physical resource among "owners" may be a convenient starting point in locating the distribution of proprietary authority in the countryside, its use as the only indicator of the distribution of this authority in the rural sector may be misleading.

The Linkages among Rural Proprietors

The third dimension of the political meaning of property in rural land refers to the linkages among rural proprietors. The countryside, divided into separate properties, may be poorly or extensively linked through relationships among individual, familial, corporate, and governmental proprietors. Proprietors may compete for inputs, labor, and markets, or they may deal collectively with these problems, the organizations formed for this purpose providing formal linkages among rural proprietors. Some proprietors may participate in these organizations while others remain outside them. In some instances groups of rural proprietors may form an elite, educated aristocracy socially linked by status and family ties. In other contexts, however, landowners have little in common but the problems and rights of proprietorship, thus lacking organizational and social ties which might be useful to them in defending their proprietary interests.

In general, the better linked the proprietors, the more able they are to defend or enlarge the prerogatives of proprietorship. If and when social, economic, and technological differentiation occurs among the rural proprietors, it becomes more difficult to sustain unified class organizations, except perhaps to defend private proprietorship itself.

Whereas strong class organizations and horizontal linkages may well serve the interests of rural proprietors under conditions of homogeneous agricultural practices, laissez-faire political milieus, and a passive rural labor force, the solidarity of such linkages is threatened by agricultural specialization, technological innovation, governmental regulation, and organized-mobilized rural labor. Under such conditions the agricultural sector can be effectively divided by groups recognizing a diversity of interests among rural landowners and seeking still new sources of differentiation. The class interests of rural proprietors can be further broken up, and the class solidarity diminished, by governmental policies which discriminate between "efficient" and "inefficient" producers, by tax structures which differentiate by crop, type of land, and size of holdings, and by subsidies, export bounties, and tax credits. Thus, the determined application of piecemeal reforms can substantially weaken, as well as divide, proprietors as a class without the costs necessarily incurred by an explicit frontal attack on property itself. On the other hand, governmental policies that adversely affect rural proprietors as a class will tend to induce collective solidarity. Low prices for all agricultural commodities, high tax rates (passed on in rental agreements to tenants), and discrimination against agriculture tend to unite landowners and rural proprietors in opposition to the current regime.

Even in a diversified agricultural sector, landed proprietors will unify to combat an organized-mobilized rural labor force and, particularly, rural unionization. Seasonal peaks in the agricultural cycle—planting, harvest, vineyard maintenance, sheep shearing, and so on—make the rural enterprise particularly vulnerable to organized labor. Because strikes at peak work periods can threaten the loss of a whole year's production, rural unionization, de jure or de facto, will tend to mobilize rural proprietors as a unified class to defend their prerogatives. In a rural sector dominated by traditional latifundia and a landed aristocracy or oligarchy, a mobilized rural labor force will generally be met with concerted class action on the part of the rural proprietors dependent upon non-familial rural labor.

The political capability of farmers to extirpate rural labor movements without resort to the coercive capability of the nation state is a critical measure of the strength of rural proprietors as an autonomous class and of their ability collectively to control the countryside. When this capability does not exist, or has been eliminated, farmers can control mobilized rural labor—or prevent its mobilization—only through the use of public police forces or military intervention.

Also of critical importance is the proprietors' capability to prevent governmental intervention where such intervention would be to their disadvantage. The dependence of farmers on governmental institutions in this situation is clear. Without control over the governmental apparatus, especially those institutions which might adversely affect the scope and domain of their proprietorship as individuals and as a class, the prerogatives of proprietorship cannot be successfully defended. At this point, the linkages of the various proprietors to nonrural interests and to the civil governmental apparatus is of particular concern.

Thus, when discussing the political meaning of property in rural land, the extent and quality of linkages among rural proprietors or groups of proprietors must be ascertained. Reference must be made to social and cultural ties as well as to the existence of formal class organizations which attempt to defend proprietary interests. An important determinant of the solidarity of such class organizations will be the relative differentiation or homogeneity of the rural sector and the types of external threats impinging on the rural proprietors as a class. The capability of rural proprietors to discipline collectively the rural labor force is also of concern. Once this capability disappears, landowners become a class dependent upon the authority of civil government in order to maintain the prerogatives of property in rural land.

The Linkages of Rural Proprietors to Urban Interests and National and Regional Governmental Institutions

Proprietorship of rural land takes on a different meaning when the proprietors have permanent residential, social, familial, economic, and political ties to urban centers. When landowners and rural proprietors depend on urban-centered governments to uphold their proprietary authority, then their participation in national and regional legislatures, the judicial system, political parties, administrative agencies, the church, the police, and the armed forces is a necessary strategy to protect the scope and domain of their proprietorship. Ties to urban-based interest groups and economic enterprise as well as control over the instruments of mass media may also serve to reinforce the power of landowners. It is also essential to determine, therefore, whether rural proprietors are themselves urbanites and, if so, with what kinds of commercial and industrial interests. In the case of Latin America, Solari has correctly pointed out the urban-rural character of the upper classes:

> This character tends to be more or less intense, depending upon the country, but it exists in all. By urban-rural character we understand herein that the rural upper class, although it obtains the fundamental part of its wealth from exploitation of the land, is composed by persons that live permanently or almost permanently in the city or as much in the city as the countryside.[16]

Within any rural sector urban linkages may vary among proprietors, and with this variation the political meaning of property in rural land changes. The greater the qualitative or quantitative variation in urban linkages among rural proprietors, the less likely it is that proprietorship of rural land per se will be the basis for class organization or membership in class-oriented political parties. Since there are different types of proprietors, with different proprietary rights and different sorts of linkages to urban and governmental institutions, the political meaning of property in rural land is also quite varied.

The capability of landowners and rural proprietors to control the extent and content of penetration by urban-centered institutions into the countryside is also important. Religious and educational institutions, for example, may offer firm support for particular types of property systems through indoctrination or political socialization. If landowners fail to control the ideological-religious teachings of these institutions, it is possible that customary perceptions of the authority of rural proprietors as legitimate may be replaced by other perceptions which are less supportive of or frankly subversive to the existing order. In this regard the linkage of rural proprietors to religious and educational institutions through family relationships, monetary control, political parties, or governmental policy is crucial to the maintenance of the scope and domain of proprietary authority. If the perceived legitimacy of property rights is undermined or questioned where before it was not, only physical coercion may then suffice to prevent the loss of customary proprietary prerogatives.

In the same way, the introduction of mass media—magazines and newspapers, transistorized radios, television, mobile cinema—into the countryside makes control over the content of the media essential to the landowners. The dissemination of "subversive" ideas into the countryside can only serve to undermine the basis of proprietary authority and may provoke overt challenges to the existing political order in the rural sector.

Finally, the commercial and technical dependence of rural proprietors on urban centers, especially after the appearance of commercial agriculture, makes the linkages of rural proprietors to sources of credit, agricultural inputs, technical services, and markets a critical constraint on the political meaning of property in rural land. Where rural proprietors are well linked to urban enterprises and governmental purveyors of goods and services, or are themselves bankers and stockholders in agribusinesses, their political capabilities are quite different than is the case where such linkages are poor or nonexistent. When rural proprietors have little control over urban-centered determination of prices for agricultural inputs, the availability and rates of credit, tax and production incentive policy, product pricing, and farm-labor legislation and administration, then rural proprietorship may be quite limited in political significance. On the other hand, where certain rural proprietors can dominate policymaking in areas of economic concern to agriculture, or to other sectors of the economy, rural proprietorship carries with it a great deal of political weight. Even in a highly industrial, complex economy, it may be possible for some rural proprietors to dominate national policymaking in a number of areas through rural-urban linkages in commerce, education, religious institutions, political parties, and governmental agencies. These linkages, in turn, may reinforce the political power of rural proprietors in the rural sector.

Linkages among Rural Laborers

Another possible political constraint on rural proprietors is the rural labor force itself, which in times of labor scarcity can often demand better working conditions and salaries. However, unless rural labor obtains some institutionalized leverage over (1) governmental institutions, (2) individual proprietors, and (3) the class of proprietors of rural land, its gains can only be temporary. Clearly, these three possibilities are interdependent, but in some cases local conditions may provide unique opportunities for rural labor to assert itself to individual proprietors with little spillover to other proprietors. Similarly, organized rural labor may effectively deal with groups of proprietors in the absence of or despite governmental intervention. As a rule, the effective governmental regulation of proprietorship depends for its success on the organized efforts of rural labor and its allies.

It is the landowner's preoccupation that the limits placed on the authority of property and the obligations of proprietorship with respect to rural labor be kept to a minimum and that the rural labor force be prevented from taking collective action in order to force a redefinition of these obligations. This is the basic structure of conflict in the countryside. Where the class of proprietors is horizontally linked and integrated into the national governmental apparatus but rural labor is not even organized at the unit of production—that is, the individual farm unit—there is little hope for dispersal of political power in the countryside. Further complicating the position of the rural work force, some rural laborers may also be small proprietors, tenants, or sharecroppers, or may exercise other proprietary functions. The mixed status of the rural worker-proprietor mitigates association of the rural laboring classes into unified functional or class organizations.

Rural laborers may share family ties, bonds of fictive kinship (*compadrazgo*, for example), or other associational linkages not based on class. Migrant workers, however, usually lack even these social ties in most of the places they work. On occasion, primary social linkages or ad hoc committees provide an organizational basis for collective action against estate owners, merchants, or other groups against whom rural labor harbors grievances. More commonly, however, the lack of rural syndicates or cooperatives deprives rural labor of effective means to challenge the owners of large estates or to deal on favorable terms in either labor or commodity markets.

Linkages among Rural Labor, Urban Interests, and Governmental Institutions

Since the rural proprietors' favorable relationships with national and regional governmental institutions enable them to maintain or increase their hold over the means of production and their authority over the rural labor force, rural labor has incentives to form alliances with other groups and classes which seek to capture the national governmental institutions and to redistribute or redefine the authority of proprietorship. In order to improve its position, rural labor must either benefit from reformist policies over whose content and extent it has little control, or actively join in the political struggle to divest the current proprietors of some or all of their prerogatives. Only when organized rural labor participates actively in the political struggle in the countryside is there the possibility of a comprehensive redefinition of property and an effective redistribution of property rights. The content and extent of the redefinition of property depends in great part on the alliances which rural labor forms with other groups and classes in the wider social network. In this context, the urban linkages of rural labor become important determinants of the nature of reforms intended to alter rural proprietorship.

Once the determination of property rights passes from local or regional institutions to the arena of national politics, or even international politics, rural proprietors can maintain or extend their vested interest in property only by controlling or at least exercising veto power over the actions of national governmental institutions as they did in the past over local or village institutions. As the determination of the scope and domain of proprietorship is no longer a strictly local matter (and tends to be progressively less so), the struggle in the countryside is transferred in part to the national arena. Both the motivation and autonomy of nonrural groups and classes challenging the position of rural landowners and proprietors become crucial to the political restructuring of the countryside and to the gains (or losses) to be afforded rural labor. Revolutionaries, utopians, or other elements with sweeping visions of social transformation tend to employ different strategies and have a greater propensity to redefine basic property concepts themselves. Such supporters of rural causes may prove quite helpful to rural labor, or they may seek to transform it if they see "peasant mentality" as an obstacle to be overcome. Rural labor, in the absence of a peasant militia or other such self-defense forces, cannot usually defend its interests from either the visions of allies or the reactions of the proprietors of large rural estates and of commercial farmers. Only under very special circumstances can the rural labor force itself become the arbiter of this struggle. That such an opportunity for rural labor became a possibility in Chile in the late 1960s makes the agrarian question and the rural labor movement in Chilean twentieth-century politics an especially interesting historical case study.

2
Chile, 1919-1931

It is a country held in large estates, and seen in the broad it looks empty; for the landlord's house is far back from the road, and the wretched brown hut of the *roto* is hard to see. But it gives the essential picture of Chilean society, a society divided into two classes—an upper class that possesses and enjoys and a lower class that labors and obeys.

Mark Jefferson, 1921

In the period 1919-1931, Chile experienced a severe constitutional and institutional crisis. The constitution of 1833 no longer provided a satisfactory framework for an increasingly urban, modernizing, national polity. The social and political forces that in the nineteenth century and early twentieth had threatened, and even eroded to some extent, the power of the rural elite gained increasing impetus. Monolithic control by an agroindustrial oligarchy over governmental institutions gave way to the challenge of an expanding middle class and a radical activist labor movement. The increased participation of previously excluded sectors exceeded the capacity of the existing institutional apparatus to provide positive resolutions. From 1924 to 1931 military caretakership and a quasi-legally elected military dictator replaced the lethargic Chilean Congress as the arbiter of national politics.[1] As Frederick Pike has commented concerning the initial stages of this period:

Chile may have been closer to civil war in 1920 than at any time since 1891. Economic dislocation following the end of the First World War had resulted in vast unemployment, in strikes, and in labor violence. In this troubled ambient, anarchists and communists were working to bring about genuine revolution and class warfare. The government in 1919 had found it necessary to declare a state of siege in the depressed mining region. The middle of the following year in far southern Magallanes a number of striking workers were shot down as they attempted to flee their union building, which had been set on fire. At about the

23

same time, in the area just south of Concepción, an eighty-three-day coal workers' strike ran its course. Even the most conservative elements in Chile began to wonder how much longer the proverbial patience of the lower classes could be relied upon. There were unmistakable indications that unless the ruling sectors made at least a few conciliatory gestures to the masses a wave of violence might sweep the land that prided itself on stability and order.[2]

Underlying this crisis of the existing political order was the so-called social question,[3] which turned on the prerogatives of property, the role of government in society, and the exploitation of the working class. A small but militant working-class movement, based in mining centers, among railroad and port workers, and to a lesser extent among urban factory workers and artisans, pressed the capitalist regime for reform. Working-class periodicals, the organization of unions and societies of resistance, and strikes and protest were all met with frequent repression by police and the armed forces. Government agents destroyed printing presses and dealt with union leaders and strikers as criminal subversives. Conservative elements in Chile saw the insurgency as an imported Bolshevik conspiracy. But, as Luis Recabarren[4] pointed out to his colleagues in the Chilean Congress, the mobilization of the Chilean working class did not entail imitation of the Soviet or Mexican example: "since 1916 there have been those in Chile who preached the establishment of the social regime presently constituted by the Russian Soviet, a year before the system was established there in 1917."[5] The challenge of the social question went well beyond improved working conditions and higher wages. It entailed a fundamental challenge to the existing regime of property and to the political system constructed to maintain that regime.

While organized workers in urban and mining centers had engaged in sporadic conflict with their employers since the last half of the nineteenth century, the challenge to proprietorship in the rural areas by an organized working class began to be felt seriously only after World War I. From the outset, the challenge of rural labor to the hacendado was an extension of the struggle of the national labor movement against the existing regime of property.

In the period 1919-1931 rural proprietors experienced the first serious delimitations of their proprietary authority and political power in the countryside both through governmental regulation and the activism of organized campesinos. The present chapter describes the nature of the system of property in rural land which came under attack after 1919 and suggests the political meaning of property in rural land in Chile at the beginning of the period 1931-1973, which is treated in the remainder of this study. Because certain aspects of the political meaning of property in rural land in this period have been comprehensively treated in other studies, for example, the exclusive customary prerogatives of rural proprietors, these issues are discussed only briefly below. Other aspects such as the territorial jurisdiction of rural proprietors and their obligations toward rural labor receive more detailed treatment in the present study.

The Legal Authority of Rural Proprietors

The foundation for the Chilean property system resided in the nation's political constitution. The constitution of 1833 guaranteed

> the inviolability of property of all kinds, whether belonging to individuals or communities. No one shall be deprived of his property or any part thereof, however small, or of any right therein, except by virtue of a judicial decision, or when the interest of the State, declared by law, requires the use or condemnation thereof; but in this case proper indemnification to be determined either by agreement with the owner or by valuation made by a jury of competent men shall be previously made.[6]

The Chilean Civil Code (1855) defined property as follows:

> Dominion (also called property) is the positive real right in a corporeal entity, to use and dispose of it arbitrarily, so long as the law or the rights of third parties are not violated. [Article 582]
> Over noncorporeal entities there also exists a sort of property. Thus, the usufructor has property in his right to usufruct. [Article 583][7]

The civil-code tradition of property created a proprietorship characterized by Andrade Geywitz as the "triumph of the Roman concept—*usus, fructus y abusus*—of private property."[8]

Limits on proprietorship derived either from the rights of third parties or from specific constitutional or legislative prohibitions. In the specific case of property in rural land, the Civil Code restricted the rights of landowners in regard to subsoil minerals and other sorts of public property (*bienes nacionales*) like navigable streams, lakes, and beaches (Articles 589-601). The rights of third parties mentioned by the Civil Code generally referred to the rights of other landed proprietors. These rights, in the form of servitudes (*servidumbres*) on landed estates, included all "limits placed on a property to the benefit of the proprietor of another property" (Article 821). These servitudes took two principal forms—positive servitudes, which entailed the obligation to allow specified actions such as, for example, to allow a neighbor access to a public road through an adjoining piece of property; and negative servitudes, which prohibited specific behaviors such as building a fence above a determined height.

Except to respect the rights of other landed proprietors, neither the Civil Code nor other national legislation before 1925 restricted the rural proprietor's discretion in land use, land management, farm management, or alienation of rural landed property. No penalties existed for nonuse or inefficient use of agricultural land. Taxes on agricultural properties, a potential indirect regulation of nonuse of land, failed to provide enough revenue to pay the salaries of the police charged with maintaining order in the countryside, let alone to act as an incentive to production. Until 1925 rural proprietors remained practically unconstrained in their ability to "enjoy and dispose of [the land] arbitrarily."

The political and constitutional crisis facing Chile after World War I led, in 1925, to the adoption of a new constitution. As adopted, the new constitution revised the 1833 text in regard to property by declaring that

> the exercise of the right of property is subject to the limitations or principles that the maintenance and advance of social order demand, and in this sense, the law may impose servitudes for public benefit in favor of the general interests of the State, of the health of the citizenry and of the public welfare. [Article 10]

Hailed as a considerable subordination of property rights to the general interest, the provisions added little, if anything, to the Civil Code's recognition that property could be restricted through legislative acts. José Guillermo Guerra, participant in the process of constitutional revision, declared:

From the first moment a tendency could be noted favoring the maintenance, in all its integrity, of the existing consecrated concept of property rights, with all the prerogatives that emanate from it, along with accentuating, slightly, its subordination to the collective interest. [Also noted] was an inclination to promote the subdivision of arable land.[9]

Guerra proposed the following wording for Section 10 of the new constitution:

The inviolability of the right of property with the limitations established by law.

In those cases required by the utility of the State or Social needs a law can authorize the expropriation of species or determined objects, previous payment agreed upon with the owner or determined by the tribunals of justice.

The Congress shall enact laws that facilitate the subdivision of landed property and that subject uncultivated lands to special taxes.[10]

Landowners resisted this effort to limit their proprietary authority.[11]

As a compromise solution, the new constitution essentially retained the landowners' extensive authority to enjoy and dispose arbitrarily of rural property, while Article 14 added the obligation of the state "to favor the suitable division of landed property and the creation of family holdings." The requirement that prior cash payment for expropriated properties precede transfer effectively precluded any large-scale program of land distribution without a deliberate policy of monetary inflation.

Following promulgation of the constitution of 1925, two further initiatives of significance affected the authority of rural proprietors over their rural properties. Law 4.174, which amended Decree-Law 755 of 1925, established the principle of punitive taxation against poorly exploited or abandoned properties. In the case of poorly exploited farms, the law stipulated a tax penalty of approximately 30 percent, to be applied at the discretion of the president of the Republic. Commenting on this legislation, the authors of *La Tributación Agrícola en Chile, 1940-1958* noted that

with the exception of the practically unapplied Presidential authority in regard to underutilized farms, there did not exist in law 4174 a criterion of increased productivity. The defects of the system of periodic re-evaluation created a legalized evasion since, while tax rates remained the same or increased slightly, land valuations were progressively underassessed.[12]

Thus, the principle of restricting nonuse of rural property through punitive taxation failed, in its application, to limit effectively the capablility of landowners to enjoy and dispose of the land as they desired. In practice, nonuse or underutilization of farm land brought no meaningful sanction.

The second legal redefinition of rural proprietorship in the period 1925-1931 appeared in Law 4.496 of 1928,[13] which declared it to be of "public utility"[14] to establish agricultural colonies in order to subdivide rural property, intensify and organize production, support the establishment of family holdings, and increase the country's population. Under the terms of Law 4.496 the state could acquire uncultivated land or extensively cultivated land in order to establish agricultural colonies. Despite the moderate nature of the law, landowners resisted it as a threat to the existing system of property and social order.[15] The provisions allowing expropriation of land not "intensively cultivated" brought particularly adverse reactions.

The law provided for discretionary, not mandatory, expropriation of poorly worked or abandoned farms. In practice the agency charged with administering the program—Caja de Colonización Agrícola—did not exercise the expropriation authority. Land was acquired at market prices and sold on credit to colonists (*colonos*). Agricultural laborers and inquilinos rarely acquired land parcels.[16] In effect the Caja became just another buyer in the land market.[17] With the onset of the economic depression, some policymakers saw colonization as a way to absorb unemployed miners and urban elements, both as colonists and bureaucrats.[18] Never in these years did the Caja threaten the existing system of land tenure nor the legal discretion of rural proprietors to enjoy and dispose of the land as they desired.[19]

Thus, until 1931, despite the emergence of a potential legal basis for altering the proprietary discretion of landowners over disposition and use of landed property, no effective delimitation took place. The introduction of the principle of punitive taxation and selective expropriation of nonproductive farms represented important legal precedents in regulating and redefining the authority of proprietors. The newly established constitutional obligation of the state to create family holdings and subdivide rural properties was also an important formal change in the system of rural property. But in 1931 landowners generally operated (or failed to operate) their rural properties free from the intervention of external authority.

Legal and Customary Territorial Jurisdiction of Proprietors of Rural Land

In 1919 the Chilean countryside remained dominated by large, extensively exploited haciendas. The hacienda system included a pattern of resident labor supplemented by temporary wage hands in peak seasons of agricultural activity. The resident laborers comprised various categories of inquilinos, *voluntarios* ("volunteers"), specialized workers, and administrative personnel. The inquilino, and inquilinaje as an institution, provided the foundation of the hacienda labor system.[20] In the nineteenth century inquilinos rarely received money wages; rather, in exchange for their labor and the labor of their families on a determined number of days, the landlord provided housing, land to work, pasture rights, and food rations. Into the twentieth century the inquilino remained a small producer on allotted land, receiving in-kind and perquisite payments (*regalías*). By 1919 some inquilinos also obtained a small cash wage, well below the market rate, to supplement the regalías.

Inquilinos were not bound to the land. Debt peonage, common in the Andean highlands during the same period, played little part in the Chilean hacienda system. Labor mobility in the late nineteenth century increased as mining and urban enterprises attracted rural workers. Railroad construction gangs were also recruited in the countryside. In this sense the Chilean hacienda system in 1919 could not be characterized as a feudal system. Any authority exercised by the landowner over the rural labor force derived from a national system of property law, national and local mechanisms for enforcement of property rights, and the customary patterns in particular haciendas or agricultural regions.

An additional intervening influence was the national and regional labor markets. With the expansion of the nitrate fields, other mining sectors, and urban enterprise, sectoral conflicts for labor provided campesinos with temporary leverage in obtaining better working conditions and higher wages. The Chilean Labor Department attempted to balance the demands of nitrate interests against those of the rural proprietors in regulating the labor recruiters (*enganchadores*) who roamed all over Chile to entice workers to go north to the nitrate fields.[21] Especially in the southern cereal-producing areas, landowners made increasing use of recruited seasonal workers (*enganchados*) for the harvest. These developments gradually increased the importance of wage labor in agriculture, at least on a seasonal basis.

In 1919, however, inquilinaje remained the foundation of the rural labor system. Landowners still sought to settle more inquilino families on their properties. Illustrative is a letter from the Sociedad Vinícola del Sur to the Labor Department requesting "three common inquilino families able to cultivate wheat and vegetables, and to do work in the vineyards. Two families containing men capable of producing charcoal [*carbón de leña*] ... and a family with a barrelmaker/carpenter."[22] The letter goes on to list the conditions of work and pay offered to the workers:

> Each family must provide the fundo one worker each day of the year at the rate of 50 centavos a day; the other individuals living in the house also have the obligation to work in the hacienda, earning whatever wage is paid to nonresident laborers [*forasteros*], currently 80 centavos, although prior to the current crisis this rate reached 1.50 pesos. The women and children in each house are also obligated to work when called upon, except for the housewife [*dueña de casa*]. These will be paid 50 centavos, respectively.
>
> The fundo will give each head of family, without charge, one *cuadra* of hill land to plant wheat and in lowlands [*vega*] enough land to plant two *almudes* of beans. In addition, near the house, a small plot is provided for vegetables. Each family has a right to maintain four head of cattle and one horse in the hacienda. In the season of vineyard plowing they must work their oxen for the fundo and they must use their horse for work-related travel.
>
> If an inquilino wants to sharecrop wheat, he can do so with his own implements and seed. At the harvest he replaces his seed and divides the remainder with the hacienda. The hacienda's share must be cleaned and delivered to the storehouse. Each sharecropper must also provide a cart of straw to the hacienda.
>
> If, instead, he wishes to rent land, that is also possible, paying the hacienda three *fanegas* of wheat per *cuadra*. *Chacras* [beans, potatoes] can only be sharecropped under the same terms as wheat. ...

The first task for these new workers will be constructing their houses. We will loan them carts and oxen and all the necessary elements available in the farm—wood, branches, straw for roofing, etc. While they are building their houses they can stay in warehouses [*galpones*] and we will give them food rations.

We understand that the government will provide free transportation for these people to the closest rail station, and we will pick them up from there.

. . . these conditions, at first sight not too advantageous, are superior to those generally enjoyed by the workers in this region. . . .[23]

From 1919 to 1931 landowners continued to settle resident labor on the haciendas. In 1931 the hacienda-resident labor system still dominated the Chilean countryside though increasing numbers of temporary and seasonal wage hands presaged some alteration in the basic arrangement. Over the resident labor force, the rural proprietor exercised no formal jurisdictional authority. Legal territorial jurisdiction had disappeared entirely except for the rights of the landowner to regulate entry and exit into his property.

In practice, however, property rights provided the hacendado extensive authority over the resident rural labor force through the labor "contract." Prior to 1928 the lack of specific legislative prohibitions in regard to the nature of the rural labor contract meant that the landowner could require whatever the market would bear, short of slavery, as a condition of employment and residence within the hacienda.[24] The only prohibition referred to the manner of payment, forbidding the use of scrip (*vales*), and was widely violated.[25]

Although specific conditions varied from hacienda to hacienda, it is possible to construct a general image of the scope and domain of authority still exercised by landowners over the resident rural labor force in the late nineteenth and early twentieth centuries. Historically in Chile the proprietary authority of landowners over the rural labor force was quite extensive.[26] The well-known *Manual del Hacendado Chileno*, published in 1875—even if we assume that it contained prescription rather than an entirely accurate description of existing conditions— allows us to estimate the scope and domain of authority which landowners believed they could reasonably claim over rural labor at the end of the nineteenth century.

The *Manual* details the obligations of each type of hacienda resident, from administrator to nonspecialized peon, indicating their responsibilities and positions in the hierarchy of the hacienda system. In the present context it is of interest to limit discussion to the main element of the hacienda labor force— inquilinos and the various types of specialized workers such as *carreteros, potrerizos,* and *vaqueros* who were simply inquilinos or peones assigned to specific tasks such as carting, caring for the pastures and animals, rodeo, and round-up.

The *Manual* divides the inquilinos into three categories according to personal wealth, labor obligations to the hacienda, and, correlatively, the land allotments, pasture rights, and other perquisites which they enjoyed. Whether "inquilino primero" or "inquilino tercero," however, all the inquilinos had to provide, either directly or indirectly through the replacement (*reemplazante*) paid by the inquilino, labor service to the hacienda in specified amounts—that is, one per day, two per day, and so on—and additional services such as planting, harvesting, shearing, and grape harvesting during critical agricultural seasons, depending upon the production pattern in the hacienda. In addition, all inquilinos except those of first class (*de a caballo*) were required "when much work existed, to make available to the hacienda all those persons living in their house—at the same wage paid to a day laborer [*forastero*]." The third-class inquilino, poorest and with the least access to land and pasture rights for animals, had to perform, in addition, "whatever occasional service is asked of him. . . ."

The *Manual* considered the inquilino's wife and daughters

> equally useful in many labors . . . and they should be obligated to make bread, prepare food, milk cows, make butter and cheese, shear wool, sew and mend sacks in the bagging of wheat . . . and other labors in which they not only can be substituted for men, but can be so with advantage. The salary or daily wage of each is arranged in relation to what the men earn. . . .
> It is not possible to excuse women from work because in times of scarcity of peones the hacendado may see his work schedule delayed. Likewise, the advantages of forcing women to earn their way are well known, since for an inquilino they are onerous due to their little income, and uniting the efforts of all . . . they will better their condition.[27]

The obligation to provide family members and other residents of the inquilino's house as workers at the command of the hacendado was not only a significant political attribute of the proprietor but represented an economic burden to the rural laborer, who was often forced to leave his own agricultural pursuits until nightfall or the early morning. The inquilino's harvest came at the same time as the hacendado's, and his cows also had to be milked and his vegetable garden tended. Thus, there existed a persistent internal struggle within the hacienda between the hacendado economy and the campesino economy for the use of existing labor resources. As long as the hacendado's proprietary authority extended customarily to other family members and remained unregulated by external legal norms, the campesino enterprise depended entirely on the benevolence of the patrón. However, as long as some inquilinos retained the right to send reemplazantes they could maintain a relatively prosperous campesino enterprise, based especially on capitalization through livestock husbandry on allotted pasture land. This also meant that the hacienda's internal organization nurtured a differentiated rural labor force and that the peon or reemplazante—not the inquilino—was the most impoverished of rural workers. The hacendado's proprietary authority, while legally unlimited, did distinguish among the types of rural laborers and did recognize, customarily, some limits to its legitimate authority vis-à-vis certain privileged or specialized workers. But even this customary delimitation alleviated only slightly the worker's subjection to the hacendado's extensive proprietary rule.

Thus, for example, the potrerizos, in charge of the pastures and animal herds, also had "to work within or outside the hacienda whenever ordered, without exception as to day or hour." Like other hacienda residents they were "forbidden to engage in personal or other labors without the permission of the patrón." In addition, these workers had to insure that "the locks on the pasture gates are always locked, not permitting that any person enter without superior orders. They will also prevent non-hacienda residents from traveling through the hacienda, except on public roads, and prevent also that they spend the night within the hacienda."

Essentially, the hacienda regime obligated all members of the households of nonadministrative personnel, including women and older children, to work at the orders of their hierarchical

superiors, day or night, at whatever task assigned them. At the
harvest, children as young as five or six were also called to
work. That the landowner's agents even controlled entry and
exit into the rural property meant, in some rural communes,
de facto territorial sovereignty over large proportions of the
administrative jurisdiction. Administrators applied fines for
misbehavior or unsatisfactory work performance. Banishment
(*i aún arrojado de la hacienda*) supplied the ultimate sanction
(short of very occasional murders) for disobedience or insurrec-
tion. Some haciendas also maintained their own jails.

From the end of the nineteenth century to 1931 the overall
hierarchical organization of the Chilean hacienda changed little.
There did occur some homogenization of the inquilino's work
obligations and a gradual decline, at least in some properties,
of pasture rights and land allotments. Still, in 1931 the hacienda contained a diverse rural labor force, with a privileged
minority of inquilinos having, in effect, substantial agricultural
enterprises of their own. But even these privileged few remained subject to the legally unlimited authority of the hacendado. With little or no notice they could be forced to leave
their homes or to move or sell their belongings without compensation for improvements made on the plots of land where
they were born, raised, and had lived for years and even generations.[28]

While the hacienda was organized hierarchically, it should not
be mistaken for a bureaucratic organization or system of authority. Relationships among members of the system were not
defined by impersonal rules and routinization of task performance but rather by the transfer of proprietary prerogatives—
personally—to agents of this personal authority. Neither, however, should personalistic rule be confused with paternalism.
Paternalism is often mentioned as an element which ameliorated the exploitation of rural labor in Chile; it is argued that
the patrón cared about his workers and saw to it that they
weren't too bad off. George McBride, author of the most
often cited work on rural Chile, suggests as late as 1935 that

> the traditional relationship that exists between the inquilino and the
> hacendado—between master and man—somewhat ameliorates the
> hardships of the inquilino's condition. The landowner is not only
> employer, he is also patrón. The system is quite patriarchal in its

actual operation. The inquilino usually feels a sense of loyalty and even of devotion to the farm owner. The latter in turn looks upon the inquilinos as his wards, almost as his children. He regards them with solicitous care.[29]

And Sergio Gómez, writing in 1971, argued that the inquilinos generally distinguished between the "protective and rewarder" sphere of the patrón and the repressive sphere of the administrator.[30] However, by World War I the personalistic, arbitrary, and coercive nature of proprietary authority had become apparent through the veneer of paternalism. Indeed, daily or even monthly direct contact between landowner and rural labor had been eliminated.[31] Control over the labor market, monopoly of land resources, and support of the coercive capability of the nation state held the hacienda system together. Paternalism, traditional authority, and loyalty of the work force made the everyday operation of the hacienda community depend less upon naked force, but the system clearly rested on the poverty and powerlessness of labor and the coercion of landed proprietors.[32]

The typical hacienda in Chile before 1931, thus, was a political community in which the landowner claimed authority over most aspects of the campesino's life. It recognized only slight demarcation between its authoritative jurisdiction and the private lives of the rural resident labor force, although in comparison with the feudal lord's authority to restrict marriages or with the *droit du seigneur*, the Chilean hacendado exercised a more limited rule. Authority was personalistic and arbitrary, despite structural organization that resembled, at least in the larger haciendas, a hierarchical bureaucratic organization. Members of the labor force were expected to deal individually with the landowner or his representatives. Severe sanctions or banishment met any effort to constitute associations of laborers, even on an ad hoc basis.

The customary linkage of the proprietor to rural police and judiciary carried on into the twentieth century. Many of the rural police posts were located within the haciendas and even were subsidized by proprietors. Police officers received food, lodging, and other perquisites directly from the local hacendados. The police served, in effect, as agents of rural proprietors.

The rural labor force was well aware of the landowners'

control over the local police contingents. Indicative is a labor inspector's report detailing the development of a strike movement in the province of Colchagua in 1924:

> The creation of a national police [*carabinero*] post in Chimbarongo would permit, in our judgment, the more effective guarantee of public tranquility, since the workers, on the one hand, have no faith in the police because they are municipal and depend upon the municipality, and the councilmen and mayor are at the same time the owners of the fundos; on the other hand the patrones have requested national police because they believe that the municipal police would be insufficient to repress a workers' movement which acquired more than modest proportions.[33]

Landowners' exercise of police and judicial power extended beyond the central valley and also to the nonhacienda resident population. South of Ñuble in the region of expanding cereal production and employment of large numbers of seasonal workers for the harvest, landowners continued to dominate local police authority and to act as magistrates.[34]

After World War I the national regime made some efforts to intervene extra-legally in management-labor relations in order to deal with the demands of rural labor, especially in the localized districts where rural unions (*consejos federales de agricultores*) organized by the Federación Obrera de Chile (FOCH) promoted strikes (see chapter 5). The landowners and rural proprietors defended their customary and legal prerogatives against administrative intrusions. The landowners' rejection of governmental intervention and the effort to protect their customary authority over rural labor is illustrated by a rural labor dispute in Aconcagua. The governor of the department in which the conflict occurred offered to mediate the conflict in the following terms:

> A committee of inquilinos from your fundo presented itself at this Gobernación and communicated the fact that difficulties have occurred between you and your inquilinos, concerning conditions of work. They requested assistance in convening a meeting to solve them.
> The undersigned, in accord with the dispositions of the Decreto Supremo No. 4353 of 14 December 1917, requests that you come to a meeting at this office tomorrow at 3:00 P.M., in order to solve the problem to which I allude.[35]

On the same day, the landowner answered the governor in the

following terms, making clear that he, the landowner, would handle problems within his private property as he saw fit:

In answer to your Oficio No. 397 of today, I must inform you that you have been poorly informed concerning the existence of difficulties with the inquilinos of this hacienda. Some of these have not complied with their labor obligations and I quickly replaced them, in order to conform with the desires recently manifested by the Government of intensifying agricultural production. . . .

. . . Until the Labor Code is passed as law . . . I esteem that there is no other legal avenue open to private citizens [in such disputes] than to recur to the courts of law [*Tribunales de Justicia*]. The decrees that have been made or [in the future] are dictated concerning these types of problems, cannot have an obligatory character, if their dispositions are not accepted by both parties.

I recognize the spirit of conciliation which has moved you . . . but I believe, for the reasons given, the occasion does not call for leaving the solution of the difficulties that may present themselves to authority other than that which the law establishes.

The ignorance in which the major part of our agricultural workers live induces them frequently to believe in the false images presented to them by individuals without conscience or merit, which also usually leads them to carry out acts which are punishable under the law. For this reason, I take this opportunity to request that you adopt the means you deem prudent, to avoid any violation of private property.[36]

The next day the governor again wrote to the hacendado, acknowledging receipt of the answer, and again urged him to consider conciliation. The governor wrote, in part:

the undersigned agrees with your analysis of the legal situation. . . . But . . . the undersigned has the obligation to put into practice the cited decree. For this reason, and those of moral character, it will not surprise you that I again propose to you that you accept the terms of conciliation proposed by the undersigned.

If, for some reason of which the undersigned is not aware, you do not desire to come to this Gobernación . . . allow me to propose a Tribunal of Arbitration to resolve these difficulties, sending to me with the bearer, the name of the person you designate, in accord with the cited decree. . . .[37]

Lacking any binding legal authority to deal with the hacendado, the governor could only urge that he accept the government's intervention in a matter involving the exercise of proprietary authority vis-à-vis rural labor. The landowner responded:

Making reference to reasons of moral character, which you do not enumerate, you again propose that I attend a meeting to study the

labor petition that has been presented or that I accept, instead, constitution of a Tribunal for Arbitration. . . .

In answer . . . I am sorry to say that I cannot accept your proposals,
as well meant as they are, because I deem it more convenient to follow
existing legal prescriptions, until they are modified. . . .[38]

This case illustrates the landowner's concept of proprietorship and the existing legal limitations on governmental intervention to regulate the jurisdiction of proprietors over rural
labor. The prerogatives of private proprietors—the definition
of private property—made trespassers and criminals of laborers
who challenged the existing wage bargain or collectively presented a labor petition. Governmental officials, in this case the
governor, could only appeal to supposed moral concerns of
the proprietor, essentially pleading with him to accept mediation. The landowner's answer was a demand that the governor
"adopt those measures deemed prudent to avoid violations of
the rights of private property." The labor contract, generally
verbal, became in reality an act of submission to the diffuse
and extensive authority of the rural proprietor.

Only the existence of alternative employment opportunity,
migration, or collective action on the part of rural labor to
force landlords to redefine their authority could—at least
temporarily—reverse the directions of dependence. In such
instances rural proprietors did not hesitate to complain to
governmental authorities. In some cases, nevertheless, with the
expansion of commercial agriculture campesinos could explicitly use the threat of migration to win concessions from rural
proprietors. For example, the intendente in Cautin reported
in 1929:

As I told you last year, Mr. Minister, there is a labor shortage which
is prejudicial to the landowners. The workers have demanded higher
wages, threatening the landowners with leaving their labors if their demands are not met. Due to the risk of losing their crop in this southern,
rainy region, the landowners have had to raise the workers' salaries.

A notable influence of the above has been the announcement of
labor recruitment [enganches] for the north. Although the workers
from the south don't like to work in the north [nitrate fields] they
take advantage of the opportunities offered in order to pressure their
employers.[39]

Similarly, in the same month, the intendente in Bio Bio

Province reported that rural workers recruited to work in the region of Mulchén stopped work in demand of higher wages, refusing to recognize the validity of labor contracts which they had not signed. Only intervention of governmental authorities convinced the campesinos to go back to work.[40] The threat of migration or leaving the harvest on one farm to go to another was not as easy for resident labor to make as it was for the migrant. For the resident worker, leaving the hacienda meant leaving a lifestyle and family ties behind. This gave the hacendado greater leverage in dealing with resident labor.

Landowners exercised somewhat less authority in the case of peones or smallholders who worked seasonally or part time for wages. The peon was already alienated from the means of production and became part of the expanding rural proletariat. The cost of his freedom from the permanent political authority of the landowner entailed constant movement, miserable living conditions, and lack of community ties or the minimal security guaranteed by the hacienda. The smallholder, who augmented his income with employment for wages or perquisites (grazing rights, firewood, sharecropping, and so on) on the hacienda, remained more closely linked to the proprietary authority of the large landowner than did the nonresident peon or migrant worker. But since their dependence on the hacienda was not strictly hierarchical nor entirely inclusive, these smallholders were potential clientele for any external agents that challenged the hacendado's control over land and water resources or sought to replace functionally the hacendado as the source of credit, agricultural inputs, or market for the campesino's produce. In the short run, however, the campesino's continued dependence upon the landlord for a wide variety of goods and services and employment overshadowed the latent antagonism between hacendado and smallholder.

Efforts by individual campesinos to delimit further the customary jurisdiction of proprietary authority were not uncommon. Such efforts might be undertaken through personal negotiation with the hacendado or with his agents. Since such renegotiation depended entirely on the unilateral and personalistic criteria of the patrón, however, the plight of the workers who refused to submit was difficult, as the letter from such a worker to the Interior Department in 1927 indicates:

For 35 years I have been an inquilino in Fundo Lo Arcaya in the Commune of Pirque, Department of Maipo. . . . Today, with no reason, they asked me to leave the house in which I was born. . . . The reason is that my wife refuses to milk the cows. She has four children and can't leave the house alone. Besides, I pay my *obligación* as inquilino and there is no reason to increase my obligations [*no tienen por que obligarme más*]. It is a great injustice that they treat me in this form after I spent all my energies working in this fundo.

Comandante Armando Gonzalez deals with these complaints unjustly, always ruling in favor of the landowners.

I ask for justice.

Luis Martinez M.

Correo Puente Alto[41]

In 1927 the authority of the landowner to require the inquilinos to provide the hacienda family labor remained almost irresistible. If the inquilino's wife would not milk cows, the family could be forced to leave the hacienda.[42] However, the semifeudal characteristics of this system did not mask the modern national foundation of rural proprietorship. Rural proprietors did not maintain legal manorial courts, and their actions in reference to rural labor remained subject to the authority of the national court system. Landowners maintained prerogatives because they dominated national governmental institutions, not because there existed no effective central authority.

During the post-1919 period, as the landowners' control over the national government started to decline, a variety of bureaucratic organizations began penetrating the countryside to delimit the de facto as well as de jure jurisdiction of rural proprietors. The hacendados resisted this intrusion, for the most part successfully, but complaints by rural laborers to the Labor Department over unpaid salaries or inequitably distributed crop shares became more common. The landowners recognized that the bureaucratic thrust into the countryside, with the efforts at regulation of their power, threatened the customary scope and domain of proprietary authority.[43]

In 1931, however, the conflict was still emergent. The gap between legal jurisdiction of proprietary authority and de facto jurisdiction remained a problem of extending the benefits of existing legislation to the rural labor force, and facilitating the campesinos' access to the administrative and judicial agencies responsible for law enforcement. Insofar as this gap remained

wide, the customary scope and domain of proprietary authority vis-à-vis rural labor greatly exceeded even the broad legal
definition of proprietorship.

Legal and Customary Obligations of
Landowners toward Rural Labor

Before 1917 and the enactment of the first labor law applied
to the countryside (compensation for industrial accidents), the
only legal obligations of rural proprietors toward campesinos
concerned compensation for labor. The legal obligation arose
from the Civil Code's generic provisions with respect to contracts (Libro IV) and rental of rural properties (Title XXVI of
Libro IV, especially section six). Interestingly, the Civil Code
did not recognize labor rents, distinguishing between payments
in money and payments in kind obtained from the thing
rented, that is, produce. Thus, the traditional understanding of
inquilinaje as a labor rent was a customary arrangement not
sanctioned by civil law.[44] In either of these cases, however, legal remedies or enforcement of violated contractual obligations
—almost invariably verbal—required court orders. The inability of rural labor to make effective use of the time-consuming,
expensive, judicial system to sustain their claims made even
these rights illusory.[45] A report by the intendente in Cautín
Province in 1929 is to the point: "the workers are obliged to
seek out lawyers . . . who because of the small amounts involved and because the workers are not able to pay the costs
of litigation are not interested [in these cases]."[46]

In 1924 the implementation of the so-called social laws
(Laws 4.053-4.059) provided, at least formally, the legal basis
for governmental intervention in labor-management relations.
The laws required written labor contracts, mandatory labor
conciliation and arbitration, social security and medical services, and legal recognition of labor unions. Except for the social security provisions (Law 4.054, discussed below), the social
laws systematically excluded rural labor from these benefits.
Labor courts, established in theory so that workers might rapidly and at low cost adjudicate their claims against employers,
were explicitly denied jurisdiction over agricultural workers,
leaving rural labor recourse, as before, only to the ordinary
civil courts. While the gradually expanding labor bureaucracy

and other governmental officials attempted to deal on an ad hoc basis with conflicting claims between rural proprietors and rural labor, the politico-legal framework effectively excluded rural labor from obtaining legal remedy.[47]

In 1928, in part as a result of the growing number of complaints by governmental officials forced to deal with rural labor problems in the absence of effective legislation, the Ministerio de Bienestar Social issued the following circular on May 25:

> Frequently the functionaries of the Labor Department receive complaints from agricultural workers, asking for their intervention to obtain what they believe to be justice in [conflicts with] their patrones. Repeatedly, this ministry has been consulted as to whether these complaints should be heard by the Labor Department and the legal norms, or other norms, which should be applied in processing and resolving [these complaints].
>
> Alluding concretely to the law of labor contracts No. 4053 it is necessary to recall that section two of Article I declares that it does not apply to agricultural labor.
>
> Despite the above, this Ministry, inspired by the principles of justice which constitute its *raison d'être*, believes that it is not possible to leave a large proportion of the working class unprotected by the government. . . .
>
> In accord with the above, [you are to] order the functionaries of the Secretaría de Bienestar Social within your jurisdiction to process the complaints of agricultural workers, seeking to obtain solutions in the role of "amigable componedor," inspired in the general spirit of justice and equity of labor legislation.[48]

"Amigables componedores" had no legal authority to sanction proprietors, making explicit the nonavailability of legal remedy to rural labor. Nevertheless, the informal entrance of the Labor Department and the Ministry of the Interior into the regulation of rural proprietors (through its provincial and departmental agents, the intendentes and gobernadores) foreshadowed the post-1931 situation of the formal extension of labor law to the countryside.[49]

Also in 1928 the Labor Department formally intervened to regulate labor contracting (*enganches*) in the countryside. The *Reglamento de Enganche*, which sought to prevent the customary abuses[50] of labor contractors and landowners, subjecting such agreements to written contracts,[51] was the first mandatory intrusion of written agreements between hacendados and rural workers. It applied to nonresident, seasonal workers, not to the resident labor force. Its lack of enforcement provisions led the secretario de bienestar social in Bío Bío to remark in 1931:

I take this opportunity to advise . . . of the difficulties in obtaining compliance with Reglamento No. 1636 concerning *enganches* of agricultural workers. When the moment comes to apply it, to insure compliance or apply sanctions against patrones, the Governor, who according to the Reglamento should proceed quickly and summarily . . . does not have the means necessary to act effectively. . . . Suppose that the governor orders the patrón to pay the contracted salaries and the latter refuses to do so. What can he do if the Reglamento stipulates neither procedures nor sanctions [for such cases] .[52]

The secretario was answered by his superior as follows:

Said Reglamento does not establish sanctions that permit the governors to require compliance. This omission, in reality, limits the efficacy of the dispositions it contains and, therefore, there remains no other remedy than the good judgment [*buen criterio*] of Labor Department functionaries in order to obtain, through conciliation, the required compliance. In the event it is not obtained, the affected parties would have no other remedy than to recur to the ordinary courts, since agricultural workers are not covered by the dispositions of Law 4.053, concerning Labor Contracts.[53]

Unenforced legal obligations represented little immediate benefit for rural labor. Yet they indicated a gradual tendency for the national government to intervene formally in order to create obligations for landowners to the rural labor force.

Still, before 1931 only the provisions of the social security law (Law 4.054) offered a basis for formal intervention of government authorities to regulate specified relations between hacendado and resident workers. Law 4.054 (1924) provided for the first formal permanent inspections of haciendas by governmental officials in order to secure fulfillment of legal obligations of landowners toward the rural labor force. Briefly, the law provided obligatory social insurance for illness, permanent disability, and old age. Workers contributed 2 percent of their wages, employers another 3 percent, and the government an additional 1 percent. The law required all workers earning less than 8400 pesos a year to register in the Caja de Seguro Obligatorio. The Social Security Administration issued small books (*libretas*) and required employers to buy stamps to paste in these as proof of fulfillment of their obligations.

A principal practical problem of the law's application concerned evaluation of the perquisites and in-kind payments (*regalías*) which constituted the major component of rural labor's wages. The general lack of accounting in rural Chile presented further difficulties (landowners were exempt from the provisions of the commercial code requiring accounting procedures for tax purposes). Serious application of the law, thus, did not begin in the countryside until 1927 and only became extensive after 1930.

Landowners made efforts to avoid compliance or to circumvent the law's provisions.[54] Some proprietors argued that since the use of the land allotment was not remuneration for labor but rather a gratuity provided by the employer, there should exist no obligation to pay taxes on the regalías as established in the Agricultural Reglamento.[55] Luis Correa said of the law (and of its companion legislation for empleados, Law 4.059):

> From the start, this complicated system [Law 4.054 and its administrative application] brought serious resistance from the landowners unaccustomed to these procedures [*tramitaciones*].
>
> Once the law was passed, the difficulty of providing effective medical service to agricultural workers because of the long distances involved in reaching them, became apparent.[56]

Sometimes the landowners' resistance took the form of noncooperation or simply ignoring the law's provisions;[57] sometimes governmental officials obtained halfhearted compliance. Despite landowner resistance, however, coverage for rural workers under the law was gradually extended into the countryside even before 1931. Illustrative is the excerpt from one labor inspector's monthly request for per diem, as presented in Table 1. No composite data are available from the Labor Department on rural inspections completed in the period 1930-1931, but incomplete sets of monthly reports suggest that inspectors had contacts with the owners of about 1000 to 2000 farms per month, depending upon weather and available transportation.[58]

The importance of these visits went beyond application of the social security legislation. The legal measures and administrative apparatus around Law 4.054 permitted the initial penetration of inspectors, thus making rural laborers aware of the few legal rights they had and reminding landowners of their legal obligations.

As with the *Reglamento de Enganche*, however, enforcement provisions were quite weak. Inspectors often requested that rural proprietors be fined for violation of the law but suffered the sort of frustration suggested by Fernando Ullmann, secretario de bienestar social in Chiloé in 1931:[59]

> 1) In many cases the fines submitted by Labor Department personnel for consideration by the Administración General de la Caja are modified. . . . By reducing the fine, without taking into account the seriousness of the violation, the affected persons do not feel the weight of the law, and in consequence, continue to break it.
> . . . in such conditions, naturally the violaters not only evade the law but in many cases communicate . . . their state of impunity, thus influencing others not to comply.[60]

As early as 1929, in the Annual Report of the Labor Department, the need for administrative fines, subject to judicial appeal, as well as jurisdiction for labor courts in cases involving agricultural workers, was suggested as a means to make more effective sanctions against violation of social legislation in the countryside.[61] Lack of this power, and the generally low hierarchical position of inspectors in the countryside, allowed landowners to ignore local inspectors when unable to convince them to ease up on enforcement.

In contrast to the extension of legal obligations, customary obligations of landowners toward rural labor had gradually deteriorated in the late nineteenth century.[62] Mark Jefferson wrote in 1921:

> In Chile the peasant is an inquilino. . . . He has a pretense at wage, the use of an acre or two of land, a wretched hut of unbaked bricks with roof of thatch, the privilege of using some animals from the farm, and fairly feudal obligations to serve all the needs of his master's house, he and his family too. In return the inquilino does what work the patrón asks of him. He toils hard and lives miserably, but life is assured him and his invariably large family. Under the Creole system he may always count on a good deal of advice, on care in sickness, when medicine and personal attention will be provided, and on help and protection in special adversity. The patrón does not mind how wretched the state in which his inquilino lives but would be ashamed to let him starve. I am not sure that this obligation of the patrón is made as much of in Chile as in other Creole society.[63]

The most salient aspect of these "obligations" on the part of the landowner was their unilateral revocability. In this sense

TABLE 1 LABOR INSPECTOR'S MONTHLY REPORT

Oct. 1931	Per diem	Inspections	Observations
1	$10	Hacienda San José, property of Carlos Toro Concha	Examined libretas and attended some complaints
2	10	Brush factory of German Muñoz in Panquehue & Hacienda San Luís, Luís Rivera	Attended 2 complaints and examined 15 libretas, and 14 libretas in Fundo San Luís
3	10	Fundo El Escorial of Santiago Carey	Examined libretas
4	10	Vineyard Los Hornos de Panquehue	Attended complaints, examined 42 libretas
6	10	Bakery owned by Amalia Mardones in Panquehue & Vineyard Modelo of Hijinio Arancibia	Examined libretas
7	10	Fundo El Molino de lo Campo owned by Ricardo Larraín Bravo	Attended complaints and examined libretas
8	10	Chacra Los Maitenes owned by Pedro Zamora in the Calle Real	Attended complaints and examined libretas
9	10	Chacras El Tambo & Algarrobo owned by Pedro Zamora & Ramon Muñoz, respectively	Attended complaints and examined libretas
10	10	Sector of Tierras Blancas	Examined libretas and attended complaints
11	10	Fundo Las Casas & Maria Auxiliadora in Panquehue, property of José Olivares	Attended complaints and examined libretas

22	10	Chacra Cancha El Llano, property of Serapio Vargas	Examination of libretas
24	20	Sector Catemu (Chagres) "El Ñilhue"	Went as ordered in providencia No. 14, 14 October, from the Secretaría de Bienestar Social de Aconcagua
25	20	Sector Catemu Fundo Los Cerrillos, property of Alfredo Riesco	In these fundos I examined the installations & different work areas and examined the libretas
25	20	Sector Catemu Fundo Las Compuertas of Johnson Gana, Fundo Las Varillas of Enrique Garcia Huidobro	
27	20	Continuation Sector Catemu, Hacienda Las Vacas of the Cía. General de Tabacos, Hacienda Sta. Rosa of Ignacio Garcia Huidobro, Hacienda El Arrayán of Manuel Gilisasti	In these fundos I visited the work areas and examined the libretas
29	10	Vineyard Errázuriz, Panquehue	I went in compliance with orders to talk with Mr. Perez Verdugo "depositario del fundo" to arrange the situation of the workers in regard to libretas which were not up to date
30	10	Fundo La Placilla & El Olivo of the Sucession Esteban Ahumada	I inspected the diverse work areas & examined the libretas
Total	$190	(San Felipe, December 11, 1931)	

SOURCE: From "Planilla de viáticos del Inspector del Trabajo de San Felipe Señor Victor Pica Rodríguez durante el mes de octubre," *Providencias* 1, 1931, 1-310, 1-16 enero.

they weren't obligations at all but "benevolences" or re-
sponses to the labor market.[64] Jefferson overemphasized the
supposedly feudal nature of this arrangement but captured the
essentially limited nature of proprietary obligations to rural
labor; often only the shame of the landowner restricted his
actions with reference to rural labor.

Customary obligations varied from farm to farm and according to hierarchy within the hacienda.[65] Length of residence,
quality of work, obedience, and other personalistic criteria
helped to determine the goods and services made available by
the landowner to each resident laborer. For example, within the
category of sharecroppers, landowners sometimes provided
seed, tools, work animals and other implements, while in other
cases all these were the responsibility of the campesino. Quantity and quality of food rations, housing, pasture rights, and
other perquisites also varied from hacienda to hacienda and
within each hacienda.

In addition to the work "contract" per se, landowners sometimes established rural schools and health clinics, supported a
church or rural missionary work, and provided credit to the resident labor force. All these services were provided (or not provided) according to the unilateral decision of the landowner.
The customary paternalism, so often cited in accounts of the
traditional hacienda, might also include gifts at Christmas and
bonuses on other fiestas. The patrón also maintained, or allowed a concessionaire to maintain, a company store (pulpería)
as a "service" to the resident population. A report signed by
the intendente and secretario de bienestar in Valdivia in 1929,
suggested the following about the pulperías:

> [Almost] 90 percent of the difficulties produced between patrones
> and agricultural workers arise from the settlement of the account at the
> pulpería. Almost always the worker impugns the prices . . . as occurred
> in the past in the nitrate fields.
> These difficulties could be avoided through a legal disposition which
> permitted the Secretarios de Bienestar Social and labor inspectors to
> regulate or control the price of the articles sold in the fundos. . . .[66]

Thus, the pulpería also frequently entailed further exploitation
of the campesino by rural proprietors.

The period 1930-1935 marked the high point for both the
absolute and relative numbers of inquilinos in the rural work

force. In 1930 there were 104,569 inquilinos (20.6 percent of the population active in agriculture) and in 1935, 107,906 inquilinos (20.5 percent of the population active in agriculture).[67] The situation was in flux, however, as the definition of inquilino changed in regard to his obligations and perquisites. For example, in some areas inquilinos had allotted land, pasture rights, and the right or obligation to send a reemplazante; on some farms, however, the right to send a reemplazante disappeared. No systematic data exist to provide a national picture of the specific perquisites and obligations of inquilinos.

Some indication does exist, however, that at least in some areas wages played a more important role than they had previously, and in some cases inquilinos became more dependent on money income and somewhat less so on in-kind or perquisite payments.[68] In general, however, these cases seem an exception. As late as 1938 a description of Fundo San Víctor in ConCon (Valparaíso Province) indicates the continuing dominance of the customary system of inquilinaje:

> to each [inquilino] is turned over more or less 2½ cuadras of flat irrigated land in exchange for a small annual payment, on the conditions that the inquilino provide a peon to the farm for a specified number of days during the year, a team of oxen during the planting season, and clean the irrigation canal where it crosses the land he occupies. In addition he is required to perform various miscellaneous duties appropriate for inquilinos, for example, working the round-up and running errands to town. . . .
>
> The peon that the inquilino provides the farm receives a salary of 3 pesos [daily], a bread ration of 250 grams and a ration of beans of more or less one-half kilo.[69]

For the rural proletariat, the peon, day worker, or migrant—in contrast to the inquilino—the customary obligations of the landowner were expressed in a temporary verbal labor agreement concerning the daily wage or piece rate, which usually consisted of food rations and money wages.[70] Frequently these laborers slept under the stars, the proprietor not even providing barracks.[71]

Exclusive Legal and Customary Prerogatives of Landowners

Exclusive prerogatives accruing to landowners as part of rural proprietorship are difficult to disaggregate from the benefits derived from high social status, wealth, education, and from family position more generally. Because the tendency for successful commercial and mining interests to buy rural property and form a semi-integrated ruling elite became apparent in Chile early in the nineteenth century,[72] it is not entirely possible to separate the exclusive prerogatives of rural proprietors from those of the propertied class in general. One can identify, however, certain customary benefits which accrued to rural proprietors particularly. First, and perhaps most important, landowners dominated local governmental institutions (municipalities) and police forces.[73] After the so-called Revolution of 1891, which reasserted local and parliamentary authority at the expense of presidential and central authority, the municipalities were essentially delivered (Ley de Comuna Autónoma, 1891) to local notables, who in the rural areas were the landowners.

The overall Chilean political system at this time operated, simplistically conceived, around a large national trough—the national budget—derived principally from export revenues and duties. Congressmen and administrators from different regions and localities contested over the division and distribution of these resources. Congressmen from the provinces depended for their election upon (1) landowners' mobilizing "their" inquilinos to vote, (2) control over the local computation of votes, (3) political composition of the current congress, which was responsible for reviewing the election and confirming candidates, and (4) the extent of electoral intervention by the ruling government administration.[74] While coercion—threat of expulsion, or loss of perquisites—had some effect in obtaining the votes of rural labor, by the second decade of the twentieth century vote buying (cohecho) played a more prominent role.[75] The system rested on campaign funds diverted through local channels to landowners who, in turn, paid their laborers to vote according to the landowners' instructions.[76] The landowners' key position for these transactions (in control of fifty, one hundred, or more votes) provided them leverage for receiving preferential legislative and administrative treatment even when their surname or wealth would not have automatically guaranteed such preference.[77]

Electoral control by landowners, though challenged by middle-class and working-class parties, continued into the post-1931 period and represented an added source of political power for rural proprietors. With it came control over national expenditures in local areas, administrative appointments (and removals), and access to business opportunities. In addition to the customary benefits of rural proprietorship, operation of Chile's credit and monetary systems provided subsidies to hacendados that added to the political meaning of property in rural land.[78] As Stevenson has pointed out: "Among the various exploitive techniques of the oligarchs, probably the most subtle and at the same time the most effective was the systematic depreciation of the Chilean currency. . . . By depressing the currency the aristocrats could continue to pay the salaried and wage-earning classes the same money wage, while increasing the number of pesos they themselves received for goods sold in the world market."[79]

Naturally, some caution must be exercised in generalizing about the effects of such policies on rural labor, particularly in the case of campesino proprietors, including inquilinos and sharecroppers, who relied heavily upon their production rather than upon a money wage for income. For example, as late as 1937 inquilinos in Hacienda Mariposas in Talca Province earned only one-seventh of their total annual wages in cash.[80] Still, the large landowners were a principal beneficiary of the inflation in terms of both increasing land values and commodity prices relative to wage levels.[81] Negligible rural property taxes and a rail freight system designed to subsidize farmers were also parts of the package of benefits customarily afforded rural proprietors.

But prerogatives were not uniformly distributed among proprietors, nor was the basic resource—the land—over which proprietorship was exercised. It is necessary now to turn to the distribution of proprietary authority in the Chilean countryside from 1919 to 1931 in order to better understand the political meaning of property in rural land.

Distribution of Proprietary Authority in the Countryside

Distribution of proprietary authority in rural Chile in the period 1919-1931 was at once highly concentrated and quite dispersed, as a result of the extreme concentration of landed property in a small number of large estates and the dispersion of proprietary authority in very small parcels of land among a great number of smallholders, smallholder coproprietors (*comuneros*), and indigenous populations in reservations. In addition, within the hacienda, inquilinos, medieros, and other agricultural laborers carried on their own agricultural enterprises.

Cadastral surveys and census information for this period are far from reliable, with estimates of the number of different-size properties and the land area they occupied differing substantially. In a presidential message in 1919 Juan Luis Sanfuentes estimated that Chile contained 4501 properties of 200-1000 hectares, 1038 properties of 1000-5000 hectares, and 248 properties of more than 5000 hectares.[82] Only five years later the Oficina Central de Estadística provided the information that there were 7236 properties of 210-1000 hectares; 2080 of 1001-5000 hectares; and 570 of more than 5000 hectares. In a period of relatively little change in rural landholding patterns, this much difference must be attributed to error, not to subdivision or expansion, as the figures would indicate for the 1000 to 5000 hectares and the above-5000 hectares categories. Because the data are inadequate, it is possible to estimate only the number of units in the various categories of landed property. In any case, even given the range of error, all estimates support the proposition that vast amounts of the available agricultural land were concentrated in relatively few rural properties.

For the country as a whole, using the data from the Central Statistical Office,[83] the distribution of landed property is shown in Table 2. The data include only properties in the narrowest sense. Unregistered properties, informally subdivided

TABLE 2   DISTRIBUTION OF AGRICULTURAL PROPERTY, 1924

Size in Hectares	Number of Properties	Percentage of Total Properties	Area in Hectares	Percentage of Total Area
Less than 5	46,136	42.5	73,069	0.28
5-20	27,475	23.3	292,411	1.10
21-50	13,853	12.7	470,414	1.80
51-200	12,503	11.5	1,288,048	5.02
201-1000	7,236	7.3	3,242,582	12.80
1001-5000	2,080	2.0	4,245,124	16.70
Above 5000	570	0.7	15,813,796	62.30
Total	109,853	100.0	25,425,444	100.00

properties, tenancies, sharecrops, squatters, and others are not taken into account. Thus, the extent of smallholds is considerably underestimated. Likewise, the internal proprietorships within the haciendas—inquilino-held land or sharecrop land—is not accounted for. On the other hand, the concentration of ownership of land is also understated, since many hacendados had several large estates.

Recognizing the biases, and taking the data only as indicative of magnitude, we find that, at most, 3 percent of all rural properties encompassed 79 percent of the agricultural land; and 10 percent of the properties concentrated over 90 percent of the agricultural land. In the central valley (Coquimbo to Bío Bío), McBride, citing the Anuario Estadístico, Agricultura (1925-1926), reported that 375 properties, representing .45 percent of all holdings in the valley, contained 52 percent of the agricultural land in the area.[84]

While ownership of small parcels insufficient to occupy even family labor full time was of a different order than ownership of the large haciendas in the central valley, almost all proprietors could make land use decisions, management decisions, alienate or transfer their properties, or leave their lands fallow at their own discretion. Where coproprietorship existed these decisions still remained in the hands of private individuals, distributed within the enterprise according to the type of proprietorship in question—rentals, sharecrops, allotted land, or pastures. But the decisions made by the vast majority of these proprietors, individually, had little impact on the national political community or economy. The small minority of hacendados provided the bulk of agricultural products and controlled the labor market in the countryside.[85] The hacienda remained the major source of supplementary employment for nearby smallholders and of seasonal labor for the numerous afuerinos or forasteros. In this respect, the political meaning of the atomized smallhold proprietorships, that is, the capability of these proprietors to influence or control the behavior of other Chilean citizens and residents, remained insignificant. Employing little nonfamily labor, generally with few, if any, resident laborers, the nonhacienda proprietors exercised little economic and political influence. Despite the relative dispersion of proprietary authority in the rural sector, the scope and domain of this authority were quite limited physically for most rural proprietors. In contrast, the large landowners enjoyed the extensive legal rights of all rural proprietors and could exercise these rights in relation to vast tracts of agricultural land and a large proportion of the rural population, who resided within haciendas or fundos. In some rural districts no rural inhabitants lived outside these rural properties, for example, María Pinto or Zapata in Santiago, and Tunca in Rancagua.[86] Thus, the hacendados had within the permanent domain of their extensive proprietary authority up to 75 percent of the rural population in the central valley.[87] On a temporary basis, their authority extended to perhaps 100,000 more migrant and seasonal workers.[88] In addition, the hacienda dominated the surrounding smallholders through control of irrigation, credit, services, and supplementary employment.

The concentration of agricultural land in relatively few large haciendas provided hacendados with a firm base for political control of the countryside. In 1930, prior to the increased subdivision of rural properties which occurred from 1930 to 1960,[89] a program which expropriated only 375 properties in the Chilean central valley could have placed under governmental control over 50 percent of the valley's agricultural land.

Somewhat ironically, President Juan Luis Sanfuentes, publicly chastized by a journalist in 1916 for the plight of agricultural labor in his own hacienda in the province of Talca,[90] proposed land reform legislation in 1919 to remedy the evils of concentrated property rights in rural land. Despite the fact that the legislation proposed by Sanfuentes provided in its first article for the veto power of landowners over subdivision, Sanfuentes recognized the division of Chilean rural society into proprietors and "that vast army of inquilinos who follow their orders." He antedated by more than fifteen years McBride's often-cited characterization of Chilean rural society as one comprised of two classes: master and man.

Internal Distribution of Proprietary Authority in the Hacienda Enterprise

Until 1931, corporate farms, cooperatives, and other types of collective proprietorships, excluding undivided inheritances, were a relatively insignificant feature of Chilean agriculture. On the large haciendas hierarchical authority systems peaked in the position of administrator or with the hacendado himself. Rural enterprises appeared simply as hierarchical organizations with decision-making capabilities centered in the patrón or his agent.

This picture of the hacienda system, however, is somewhat misleading. Chilean haciendas, through indirect land management—rentals, sharecrops, and labor tenancies—almost always included an internal campesino economy. As late as 1955 the "tenant Peasant Enterprises contributed slightly less than half of total output of the Hacienda System in Chile."[91] Thus, while the hacendado had almost exclusive proprietary authority within his rural property, he delegated many of the day-to-day decisions to his agents and to individual campesino enterprises. The economic output of the hacienda depended upon numerous small producers in addition to the land farmed directly by the hacienda enterprise. Generally, however, the landowner obtained agricultural inputs and passed these onto the campesino. Likewise, the hacendado bought the campesino's harvest and performed the marketing function. The campesino often exercised only limited proprietary functions, even on sharecrop land. Still, decision making about production, work routine, quality of work, and marketing was more dispersed than the formal concentration of proprietary authority suggested. During the period 1919-1931 the campesinos in some haciendas sought to increase their own proprietary discretion, insisting on performing their own marketing functions; seeking credit from merchants or middlemen, or otherwise bypassing the hacendado in regard to production and management of their sharecrops or tenancies.[92]

The challenge to concentrated proprietary authority in rural land, thus, could attack the hacienda system through either the subdivision of existing properties and their redistribution or the redistribution of proprietary authority within existing hacienda systems. The second of these, a persistent struggle between the hacendado and internal campesino enterprises, is often overlooked in discussions of land reform.[93]

Linkages among Rural Proprietors

The small group of hacendados that in 1924 controlled 80 percent of Chile's agricultural land was, in addition to a privileged propertied class, a closely associated, urban-dwelling, social aristocracy. Common economic interests, family and social ties, and common educational experiences linked landowners. In this respect, President Sanfuentes' comparison of the hacendado class to the English rural aristocracy prior to World War I is perhaps appropriate.[94] Through several agricultural societies, the hacendados played an active role as an organized interest group in national politics since the mid-nineteenth century. When Congress or the Executive considered policies which might affect the rural sector, the agricultural societies received formal notification and were asked for their observations. Thus, for example, in 1928 when the government considered application of Law 4.053, regarding labor contracts and the special situation of rural labor, the minister of Bienestar Social sent the following note to associations of rural proprietors:[95]

> The Subcommission of the Commission designated by the Supreme Government to study the Social Laws, has agreed to study along with the Law of Labor Contracts, the special conditions of rural labor. . . .
> In order that the Subcommission . . . can study the conditions of agricultural labor . . . I urge you to send to this Commission [*Inspección General del Trabajo*] the observations you might have on the ideas proposed. . . .[96]

Smallholders, inquilinos, sharecroppers, and other campesino proprietors, generally unorganized in formal organzations, received no such invitation to participate in national policy-making concerning rural labor law.

The hacendados kept each other well informed about "troublemakers" within the rural labor force and collectively resisted the first efforts of rural labor to challenge the extensive authority of landowners in the post-World War I period. During this period the hacendados organized a parasyndical organization called La Unión Agraria, which sought to unite all the "agricultores" of the country; defend the general interests of agriculture before public opinion; work toward the organization of agricultural credit, rural banks, cooperative societies, economical freighting, and, in general, for the realization of all those ideas directed toward agricultural development and social well-being; and to exercise influence over the public authorities so that they would make effective the aspirations of this society. In addition, the members agreed "to exert influence within their respective political parties, so that the designations of candidates to the national congress fall to citizens that sustain the ideas of protection and development of agriculture which the Unión Agraria aspires to realize."[97]

The Unión Agraria linked hacendados to defend them from attacks on their proprietary authority and to protect the interests of the hacienda system in national and local policymaking. When the first wave of labor conflicts hit the countryside in the period 1919-1925, the Unión Agraria, along with other agricultural societies, united hacendados to resist recognition of rural labor unions and to eliminate "agitators" from the rural work force. For example, in a labor conflict in Fundo Santa Adela in Chimbarongo (Colchagua Province) in 1924, the campesinos included in their labor petition a request for "recognition of the Federación Obrera de Chile in order to have a delegate who represents us as organized workers." (See chapter 5 for a further discussion of the role of FOCH in the countryside.) The proprietor answered the petition: "The fundo declares that it does not recognize the Federación Obrera de Chile because the General Administrator is a member of the Unión Agraria, which prohibits its members from recognizing that organization."[98] The labor inspector who dealt with the conflict reported to his superiors:

> The patrones, that is the landowners of this region, declared to me that they are affiliated in an institution called "Agrarian League," which has as its objectives improvement of the conditions of farming and . . . efficiently handling the betterment of the conditions of living and labor of the workers.
>
> Those petitions of the workers that for the moment were not considered, will be considered at the next meeting of this Agrarian League.

In this way the hacendados managed their common interests in the countryside. Regional associations with national affiliation met together to determine working conditions, salaries, and obligations of rural labor.

In addition to their parasyndical and interest-group functions, landowner associations kept their members informed of technical innovations, availability of agricultural inputs, improved farm management practices, and current political debates of interest to the agricultural sector through journals like *El Agricultor* and, later, *El Campesino*. Thus, the hacendados, in addition to family, social, and political ties, maintained linkages in an information network which attempted to solidify class unity as well as to provide helpful advice for agricultural entrepreneurs.

If there existed a weakness in the linkages among this class of hacendados, it was that as pseudomagistrates they generally recognized few external constraints. Landowner associations had difficulty enforcing policies on their members. As a minority of hacendados adopted more modern agricultural techniques, sought to limit or eliminate inquilinaje and replace it with wage labor and machinery, or moved from extensive cereal-livestock operations to more specialized and intensive cropping patterns, the community of interest within the class of hacendados began to weaken. The gradual subdivision of large properties close to urban centers, increased demand for truck crops, demands by bureaucrats and an expanding urban professional element for land to enhance their status and protect themselves against inflation also foreshadowed the urbanization of rural proprietorship by groups with affiliations other than the Club de la Unión, Sociedad Nacional de Agricultura (SNA), or Sociedad de Fomento Fabril.

But perhaps most important, by 1931 it was clear that the hacendados had lost their autonomous capability to control rural labor. Landowner associations could not adequately maintain the established law and order in the countryside, even with the cooperation of local governmental officials. Control of municipal councils and local police or militia no longer sufficed to repress labor conflicts or strikes. To protect property against subversion, landowners made direct appeals to the national government to send carabineros or the military. Now only continued influence in the national regime could guarantee the status of rural proprietorship. To this end the agricultural associations directed their energies.

Linkages among Rural Laborers

Unlike the hacendados, the thousands of smallholders, inquilinos, and rural wage laborers maintained almost no formal class organizations. In the period 1919-1925 initial efforts to organize rural labor organizations and mutual aid societies achieved some success before governmental and landowner repression curtailed these activities (see chapters 4 and 5). Within the hacienda or smallholder communities, family, fictive kinship (*compadrazgo*), economic cooperation, and recreational groups linked the campesino households. Differential access to land and other perquisites provided by the hacendado stratified the hacienda community. The smallholder communities (in the sense of rural locality, not necessarily villages or towns) likewise contained various strata of campesinos linked to greater or lesser extent to the nearby haciendas through labor relations, credit, sharecropping, or dependence for irrigation water. Overall, the rural labor force was far from a unified group. The landowner's capability to give selective access to land or other perquisites to loyal or obedient workers provided an important mechanism for creating and maintaining stratification within the labor force, which in turn reduced the likelihood of formation of class organizations that might directly challenge the hacendado. By sustaining a possibility of limited upward mobility within the hacienda system—through pleasing the landowner—the hacendado created a situation of conflict among campesinos over resources that the landowner dispensed.

Linkages of Rural Proprietors and Laborers to Urban Interests and Governmental Institutions

The Chilean hacendado class has always been urban in residence, while maintaining extensive agricultural interests in the countryside. This tendency intensified in the late nineteenth and early twentieth centuries. For the large landowners, residence on their hacienda(s) was, in most cases, seasonal or periodic. In addition to urban residence the great landowners had ties of family, political party, commercial interests, and education to the hub of Chilean society—Santiago. The landowners formed so integral a part of Chilean society and politics that in 1883 the minister of hacienda requested that the SNA help to form an analagous organization to stimulate industry.[99] In effect, at government request, members of the SNA assisted in the creation of the most important industrial interest group in Chile. In the early years the *Boletín* of the Sociedad de Fomento Fabril shared the scorn of the Chilean hacendado for the "ignorant Chilean campesino" in comparison with foreign colonists brought by the government to settle in southern Chile.[100] From the outset, the Chilean hacendado class linked itself to urban and industrial enterprise. At the same time, successful merchants, miners, and industrialists bought haciendas to consolidate their upper-class status.

Indeed, this class of hacendados essentially constituted an aristocratic atavism for Chile in the early twentieth century. It dominated the Congress, executive administration, and judiciary. Also heavily represented in commerce and industry, Chile's most important hacendados were in addition Chile's most important bankers, miners, and politicians.[101] In short, the hacendados were not simply a rural class but a national propertied class whose source of political power rested in the countryside but extended to the urban sphere.[102]

In contrast, the linkages of most rural laborers to the urban sphere remained quite limited. Hacienda residents "move[d] little from one property to another. Many of them spent their entire lives in a single estate, and it is almost equally common to find families on a hacienda that have lived there for a number of generations. . . . In general the tendency has been for the farm laborer to stay on an estate, for the family to remain together."[103] Migration to the nitrate fields, coal mines, and construction sites in the countryside and towns, however, separated some campesinos from the hacienda system and provided them contacts with urban customs and class organizations. Nitrate workers or workers returning from railroad construction crews sometimes brought the experience of organized-labor resistance back to the countryside (see chapter 6). But the linkage of most rural laborers to urban financial institutions, marketing channels, and urban political organizations remained slight until 1931. Contact with governmental bureaucrats gradually increased but until 1931 was still uncommon.

The Social Question and Rural Labor

Until 1919 the dominant hacendado class had been able to limit intervention of the state in the rural sector. The high clergy of the Church was selected in the parlors of the hacendados' Santiago residences. Church missions in the countryside preached loyalty to the patrón, suffering on earth, and just rewards in heaven. Rural schools, where these existed, were staffed by landowner-paid teachers who also provided ideological support for the existing order and singled out potential troublemakers among the rural youth so that landowners could take punitive action.

National politics, which remained an intimate affair centralized in Congress until 1924, gave to the period (1891-1924) the often-used label "parliamentary republic." The epitome of the formal democracy which masked elite rule, this parliamentary republic has been characterized by Alberto Edwards as follows:

> The great mass of the electorate, indifferent as always, put its votes up for sale; provincial leaders, submissive to power, obligated themselves [se enfeudaron] to the different aristocratic circles of the capital; each of these had its clientele. . . . Election followed election, without changing, except in insignificant detail, the relative power of the old oligarchs who played the parliamentary game in the drawing rooms of Santiago.
>
> . . . all the great personages were fundamentally in agreement: their conflicts were predominantly personal or between small circles, not over differing interests or doctrines.
>
> For this reason there does not exist a more conservative period in Chilean history. In 1918 things remained as they had been in 1891.[104]

Superficially, Edwards seems correct. But the emergent working-class movement and populist political parties, as well as the embryonic Marxist movement, belies the image of an unchanged polity. Labor conflict, a growing urban middle sector, commercial competition, and an expanding bureaucracy all threatened the integrity of the existing political order. Between 1919 and 1931 this political order collapsed, and the control of the hacendado class over national governmental institutions was eroded.

The populist agitation which accompanied Arturo Alessandri's election in 1920 was followed by more than a decade of constitutional crises. The new constitution of 1925 strengthened the executive authority at the expense of the parliament. From 1925 to 1931, however, the new formal arrangements could not be effectively implemented. A quasi-dictatorial regime (1927-1931) under President Carlos Ibáñez repressed the national labor movement but at the same time promulgated Chile's first land reform law, enacted a labor code, carried out an extensive public works program, and expanded the role of the state bureaucracy. The Ibáñez regime temporarily destroyed the decisive role of Congress in national politics. The government suppressed traditional political parties and repressed the leftist political movements. Ibáñez attempted to substitute his own party-labor movement, identified by the acronym CRAC, for the multi-party transaction system of the parliamentary republic. But Ibáñez did not bring about the end of hacendado hegemony in Chile.

Emergence of a working-class movement in urban areas and mining centers along with populist and, ultimately, Marxist political parties, upset the political balance and challenged the hacendados for control of the national governmental apparatus. The struggle of the urban labor movement and nontraditional political parties to wrest control of the national government from the hacendados gradually extended to the countryside. Rural labor joined the broader struggle against the extensive rights of private property in the means of production.

In the countryside the conflict focused on a redefinition and redistribution of property in rural land. The initial thrusts of organized rural labor in the countryside borrowed tactics from the urban labor movement and miners, tactics which included petitions, work slowdowns, and strikes, while appealing for a national redefinition of proprietary authority through a labor code, minimum-wage laws, and the right to form unions in the rural sector. In this sense the debate over a labor code in Chile in the first decades of the twentieth century focused on a basic component in any political system—the nature and distribution of proprietorship. Labor legislation or labor codes, as both the Chilean hacendados and the nascent labor movement recognized, may radically redefine the authority and power of those in control of the means of production. Thus, the landowners and the Chilean national regime repressed newly formed rural labor organizations after the short-term gains of the campesinos in the period 1921-1925 (see chapter 5).

Yet at the same time that landowners repressed the rural labor organizations, increasing conflicts in the mines, in urban areas, and in the countryside made clear the urgency of a formalized industrial relations system.[105] The government could not settle every strike with troops. Following the lead of European nations after World War I and relying heavily on doctrine from the International Labor Organization (ILO), the Chilean government finally adopted a labor code in 1931.

The Labor Code represented an initial delimitation of the
Civil Code's concept of property, particularly in regard to the
scope and domain of authority over persons in relation to proprietary interest. In the countryside the Labor Code represented
the first legal, formalized regulation of employer-campesino relations and provided a basis for rural unionization. It also provided a basis for bureaucratic regulation of proprietary authority in order to force compliance with newly created legal obligations of rural proprietors toward the campesinos.

Adopted in a decree-law by the Ibáñez regime, the Labor
Code attempted through legitimation of government-controlled
labor conflict to bridge the gap between unregulated capitalism
and calls for the revolutionary transformation of Chilean society.
The Labor Code provided a legal redefinition of rural proprietorship by introducing obligatory contractual relationships between
landowners and campesinos. No longer did the laws of Chile
explicitly exclude rural labor.

From 1931 to 1964 additional labor legislation further redefined employer-campesino relations. A product of both the continuous party competition for proletarian and middle-class votes
among a growing range of political parties and the pressure for
reform by working-class organizations, the legislation gradually
reduced the proprietary authority of landowners over the rural
labor force. From 1931 to 1964 landowners sought to evade,
resist, and modify the limitations imposed on rural proprietorship, to repress the labor movement which challenged proprietorship, and to control the votes of rural labor and thereby
maintain control of the national political apparatus on which
property in rural land depended. The history of this struggle
is discussed in the following chapters, which focus first on labor
legislation, next on the rural labor movement, and then on the
role played by political parties and the urbanization of the
countryside in disrupting the traditional system of property in
rural land.

2
The Political Transformation of the Countryside: 1931-1964

Introduction

The events described in the next four chapters took place in the years 1931-1964. The discussion of the conflict between capital and labor, rural proprietors and rural workers, focuses in turn on labor law, rural unions, and the broader Chilean political context, including the role of political parties in the transformation of the countryside. Thematic treatment leads the reader over the same time period several times by different routes. To avoid confusion and to help the reader shape an overview of this period, the time-line that follows marks major events discussed in part 2 of the book. It may be referred to, on occasion, when the reader wishes to step back from detail and place the discussion in the context of the overall history of the period.

1931	Labor Code adopted (chapter 3)
1932	Arturo Alessandri takes office as president
1933	First administrative suspension of rural unionization
1934	Massacre of peasants at Ranquíl (chapter 5)
1935	Founding of Liga Nacional De Defensa de Campesinos Pobres (chapter 5)
1936	Popular Front formed
1938	Popular Front candidate Pedro Aguirre Cerda elected president
1939	Administrative order suspends rural unionization (chapters 4 and 5)
1941	President Aguirre Cerda dies in office
1942	Juan Antonio Ríos becomes president
1946	President Ríos dies in office
1946-1947	González Videla elected president with support of communists; massive wave of rural unionization and labor conflicts; Law 8.811 passed to "regulate" rural unions (chapters 4 and 5)

1948	Law passed outlawing Communist party; repression of labor movement (chapter 5)
1952	Carlos Ibáñez elected president
1953	Minimum-wage law adopted for rural workers; campesino strike in Molina (chapters 3 and 5)
1958	Electoral reform law leads to increased importance of campesino votes; Jorge Alessandri elected president (chapter 6)
1958-1962	Renewed rural labor militancy; Christian Democrats join Marxists in rural labor organizing (chapters 5 and 6)
1962	Alessandri Land Reform enacted (Law 15.020) (chapter 7)
1964	Christian Democratic candidate Eduardo Frei elected president

3

Labor Legislation
and Rural Proprietorship

A good part of the opposition [to a labor code] came from the rural aristocracy, the wealthy and cultured hacendados. . . . The very concept of labor relations was antipathetic to their way of life, a challenge, a threat, a revolt which implied an end to special status and high privilege.

James O. Morris

The creation of a normal working day is . . . the product of a protracted civil war, more or less dissembled, between the capitalist class and the working class. . . . In place of the pompous catalogue of the 'inalienable rights of man' comes the modest magna carta of a legally limited working day. . . .

Karl Marx

The Political Implications of Labor Legislation

In the history of industrial society the developing capitalist economies in Europe, followed by those of the United States and Latin America, were each subjected to a particular manifestation of the struggle between labor and private proprietors: the effort to impose limits on the proprietary authority of employers in relation to the working classes. The struggle of the working classes and their allies resulted in the formalization of labor legislation or labor codes as the capitalist state dealt with the reality of conflict and violence posed by working-class movements.

In response to working-class movements the existing regime sought alternatives to the use of police and military. In this context, industrial-relations systems evolved with unique national twists but focused upon the same basic conflicts between labor and capital. Soon specialized agencies of the state appeared to administer labor law and to institutionalize labor conflicts, that is, to limit the scope of demands by the working classes and

69

force employers to recognize the legitimacy of working-class organizations.

In the twentieth century, labor legislation and governmental intervention to regulate conditions of work, sanitation, industrial safety, minimum wages, and so on became common practice. But nowhere is such legislation self-enforcing. Even where bitter legislative conflicts are avoided in the preparation and promulgation of labor legislation, administration and enforcement of legislation often present serious problems.

Regulation of proprietorship through labor law must be preceded by both a determination that regulation is necessary and a formalization of that determination in legislation. That labor legislation may be largely symbolic because of a divergence between legal formulas and the manner of their implementation is always a possibility, especially where intended beneficiaries or potential clientele of the legislation are unorganized, poor, and politically weak.[1] Political reforms intended to replace the defunct paternalism of the precapitalist era will remain parchment barriers unless the resources necessary to carry out legislative prescriptions can be obtained by administrative agencies, and their functionaries can be made responsive to the intended beneficiaries of the legislative prescriptions. In order to secure administrative responsiveness, the intended beneficiaries of the legislative prescriptions must organize on a relatively permanent basis for collective action and vigilance of the regulators as well as of the proprietors. They must also acquire the legal tools and knowledge to confront proprietors in judicial and quasijudicial proceedings. Organization for collective action may also allow the intended beneficiaries to exercise influence on legislators as well as on bureaucrats.

Meeting these conditions in the face of the resistance of proprietary interests and the negative bias of existing institutional arrangements, especially with regard to the permanent organization of disadvantaged social groups or classes, is generally quite difficult.[2] The delimitation and regulation of proprietary authority is thus a question of political power and of mobilization of the necessary resources to make regulation effective. The difficulty of the task is the reason that legislative prescription often remains largely symbolic.

In the case of agricultural laborers and smallholders, the

difficulties are magnified, due in part to the generally precarious position of these rural groups in most modern nation states. Regulation of rural proprietorship presents tremendous obstacles which thwart the effective political organization of rural labor, not only because rural labor has neither the time nor money to organize but also because rural proprietors exercise so much customary authority in the countryside that efforts to organize expose rural laborers to severe sanctions.

As a general rule, the less politically powerful the intended beneficiaries of regulation, and the less well organized they are to eye permanently the administration and enforcement of the appropriate laws and decrees, the more symbolic (less effective) will be the implementation of legislative prescriptions intended to regulate proprietorship. Labor legislation is no exception. Despite these problems, however, labor legislation has potential for enforcement which represents a threat to proprietors. When it is enforced, it becomes an effective delimitation of proprietorship. With all its potential difficulties, from the bribing of governmental officials by landowners to the psychological identification with or deference to the landowner on the part of bureaucrats, regulation of rural proprietors can be a significant factor in improving the situation of rural labor and redefining the meaning of property in rural land.

For this reason landowners have every incentive to resist the enactment of labor law. Furthermore, if enacted, they can be expected to attempt to block or subvert its effective implementation by means of a narrow interpretation of the laws' provisions, making possible legal evasions; by delaying tactics, which permit continuous postponements of application; by participation, formally or informally, within the policymaking apparatus of the agency expected to regulate their activity;[3] by denying enforcement officials the necessary resources to carry out the legislative prescriptions on anything but a symbolic level, for example, constraining regulation through budgetary action in the relevant legislative body; by bribing officials to assure nonenforcement; by establishing internal constraints on personnel of the regulatory agency such that a sensible bureaucrat avoids particular enforcement patterns; and by making the costs of registering complaints too high for the potential clientele to bear, for example, lengthy legal procedures and exposure to

landowner reprisals. No enforcement system can work if it relies upon reports of violations from sources (workers) liable to
sanction when and if their role as informants is discovered.
Physical violence against "agitators" is another effective method
of discouraging complaints commonly used by landowners (or
mine operators) to keep the labor force in line. Finally, bureaucrats responsible for law enforcement may be made to understand by their superiors that certain specific proprietors are
not to be bothered—because they belong to the same political
party as the minister, are friends or *compadres* of their superiors, another inspector's brother, and so on. This type of nonenforcement is the most difficult to eliminate even where a
clear political mandate for enforcement exists and rural labor
is organized to defend its collective interests. In the aggregate
it is insignificant, but if the other types of impediments are removed, the injustice and corruption inherent in the last type
become more obvious.

This chapter examines the major labor legislation affecting
rural proprietors and rural labor in Chile from 1931 to 1964.
Excluded from this discussion is the problem of legislation
dealing with rural unions and syndicates, which is treated separately in chapters 4 and 5.

The Labor Code of 1931 and Subsequent Labor Legislation

The Chilean Labor Code of 1931 was not, strictly speaking, a
legislative enactment. Rather, it was a decree with force of law
(*Decreto con Fuerza de Ley 178*) which codified existing labor
legislation and introduced new sections of labor law, including
a section on agricultural laborers. The Labor Code also altered
the system of labor courts, leaving in the jurisdiction of the
Juntas de Conciliación (institutions for mandatory arbitration
and control of the right to strike by labor) matters concerning
collective labor disputes. The Labor Code, thus, represented
the last major contribution of the intervention of military-
authoritarian rule in Chile (1924-1931) which ended the period
of parliamentary dominance (1891-1924). For this reason it
did not have to run the gauntlet of congressional opposition.

The presidential and bureaucratic source of the Labor Code
caused some of the most extreme elements within the landowner class to reject the Labor Code as illegal or, at best, too

advanced for the conditions of Chilean reality. An example of
an influential landowner with this attitude was Alejandro Dussaillant, deputy in the Congress and landowner (Fundo Casa
Blanca) from Talca. Dussaillant violently resisted rural unionization and made constant efforts to have moderately active
labor inspectors transferred. He wrote in October 1932 to the
director of the Labor Department as follows:

> I am the first to recognize that every functionary must require that
> the law be obeyed. I would do the same. But in this case, *that of a law
> which threatens the very bases of civilization and progress—threatens
> the rights of property and of equity*, and the liberty of each [man] in
> his own house—I would not only apply the law moderately, but I
> would also overlook, insofar as this is possible, its arbitrary and exag-
> gerated [provisions]. . . . [emphasis added]
>   I took the occasion of my complaint against the labor inspector,
> Sr. Menzel, to make known my permanent protest concerning the La-
> bor Code, because [it] contains some iniquitous provisions, not to
> mention the fact that it originates in an imposition of force rather
> than a true law. I did what I had to do and what I will do each time
> the occasion arises. If these protests did not reach the higher officials
> of the Labor Department . . . they might imagine that the landowners,
> industrialists, and merchants of this country were in accord with this
> decree-law. . . .[4]

If Dussaillant was incorrect in his evaluation of the code's legal
status, he nevertheless accurately evaluated the code as a threat
to existing property rights.

The Labor Code, in addition to its generic provisions,[5] dealt
specifically with agricultural workers in section 8 (Articles 75-
82). Article 75 defined "agricultural workers," and Article 76
provided that agricultural workers would be subject to the general stipulations of the Labor Code and labor contracts insofar
as this was compatible with agricultural work and with the
dispositions of the rest of section 8. Article 76 also stipulated
that part of the labor contract in the countryside would always
be understood to include the landowners' obligation to provide
the worker and his family with "adequate and clean" housing.
Furthermore, it stipulated that agricultural work would not be
subject to an hourly schedule or limit but that work hours
would be determined by the nature of the work (harvest, planting, maintenance of irrigation canals, and so on) and the customs of the region. This provision meant that the customary

sunup-to-sundown work routine could be retained in the countryside.

Articles 77 and 78 regulated sharecropping, and Article 79 dealt with the contract of inquilinaje. Among other things it stipulated that the following matters should be included in the contract: (1) labor obligations of the inquilino to the landowner; (2) perquisites in land, housing, food rations, grazing rights, and so on, which the landowner was obligated to provide to the inquilino; (3) legal causes for termination of the contract without rights to severance pay and notice (*desahucio*); (4) wages in money and kind (*especies*); (5) obligation of the inquilino to provide members of his family or other workers to work in the hacienda and the responsibility of inquilino or landowner to pay these workers where such an obligation existed.

Article 80 limited the landowners' right to apply fines to rural labor by providing that with the authorization of the labor inspector the patrón could discount the daily wage of an inquilino who did not come to work or send a replacement. This section restricted landowners' customary application of fines as punishment for innumerable supposed violations of orders, discipline, or work obligations.

Article 81 explicitly prohibited landowners from requiring resident labor or sharecroppers to sell their produce to the hacendado for whom the campesino worked. It also provided that landowners must pay current market prices (*corrientes del mercado*) when buying the produce of resident labor.

Article 82 required that temporary workers be given six days' notice and severance pay, whereas inquilinos were to receive two months'. Finally, Article 92 of the Labor Code required all proprietors of firms which hired labor to prepare and have approved by the Labor Department internal regulations (*reglamentos internos*) which detailed the obligations of the work force in relation to work and continued employment in the enterprise. Thus, traditional authority and custom were to be replaced with an impersonal formal code.

These provisions, combined with the other sections of the Labor Code applicable to rural labor—including provisions for presentation of labor petitions, mandatory collective bargaining and unionization—represented a radical legal redefinition of the status of rural proprietors and rural labor. Rural proprietors were now formally subject to governmental regulation. Rural labor had formal access to the Labor Department's law enforcement machinery and to the labor courts to demand rural proprietors' compliance with their obligations. The Labor Code exposed landowners to legal labor petitions, strikes, and unionization by rural labor and obligated them to deal with these situations, at least formally, as stipulated in the Labor Code. The Code also legally obligated all enterprises with industrial unions to distribute up to 10 percent of profits to the union (Article 402). This implied a certain accountability to the workers. In the case of labor petitions, legal in all enterprises with more than ten workers (Article 502), no workers could be dismissed during the processing of a labor petition unless they damaged the firm's physical property or induced a secondary boycott (Article 509). The code prohibited lockouts (Article 542).

The Labor Code entrusted enforcement of these provisions to the Labor Department (Articles 557 and 558). Labor inspectors were granted the authority to visit all places of work, at any time of night or day. The code made the impedance of inspection visits a civil offense punishable by 100- to 500-peso fines for the first offense and 500- to 1,000-peso fines for additional offenses (Article 568). Labor inspectors also had the authority to require employers to appear at regional or local offices of the Labor Department to answer complaints by workers. Not until later did inspectors acquire the power to apply administrative fines to enforce this authority (Article 572).

Between 1931 and 1964 various additional labor laws placed further obligations upon landowners and extended legal benefits to rural labor. These included family allowances (*asignación familiar*) in 1947; minimum-wage legislation in 1953; housing codes in 1954, 1956, and 1960; fixed minimum percentage of agricultural minimum wage in cash (1953, 25 percent; 1963, 35 percent; 1964, 50 percent); paid Sundays (*semana corrida*) in 1959 and so on. Enforcement remained the responsibility of the Labor Department. Social Security inspectors and health inspectors also carried out some duties in the countryside, but for the most part the Labor Department retained responsibility for regulation of rural proprietorship vis-à-vis the rural labor force.

During the next thirty-three years (1931-1964) landowners

persistently, and to a great extent successfully, resisted effective enforcement of the Labor Code in the rural sector. The immediate response of the Sociedad Nacional de Agricultura (SNA) to the Labor Code set the tone for the next three decades. In a section of the SNA's annual report labeled "Legislación: El Código del Trabajo" the landowners declared their objections to the Labor Code's extension of benefits to workers and empleados in the countryside:

> This Code gravely injures the interests of rural proprietors. Because of this, the Society [SNA] has studied its dispositions in depth and has carried out an intense effort to convince the Public Authorities of the need for its partial or total reform in regard to the agricultural industry.
>
> In addition, to guarantee compliance with the law, it would be necessary to create a veritable army of functionaries in order to visit the fundos. . . . Such an increase in the budget is not possible.
>
> . . . given the insoluble difficulties in complying with the law, the result will be an aggravation of the differences between labor and capital.[6]

From 1931 until 1964 landowner resistance to labor legislation and to its implementation in the countryside remained implacable. Resistance took a variety of forms, each of which is treated in the case histories that follow. The cases are presented to illustrate the application of particular tactics by landowners in resisting labor law. All these tactics remained effective into the 1960s. From 1931 until 1964 only slight improvement occurred in the enforcement of most labor laws in the countryside. Not until the period 1964-1970 (see chapter 8) did application of labor legislation widely impinge on the authority of rural proprietors.

Resistance, Evasion, and Nonenforcement

Narrow Interpretation of Legislation

Ambiguities in the Labor Code gave landowners bases for denying the legality of certain provisions of the Labor Code or other labor legislation affecting the rural sector. Following are several examples which illustrate the tactics used in this type of resistance to the Labor Code.

Case 1: The Legality of Labor Petitions in Agriculture. In 1939 a landowner claimed that the sections of the Labor Code dealing with labor petitions did not apply to rural labor because agriculture is highly vulnerable to work stoppages and labor conflicts.[7] Labor petitions in the countryside, while not numerous, had been routinely processed since 1932. Even before the adoption of the Labor Code, petitions in various fundos had been dealt with through arbitration or the good offices of governmental officials. The landowner's response in this case was clearly an effort to have existing law restrictively reinterpreted during a period of intense rural labor conflict. The legal section of the Labor Department rejected a narrow interpretation of Article 76 in the following succinct terms:

> ... given the liberality of Article 502 of the Labor Code, inquilinos and agricultural workers are entitled to present labor petitions, which would be processed according to the dispositions of the Title II of *Libro IV* of D.F.L. 178 [the Labor Code].
> Consequently, the labor petition formulated by the workers of Fundo Santa Virginia is legal.[8]

In this case, the Labor Department acted swiftly by bureaucratic standards. It took fourteen days to formulate a legal opinion and send it to the labor inspector in the appropriate province. At stake was, in addition to the legality of rural labor petitions, the legal protection of workers who presented the petitions. During this period labor inspectors sent the following notification to landowners when workers presented legal petitions:

> In accordance with the law I hereby inform you that a collective labor conflict exists between yourself and the workers in Fundo [name]. Since [the conflict] occurred as the result of a labor petition presented by the latter in which they demand improved economic conditions ... no worker can be dismissed unless he seeks to destroy the property of the enterprise or incites a secondary boycott.
> Violation of this disposition is punishable by a fine of from 500 to 1,000 pesos.[9]

This meant that labor petitions in the countryside, despite landowner efforts, would not be de-legalized through narrow interpretation of legislation. In this instance, at least, legislation was not largely symbolic.[10]

Case 2: Procedural Omissions in Labor Conflicts. In 1941 campesinos presented a labor petition to a landowner more than forty-eight hours after its approval by the workers of the fundo. The Labor Code (as amended by Article 13 of Reglamento 719 and modified by Decree 606 of October 21, 1940) declared that failure to present labor petitions to the employer within forty-eight hours invalidated the petitions. A holiday had occurred within the forty-eight-hour period and the workers delivered the labor petition slightly late. To prepare another petition required reconvening all the workers to vote on the petition's content—this time with the landowner forewarned and able to exercise some influence over a number of workers, thus preventing the necessary quorum from attending the session. If the Labor Department declared the petition illegal, the landowner could legally dismiss the labor leaders and other signers of the labor petition. In this case the narrow interpretation of the law's provisions by the Labor Department supported the landowner:

> Failure to present a copy of the labor petition to the patrón within the limit prescribed in the cited dispositions signifies the omission of an indispensable procedure . . . therefore, in this case, the petition should be considered void and without legal validity. . . .
> The circumstance of a holiday within the 48-hour time limit does not alter this conclusion. . . .[11]

Taking advantage of rural labor's lack of legal assistance, landowners could in this fashion call into question the legal validity of particular labor petitions. When successful, labor leaders and other "troublemakers" could be evicted or otherwise disciplined by the landowner.

Case 3: The Meaning of "Collective Dismissals." From the perspective of rural labor, perhaps the most discouraging example of narrow interpretation of labor law occurred in reference to the section of Law 7.747 of 1943 which stipulated that "in cases of collective dismissals affecting more than ten workers . . . prior authorization from the Minister of Economy and Commerce and Ministry of Labor is necessary. . . ." In a short period of time in late 1944 the operators of Fundo Pinares in the province of Concepción dismissed 131 workers in groups of less than ten workers each. The secretary general of the Confederación de Trabajadores de Chile (CTCH) protested to the Labor Department. The Labor Department ruled that collective dismissals as defined by law meant "dismissal of workers in groups

. . . at the same time, on the same day. This group must consist of more than eleven workers. This legal disposition is not applicable when dismissals are made of groups of less than eleven workers on different days."[12] In retaliation for labor conflicts or for other reasons landowners could dismiss workers at will for "cause" so long as they dismissed no more than ten workers a day. The law which sought to restrict collective dismissals was, thus, subverted through narrow interpretation.

With the introduction of new labor legislation landowners attempted to limit the number of beneficiaries and to narrowly interpret the legal extension of the new laws. Illustrative are the two cases which follow. The first was an effort in 1954 to exclude certain workers from the minimum-wage legislation adopted in 1953; the second deals with the landowners' effort to redefine the legal status of inquilinos in order to avoid social security tax obligations. In each of these cases the landowners successfully limited the law's application, meeting no resistance from a rural labor force still unequipped to permanently scrutinize legislative and administrative officials and employ legal staffs, as did the landowners, to protect their interests.

Case 4: The Working Status of Milkmaids and Cooks. In April 1954, the SNA wrote to the director of the Labor Department, "This society requests that the Labor Department confirm its understanding that . . . the law does not require payments of the minimum salary to those workers who do not work a full day [sunup to sundown] such as milkmaids and cooks."[13] As early as November 1953 the SNA had made an intensive effort to minimize the impact of minimum-wage legislation in the countryside.[14] Now it sought to exclude the most exploited of all rural labor, the wives and daughters of the campesinos, from the provisions of the minimum-wage legislation. Article 9 of the law which established minimum wage for rural labor stipulated that it applied to those who worked a complete shift according to local custom. What was a complete shift for a milkmaid or a cook? The question was not even asked—because no legal representative of rural labor raised it.[15] Perhaps it would have made no difference. But in the case at hand the Labor Department simply ruled in favor of the landowners, who acted under advice of legal counsel: "As established in Article 9 of

DFL 244 only those workers completing a full shift . . . have a right to the minimum salary. The workers to whom you allude in your inquiry, because they do not complete a full shift, do not have a right to the minimum salary."[16]

Case 5: When an Inquilino Is Not an Inquilino. In 1961 the SNA, citing jurisprudence of the labor courts and the text of labor law, wrote to the Labor Department objecting to an interpretation of the status of inquilinos adopted by the Social Security Administration.[17] The SNA argued that, in order to be considered an inquilino, a worker had to possess the following attributes: housing for himself and family; an allotment of land to plant for his private use; and authorization to send a replacement (*reemplazante*) if he did not come to work. The Social Security Administration had ruled that all workers provided housing and allotments of land to plant were, in fact, inquilinos. In some farms the right to send replacements had been eliminated over a period of years; the reintroduction of this requirement would have seriously reduced the number of inquilinos. Naturally, since the law guaranteed inquilinos two months' severance pay and notice in the case of dismissal (as opposed to six days for voluntarios or other laborers) redefinition of "inquilinos" as the SNA desired meant not only liberation from taxes (taxes had to be paid for days inquilinos did not work, but not for the missed working days of other classes of rural labor) but also an easier time in eliminating unwanted hands. (The Labor Code did explicitly include as part of the definition of inquilino, ". . . entitled to send a replacement.")

The Social Security Administration argued that, taking into account Article 79, which in discussing the inquilino contract included the phrase "if such an obligation [sending a replacement] would be convenient," the elimination of this single part of the labor contract did not destroy the status of inquilino.[18]

The SNA lawyer sent a copy of the Social Security Administration's resolution to the Labor Department. Clearly disturbed by the Social Security Administration's intrusion into the Labor Department's area of authority, the Labor Department reversed the other agency's findings and ruled that all rural laborers without the obligation (or right) to send a replacement were not inquilinos.

In each of the above cases legal interpretation which narrowly construed legislative and administrative provisions worked to the disadvantage of rural labor. The campesino had no representation in the legal decision-making process. The landowners, in each case, presented the Labor Department a brief prepared by its legal counsel. Under such conditions regulation of proprietorship by a nonideological technocratic bureaucracy was nearly impossible. Rural labor did not speak the language of the Labor Department's legal section. Rural proprietors employed agents who knew the language quite well. Even into the 1960s narrow formalistic interpretations of legal norms ameliorated some of the ostensible constraints on rural proprietorship imposed by labor law.

Legal Evasion

Legal regulation that rests on definition and formal arrangement can be subverted by changing the formal aspects while maintaining the substance of customary arrangements. Chilean landowners understood this principle quite well and used it where possible to avoid the burdens of regulation and taxation. A single example suffices to illustrate the efficacy of such a strategy.

The Labor Code did not consider sharecroppers, unlike inquilinos and other rural laborers, as dependents. That is, rural proprietors were not liable for social security taxes, insurance policies for work accidents, minimum wage payments, and so on, for "independent" sharecroppers. On an informal basis landowners could insist that an inquilino accept the status of sharecropper while agreeing to fulfill the same labor obligations previously fulfilled as an inquilino. If the campesino refused, the landowner could, with appropriate notice, dismiss him.

Case 6: "On Comodato." In Osorno in 1954 the landowner of Fundo Millantue adopted the following contract of *comodato:*

1. [Landowner] gives in "comodato" a piece of land of more or less one cuadra . . . to [worker] . . . who declares he received the land to his satisfaction.
2. The *"comodatorio"* [worker] can use this land with his family, but cannot rent it nor deliver it to third parties. . . .
3. Termination of this "comodato" and restitution of the land shall not

take place prior to one year from today.

4. The "comodatorio" declares that he is not an *empleado* nor worker of [landowner] but that he works independently in various activities of his own.

The document was signed by the landowner and contained the thumbprint of the worker. The local labor inspector, becoming aware of this arrangement in 1956, wrote to the director of the Labor Department for clarification of the status of such a contract, which he saw as being developed "with the exclusive purpose, to my way of thinking, of evading the social laws and especially the obligations arising from the labor contract with agricultural workers."[19]

In response, Oficio 02177 from the director of the Labor Department pointed out that " 'comodato,' or loan of use, is a contract in which one of the parties delivers to the other, without charge, a product, a good, or piece of land to make use of, with the obligation to return the same after a determined period of time."[20] The Labor Department considered such contracts legal unless the beneficiary of the comodato had obligated himself to perform services in exchange for those benefits. In such a case a labor contract would be needed. If this could be demonstrated, then the comodato could be challenged and a labor contract insisted upon. If, however, the comodatorio (the worker) denied any commitment to perform services for the landowner, then no challenge to the arrangement could be made. A legal evasion of the law was possible as long as the landowner made clear to the campesino that he would rather run cattle on the land than to bear the costs associated with a labor contract. The campesino's choice came down to acting in collusion with the landowner or leaving his home.

Such legal evasions also became popular among landowners during periods of labor conflicts. For "purely commercial" reasons landowners often decided to change the mode of production within their fundos, employing sharecroppers instead of inquilinos. From the Popular Front period onward (1939-) landowners used this mode of dealing with labor disputes in which the rural labor force sought to obtain better conditions of work or enforcement of labor legislation.

Case 7: La Tercera and La Cuarta de Longaví. Fundo La Tercera in Longaví and the nearby Fundo La Cuarta were rented to Gellona, Ossa y Cia. Exploitation was carried out through the traditional system of use of inquilinos and voluntarios. During 1939 and 1940, with the wave of unionization which took place in this region (see chapter 5), the campesinos in these farms joined a rural union, "Los Cristales," affiliated with the CTCH, and presented labor petitions to the fundos' renters. After dealing in the short run with the conflict, the renters proceeded to notify all the inquilinos at the end of the harvest that the fundo intended to change its mode of production. Instead of the normal cropping pattern the administration planned to turn most of the land in both farms over to sharecroppers. The proprietors informed the inquilinos that they were welcome, of course, to become sharecroppers if they so desired.[21] Under pressure from mobilized workers to comply with labor legislation and better work conditions, the landowners legally evaded the issue by changing the mode of production on the farm and introducing sharecroppers for whom no legal liabilities existed. This pattern persisted into the 1960s. The number of inquilinos steadily declined while the number of sharecroppers increased as new minimum-wage legislation and other labor laws were enacted.

Delaying Tactics

Formal adoption of regulatory codes can be accompanied by temporary provisions which give proprietors a specified time period within which to comply with the code's requirements. Such grace periods may also be requested by those to be regulated in order to allow them to comply with the law while not overburdening their financial or administrative capabilities. It is also possible, however, to adopt a deliberate strategy of requesting additional and continuous grace periods in order to avoid compliance with regulatory legislation over a rather extended period of time.

Chilean landowners represented by the SNA adopted this tactic when it could be successfully employed in order to subvert the application of legal obligations. A particularly irksome case of such a tactic involved a housing code for the countryside contained in the minimum salary regulations adopted in 1953.

Case 8: "The use of latrines is not a common practice in our countryside." A part of the minimum-wage legislation stipulated that the value of housing provided by rural proprietors to campesinos could not be discounted from the laborers' earnings unless it met certain minimum standards, including the existence of a latrine.[22] The provisions of the code were formalized in late 1954. When faced by the real possibility of not being able to charge workers for their housing—thus having to pay them higher cash salaries—the SNA wrote to the Labor Department requesting a minimum grace period of two years in order to meet the requirement of installing latrines in the vicinity of their workers' houses:

> The Directive Council of the National Agricultural Society in its last session took note of the different modifications of the Regulations concerning campesino housing proposed by the Commission studying the life and work of agricultural labor.
>
> In this regard, it is our pleasure to inform you that the Council has agreed, at this time, to request the establishment of a grace period of not less than two years so that landowners may comply with the requirement of constructing latrines.
>
> We believe that this requirement, despite its evident justice, cannot be immediately fulfilled by agriculture. The immense majority of rural houses now lack the elements which would permit a rapid and satisfactory solution to this requirement, thus making it impossible for landowners to deduct the value of housing in calculating the minimum wage, an occurrence which is, naturally, contrary to the spirit of the Commission that has been involved in establishing the minimum requirements at hand. . . .[23]

The Labor Department representative on the commission considering the housing code's application interceded. The department established a grace period for compliance until February 30, 1957.[24] In February, 1958 (one year after the end of the first two-year grace period), the department again considered the problem of enforcement of the housing provisions. The SNA again wrote to the Labor Department to request a further grace period for the installation of latrines, pointing out at the same time the great efforts that rural proprietors had made to meet the requirements of the housing code.

> Decree number 243 of the Minister of Labor . . . of 1956 . . . fixed the minimum conditions of rural housing provided by patrón to rural laborer, in order that the housing be considered as a regalía[25] and part of the minimum wage.

Article 9 of the decree in reference . . . declares that the "house must have a latrine no less than 1.50 meters deep."

Compliance with other requirements demanded by regulations has meant that a good number of proprietors [agricultores] have yet to complete construction of latrines. In addition, the Director [of the Labor Department] is aware that the use of latrines is not a common practice in our countryside. . . .

For these reasons it would be just if the Government, through a decree of the Minister of Labor, extends the grace period in which to construct latrines until January 30, 1959. . . .26

Again the extension was granted.27 Thus, until 1959 the landowners managed to obtain, through requests for grace periods, nonenforcement of regulations adopted in 1953. A temporary concession became a permanent aspect of code enforcement during the six-year period 1953-1959.

Formal and Informal Participation within the Regulatory Agency

Responsiveness to interested citizens is generally considered an important attribute of democratic administration. In regard to regulatory policy both the intended beneficiaries and those to be regulated are "interested" citizens. Often, however, the proprietors to be regulated manage to invest enough time and energy in maintaining good relationships with the regulatory agency so that the diffuse and unorganized interests of the regulatory agency's intended clientele are neglected. Administrative responsiveness comes to mean subordination of original goals to the criteria of those interests which, in theory, were to be regulated. One way in which this subordination is sometimes accomplished is through representation of those interests ostensibly to be regulated within the policymaking process of the regulatory agency.

The SNA in Chile commonly had formal representation in governmental agencies, including credit and banking institutions, as well as regulatory agencies. The SNA viewed participation in the administration of policies which affected the interests of rural proprietors as its right. When agencies failed to take this "right" into account, the SNA responded immediately to protect its status and the interests of its membership and other landowners.

Case 9: SNA vs. the Social Security Administration. In 1939

the Social Security Administration attempted to extend the benefits of social security and medical insurance to a large proportion of rural workers (particularly to the reemplazante or peón obligado) by establishing the legal liability of landowners toward this sector of the labor force. This action on the part of the Social Security Administration (having come under the control of the Socialist party at the beginning of the Popular Front period) represented a different interpretation of existing legislation, which would have made explicit the employer-worker relationship between landowner and reemplazante instead of between inquilino and reemplazante. The landowners felt that their interests had not been appropriately taken into account, as is made clear in "Notas de Actualidad" in the July 1939 issue of *El Campesino*:

> Exactly a year ago the Caja de Seguro Obligatorio wished to put into effect certain substantial modifications in the Reglamento according to which Law 4054 is applied to workers in agriculture.
> Said modifications affected the regime of taxation to which agricultural production is subject under the Social Security law to such an extent that a unanimous clamor was raised by the landowners to insist that the modifications were not put into practice. . . .
> The National Agricultural Society, representing the interests entrusted to it, made itself the interpreter of general protest and asked the Council of the Social Security Administration to revoke its decision. This was accepted by the Directors. . . .
> It was agreed, also, that the reforms of the Reglamento be studied —taking carefully into consideration the peculiarities of agricultural work and established customs and usages. For this purpose a commission was named composed of functionaries of the Social Security Administration and leaders of the SNA [*consejeros*] advised by the SNA's lawyer—in whose hands has been placed the documentation relevant to the case. . . .
> It is to be deplored that the work of this commission, which was quite advanced, did not produce concrete results. However, it is even more to be deplored that now, in abrupt fashion, the Council of the Social Security Administration has reneged on the previous agreements . . . and has resolved to put into immediate effect the same Reglamento that had been the object of repudiation this past year. . . .
> If the Social Security Administration is only interested in carrying out its plans, the landowners nevertheless maintain the right to defend their legitimate interests. . . .[28]

Initially unsuccessful, the SNA remained persistent in claiming its "right" to be a part of the policymaking process within the Caja de Seguro Obligatorio. In 1941 the Caja signed an agreement with the SNA stipulating that reassessment of regalías for tax purposes would no longer be carried out without prior consultation with the landowner organization.[29] In 1944, however, when the Caja acted in this area without such prior consultation, the SNA responded vigorously:

> . . . the Society made the Caja live up to the agreement of February, 1941, pointing out to the Caja its lack of authority to adopt unilaterally this type of resolution. . . .
> This Society, in a communication to the Minister of Health dated 10 December 1944, expressed the following:
> "From the study we made in cooperation with you and the Minister of Economy and Commerce, it became clear that the Caja has the authority to evaluate . . . the regalías provided by individual landowners. But to make a general evaluation of such regalías, it is indispensable to follow the procedure of agreements in which leaders of the agricultural societies participate."[30]

The two ministers in question accepted this interpretation of the SNA.[31] In 1947, however, the Caja again acted without consulting the SNA and the same political conflict recurred. The SNA again reasserted its "right" to be represented in the administrative body that determined the status of reemplazantes or the value of regalías.[32]

The SNA never suggested that rural labor might also have a "right" to be represented in this context. Rural labor gained such access to a regulatory agency for the first time, although only in an advisory role, through the special commission established by the Labor Department to study rural labor conditions and standards of living in the countryside in the mid-1950s. Here, however, the SNA was also represented, and the recommendations of the commission were proposals without binding force.[33]

As a rule, despite the SNA's ability to gain formal or informal participation within most governmental institutions, it seems that this was much less the case within the Labor Department. The inability of the SNA to penetrate the Labor Department successfully in this fashion led to the use of other tactics in dealing with the Labor Department as a potential regulator of proprietary authority.

Limiting Resources Available to Regulatory Agencies
The Labor Code charged the Labor Department with the task

of enforcing the code's provisions through periodic inspections, jawboning, and the application of legal sanctions. Emphasis was placed on gaining compliance, not on punitive measures. The department sought to limit the use of sanctions to cases in which conciliation failed and violators refused to meet the code's provisions.[34]

In order to enforce the Labor Code and subsequent labor legislation in the countryside, the Labor Department had to determine where violations existed, seek to convince landowners to comply with existing legislation, and apply sanctions where necessary, while at the same time seeking to insure that rural labor obtained remedy for injuries incurred because of legal violations. In order to determine violations the Labor Department could introduce permanent inspection teams to visit the countryside, respond to complaints of violation, or adopt both of these strategies. Whereas the department always considered the first alternative to be superior and from time to time introduced rural inspection plans on a local or national basis, it was never funded at a level which would have made possible systematic performance of its assigned functions.

From the first days after the Labor Code's promulgation until 1965, the Congress denied the Labor Department's requests for funds to finance rural inspection programs. Documentation of this systematic lack of support by Congress and the Executive is extensive, as illustrated by the excerpts from labor inspectors' reports presented below.

Case 10: Horses Would Help. In 1933 the labor inspector in San Bernardo (Santiago Province) wrote to his superiors as follows:

> I enclose your communication No. 1250 . . . in which you declare that in a recent visit to the fundos around the town of Buin you found that the fundos do not maintain a register of workers and salaries.
>
> I must tell you in this regard that given the extensive jurisdiction of this Inspectorate, from Lo Ovalle to Hospital, and the lack of any means of transportation available to the personnel of this office, it is completely impossible to visit all the fundos.
>
> It is indispensable to provide this Inspectorate with a pair of horses in order that compliance with existing labor legislation can be secured.[36]

Case 11: And Saddles. In March of 1936 a labor inspector in San Fernando (Colchagua Province) wrote to his superiors to inform them of rural inspection visits carried out in the province:

> I would have sent out two inspectors, but lacking saddles, reins and a horse, this has not been possible. Lack of inspection activity is felt more each day: [we have] a series of complaints which, for lack of means of transportation, have not been attended as this inspectorate would have liked.[36]

In 1939 the Labor Department named a rural inspector, and from 1939 to 1942 this single inspector (Ramiro Concha Vera) inspected hundreds of fundos from Santiago to Osorno. Revisits, to verify compliance with the instructions left by this inspector, were not common. Although such inspections were largely symbolic the department eventually cut the rural inspector's gas rations by approximately 75 percent. The reason given for the cutback was the need to conserve fuel during wartime rationing. In any case, one labor inspector with his personal car and a book of gas ration tickets could not enforce labor law in all of rural Chile.[37] Through the 1940s and into the 1950s the situation remained about the same. In 1953, in answer to a communication by the president's Special Department of Complaints concerning the number of complaints in regard to the rural sector, the director of the Labor Department responded at length:

> I should express to you that this Department has always had special interest in controlling and inspecting the application of the labor laws in the agricultural sector . . . given the fact that this is the sector least controlled and where, naturally, the laws are least complied with. Sporadic rural visits have been made in the province of Santiago and elsewhere when it has been possible to take advantage of some personal mode of transportation. However, due to the lack of automobiles or trucks specially assigned to this task, and because sufficient funds have never been available for transportation or per diem, this work is neither as complete, nor as systematic, nor as effective as we would like.
> Every year in the budget proposals, funds have been requested to take care of this necessity and, disgracefully, these have always been reduced in a disproportionate amount without consultations with this Service. . . . At the same time, the acquisition of automobiles has been requested for use in rural inspections in the province of Santiago and other provinces . . . disgracefully, this request has not been granted. . . . The deplorable conditions mentioned by you exist and will continue to exist unless the petitions of this Department are attended to.[38]

The message continues, insisting that the Labor Department cannot carry out its function without minimal support from the Congress and the Executive in the form of financial and material resources. Line personnel also felt the lack of support for their labors, as evidenced by a report from an inspector in Osorno in May 1954:

> *Lack of Personnel:* The offices under my supervision . . . have only myself, an assistant in Osorno, and one other inspector in Río Negro.
> With these few functionaries the Labor Department cannot meet workers' demands for attention or solve the various problems that develop. . . .
> *Means of Transportation:* Until now the enforcement of labor law in the agricultural sector can be considered a myth, since without personnel or means of transportation the Labor Department has not been able to realize an effective inspection program in the countryside.[39]

From provincial and departmental inspectors all over Chile similar reports and complaints continued to come into the Santiago headquarters of the Labor Department. In June 1954, faced with a decrease in budgetary allocations for transportation, the Labor Department ordered all personnel to refrain from making inspections in the countryside except in response to complaints that included a specific request for an inspection visit. All other department business was to be conducted by requesting the appearance of the involved parties at the appropriate inspectorate. This order placed a considerable burden on rural workers unable to make numerous trips to departmental offices and allowed rural proprietors to postpone or delay conciliation sessions for months or even years. The order followed the introduction of an agricultural minimum-wage and housing code by less than a year (DFL No. 244, July 23, 1953). Thus, expanded obligations of landowners toward rural workers coincided with a reduced capability of the Labor Department to insist on compliance. Some congressmen protested, but no additional resources were provided to the Labor Department.[40]

Unable to acquire funds through the Congress or in the Executive budget, the Labor Department resorted to "compulsory-voluntary" loans of vehicles from other governmental agencies. This tactic provided little relief. Cooperation was poor; at best it allowed some inspectors to make rural visits once or twice a month.[41] As recently as 1961 a labor inspector in Colchagua was forced to make an inspection visit to a fundo in the department of Santa Cruz in a cart.[42] In 1963, seemingly in desperation, the director of the Labor Department authorized the contracting of taxis[43] in order for inspectors to make inspections ordered by the headquarters in Santiago—often in response to the insistence of leftist deputies and senators like Salomón Corbalán in Colchagua (see chapter 6). In 1964 the outgoing president of Chile again eliminated funds for vehicles for the Labor Department from the national budget.[44]

Not only were funds denied for vehicles, but prior to 1964 the Labor Department's personnel were among the worst-paid government employees in Chile, and their number remained always insufficient to carry out their responsibilities. Guillermo Videla Vial, who assumed the directorship of the department under the Christian Democrats (1965) commented:

> When I entered the Labor Department it was near the bottom in respect to salaries of its personnel, and the director earned as much as a warehouse foreman in the Empresa de Comercio Agrícola. During my directorship we hired about 200 inspectors and bettered the salaries and working conditions of the personnel. It was a service that past governments tried to maintain with the bare minimum of resources. It was without means of carrying out its functions.[45]

Lack of resources limited the Labor Department to acting on complaints instead of carrying out a permanent inspection program. And even in processing complaints the department had limited capabilities for action. Alejandro Chelén Rojas, Socialist deputy and senator, confirmed the unwillingness of the proprietary interests represented in Congress to provide funds for the Labor Department:

> The labor inspectors had no resources because it was convenient to the rightist governments that they did not have them. We attempted many times through "items" in the Congress to allocate funds to the Labor Department for transportation. We were 15 against 120. Since I had a pickup truck I sometimes took inspectors to the countryside to solve problems that had come to my attention.[46]

Systematic efforts by landowners and their allies thus maintained the Labor Department as a marginal institution—largely symbolic—in its efforts to enforce labor legislation. The effectiveness of this strategy on the part of proprietary interests is confirmed by the reports of labor inspectors for the visits made to the countryside either in response to formal complaints or as part of the sporadic program of inspection.[47] Reports from these visits indicate a general ambience of noncompliance with labor legislation in the countryside, tempered by local or regional patterns that were somewhat better than the norm in certain areas.[48] In most farms not all laws were violated, but some laws were violated in just about every farm. Despite the limited credibility of the threat of sanction, due to the Labor Department's lack of personnel and resources, the threat seems to have tempered the total arbitrariness of the relationships between landowner and campesino which had been the norm before the enactment of the Labor Code. To this extent the Labor Department effectively delimited the scope and domain of proprietary authority.[49] Nevertheless, effective enforcement of the code and subsequent legislation was far from the rule.

Two good examples of the poor levels of compliance with particular laws are the cases of family allowances (*asignación familiar*) and the housing provisions of the Labor Code.[50]

Case 12: Family Allowances. In 1953, six years after family allowances had been introduced in Law 8.811, the Labor Department did a survey for its own use on compliance with the law's provisions. The reglamento for Law 8.811 (Decreto 261, April 7, 1948) specified eligibility and procedural regulations for the family allowance (Articles 23-32). The law required that each month the landowner prepare a list of workers who had worked in the hacienda, the amount of money and in-kind payments earned by each worker, and the total amount of wages paid for that month. Minimally, 7 percent of this total figure had then to be made available by the landowner for family allowance payments to the workers who had not missed any work days. If no workers had perfect attendance, no payment was required for that month. (Later the Labor Department ruled that even if only one worker had perfect attendance he was entitled to all the accumulated funds for that month.)[51] The Labor Department found that in 1953 approximately 49,790 agricultural units employed workers potentially eligible for family allowance. Of these, only 2,474 sent in the required documentation each month (which did not necessarily indicate full compliance with the payment owed the workers). That is, more than 95 percent of the agricultural units subject to the law's provisions did not even make formal efforts to comply.[52] The head of the statistical section which carried out this study reported that the "lack of transportation, lack of personnel and of funds to finance the inspection visits in the fundos, render it impossible for the provincial inspectorates to insure compliance with Law 8.811 by the patrones, thus mocking the payment of the family allowance that should justly be received by the agricultural workers of the country."[53] He suggested that a special inspector be sent to each province to make the workers aware of their rights and to insist on compliance.[54] The Labor Department had no personnel or funds to carry out this suggestion.

Case 13: The Housing Code. In the case of housing no such convenient survey exists through which to estimate the degree of compliance with the Labor Code's stipulations that "adequate and hygienic" housing be understood as an obligation of landowners toward rural labor. There is no doubt, however, that rural proprietors rarely took these provisions seriously. Except for a small minority of fundos, the comments of a labor inspector in 1936 about Hacienda Chacabuco and in 1939 for Hacienda La Dehesa (both in the province of Santiago) accurately apply to the situation even into the 1960s.

> The houses are in poor condition, many having dirt floors, bare, unpainted, or unwhitewashed walls, and roofs without ceilings.
> The majority of the houses are of adobe with thatch roofs, lacking adequate foundations and the [required] minimum of fifteen centimeters from ground to the floor.[55]

And in La Dehesa:

> The houses of the inquilinos are in deplorable condition, practically uninhabitable. They consist of three rooms, with bare adobe walls, floors of adobe bricks in poor condition, roofs without ceilings; in the rainy season water comes through the roof into the house. They lack kitchens or other rooms.
> We determined that in one of these hovels live eight adults and four children, with the negative results that are to be imagined. . . .[56]

These are descriptions of neither the best nor the worst in

rural housing. In general, and even until recent years, rural housing had not met even the most minimal requirements of the 1931 Labor Code: "hygienic and adequate." Labor inspectors could, and in response to complaints sometimes did, issue orders to landowners to correct housing deficiencies. But the normal sanction for inadequate housing consisted of prohibiting the landowner from discounting its value from the workers' earnings when calculating the minimum wage. Thus, if the landowner calculated that meeting the housing code entailed more expense than simply not charging the worker for housing—*after* this was prohibited by a labor inspector *if* an inspection visit were made —then the housing code was not enforced at all. At least this was the understanding of many labor inspectors, as illustrated in a 1960 report on a hacienda, San José de Piguchen in the province of Aconagua, that had been visited by labor inspectors in the past:

> The houses do not meet minimum hygienic conditions. The majority have no floors. They are extremely old buildings, adobe with tile roofs or roofs of zinc sheeting. However, these houses are not considered as perquisites which are discounted from earnings—so that in accord with the dispositions in effect this service has no authority to require that they be improved.[57]

Under these conditions the labor inspector normally informed the relevant health service section of his findings and hoped that the health inspector would follow up on his observations.[58] While not the routine, in some regions good working relationships between labor and health inspectors made this a viable strategy.[59] But the limited capability to make visits often meant that when inspectors did respond to complaints they found conditions like those described in Fundo Rabuco y Pachacama (Valparaíso Province) by an inspector in 1953:

> *Cabins for single workers.* [Pachacama] . . . there does not exist an adequate adjective to describe the miserable conditions of these dwellings. . . . These living quarters consist of one dark room, without beds; the workers sleep on the floor, covering themselves with sacks or with their own clothes. The floor is dirt, and the workers make fires [on it] to protect themselves from the cold and to prepare their food . . . this housing fails to meet the minimal conditions of life for a human being.[60]

This inspection, made in response to workers' complaints and to the intervention of members of the populist governmental party, Partido Agrario Laborista, took place in an area of commercial agricultural properties and industrial and mining enterprises relatively close to Santiago. It was, thus, a zone where the Labor Department was not so understaffed, as in other provinces or in less accessible rural areas. In addition, the special agricultural inspector (Boris Yopo Paiva) from Santiago's Sección de Trabajo Agrícola could intervene. Still, the region received only sporadic visits from the department's inspectors, agricultural visits being made in response to complaints or political intervention. Available resources permitted little more.

In short, the landowners and their allies effectively maintained the Labor Department understaffed and underfinanced. Ideological commitment to effective regulation of proprietary interests combined with allocation of the necessary resources to carry out the task were lacking throughout the period 1931-1964, including the Popular Front years of 1939-1941. The lack of resources, a systematic denial of the means necessary to regulate proprietors in the countryside, was the most effective instrument of the landowners in resisting the effort to make regulation more than largely symbolic.

Compensation of Officials for Nonenforcement

Corruption, including bribery, exists in almost all political arrangements. Where there is the opportunity to avoid large, legally derived costs by making smaller expenditures in bribes, individuals will sometimes use this tactic to avoid compliance. In general, at least a small number of officials will be tempted to increase their income by selling the authority of their official position, either by acting in certain ways or by not acting.[61]

Nonenforcement of Labor Code provisions in the Chilean countryside was sometimes obtained through bribery (*coima*), which took two general forms: payments for specific services rendered and monthly or semi-annual payments for advising proprietors (in a "private" capacity) how best to comply with labor laws. The latter practice was more protection service than quid pro quo payment for particular actions on the part of officials. Although it is officially prohibited, the practice still existed within the Labor Department in the early 1970s. (Inspectors who take on private "clients" in this fashion are called *asesores*.) The practice is much more common in urban areas than in the rural sector, where quid pro quo payoffs were more common.

Despite the relatively insignificant level of corruption,[62] at least compared with corruption in law enforcement and regulatory activity in other nations, Chilean campesinos often believed that landowners' noncompliance with laws was due to generalized corruption of Labor Department officials. "Se arregló con el futre" (literally, he made an arrangement with the boss) was the campesinos' frequent reaction to the slow processing of complaints that often failed to bring results because of formal requirements for documentation and the legal skills of the landowner's lawyer. The campesino's plight was real, but the cause, generally, was not corruption of Labor Department officials.

On the other hand, corruption did play an important role in the poor enforcement by Social Security inspectors of the landowner's obligation to pay monthly taxes in order to keep the workers' libreta up to date. Without this libreta the worker could not receive "free" medical attention from the health service. In general, landowners retained possession of all the libretas in a fundo. When a worker desired to go to the health clinic he would request the libreta for a particular day, giving the landowner time to bring the libreta up to date. In practice this meant that if landowners could receive grace periods from the local Social Security inspectors they could work for months or years with the money deducted from the campesinos' wages.[63] Likewise, if the local Social Security inspector cooperated with the landowner in determining the amount owed for family allowance payments, very large amounts of money could be withheld, a portion of which the landowner could make available to the social security official. These practices were directly detrimental to rural laborers and were more common than the periodic scandals within the Social Security Administration might have suggested. Indicative is the fact that when special rural inspection teams went into the countryside in the first years of the Christian Democratic administration (1964-1970) various large deals involving Social Security officials and landowners were broken up. Several officials were tried on criminal charges and sent to prison.[64]

In perspective, however, the nonenforcement of labor legislation in the countryside during the period 1931-1964 owed
little to institutionalized corruption. Corruption occurred but
did not constitute a widespread source of noncompliance
with rural labor legislation. When inspectors did go to fundos
in response to complaints, or attempted to conciliate labor
conflicts, they generally made a sincere effort to come to a
reasonable and fair solution. However, the reasonableness of
solutions was bounded both by existing law and the current
ambience in the countryside—factors which remained rigged
against rural labor. For example, even in the labor courts (and
these did not exist in all areas), labor cases involved so considerable an investment of the complainant's time and effort
(missing work days, going to town to talk to the labor inspector only to find that he was making inspections in a nearby
town or rural district, and so on), that the rural worker who
lived from hand to mouth could not, in practice, make use of
potential legal remedies. The frustration of dealing with the system often led the campesinos to see it as an *arreglo* (arrangement) between landowner and labor inspector. In fact, except
for very special cases, the landowners did not need to bribe labor inspectors. The existing legal system and administrative
process was corrupt not because the labor inspectors received
bribes but because it relied on private lawyers, lengthy legal procedures, a formal language that the campesino often did not
understand (most nonlawyers or administrators did not) and
prevented labor inspectors from discharging their offices for
want of funds. It wasn't that the labor inspector "se arregló
con el futre" but that "el futre al sistema lo tenía arreglado"
(the boss had arranged the system).

Internal Incentives Mitigating Code Enforcement

The vulnerability of regulatory officials to their superiors and
the vulnerability of their superiors to the dominant political
interests external to the administrative agency can produce a
tendency to ignore certain routine violations of law or to adopt
less than rigorous enforcement tactics. On the other hand, pressure in the form of ideological commitment and explicit orders
to enforce laws to their full extent can produce a milieu in which
regulation of proprietorship becomes relatively strict. Routinely,

most regulatory agencies come to informally identify certain acceptable violations which inspectors will ignore unless external constraints, such as mass media exposure, intervention of political parties or individual politicians, or formal legal action prevent overlooking them. Other violations, because they are highly visible and easy to use as standards of measurement for agency performance or for justifying funding, are fairly well enforced. In turn, individual inspectors or law-enforcement personnel give priority to the enforcement of certain laws for personal or institutional reasons. For the individual inspector, however, his assessment of the response of his superiors when he does attempt to enforce legislation seriously constrains (or supports) his attitudes and behavior in his daily work.

National political authorities outside the Labor Department in the period 1931-1964 did not, in general, give high priority to Labor Code enforcement in the countryside. This is confirmed by the low level of resources committed to the department for its functions and to the generally acknowledged exposure of labor inspectors who attempted to insist on compliance by influential landowners. Legislators, party officials, interest groups, or other governmental officials often pressured the Labor Department to set aside administrative orders or fines. At times such reversals occurred without the consent of the labor inspector involved. On other occasions the inspector received orders to reconsider his findings and issue new instructions.

Despite these possibilities, and the covert sanction of reassignment to less favorable posts for uncooperative inspectors, the formalism inherent in the Labor Department afforded some protection to inspectors who for ideological or professional reasons insisted on strict compliance in their assigned areas. While often viewed as overzealous, if such inspectors could justify their actions within the existing laws and regulations in addition to thoroughly documenting the violations they reported, they generally received support from their superiors against attacks from sources external to the department. In this sense, there never existed a general cynicism or climate of noncompliance within the Labor Department. But almost from the beginning labor inspectors were transferred to different posts when they created too much hostility among landowners in particular regions. Reassignments sometimes brought promotions—a formal recognition of the inspector's correct performance of his assignment, if admittedly an informal recognition of the landowner's claims that the inspector had been overzealous.

Case 14: Inspector Menzel vs. Landowners in Molina. Carlos Menzel, a labor inspector in the Talca (Molina) region in 1932, helped to form several of the first legally recognized rural unions in Chile in vineyards belonging to some of the region's most influential landowners, including a congressman named Alejandro Dussaillant. Menzel also required the landowners to comply with labor legislation. Dussaillant wrote numerous letters to the Labor Department, denounced Menzel as a subversive Bolshevik, and demanded his removal. He insisted that Menzel had exceeded his authority, did not provide adequate attention to the workers coming to his office, and had otherwise acted in illegal, corrupt, and unacceptable ways. He also accused Menzel of chronic drunkenness. In short, Menzel became a *cause célèbre* and a definite source of conflict for his superior, provincial inspector Jorge Weltz. Weltz, notified by Santiago headquarters of accusations against the local inspector, investigated the case and then fully supported Menzel in his claims against the landowners. Summing up his findings, Weltz wrote: "[The landowners] are extremely interested in obtaining the transfer of Sr. Menzel from this Department. . . . The reason for this is that he has required them to comply with labor legislation to which they offer a certain resistance."[65]

The landowners responded by suggesting that Weltz also was a subversive and a friend of Menzel, so that it was only natural for him to defend his colleague.[66] As the case became more problematical for the Labor Department, Alfredo Bañados, a career functionary who had helped prepare the Labor Code, was sent as "inspector visitador" to investigate the entire case again. Bañados had instructions to carry out a full investigation based on the sworn testimony of all involved parties and relevant witnesses.[67] Part of his instructions included the preface that the investigation was to be made because the Labor Department "must offer the maximum of guarantees to all interested parties and act at all times to assure impartiality, competence and judgment of the functionaries pertaining thereto."[68] In short, the case involved an administrative investigation, not merely a simple accession to landowner demands for sanction against inspectors who caused problems. Bañados confirmed the judgment of the provincial inspector, vindicating the action of the local labor inspector. In closing the case the director of the Labor Department declared:

> In attention to the report by the visiting Inspector Sr. Alfredo Bañados, which establishes the unjustified nature of the denunciations against the Provincial Inspector of Talca, Sr. Jorge Weltz, and of the Department Inspector, Sr. Menzel, and demonstrates that they fulfilled their obligations to both give impetus to and obtain strict compliance with labor legislation: This authority approves of this report in full. The case is closed. The conclusions of this investigation were made available to inspectors Weltz and Menzel and to the parties who made the denunciation.[69]

Thus, even as early as 1932, labor inspectors were not necessarily totally exposed within the Labor Department itself if and when they attempted to enforce the Labor Code. Early development of a functioning administrative review process for accused inspectors and a technical sense of mission by a growing cadre of career bureaucrats somewhat protected officials in these kinds of cases.[70] This became more common as the bureaucrats themselves became organized in associations which were the functional equivalent of unions which were prohibited in the public sector.

Still, in the early period and even into the 1960s, rigorous code enforcement was not the rule. Only in areas where individual inspectors had ideological, professional, or personal committments to code enforcement did landowners begin to generally comply with labor law. Of importance, nevertheless, is the fact that inspectors of this sort were not easily removed from the department nor routinely punished.

Discouraging Complaints

Since the Labor Department had to rely on processing complaints rather than systematic preventive inspections, it was in the landowner's interest to prevent complaints and thereby avoid any contact at all with labor inspectors. Landowners could legally dismiss day workers with six days' notice and inquilinos with two months' notice. The threat of dismissal undoubtedly restricted the willingness of some rural laborers to register formal complaints, especially when they knew that a formal complaint might involve a long, drawn out process and substantial investment of time and effort. Blacklists maintained by the landowner associations provided additional sanctions against potential "troublemakers."

Despite these deterrents (not limited in any case to the rural sector), rural laborers consistently and in relatively high numbers registered their complaints with the labor inspectors and took their cases to the labor courts. Unfortunately, data have not been collected to determine what types of rural workers tended to register complaints—day workers, inquilinos, sharecroppers, migrants, and so on. Collection and analysis of such data would give insight into the relative control by hacendados over the diverse strata of rural labor in the period 1931-1964 as well as a sense of alterations in patterns of interactions, by strata, over time. For the years 1946-1949, however, data are available on complaints registered which at least separate agricultural workers in general from other types of workers, empleados, and household servants (see Table 3).

TABLE 3   FORMAL COMPLAINTS TO LABOR DEPARTMENT, 1946-1949

	1946	1947	1948	1949
Empleados	2,084	1,808	1,885	1,703
Workers	11,270	13,193	13,067	10,848
Agricultural workers	4,669	6,272	5,521	4,440
Household servants	3,992	4,025	4,331	3,987
Total complaints	22,015	25,298	24,804	20,978
Agricultural workers as percentage of total	21	25	22	21

SOURCE: Brian Loveman, "El mito de la marginalidad: Participación y represión del campesinado chileno" (Santiago: ICIRA, 1971).

During these years agriculture occupied between 30 and 35 percent of the actively employed population, including hacendados, other proprietors, and administrative employees. Formal complaints by agricultural laborers did not dip below 21 percent of all complaints registered during this four-year period and averaged about 22 percent. These four years included a period of active unionization and labor conflicts in the countryside (late 1946 to mid-1947) and a period of anti-labor repression (mid-1947 to 1949) in which labor conflicts declined significantly (see chapter 4). This, seemingly, did not affect the relative share of complaints by rural workers although the total number of complaints declined by about 33 percent from 1947 to 1949.

Labor inspectors treated complaints routinely, not as aberrations or rural rebellions. Typical of the routine handling of these complaints is the following labor inspector's report from Hacienda Huechun Alto (Melipilla, Santiago Province) in 1939:

> In attention to your telegram No. 668 in relation to a presentation made to the Minister of Labor in regard to the dismissal of thirteen workers from Hacienda "Huechun Alto," the property of Joaquín Prieto Concha, I can inform you as follows:
>
> On the thirteenth of February two dismissed workers presented themselves at this inspectorate to claim their right to severance pay and payment for planted crops. These complaints were registered as numbers 34 and 35 in the "Libro de Reclamos Generales," citing the parties to a reconciliation session for the 18th of the same month. The day and hour were noted on the citation, and the two workers arrived here as did the administrator [of the fundo] in the company of ten other workers who had been dismissed. In the presence of the undersigned, [the administrator] declared that the workers had been dismissed because their services were no longer necessary, and that he had authorization from the patrón to pay them whatever monies the law determined was owed to them. The complainants accepted this procedure. ... All the workers received their corresponding severance pay in my presence, to their entire satisfaction, as is certified in the Libro de Reclamos Generales in this inspectorate, where they stamped their respective signatures in acknowledgement of acceptance.
>
> With respect to the workers who had crops to harvest and wished to leave the hacienda immediately, these [crops] were evaluated in common by the parties in my presence, and those who did not accept this procedure were authorized to remain in the hacienda until after the harvest.
>
> In a casual inspection effected in the hacienda yesterday, I found that six of these workers still remain in the hacienda ... they are authorized to work outside the hacienda whenever they desire.[71]

Such complaints, 4000-6000 per year (1946-1949) were handled routinely by the Labor Department, but campesinos did not always obtain favorable outcomes. And even when the formal outcome favored the worker, the campesinos still might be losers, as when forced to leave the place of their birth or their homes. Nevertheless, workers continued to use formal complaints as a tool for forcing landowners to fulfill their legal obligations.

This is not to say that both intimidation by landowners and the frustrations involved in the formal complaint process did not prevent rural laborers from registering complaints. Rather, even given the level of intimidation which existed, campesinos made formal complaints which the labor inspectors processed as part of their normal duties. If, however, all the subtle (and not-so-subtle) intimidation by the landowners (dismissals, refusal to provide sharecrop land to "troublemakers," reduction of perquisites, and so on) had been removed, it is probable—as occurred after 1964—that the Labor Department would have been unable to meet the demands of the resulting heavy case load. Indeed, in the period 1931-1964, the department was hard pressed to deal with the number of complaints registered in rural areas. When, after 1964, leftist political parties and the Christian Democratic government itself stimulated large numbers of formal complaints by rural labor, the department was unable to deal with the work load and appointed a large number of new labor inspectors (see chapter 9).

Physical Violence and Resistance to Labor Inspections

When proprietors feel that they are the law, denial of the legitimacy of the authority of regulatory agencies may occur. Although by 1931 no serious challenge to the authority of the central government existed in Chile, some landowners did physically resist inspection visits and deny labor inspectors access to their territory (property) and to the required documentation concerning labor contracts, salaries, and social security payments. Physical attacks on labor inspectors occurred rarely, though the possibility of attacks always existed. The cases which follow are illustrative.

Case 15: Use of Physical Force. A labor inspector in the province of O'Higgins in 1938 attempted to process a number of complaints registered against a particular landowner by various rural laborers. The landowner refused to come to the labor inspectorate for the necessary conciliation procedures (*compa-rendo*). The labor inspector then sought to reach a solution in the case because he felt that the workers (migrants) could not afford the time and cost of processing the complaints through the labor court. He went to the landowner's hacienda and then to a nearby hacienda which the landowner was visiting. He suggested to the landowner that some agreement might be reached in the case, but the landowner,

> answering me in an insolent manner . . . incited the persons nearby to throw me off the property. Although I mentioned to him the authority vested in labor inspectors by the law, they proceeded with violence . . . throwing an adobe brick at my head. . . .[72]

The labor inspector left the scene and informed his superiors of the incident. The workers' complaints were sent on to the labor court.[73]

Case 16: And Coercion. In 1940 a labor inspector in Curicó made an inspection visit to Fundo Huañuñe. The fundo's overseer met the inspector and escorted him around the grounds and buildings. After completing the tour the inspector was taken to an office where he intended to fill out the forms concerning the visit and to obtain the necessary documentation. After filling out the forms, he attempted to return to the section of the fundo where the inquilinos' housing was located. The overseer physically impeded him from doing so, indicating that he had received a telephone call from the landowner in Curicó instructing him (the overseer) to prevent continuation of the inspection. The inspector then attempted to go out on the public road and inspect the houses located there. Trying to leave the fundo he found the gates locked. The overseer announced to him that he was being held until the landowner arrived from Curicó. The landowner arrived in the company of a police lieutenant and two policemen.

> Upon his arrival [the landowner] heaped upon me an infinity of gross insults . . . and if it hadn't been for the intervention of the police officer . . . the undersigned would have been a victim of still more insolence on the part of this "gentleman" [*caballero*].
>
> In virtue of the intervention of [the landowner] and in . . . order to avoid further consequences, I left the fundo at four o'clock, leaving unfinished the inspection visit I had begun in the morning.[74]

In this case the labor inspector brought formal charges against the landowner under Article 568 of the Labor Code (impeding the visit of a labor inspector) and also filed criminal charges. The workers' houses, however, were not repaired.

It should be emphasized that these cases are not typical of landowner response to visits by labor inspectors. Infrequent as they were, however, individual cases continued to occur throughout the period 1931-1964. The incidents indicate resistance by some landowners to any redefinition of the meaning of rural proprietorship and the authority of rural proprietors. For these landowners, private property meant that governmental regulation did not extend into the territory of their proprietary domain. The use of force by landowners also indicated, however, that in some cases, despite all efforts to evade or subvert application of labor law, labor inspectors insisted on compliance. Physical force, the least subtle and, over the long run, the least effective manner of resistance to labor legislation in the Chilean context, represented an anachronistic response by landowners unable to otherwise impede the increasing restriction of proprietary authority contained in labor law.

Labor Legislation and the Redefinition of Rural Proprietorship: An Overview, 1931-1964

From the adoption of the Labor Code in 1931 until 1964 the Chilean Congress and various administrative agencies formally redefined rural proprietorship through a number of laws and their respective regulations. Slowly, the obligations of rural proprietors toward rural labor increased and the proprietary authority of landowners over rural labor was restricted. The Labor Code required landowners to enter into written contracts with rural laborers. This obligation legally ended the customary oral labor agreements that provided no formal protection for the campesino and allowed labor relations to depend upon the whim of the hacendado. The Labor Code also delimited the scope of proprietary authority by somewhat restricting the right of landowners to dismiss and evict campesinos, regulating the application of fines, and introducing the concept of formal regulations (*reglamentos internos*) that defined the rights and obligations of employer and workers within the enterprise.

Subsequently, additional labor legislation further restricted the scope and domain of proprietary authority. Minimum-wage laws, social security provisions, housing codes, health codes, and unionization laws all contained formal delimitations of rural proprietorship. By 1964 the legal prerogatives of rural proprietorship vis-à-vis rural labor had changed radically from the situation in 1931. Formally, the hacendado no longer exercised the unregulated authority of a nineteenth-century landlord but rather that of an employer in a twentieth-century Western industrial society. This legal transformation corresponded to the gradual and more general legislative regulation of capitalist enterprise within the Chilean polity.

Lack of enforcement of regulatory provisions, however, produced an ever widening gap between the legal definition of proprietorship and its practice in the countryside. This meant that rural proprietors enjoyed an important economic subsidy from the nonenforcement of labor law. The subsidy allowed landowners to retain customary modes of production. It also meant that the possibility existed for a future government to alter radically the economic and political structure of the countryside by simply enforcing existing law. Law enforcement, in this context, would represent a revolutionary measure.

As the foregoing suggests, regulation of the proprietary authority of landowners through labor legislation was less than perfectly administered. In many areas regulation remained largely symbolic. Yet certain basic restrictions on proprietorship had been generally accepted by 1964. The legitimacy of labor legislation was no longer in dispute. Because the Labor Code and succeeding labor legislation were recognized by landowners as formal constraints on their proprietary authority, landowners resisted further legislation and attempted to subvert the administration and implementation of existing regulations.

Private Property and Labor Law

The landowners always made clear that the basic conflict surrounding labor legislation remained the scope and domain of proprietorship—"private property." Thus, in opposing the adoption of Labor Department-imposed *reglamentos internos* that specified the rights and obligations of employers and workers in the rural enterprises, the landowner claimed that reglamentos internos should not be applied in the countryside because of the "special nature" of agriculture.[75] Between 1931 and 1935 legal debate within the Labor Department and the Consejo de Defensa Fiscal finally resolved that reglamentos internos should indeed be required in the rural sector. The department confirmed a temporary resolution to this effect in September 1934.[76] In 1936 the Labor Department distributed the first model reglamento for use specifically in the countryside.[77] The model contained a list of the types of clauses that should be included in the reglamento but did not, for the most part, include substantive recommendations.[78]

The most important aspect of such reglamentos and their processing by the Labor Department was that they implied a formal recognition by the landowner of a legal delimitation on proprietary authority and acceptance of legal obligations toward rural labor. The requirement for written labor contracts reinforced the formalization of landowner-campesino relations. While not universally enforced, labor contracts were introduced into most of Chile's larger, commercial fundos. Violations normally consisted of not having contracts for all workers on a farm, especially for migrant workers or temporary hands. Only infrequently did fundos, after 1940, maintain no labor contracts at all.

That the landowners understood the implications of the reglamentos internos as formal delimitations on the rights of proprietorship is demonstrated by a letter written by the representative of the Northern Agricultural Society (Sociedad Agrícola del Norte) to the Labor Department in 1940. The society had proposed a model reglamento for use by its members in their rural properties. The Labor Department took issue with a clause in the reglamento which prohibited visits to the agricultural workers within the hacienda or group gatherings in the worker's house (other than of the family) without authorization. The representative of the society argued: "I would suggest that the proposed wording be retained since these fundos are private property and, in consequence, the owner has a right to object to the presence of particular persons on it."[79]

Making clear the issue in this case, the Labor Department responded that private property was not an absolute right, but a set of rights bounded by the constraints of labor contracts and other legislation:

> This Department maintains its point of view in regard to this section. While it is true that the fundo is private property, this cannot be taken in an absolute sense, given the reality of life in the countryside. The worker receives, in exchange for his labor, remuneration and regalías, one of which is the right to a house. From the moment in which the labor contract becomes operative, the worker's house becomes private property [*un recinto particular*], a condition which continues until the termination of this contract, and other persons should be allowed access to it without too many limitations.[80]

Again, however, despite formal delimitation, the de facto discretion of proprietors remained extensive. The seeming victory for the workers was not generally accepted or enforced. In 1962, in a highly commercial fundo linked to the SNA itself, the proprietor still denied the workers the right to have visitors in their homes. The "right" of landowners to control entry and exit to their private property was challenged only when labor inspectors, in response to complaints or in dealing with collective labor conflicts, visited particular properties.

From Mallarauco (Santiago Province) in 1962 a labor inspector reported (Fundo California):

> *Prohibitions on Visits:* Visits are allowed, but only with prior written authorization of the patrón. Violation of this rule constitutes cause for immediate termination of the labor contract.
>
> Orders have been given to eliminate this clause [since] causes for termination of the labor contract are only those established by law. . . .[81]

Formally, the labor code and subsequent labor legislation substantially delimited the scope and domain of authority of rural proprietors vis-à-vis the rural labor force. In practice, as a result of nonenforcement, this authority remained quite extensive but vulnerable to massive enforcement efforts. The gap between formal requirements and practice varied from law to law, but coincided generally with the inability of rural labor to effectively demand enforcement and of the Labor Department to respond to such demands—even had rural labor and its allies been appropriately mobilized. The disjunction between the legal limits on rural proprietorship (and the obligations of landowners toward rural labor) and the existing situation in the countryside—the extent to which labor law was symbolic—was perceptively noted by a career functionary (Julián Gonzalorena) of the Labor Department on special assignment in the countryside in 1965:

The labor conflicts and discontent shown by agricultural workers can be traced to the lack of timely and efficacious inspection and enforcement on the part of the Labor Department, due to the lack of money, personnel, and transportation.

. . . The campesinos, insofar as I have been able to tell in the conflicts I have been dealing with, ask only that the landowners comply with the law.[82]

Closing the gap between law and practice, making regulation of rural proprietorship more effective and less symbolic, depended substantially on mobilization of rural labor to demand that their legal rights be respected; that political parties and the urban labor movement support these demands; and that the Labor Department have resources for effective enforcement of labor legislation. These requirements were not isolated but mutually reinforcing—without all of them labor law would remain, if not "largely symbolic," at least symbolic in part.

From the landowners' perspective, labor legislation and the unionization of the labor force represented a difficult problem. In the first place, effective transition from the role of patrón on a hacienda to that of employer in a rural enterprise entailed fundamental changes of the landowners' perceptions of their own position in rural society. It also required recognition of the campesinos' rights to bargain collectively, to challenge formally the orders of the proprietor on the basis of norms external to the hacienda and, more generally, to participate in the determination of work routines and wage levels or even to share in the distribution of the economic surplus produced by the rural enterprise. Compliance with labor law required the landowners to rethink the basis of the legitimacy for their own authority and to modify profoundly their behavior in dealing with rural workers. An alteration of existing human relationships of this magnitude involves changes in the underlying world view of both landowners and rural workers. Such a change could not be expected to occur overnight. Existing psychological and sociological orientations were serious obstacles to rapid acceptance by proprietors of the implications of labor law.

Second, even after labor law was accepted, the economic costs for the landowners of complying with labor law were quite high. Creation of rural unions made it probable that the cost of labor would increase still more. This dilemma would not have been so serious if governmental economic policy from 1938 onward had not discriminated against agriculture. National economic policy prevented farmers from recovering increased labor costs by passing these on to consumers as higher prices. A program of induced industrialization depended upon relatively low domestic food prices. Governmental policy involved subsidization of foreign producers of agricultural commodities and discrimination against domestic producers in order to maintain relatively low food prices in urban Chile. Thus, labor law and rural unions represented threats both to the political status of rural proprietors and to the economic viability of rural enterprises, given the constraints of existing development policy adopted by the national governments.[83] In this context, even if rural proprietors generally desired to comply with labor law or felt obligated to improve the situation of rural labor—for which there is little evidence—the economic constraints discouraged this type of strategy in dealing with the rural work force.

To meet the economic and political challenge of labor law, in addition to the patterns of resistance and evasion discussed above, landowners adopted a dual strategy of substituting share-cropping arrangements for inquilino labor rents and using more wage labor (*afuerinos, voluntarios*) relative to permanently contracted resident labor (*inquilinos*). Introduction of share-cropping legally eliminated employer-worker relations, freeing the landowner from the payment of social security taxes and family allowance contributions[84] (see cases 5 and 6 above). With adoption of the minimum-wage provisions (1953), land-owners began to consider more closely the relative costs of different kinds of labor inputs (inquilinos, sharecroppers, wage workers, part-time wage workers, and so on). Between 1955 and 1965 the amount of land given to sharecropping in the central valley increased by 46 percent while the number of sharecroppers declined by about 10 percent.[85] The available data does not discriminate between internal sharecropping, within haciendas, and sharecropping on a single-enterprise farm. Still, the direction of change indicates a move toward increased sharecropping both within the haciendas and on other types of production units. At the same time, the landowners sought to reduce the number of permanent resident workers who still paid what might be considered a labor rent for allotted land, with machinery and wage workers.[86] Agricultural workers with an annual contract and an hourly, daily, weekly, monthly, or piece-rate wage did not, however, exist on a wide scale in Chilean agriculture. Thus, the move to reduce the relative number of inquilinos was an effort to eliminate fixed operating costs imposed by social security and family allowance payments (22 percent of labor costs),[87] and to a lesser extent to increase profits by substituting either direct management or sharecropping for labor rent tenancies.

While the early estimates on the relative number of inquilinos in the agricultural labor force are somewhat misleading, because of changing legal definitions of "inquilino" (see case 5 above), between the agricultural censuses of 1955 and 1965 the number of inquilinos officially decreased from 82,367 to 73,938. The decrease represented a decline in the inquilinos' relative share of the population active in agriculture from 12.4 percent to 8.4 percent.[88] Supporting the thesis that to a certain extent the desire to recover land from the internal campesino enterprises also contributed to pressure for the replacement of inquilinos with other forms of labor is Schejtman's finding that, whereas in 1955 some 111,790 rural workers and administrative personnel obtained land allotments, by 1965 only 62,017 rural workers and administrative personnel enjoyed *regalías de cultivo.*[89] Kay estimates that by 1964 only 46,500 inquilinos still received land allotments as a component of their wage.[90] This meant, overall, a decrease of 44.5 percent in the number of rural workers and administrative personnel receiving land allotments and of 36.6 percent in the total area given over to these regalias de cultivo.[91]

Between 1953 and 1964 the increasing legal minimum cash salary obligations of landowners to rural workers entailed a progressive underevaluation of in-kind payments, including land allotments, if the landowner allowed the workers to retain the customary land allotments and pasture rights and paid 50 to 75 percent of the legal minimum in cash. It is in this context that the landowners' persistent resistance to rural unions must be understood. Fearful of losing political dominance in the countryside and, especially after 1953, facing increased legal obligations to the work force, landowners sought to prevent the development of rural labor organizations that might force them (1) to comply with labor law, (2) to respect the customary benefits of rural workers, (3) to improve living and working conditions for the campesinos, and (4) to relinquish their political control of the countryside.

Thus, the lack of effective organization on the part of rural labor, necessary if the regulation of proprietorship was to become effective, was no accident. Chilean campesinos attempted to organize themselves at various times during the period 1919-1964. Recognizing that labor law, and particularly rural unions, represented a threat to their status, their power, and to the economic viability of the existing rural enterprise, landowners bitterly resisted these organizational efforts, seeking to repress the challenge to rural proprietorship inherent in an organized rural labor force.

4

Rural Unions:
The Politico-Legal Struggle

The struggle between capital and labor that led to elaboration of labor legislation and eventually to the Labor Code of 1931 provided also the legal basis for rural unionization. Prior to 1924 and the promulgation of Law 4.057 there existed no legal basis for unionization of any kind in Chile. After World War I, however, the government tolerated some union activity in the urban sector, the mines, and the railroads. In 1924 the cluster of social laws (Laws 4.053-4.059) included procedures for the formation of legally recognized government-regulated labor unions. Law 4.057, which specified the conditions for legal recognition of unions, did not except agricultural unions, but Law 4.053 (concerning written labor contracts) explicitly excluded rural labor. Thus, application of the unionization provisions in the countryside was legally ambiguous.[1]

The only rural labor union to obtain legal recognition (*personalidad jurídica*) under the provisions of Law 4.057 was the Sindicato Profesional de la Industria Ganadera y Frigorífico de Magallanes (Decreto Supremo 2218, 29 octubre 1929). This union, formed in the second decade of the twentieth century, represented workers in the meatpacking plants as well as laborers who resided and worked in the countryside of Magallanes—sheepherders, sheep shearers, butchers, and so forth. It also included workers not linked to the hacienda-dependent social structure of central Chile. For both these reasons it was never a typical agricultural union. Furthermore, between 1931 and 1967 the Labor Department and the organized workers rejected periodic efforts to have the union formally defined as agricultural.[2] Eliminating this exceptional case, we can say that no legally recognized rural union existed in Chile prior to adoption of the Labor Code in 1931.

113

The Labor Code and Rural Unions

The 1931 Labor Code provided the following:

Article 362   The right of association in unions is recognized for all persons of both sexes, older than 18 years of age, who work in the same enterprise or place of work, or who pursue the same occupation or profession, whether manual or intellectual.

Article 363   These unions may be of employers, *empleados* or workers, or mixed, or of persons who exercise independent professions or occupations. These unions are "industrial" or "professional."[3]

Article 379   Industrial and professional unions will be considered legally constituted once they are granted legal recognition by the President of the Republic.

Because industrial unions included all workers in the same firm, whatever the enterprise (Article 381), a union which grouped rural workers in a single farm took on the name "industrial union" the same as that formed by workers in a shoe factory. Professional unions associated people engaged in the same profession, craft, or similar or related labors (Article 407), and under this provision it became possible to form "professional unions" of agricultural workers from different farms. Either type of union could represent its members in labor conflicts and collective bargaining.

No section of the Labor Code which dealt with unionization explicitly excluded rural labor, and in the period 1931-1933 campesinos formed several legally recognized unions in the countryside (see chapter 5). When landowners realized that at least some labor inspectors took literally the Labor Code's provision on unionization, the landowner associations acted to prevent the development of rural unionization and to destroy the unions already formed. In addition to making reprisals against union leaders and organized workers, the landowners presented legal arguments contending that the Labor Code's provisions did not apply to rural labor.

Administrative Repression of Rural Labor

The first formal challenge to the legality of rural unions seems to have occurred in the case of Hacienda Las Palmas de Ocoa, operated by Monte Alegre (Chile) Ltda. A leftist deputy, Emilio

Zapata Díaz,[4] had been active in attempting to organize the campesinos in this farm and to secure compliance with labor law by the hacienda's administration. When the campesinos' complaints led to a labor inspector's visit to the hacienda in order to verify the owners' violations of labor law, the hacienda's administration protested to the director of the Labor Department and also complained that Labor Department personnel were allowing formation of a union in the hacienda. The administrators threatened to terminate production in the farm if the situation was not "arranged."[5] The director of the Labor Department responded to the farm operators on February 11, 1933:

> I have in my possession your communication concerning [the organization of agricultural unions] . . . . the matter which you discuss is being studied by the appropriate authorities in the Labor Department, who are giving it their special attention. In these circumstances, the undersigned deplores the fact that . . . you express a certain compulsion and even resolution to pressure the authorities.
>
> In relation to the intervention of a labor inspector, I want to tell you that in the case at hand, a complaint arrived at the Labor Department . . . which inspector Julio Cesar Rojas, of definitive Conservative affiliation . . . was designated [to investigate]. Deputy Emilio Zapata offered to accompany the inspector . . . who refused the offer.
>
> The above is all that I can tell you for the moment, reiterating that the matter is receiving our closest attention and will have a rapid and definitive resolution.[6]

The hacienda's proprietors again wrote to the Labor Department on February 24, 1933, insisting on a resolution of the unionization issue.[7] The department replied that on February 10, 1933, the legal right to form rural unions had been administratively suspended, with the knowledge and approval of Chile's president, Arturo Alessandri, and the minister of labor.[8] The order to suspend rural unionization, an ambiguously worded telegram-circular to Labor Department personnel, read as follows:

> This Department, in conjunction with the Government, is studying activities related to the unionization of workers in rural properties. Since there exist complex difficulties in carrying out these legal provisions, this Department orders you to refrain from assisting in the constitution of organizations of this type until you receive definitive and precise instructions.[9]

In response to landowner pressure the Labor Department had suspended the Labor Code's rural unionization provisions.[10] How did this come about?

During the same period the National Agricultural Society (SNA) had also moved into action. The directors of the landowner association wrote to the Labor Department in early February, rejecting the legality of rural unionization and the application of other provisions of the Labor Code in the countryside:

> The National Agricultural Society has received complaints from different parts of the country to the effect that some labor inspectors are insisting on application of the legal dispositions concerning unions in the agricultural sector.
>
> Union organizations are covered by the dispositions of Section III of Decree Law No. 178 of the Labor Code.
>
> Article 362 establishes the right to organize unions for those employed in the same enterprise or place of work.
>
> Article 381, in turn, provides that the workers of any mining, nitrate, transport, factory, manufacturer, shop and other industrial and commercial enterprises can form a union. . . . The enterprises mentioned are entirely different from agricultural enterprises. [Also mentions Articles 382, 384, 402, and their applicability to agriculture.]
>
> The functionaries who formulate this class of demands act, perhaps, on the basis of an erroneous concept about the true meaning of the term industry and believe that it includes agriculture. This . . . constitutes, without doubt, an error. . . .
>
> . . . In the name of this Society I request that you impart the necessary instructions so that compliance with the cited dispositions is not required in agricultural labors, because they are not applicable to them.[11]

The SNA continued to make its case during March despite the temporary de facto suspension of the legal rights of rural labor to organize unions. At the end of March 1933, an internal memorandum of the Labor Department indicated the position that the department would take on this issue:

> . . . In effect, Article No. 362 of D.F.L. 178 of May 13, 1931, which is fundamental in regard to the "right of association in unions" does not establish any exceptions to this right . . . but confirms it amply without other limitations than those of age. . . .
>
> Besides, Article No. 362 of the cited D.F.L. No. 178 is in absolute agreement with Article 10, No. 5 of the Political Constitution of the State that assures "the right of association without prior permission and in conformity with the law."

To exclude the campesinos from the unionization law, along with disregarding the rights recognized in Article 362 of the Labor Code, consecrated by Article 10, No. 5 of the Constitution, would also mean creation of a privileged position for other workers in relation to the agricultural worker, in open violation of Section 1 of the above-mentioned Article 10 of the Fundamental Charter of the Republic, which establishes that in Chile there exists no "privileged class. . . . "

Considering the arguments of the National Agricultural Society that the expressed legal dispositions are not applicable to it, it is appropriate to remark that economic science considers as industry all processes of work "carried out in habitual and determinate form with the end of producing or obtaining goods and wealth" (Daniel Martner, Economía Política). According to this, agriculture possesses all the characteristics necessary for it to be considered an industry.

Analyzing the problem . . . there is no doubt that the agricultural worker has the complete right to unionize [in professional or industrial unions] because they are workers in industrial enterprises . . . [that is] the exploitation of a fundo or hacienda.[12]

On May 15 the Consejo de Defensa Fiscal (a kind of administrative supreme court) also ruled against the SNA:

You have requested a report by this Consejo concerning the legal opinions formulated by the National Agricultural Society to the Labor Department, in a request in which it is asked that compliance with the dispositions of the Labor Code concerning union organization not be enforced in agricultural enterprises.

. . . the agricultural industry and its labors present modalities of labor that are unique and which distinguish them from other industries and labors, but this Consejo holds that these peculiarities are not sufficient to sustain the opinion that the cited dispositions are not applicable. It is undoubtedly the case that organization and regulation of agricultural unions will offer difficulties and will require preferential attention by the organisms charged with overseeing them, but these difficulties cannot be causes that allow denying to those working in agriculture the right to associate in unions and enjoy the accompanying benefits.[13]

The SNA continued to insist on a reinterpretation of the legal status of rural unions, carrying its argument once again to President Alessandri and to the minister of labor.[14] Given "new evidence" presented by the SNA, and under political pressure, the Consejo de Defensa Fiscal nevertheless again ruled against the landowners.[15] The legal technocrats in the Consejo de Defensa rejected the landowners' brief. Despite these legal victories for rural labor, the telegram-circular of early 1933 that suspended the constitution of rural labor unions was never formally retracted. No new rural unions gained legal recognition until 1937.[16]

In 1937 and 1938, in anticipation of the presidential elections of 1938, and with the telegram-circular seemingly forgotten if not officially retracted, new efforts were made to establish legal rural labor unions in the Chilean countryside.[17] In the first months of 1939, as part of the popular mobilization that accompanied the victory of the Popular Front candidate, Pedro Aguirre Cerda, the Labor Department registered over 170 formal labor petitions in the rural sector (compared to 6 in 1938). During the same period campesinos organized over 200 rural labor unions, perhaps 75 percent according to legal norms.[18]

Extremely concerned with the wave of rural unionization and labor petitions, the SNA again appealed directly to the president of the republic—as it had done in 1933—to stop the continued formation of labor organizations in the countryside and to consider the need for special legislation in this sector of the economy.[19] President Aguirre Cerda acceded to the landowners' demands, naming a "comisión-mixta" of landowners and representatives of rural labor.[20] Formally, the president himself presided over the commission and instructed it to study rural unionization and to prepare a legislative proposal for consideration by Congress. In order to arrive at this temporary settlement, the SNA agreed to attempt to prevent its members from dismissing workers and throwing them off the land, as they had been doing in retaliation for unionization and presentation of labor petitions. The Confederación de Trabajadores de Chile (CTCH) and the political parties of the Popular Front government responsible for stimulating the rural unionization movement—especially Socialists and Communists—agreed to a temporary halt in the unionization drive.[21] Again, political negotiations at the presidential level resulted in the suspension of the legal right of rural labor to organize unions. To the discredit and (later) confessed sorrow of Chilean leftist politicos, an arrangement that sacrificed the rural labor force in the name of supporting the Popular Front government was made possible by the participation of the Communist party, the Socialist party, and the CTCH.[22]

In response to this political deal and at the orders of Aguirre Cerda, the Labor Department issued the following telegram-circular:

> Considering that the President of the Republic has ordered the organization of the Mixed Commission of Patrones and Agricultural Workers to study campesino unionization in conjunction with other problems of agrarian life, and the Political Parties of the government coalition have agreed that to continue the formation of unions could make difficult the solutions sought, the following Ministerial Order has been issued:
>
> While the Special Mixed Commission of Employers and Agricultural Workers is functioning the Labor Department will suspend all activity [*tramitación*] related to the constitution of agricultural unions. Communicated to you for your strict compliance without prejudice to complementary postal instructions.[23]

Whereas the telegram-circular explicitly limited the suspension of the labor inspectors' necessary cooperation in the formation of legally recognized rural unions to the period during which the special commission functioned, termination of the commission provided no relief for rural labor. Congress took no action on the legislative project, and the ministerial order which suspended rural unionization remained in effect.[24] For the next seven years—until November 15, 1946—this "temporary" suspension of the participation of Labor Department officials in the formation of rural unions (participation formally necessary in order to organize legal unions) mocked the Chilean constitution, the Labor Code, and the prior ratification in 1925 of International Labor Organization (ILO) Convention No. 11 concerning freedom of association for rural labor. The suspension of rural labor's legal rights was maintained despite pressure from within the Labor Department (especially from the Legal Section, where Hector Escríbar M. persistently rejected the circular's legal validity) to have it rescinded.

Despite their initial agreement to the suspension of rural unionization, by 1940 elements within the CTCH leadership as well as a group of deputies within the Socialist party (who eventually were to leave the Party and form the Partido Socialista de Trabajadores [PST])[25] recognized their error in acceding to the landowners' demands in exchange for a promised end to dismissals of inquilinos and agricultural laborers.[26]

In October 1940 Bernardo Ibáñez A., secretary general of the CTCH, sent the following letter to the minister of labor:[27]

> The majority of our CTCH organizations have directed communications to this General Secretariat in which they ask that we request from the Minister of Labor a declaration in regard to the legislative proposal concerning campesino unionization.
>
> They remind us that the Minister, in the speech he delivered at the inaugural session of our First National Conference, declared that if the Congress did not dispatch the law before the 15th of September, the Minister of Labor, in accord with the Government, would proceed to decree the unionization of the campesinos in accordance with the dispositions of the Labor Code.
>
> Since the date set has passed, our comrades from the provinces wish to know the definitive decision of the Minister of Labor in this regard and they ask for reports from our National Directorate.
>
> We would greatly appreciate it if you would communicate to us what has been determined in respect to this problem in order to inform the interested parties.
>
> Awaiting your appreciated response. . . .[28]

But still the ministerial order which suspended legal rural unionization was not rescinded.

In 1941 President Pedro Aguirre Cerda died in office. His successor, Juan Antonio Ríos, proved much more conservative than his predecessor in regard to rural labor and the Communist party. The proposed legislation on rural unionization recommended by Aguirre Cerda's special commission, which labor representatives Emilio Zapata and Carlos Acuña had left in protest over the content of the proposed legislation, was delayed in the Congress. Next the president withdrew the legislation from Congress and sent it to the Consejo Superior del Trabajo, an advisory body, for further study. The Consejo considered the legislation from April 22, 1943, to almost the end of 1944. During this time the temporary suspension of the rights of rural labor to organize unions remained effective.

The commission of the Consejo Superior del Trabajo on Agriculture, on which the SNA maintained permanent representation, began to consider rural unionization legislation by reviewing the provisions of the law proposed by Aguirre Cerda and the counterproposal of Emilio Zapata. After the first two sessions Zapata's proposal received no further mention. The Aguirre Cerda project served as a permanent basis for a revised legislative proposal during the remaining year and one-half of the Consejo's work on the rural unionization legislation.

The positions taken by the SNA representative in these sessions revealed the landowners' fundamental resistance to rural unionization and their desire to maintain in effect the illegal decree that prevented rural unionization. For although the SNA participated in the 1939 special commission which recommended the legislative proposal that the Consejo Superior del Trabajo was now reconsidering (after a four-year delaying action in Congress by the landowners and their allies), the SNA representative, Jorge Rodríguez Merino, began the second round of discussion by rejecting any legislative or administrative action on rural unionization. Rodriguez informed the Consejo "that his constituents [the SNA] reject any initiative which tends, actually, to promote unionization of the campesinos. . . ."[29] The SNA representative made clear that as a matter of principle the landowners did not feel that any action should be taken on rural unionization, that is, that the temporary suspension of the rural laborers' legal rights should not be rescinded and no new legislation introduced. But the landowners agreed to participate in the commission's deliberations because "there exists an evident majority within the commission which desires to begin study of the regulation of rural unionization."[30]

Marcial Caceres, representing labor in the commission (Caceres was affiliated with the CTCH but not with its rural department nor with rural labor), responded to Rodriguez by reminding him that the Labor Code extended the right to organize to rural labor and that this right had been formally recognized in the past:

> . . . to speak of the inopportunity of legislation concerning campesino unionization, is to forget that the Labor Code recognizes the right of the rural workers to form unions. . . . The Labor Department and the Consejo de Defensa Fiscal have recognized the existence of this right, and the Supreme Court has ruled valid this [type of] union organization. In addition, to deny this right is to violate an agreement validly contracted by the State upon subscribing to the conventions of the International Labor Office.
>
> The exercise of the right of union organization in the countryside is today absolutely necessary since only through organization can agricultural workers improve the miserable conditions in which they live and end the abuses of the landowners. . . .

The working class, in deference to the Government, has not insisted to date on the unconstitutionality and illegality of the Decree
of 1939 that suspended union organization. But it is not disposed
to continue on this plane . . . if the Campesino Unionization Project
submitted for consideration by the Consejo Superior del Trabajo is
not soon dispatched.[31]

Direct representatives of rural labor appeared only once
during the year and one-half of debates over the proposed rural
unionization legislation in the Consejo Superior del Trabajo.
José Augustín Valenzuela, president of the Federación Industrial Nacional de Trabajores Agrícolas (FINTA) was allowed to
speak in the seventh session of the commission (July 29, 1943).
The commission reprimanded Valenzuela for speaking in terms
which the SNA representative on the commission found objec-
tionable, and even Marcial Caceres apologized for Valenzuela's
lack of respect ("*cultura suficiente*"). In reading the summary
of Valenzuela's comments, however, one finds that the only
strong language seems to be the suggestion that "reactionary
hacendados, pro-fascist enemies of the *patria* were those who
opposed the association of campesinos in unions."[32]

Throughout the sessions Caceres, and Valenzuela when he
appeared, took the position that special laws were not necessary for rural unionization. The existing Labor Code simply
needed to be implemented in the countryside. Jorge Rodríguez,
the SNA representative, responded that the study of special
dispositions concerning campesino unions was initiated with the
understanding that the matter of application of the Labor Code
to agriculture would remain *sub-lite* because the governmental
decision to suspend the application of this legislation in the
countryside originated in studies that indicated the inadequacy
of existing unionization provisions for agriculture.[33] Marcial
Caceres responded in turn by insisting that the suspension of
rural unionization through an administrative order was an arbitrary and illegal act and that, therefore, at least those unions
formed in 1939, prior to the suspension order, should be immediately recognized by the government.[34]

The Consejo, despite the arguments of its members, considered the proposed Aguirre Cerda legislation section by section—
almost word by word—during the next sixteen months. From
time to time, however, the SNA representative reminded the

commission that the landowners believed that no legislation in this area was justified. When the commission finished its deliberations, the resulting proposed legislation restricted even further the ability of rural labor to organize than had the original legislative proposal of 1939.[35] The SNA representative had even brought to the sessions of the Consejo a proposal for mixed unions composed of three representatives of rural labor and two landowner appointees.[36] As late as the twenty-seventh session, the SNA representative again argued in principle against any legislation that would permit agricultural unions. Rodríguez declared that upon initiating the study the previous year he had pointed out that the agricultural societies considered ill-omened any union organization in the countryside and that this opinion had not changed. He made this declaration "in the fear that it could be supposed that by participating in the discussion of the proposal's particulars, this would signify renunciation of the basic principle sustained by agriculture: that we consider profoundly pernicious the organization of campesino unions."[37] The last session took place on November 16, 1944. The Consejo sent the proposed legislation on rural unionization to the Congress, where it languished until 1947. The "temporary" suspension of the legal rights of rural labor remained in effect.

In 1946, with the death of Juan Antonio Ríos, Chile again faced presidential elections. As in 1939 the political parties of the Left and the CTCH began to mobilize rural labor to present labor petitions and reactivated the issue of rural unionization. Elimination of the ministerial order suspending rural unionization became a campaign issue of Gabriel González Videla, the Left-supported candidate of the Radical party. Elected to the presidential office with the cooperation of the Communist party (which occupied ministerial posts in the first months of the González Videla administration, something it had not done in the Popular Front government), González Videla rescinded the order for temporary suspension of rural unionization[38] and thereby fulfilled a campaign promise to the Left.[39] His election in the Congress, however, was obtained through a bargain with the rightist Liberal party, which essentially turned on a single issue: the prevention of rural unionization or, at the least, unionization on terms previously approved by the Liberal party.[40] González Videla agreed that in exchange for the Liberals' votes no legislative project concerning rural unionization would be presented to Congress without prior consultation with the Liberal party.[41] Again, as in 1933 and 1939, the issue of rural unionization had to be dealt with at the presidential level and as a central focus of Chilean national politics.

In revoking the order which suspended rural unionization, González Videla made clear at the same time that this area of policy should be the subject of special legislation. Despite apparent internal contradictions within the González Videla cabinet,[42] the massive wave of unionization and accompanying labor conflicts[43] made special legislation of immediate and urgent concern to landowners, and to the political parties of the Right in the Congress which represented their interests. Deputy Pereira Larraín (Conservative party) declared in Congress during this period: "The repeal by the Government of the circular that suspended rural unionization transformed the solution of this problem into an urgent necessity. . . ."[44] By July 29, 1947, Law 8.811 had been rushed through the Congress. Once again, massive mobilization of rural labor, organization of rural unions, presentation of labor petitions, and strikes in the countryside had been met with legal restrictions.

Legislative Repression of Rural Labor: Law 8.811

Law 8.811, based on the Aguirre Cerda proposal as modified by the Consejo Superior del Trabajo (after further modification in the Congress), hindered the legal organization of rural labor from 1947 to 1967.[45] It represented, instead of the Campesino Unionization Law (Ley de Sindicalización Campesina) as it was officially proclaimed, a legal repression of the right to organize, which rural labor had theoretically enjoyed since promulgation of the 1931 Labor Code.

In order to understand the regressive nature of this legislation it is useful to compare important sections of Law 8.811 with the equivalent material in the Labor Code:

Campesino Unionization Law (Law 8.811) Article 16	Labor Code Article 381
Rural unions can be constituted in all agricultural properties	The workers (over 18 years of age) of any enterprise (Article

having more than twenty workers older than 18 years of age,
with more than one year of
consecutive service in the same
farm, which represent at least
40 percent of the workers of
the farm. At least ten workers
must know how to read and
write.

362) which registers more than
twenty-five workers can constitute an association that will take
the name "sindicato industrial."

The Labor Code (Article 381) did not require literacy, consecutive service, or minimum proportion of permanent workers to
nonpermanent workers in order to organize labor unions.
Whereas under Law 8.811 (Article 16) rural unions could be
organized with twenty workers instead of twenty-five, as stipulated in the Labor Code, the workers were required to have
been in the farm for over one year and represent 40 percent of
the workers on the farm; at least ten of them had to be able to
read and write. Jorge Rogers, then Falanje deputy for Chiloé
Province, argued that the requirements would eliminate the possibility of establishing legally recognized unions in more than 85
percent of Chile's rural properties.[46] Landowners could maintain nineteen permanent workers (not including sharecroppers)
or convert inquilinos to sharecroppers, and thereby prevent
unionization. Obtaining data from the Caja de Seguro Obligatorio—based on farms which paid social security taxes (approximately 15,000)—Rogers found that only 1,985 farms permanently employed more than twenty-five workers. He went on to
say in the congressional debate: "The project in debate, as it is
conceived, is a project for the repression of rural unions. . . .
The solution which has been found for the problem of rural
unions is that there should not be unionization."[47]

In addition to the obstacles to rural unionization mentioned
by Jorge Rogers, the new law provided that "the workers who
wish to unionize must express this decision in a meeting where
55 percent of those present vote favorably, and in which no
other elements than the interested workers can be present"
(Article 17). The law allowed no labor organizers or outsiders
to instruct the campesinos in the legal requirements necessary
to constitute a rural union. The law required the workers to
notify the labor inspector and the landowner of their intentions.

The landowner could legally deny permission for the union to meet in the farm, in which case the labor inspector might give permission for the union to function outside the boundaries of the hacienda (Articles 9 and 17). Within five days of the union's formation the labor inspector had to officially notify the landowner of the organization's existence, ostensibly for the protection of rural labor.

In addition, the law provided that rural unions might be dissolved, among other reasons, for violating the norms for mandatory conciliation and arbitration in agriculture; for strikes; if the farm, because of change in production, employed permanently less than twenty-five workers during one year; by agreement of 55 percent of its members; and if the number of members was reduced to less than twenty (Article 46). The landowner or any single member of the union could ask the labor court of jurisdiction to dissolve the union if the appropriate circumstances existed (Article 47).[48] The labor court was given a ten-day limit to rule in such cases (Article 48).

None of the latter provisions applied to other unions according to the 1931 Labor Code. Further, because union officers did not receive the customary *fuero* (immunity from dismissal) in rural unions, in contrast to provisions for all other labor unions, labor leaders could simply be thrown off the land as soon as labor conflicts were resolved. (Short-term immunity from retaliation applied during the processing of labor conflicts.) The law specified procedures for collective bargaining and labor petitions so restrictive as to almost preclude them (Articles 52-69). That labor petitions were forbidden during the planting or harvesting seasons, which were a minimum of sixty days each in each zone or region, precluded legal labor conflicts during at least four months of the year—and at the most strategic times for rural labor to make good their demands. The law outlawed strikes in agriculture. (As late as 1946 legal agricultural strikes took place in Chile.) Thus, the landowners and their allies eliminated another instrument through which rural labor could legally assert collective demands. If over 55 percent of the unions' membership illegally went on strike, the union could be dissolved at the request of any single member, the landowner, or the labor inspector. Punishment for crimes against the "right to work" (*contra la libertad del trabajo*) of other laborers consisted of mandatory jail terms (one to sixty days) (Article 71). Violations of this section included threats against the workers or landowner by the respective union; any act intended to impede the workers from coming to work; any act that impeded normal milking operations; and any act that tended to destroy or destroyed the materials, instruments, or products of work or commerce, or which caused their deterioration or a decrease in their value (Article 70). Similar provisions applied to nonrural unions with the important exception that strikes under some conditions were legal—changing substantially the meaning of "right to work" and therefore of criminal behavior.

Finally, the law required all rural unions formed prior to the passage of Law 8.811 to conform to the provisions of Law 8.811 or be dissolved. The SNA declared that ". . . the danger of extending workers' conflicts and social resistance to the countryside, by virtue of a poorly considered generalization of the Labor Code, has been reduced and regulated by Law 8.811. . . ."[49]

The logical outcome of this legislation, the almost impossible task of forming legally recognized rural unions and presenting legal labor petitions, reached its extreme expression in 1963 in a conflict in the province of Aconcagua. The Labor Department ruled that in some farms—those which plant and harvest year-round—no labor petitions were legal. The campesinos wrote to the Labor Department from Fundo Santa Marta de Longotoma as follows:

> We have presented a labor petition to our patrón, which has been submitted for recognition to the Arbitral Tribunal. The Tribunal has ruled that the petition was presented during the period of harvest and planting in the fundo.
> Article 470 of the Labor Code states that the periods of planting and harvesting will be determined by Regulations for each zone, and not by what is being planted or harvested in each individual fundo.
> This is the basis for our appeal. We request that the Director of the Labor Department inform us in writing concerning the dispositions of the Reglamento for the zone in which Fundo Santa Marta is located . . . or what guidelines should be followed, in case the referred-to Reglamento does not exist, in a fundo like the one mentioned, in which there is year-round planting and harvesting.[50]

The Labor Department's tortured, bureaucratic response confirmed that, pushed to its logical extension, the Campesino

Unionization Law indeed prohibited labor petitions as well as strikes in farms where planting and harvesting went on all throughout the year:

> Your presentation of the 22nd of this month has been received. . . .
> In this regard I inform you that:
> . . . This Reglamento in its Article 33 declares the following:
> "The periods of planting and harvesting will be determined in each case by the respective Provincial Agronomist, at the request of any of the parties in conflict."
> . . . In regard to the fact that the fundo in question is engaged in year-round planting or harvesting . . . Article 470 of the Labor Code says the following:
> "Labor Petitions shall not be presented during periods of planting and harvesting, which shall be fixed by Regulations for each zone. Each of these periods shall be a minimum of sixty days.
> "These labor petitions shall be presented only once a year."
> From this precept it is deduced that in a fundo with the characteristics indicated, labor petitions cannot be presented.
> Despite the above, given that you will appeal the ruling of the Tribunal of Arbitration, this problem could be submitted for the consideration of the Tribunal that will hear the appeal.[51]

The so-called Campesino Unionization Law served simply to deny not only the right to strike but also the right to present legal labor petitions. Rural labor found itself in a worse legal position than in 1924 and stripped of the gains formally made in the Labor Code of 1931.[52] In order to maintain the existing political order, the national regime essentially outlawed the rural labor movement. This legal repression was formally maintained until 1967.

Soon after the passage of the Campesino Unionization Law, the González Videla government veered further toward the political Right, breaking with the Communists especially because of their leadership in rural labor unionization and stimulation of rural and industrial strikes. The anticommunist legislation which followed was effectively applied to repress the rural labor movement. Law 8.837 gave the president extraordinary powers to deal with "subversion." In 1948 the so-called Law for the Permanent Defense of Democracy (Law 8.987) outlawed the Communist party, excluded its members from participation in the labor movement, and set up zones of "banishment" for agitators and "subversives." The law also eliminated the Communists' right to participate in elections and ordered their names removed from voter registration lists. The law prohibited Communists from holding union offices.[53] In June 1949 an oficio-circular announced the norms which were to be enforced generally in keeping those identified as Communists out of the labor movement.[54]

Repression of leftist political parties and labor leaders, who had assisted the rural labor movement, further restricted the legal capability of rural labor to organize. Thus, for example, in Fundo San Manuel (Parral, Linares Province) in 1949 the requirements of Law 8.987 eliminated four of the five union officers. This union had been organized prior to Law 8.811, dissolved in order to comply with the new union legislation, and reconstituted in accordance with the new law. Within a two-year period the legal repression of rural labor caused the union to go through three reorganizations and then face the loss of its officers due to the anticommunist legislation.[55]

Such cases were typical. Legal repression of unions, union leaders, and the rural labor movement followed as a direct consequence of enforcement of Law 8.987. The SNA, which since the first rural unionization efforts of the period 1919 to 1925, had identified rural unions with the elimination of private property and the advent of communism, reacted jubilantly to the repression of the labor movement. In October 1947, before enactment of Law 8.987 but after the first extension of extraordinary powers to González Videla to deal with "subversion," Máximo Valdés Fontecilla, SNA president, had declared:

> I stop for a moment, gentlemen, to make a fervent plea to the landowners of my country that they, without exception, collaborate with His Excellency the President of the Republic and his Government, contributing with all their force to the extirpation of the malignant tumor that corrodes the entrails of the nation and that is called: International Communism.[56]

The Consequences of Administrative and Legislative Repression

The combined impact of the administrative suspension of rural unionization, Law 8.811, and Law 8.987 on the rural labor movement is indicated, in part, by the drastic decline of labor petitions presented in the countryside (see Table 4). From marginal activity in the years 1932-1938, rural labor during the Popular Front period rapidly expanded its agitation for better

TABLE 4   LABOR PETITIONS REGISTERED BY THE LABOR
DEPARTMENT IN CHILE, 1932-1950

Year	Number of Labor Petitions	Number of Agricultural Labor Petitions	Agricultural Labor Petitions as Percentage of All Labor Petitions
1932	51	5	10
1933	172	6	4
1934	125	6	5
1935	135	4	2
1936	187	1	—
1937	235	3	2
1938	248	5	2
1939	652	171	26
1940	1130	199	18
1941	892	115	13
1942	854	101	11
1943	980	83	9
1944	1110	82	7
1945	883	62	7
1946	1172	272	24
1947	1234	384	31
1948	878	24	3
1949	827	16	2
1950	818	11	1

SOURCE: Brian Loveman, "El mito de la marginalidad: Participación y
represión del campesinado chileno" (Santiago: ICIRA, 1971), pp. 10-11.

working conditions and a greater share in the economic surplus produced in the agricultural sector. Hindered by the
suspension of legal unionization activity from 1939 to 1946,
militancy gradually declined after 1940. From 1942 to 1946
the rural labor movement continued to press its demands but
received little support from the administration of President
Ríos. The continued suspension of legal unionization made
difficult the establishment of permanent workers' organizations in the countryside and left labor leaders exposed to

landowner retaliation. The number of formal labor petitions
therefore declined.

With the repeal of the ministerial order that had suspended
legal unionization, rural labor again—this time massively—
pressed its demands on rural proprietors. The repression of the
Chilean labor movement that followed the enactment of Laws
8.837 and 8.987 affected most severely the rural sector, still
the weakest link in the labor movement. Not until 1952-1953
did a temporary recovery begin, when social-Christian-oriented
labor leaders intervened in the countryside. Still, even in the
post-1953 period, and until 1967, the restrictions in Law 8.811
thwarted the organization of legally recognized rural unions.
From 1948 until 1964 campesinos formed only forty-two legally recognized rural unions.[57] When the Christian Democratic
candidate for president, Eduardo Frei, was elected in 1964,
there remained only twenty-two such unions with a total membership of about fifteen hundred workers.[58]

Labor Department personnel recognized the restrictiveness
of legal constraints on rural unions. In 1958, upon assuming
the position of *jefe* ("head") of the section responsible for labor
unions (Departamento de Organizaciones Sociales) within the
Labor Department, Juan Arrancibia severely criticized the provisions of Law 8.811 and suggested legislation to correct these
deficiencies.[59] Arrancibia's objections to the law, for the most
part, were the very restrictions that landowners had insisted
upon in order to maintain their extensive proprietary authority
in the countryside. When President Alessandri completed his
term in 1964, the legal repression of rural labor remained intact.

Repression as Reaction

In the politico-legal context for rural unionization, perhaps
the most significant aspect of this entire period (1931-1964)
was that legislative and administrative acts by the national government were reactions to concrete efforts of rural unionzation.
In the most literal sense governmental policy was reactionary.
Rural unionization and labor conflict induced the negative response of rural proprietors who insisted—with success—that the
national regime move to legally de-authorize rural unions or
make their organization virtually impossible. This occurred in
1932-1933 in response to the first legal unions in the province

of Talca. It occurred again in 1939 in reaction to the wave of unionization that accompanied the Popular Front. In 1947 landowners again moved to legally restrict rural unionization in response to the massive unionization drive which accompanied the first months of the González Videla government. In 1953, 1959, and 1962 the landowners insisted that the provisions in Law 8.811 be strictly enforced in response to labor conflicts in the countryside promoted by unions without legal recognition.

Invariably, the landowners saw rural unionization and communism as synonymous—and as the most direct threat to the customary prerogatives of rural proprietorship.[60] But throughout this period existing legislation and administrative policy did not, a priori, prevent rural unionization. It was enacted and implemented to repress rural unions which had, for the most part, already been constituted in accord with existing legal norms. When, despite existing laws and administrative regulations, rural labor did legally organize and present collective demands to the landowners, the existing political regime responded with more restrictive laws or regulations to meet the challenge to the prerogatives of property in rural land. Whether through illegal administrative decree or restrictive legislation, the national regime maintained itself and the position of the hacendados through "legal" repression of rural labor.[61] The following chapter details the character of the struggle in the countryside that brought landowner and governmental repression during this period.

5

Rural Unions: The Struggle in the Countryside

Those that cause indiscipline by inciting the other workers to demand higher wages, more food or less hours of work will be severely punished or even thrown off the hacienda.

Manual del Hacendado Chileno, 1875

It is the large estates, generally unproductive, that produce discontent and poverty and it is these large estates that we will eliminate when we are able to throw from power the current exploiters [of the people].

Luis Emilio Recabarren, 1923

The Agarian Reform is not Frei's but is a product of the years of struggle and the suffering they imposed upon us [de los palos que nos dieron].

Emilio Zapata Díaz, 1971

Most treatments of the pre-1964 rural scene in Chile take for granted Christian Democratic claims that "the Chilean campesino initiated his process of liberation in the government of ex-President Frei. More than one hundred years of dependence began to be replaced by a free, responsible life."[1] In fact, the process of liberation of the Chilean campesino has been a long, uneven struggle which was always a part of a larger politico-ideological challenge to the existing system of property in Chile. Until 1964 each wave of rural unionism met repression and defeat through the combined efforts of national governments and the landowners. The national regime employed its administrative and legislative power to destroy rural unions (see chapter 4). Landowners used violence against the campesino's person and property, threatened eviction from tenancies or sharecrops, destroyed crops, and blacklisted persons to prevent future employment and to break rural unions.

In addition, often to their eventual disadvantage, campesinos were a part of the sectarian battles between competing leftist

133

groups and movements. Rural labor shared the frustration of the Chilean working class as the political Left periodically seemed to turn on itself in fratricidal conflict. At several key junctures rural labor organizations decided the short-term outcomes of these battles between competing popular movements. The Socialist victory in the first national congress of the Confederación de Trabajadores de Chile (CTCH) (see p. 163) is a case in point.

This chapter examines the active struggle of rural labor from 1919 until 1964 to organize itself and to delimit the proprietary authority and political power of rural proprietors. The historical treatment focuses on the relationships among Chilean national politics, the urban labor movement, and rural labor. The activism of rural labor and its allies was a key component in the national labor movement's challenge to traditional concepts of property and property rights. The serious nature of this challenge gave rise to national political solutions which emphasized repression of the rural labor movement.

The First Wave of Rural Unionization

In the post-World War I period, working-class organizations explicitly attacked the unchallenged control of propertied classes over Chile's national life.[2] Most important among these was the Federación Obrera de Chile (FOCH). From its founding in 1909 among the railway workers in Santiago, the Gran Federación Obrera de Chile (shortened later by deleting "Gran") developed by the end of World War I into a Marxist-dominated, revolutionary working-class organization. Between 1919 and 1925 FOCH began to penetrate the countryside, challenging the hegemony of the hacendados. Thus, the first organized challenge by rural labor organizations to the hacendados formed part of a larger attack by a national labor movement on the system of property relationships which served as the foundation of Chile's existing political order.

Certainly in the nineteenth and early twentieth centuries sporadic resistance by rural labor to poor working conditions, low wages, or encroachment of the haciendas on communal or individual campesino properties gave rise to landowner-campesino disputes. But no social history of nineteenth-century Chile treats this subject.[3] Balmaceda's warning to the hacendados that

"those who insubordinate the other workers so that they will
not work except for a determined wage or demand increase in
food rations and diminution of work hours will be punished
severely or even thrown off the hacienda" was surely not a prescription for a merely hypothetical situation.[4] There can be no
doubt that occasional resistance did in fact take place. The extent of the resistance cannot at present be determined.[5]

In 1911 the *Boletín de la Oficina del Trabajo* for the first
time officially recorded a labor conflict in the countryside
which involved a strike by forty workers.[6] The workers demanded immediate payment of back salaries. Settling the strike
on the same day, the hacendado agreed to pay the workers
every two months. Previous conditions are not recorded.

No more rural conflicts appear in the *Boletín* until 1919,
when three strikes were recorded in rural Aconcagua. The next
year the Labor Office[7] listed five strikes in the countryside.[8]
FOCH supported each of the latter movements. By 1921, according to a study by the Labor Office, FOCH had organized
rural labor organizations from Coquimbo to Valdivia.[9] In addition, Consejos Federales de Oficios Varios included campesinos
in O'Higgins, Colchagua, Curicó, Talca, and Linares.[10] Into
1921 FOCH continued stimulating labor petitions and strikes
in the countryside.

In May 1921 the National Agricultural Society (SNA) sent a
letter to President Arturo Alessandri which declared in part:

> To this difficult situation in which agriculture finds itself has been
> added the unconscionable propaganda being made in the countryside
> in the name of Your Excellency, trying to federate inquilinos and agri-
> cultural workers, and promising them the abolition of property, the
> distribution of land, and installation of the Soviet regime.
> ... The National Agricultural Society appeals to Your Excellency
> because of this danger and has confidence that through Your Excellen-
> cy's efficacious action these dangers can be averted, and implores that
> you ... recommend to the authorities that they strictly comply with
> laws protecting property and life and guaranteeing the functioning of
> the agricultural industry; that you use the legislative means which Your
> Excellency considers necessary to better the conditions of agriculture
> and the well-being of the proletariat of the countryside while avoiding
> further labor disturbances.[11]

Alessandri, despite the populist rhetoric of his campaign, agreed
with the landowners that

> Before all, and above all, it will be necessary to maintain order
> and security of life and property in the city and the countryside; be-
> cause respect for property and the right to work are fundamental to
> the prosperity of nations.
>
> I condemn in the most energetic form the work of agitators and
> disturbers of order and of work and I consider them the enemies of
> the people (*pueblo*) and of the Republic's progress.[12]

In the same letter Alessandri continued:

> ... To the workers of the countryside I say [that] it is not advis-
> able that they federate under the same rules and direction as workers
> in the cities ... all use of violence by patrones and workers ... is to
> be condemned, as it impedes those who wish to do so from working
> and because the right to work is just as sacred and more useful than
> the right to strike. All propaganda that leads to violence or distur-
> bances, that speaks of redistribution of land or of social revolution is
> to be condemned, because to do so is to attack the prosperity of the
> nation and its constitutional life.[13]

Alessandri's answer, paternalistic and sympathetic yet
staunchly defensive of the property rights of the threatened
landowners (and including a suggestion that landowners sponsor
unions to create "solidarity in the countryside") seemed, at
first glance, an overreaction to the still localized challenge of
rural labor to the landowners. Nevertheless, the matter seemed
to justify the SNA's concern. In every strike or labor petition
supported by FOCH, the workers at least partially succeeded
in forcing the landowners to meet their demands unless the government used police to break the strike or the landowner could
convince local officials to authorize municipal police to throw
"agitators" or participating workers off the hacienda.[14]

Between 1919 and 1925 FOCH-oriented campesino organizations presented labor petitions and carried out strikes in over
forty haciendas. In 1922 FOCH threatened to carry out strikes
simultaneously in three hundred farms.[15] Illustrative are the
developments in Hacienda Aculeo in early May 1921.[16] The
Provincial Junta of FOCH in Rancagua wrote to the Minister
of Interior, Pedro Aguirre Cerda, as follows:[17]

> The workers of Hacienda Aculeo, property of Miguel Letelier Espi-
> nosa, have been incorporated into the FOCH, forming Consejo Federal
> No. 6 in Rancagua. This simple and legitimate resolution by the work-
> ers, to associate themselves in order to collectively help one another

and defend themselves from the vicissitudes of life, has been taken
by the proprietor of Hacienda Aculeo as a demonstration of hostility against his interests, and as probable consummation of dis-
orders and threats to property, and so to this effect, he has taken reprisals against the federated workers, notifying ten inquilinos that as of
April 29 they have eight days to leave the Hacienda. As if this were
not enough, on the 30th of the same month he notified twelve more
inquilinos that they must leave the Hacienda, with the same time limit,
under pain of being evicted with force by carabineros whom the Minister has placed at the disposition of this industrialist.[18]

Landowners responded to the organization of rural labor, the
presentation of labor petitions, and the strikes in the countryside with massive dismissals, enforced by police when campesinos refused to leave the haciendas. In the years 1921-1925 a
pattern which persisted throughout the rest of the period under
consideration was established. Campesinos made short-term
gains through labor disputes; shortly thereafter, landowners retaliated with evictions, blacklisting of labor leaders, or "changes
in modes of production for 'purely commercial reasons' "—that
is, switching from crops to livestock or to sharecropping arrangements in order to eliminate dependence on numbers of permanent workers.

FOCH intervention in the countryside during this period set
a pattern for the rural labor movement for the next fifty years.
First, rural labor activism formed part of a wider ideological
and political attack on existing property relationships and on
the existing governmental regime. The activism of rural labor
took the form of labor petitions, work slowdowns, strikes, sabotage of production, and physical resistance to evictions. Repression of rural labor resulted from national governmental intervention through proposed new legislation, administrative
innovation (the Yáñez decree and subsequent "voluntary" arbitration measures), and the use of coercion—the carabineros—
to support the rights of rural proprietors and defend the prerogatives of private property.

FOCH also began a service and recruitment campaign which
was to characterize both Marxist and Catholic rural labor organizations in the future. The service entailed processing individual and collective complaints by campesinos and asking the
Labor Department or other governmental agencies to investigate
the legality of landowner behavior or to remedy wrongs done

to workers. Handling individual claims for back salaries, inequitable division of crop shares, or other problems provided a
means to recruit clientele, diffuse FOCH propaganda, and increase membership in the countryside. The important role of
mediator among campesinos, campesino organizations, landowners, and the national regime became a typical function of
rural labor organizations during the next half century.

Likewise, FOCH's use of letters addressed to Chile's president
to state claims and problems of rural labor became a common
political tactic.[19] FOCH's appeal to Alessandri was followed by
similar communications by various campesino unions and the
Liga Nacional de Defensa de Campesinos Pobres, CTCH, ASICH,
and CUT—all national labor organizations which followed FOCH
in later years. FOCH's penetration into the countryside thus set
the tone and style for a national political struggle between rural
labor and rural proprietors to be waged in the coming decades.

Landowner reaction to FOCH similarly set the tone for the
next fifty years. Landowners reacted immediately and collectively to the threat of an organized labor force.[20] They agreed
to expel agitators and not to accept the presence of federated
inquilinos or workers in the haciendas. In addition, they deleted
customary perquisites and land allotments, shifted temporarily
to less labor-intensive modes of production in order to justify
dismissals of workers participating in the labor movement, dismissed labor leaders or "agitators" and appealed for police protection for the "right to work" for strikebreakers. When workers refused to leave their homes, landowners then requested
court orders (or moved without such orders) so that police
would evict inquilinos and other workers from the hacienda.
Except in isolated cases where the syndical organization could
be sustained, any short-term gains won by rural labor through
activist tactics were lost in the retaliation which followed. At
the end of the harvest, landowners simply failed to renew contracts of inquilinaje and told the workers to leave the haciendas.
The pattern was to be repeated over and over again in the waves
of rural labor conflicts throughout the next five decades.

What, then, did campesinos seek in the labor petitions presented to rural proprietors in the period 1919-1925? The petitions generally combined demands for the recognition of the
recently formed labor organization (FOCH consejo), the elimi-

nation of traditional obligations and toll charges, improved wages, housing, food rations, land allotments, the reestablishment of traditional prerogatives (for example, land allotments and pasture rights) recently eliminated by the landowner, and nonretaliation (or the rehiring of already dismissed personnel).[21] Illustrative is a labor petition from Hacienda El Melón in Valparaíso in 1921.[22] After presenting a copy of the labor petition to the landowner, the campesinos sent a copy of the petition with the following letter to the intendente of the province:

> The Consejo Federal No. 2 of El Melón wishes to inform you that on the 14th of the present month this Consejo Federal presented a labor petition from the workers of the fundo El Melón pertaining to Señor José Mass, who returned the petition immediately, refusing to discuss any of its points. Because of this attitude the workers have agreed to bring the matter to your attention so that you might speak to the parties and if necessary submit our petitions to arbitration in conformity with the Yáñez decree.[23] We await your reply before declaring a strike and we append a copy of the labor petition.

1. Recognition of Consejo Federal No. 2.
2. Immediate dismissal of Hugo Otaegui O. [an administrative employee] for constant provocation of the federated workers.
3. Removal of overseer Lorenzo Saavedra because of his hostility toward workers.
4. Re-employment of dismissed inquilinos.
5. Raise in salary to three pesos for the inquilinos and voluntarios.
6. Eight hours of work on the following schedule: seven to eleven a.m. and twelve to four p.m.
7. That we not be obligated to loan our oxen to the haciendas as this is prejudicial to the interests of the inquilinos, taking time from our own agricultural labors.
8. That pasture rights for oxen of the inquilinos and other animals that the inquilinos set to pasture be charged at the same rate as in the past.
9. That the non-irrigated hill land be available to plant under the same conditions as in the past.
10. That the sierra be available as before for animal husbandry.
11. Freedom to sell our products [that is, not necessarily to the landowner].
12. That seed be loaned to us and that it be discounted before the distribution of the harvest [out of the total harvest, not just the inquilino share].
13. That the carters [carreteros] not be charged four pesos per trip because this is unjust. . . .

14. That preference be given to inquilinos over outside workers in assigning sharecrop land, and that those who need to plant be given good land.

The labor petition was a combination of reactions to deteriorating conditions—efforts by the proprietor to encroach on the campesino enterprises through decreased land allotments, pasture rights, and other perquisites—and demands for innovations and improvements in working conditions. The workers also sought recognition of their labor organization, nonretaliation (rehiring of dismissed inquilinos), and elimination of traditional labor obligations to the hacienda (for example, provision of ox-teams for hacienda labors). Other FOCH-oriented labor petitions for the same period contain much the same demands, always including the demand for recognition of the FOCH consejo.

The proprietor's response to several of the inquilinos' demands, including those for a shorter work day and higher wages, indicated that the labor petition in El Melón was a part of a broader, national political movement which challenged the existing system of property in Chile. He responded that the farm would "accept what would be stipulated in the Labor Code. To this effect the parties will wait the thirty days which it can be supposed its promulgation will be delayed."[24] (In fact, no Labor Code was adopted until 1931.) FOCH's labor activity in the countryside was an element in its national campaign to alter, through legislation and direct confrontation, the prerogatives of proprietorship. In this sense, the campesinos, in addition to attacking the traditional authority of proprietors in rural land, participated, if unknowingly, in an effort to alter relationships between the propertied classes and the labor force on a national scale.

By 1924 FOCH seems to have escalated its demands for recognition to include recognition by rural proprietors in general and by the Chilean government. In 1924 a labor petition presented by campesinos in Hacienda Huemul (Colchagua Province) included a demand for recognition of FOCH by the landowner, and declared that FOCH would "make this demand in all the agricultural regions of Chile with the support of its members from North to South."[25] The campaign in Colchagua in 1924 which included this labor petition was directed by Recabarren and Cruz, representatives of the Communist party in the Congress. Barría Seron reports that in 1924 Recabarren and Cruz carried out a campaign "helping to strengthen and activate the organization [FOCH] and to reorganize inactive Consejos or create some [consejos] campesinos."[26] This effort by FOCH apparently coincided with the first program for the countryside adopted by the recently formed Communist party.[27]

FOCH's penetration into the countryside declined after Recabarren's suicide in late 1924. FOCH itself suffered a violent setback in the massacre at La Coruña in 1925, when troops fired on workers, causing numerous deaths and injuries.[28] Finally, with the assumption of power by Ibáñez after the transitional period 1925-1927, the government made frontal attacks on working class organizations and leftist political leaders. The government used assassination, detention, and exile to deal with individual union or party leaders, effectively repressing FOCH and the Communist party.[29] With civil liberties curtailed, repression became the overt policy of the regime toward FOCH and its membership.[30] The nascent rural consejos, dependent as they were on urban political orientation, quickly disbanded. As will be seen, however, rural unions reappeared quickly in the same fundos and rural sectors when more favorable conditions returned. For the next half-century the regions around Choapa, Coronel-Colcura, Los Andes-La Calera, Melipilla, San Fernando-Chimbarongo, Molina, and Longaví remained centers for rural unionization and labor activism in the countryside. FOCH had begun an organized attack on the hacendados which rural labor carried on after the Ibáñez repression ended. By the time Ibáñez left the presidency a new labor code made possible the introduction of a distinctive organizational weapon to be used by rural labor in the struggle with the landowners—legally recognized agricultural unions.

The First Legally Recognized Unions in the Countryside

The unionization provisions of the Labor Code of 1931 made possible the creation of legally recognized rural unions.[31] After the promulgation of the Labor Code in 1931, campesinos formed legal unions in several vineyards in Chile's central valley in the province of Talca. These unions represent the first application of unionization legislation within the context of hacienda enterprises.[32]

The owner of one of the first unionized vineyards (Casa Blanca) was a Conservative deputy from Talca by the name of Alejandro Dussaillant (see also chapter 3). Dussaillant carried the struggle against the unions directly to the Congress. In addition, he insisted that the Labor Department dismiss the labor inspector who had assisted (as was his legal duty) in the formation of the unions in the vineyards.[33] Dussaillant also retaliated against the union members. He was supported by other landowners in the region of Molina who were also affected by the nascent organization of agricultural workers. Alberto León,[34] administrator of Viña San Pedro, a neighboring agricultural enterprise, presented a formal complaint against the labor inspector in Molina, including the charge that "by forming a union behind the back of the management of this fundo . . . [the inspector] has created animosity and lack of confidence on the part of the patrones and workers, thus failing in the mission of conciliation with which he was charged by the Labor Code."[35]

To stop the unionization drive, the landowners combined legal manipulation, attacks on inspectors, and retaliation against union leaders and members. Dussaillant claimed that rural unions were illegal because their existence rested on unconstitutional decree-laws.[36] At the same time, landowners employed physical resistance against, and noncooperation with, inspectors who sought to form legal unions. Carlos Menzel, labor inspector in Molina, reported as follows on his efforts to constitute the union in Viña San Pedro:

> Yesterday the 18th of October at 9:05 a.m. arriving "en visita" to Viña San Pedro, property of (Sucesión) Delia Ovalle de Correa (general representative in Santiago Luis Larraín Cotapos . . .) to formalize the founding of the union in this enterprise at the request of the workers involved . . . I was received by Luis Alberto León, administrator of said vineyard, to whom I respectfully explained the purpose of my visit. However, León, even before I finished explaining my mission, cursed me and then the Provincial Inspector.
> . . . León indicated to me that the infamous unionization law was a matter at the discretion of the patrones and not the workers, and that therefore the workers of the vineyards who had congregated should immediately disperse and return to their labor—although it was a holiday.

. . . Trying to calm the exaggerated reaction of this señor [I] explained that unions were formed according to the will of both parties and always, if more than 55 percent of the workers of the enterprise were in agreement, showing him the pertinent sections of the Labor Code.

[Despite the resistance of León] I proceeded to formalize the founding of the Sindicato Industrial Viña San Pedro in the open air, using only a modest table provided by the workers.

I report to you this outrage against the person of this inspector in the presence of witnesses, carabinero Luis Peralta who accompanied me, and the 92 workers who signed the act of constitution.

In addition I must inform you that Señor León has dismissed the leaders [*Directores*] of the union: José Troncoso Arroyo, José Muñoz Muñoz and Felix Guerra González without the show of any of the legal causes required by Article 376 in accord with Article 9 of the Labor Code. [They were dismissed] solely for having requested my presence to formalize the act of constitution in accord with Article 372 of the same body of the law.[37]

As owner of Fundo Casa Blanca, Dussaillant retaliated against the union in a similar manner by dismissing labor leaders and unionized workers. He also adopted a labor contract, which the Labor Department ruled illegal but which temporarily denied job security to any of the resident or temporary workers. When the union contested the legality of the contracts, which were self-terminating every two weeks and required reconfirmation by Dussaillant, the Labor Department supported the union.[38] Nevertheless, Dussaillant and the other landowners intensified their efforts to destroy the unions.

In January 1933 the union in Viña Casa Blanca complained to the Minister of Labor about persecution by the landowners:

We would like to bring to your attention that our corporation, called Sindicato Industrial Viña Casa Blanca, finds itself in an extremely difficult situation due to unjust reprisals of which we are victims. . . . We can no longer tolerate the persecutions and defamation to which we have been subjected until now. . . . Our patrón stubbornly persists in his desire to destroy our union and promises that once it is destroyed he will reimburse us for the wages which he has taken from us. . . .[39]

In 1933 Dussaillant and the other landowners in the Molina region were successful; the unions became inactive, not to be reconstituted until 1939. The labor inspector who had helped to form the unions was transferred to Curicó. The first effort to constitute legal rural unions, initially successful in the sense of obtaining legal personality, shortly thereafter met with landowner resistance which the workers could not overcome. The unions were temporarily destroyed.

Stagnation of Legally Recognized Unions: Alternative Patterns of Labor Conflict and Resistance

The period from 1932 to 1936 was one of stagnation for legally-recognized rural unions but one of growing resistance by campesinos to the authoritarian hacienda system and the political domination of rural proprietors. The most infamous incident during this period was the massacre of campesinos at Ranquil in upper Bío Bío in 1934. It was an atypical case of smallholders (*colonos*) who claimed land that was the object of extensive litigation between 1928 and 1934. These campesinos, dispossessed of their land, resisted the national police sent to quell the rebellion with force of arms. Communist party organizers were involved in the uprising but the conflict antedated party intervention. In any case, the struggle was not resistance to the hacienda system and the authority of rural proprietors per se but rather an armed confrontation over conflicting legal claims to land. Ranquíl, in this sense, was the only recorded large-scale "peasant uprising" in Chile between 1919 and 1964.[40] The uprising occurred in a frontier region where conflicting land claims and governmental unwillingness or inability to resolve a collective conflict with a long historical background led to unsuccessful efforts to relocate squatters and colonos on a broad scale. These efforts culminated in a brief but bloody confrontation which left the ranks of Chile's hacendados fearful. But the campesinos of Ranquíl were independent proprietors who had been dispossessed of their own homes and land, not resident workers in a hacienda of the central valley. The movement represented a localized peasant uprising in a conventional sense rather than an attack on or a challenge to the existing system of property. Still, the events at Ranquíl provided an impetus for the colonization law promulgated by the Alessandri government in 1935 and dramatized the plight of campesino proprietors in their relationships with the hacendado and the national regime's instruments of coercion.

Because the events of Ranquil were exceptional, the persistent, routine resistance of campesinos to the hacendado and the hacienda system in the period 1932-1936 is more significant in the present context. In a period usually noted for the continuing acceptance and submissiveness of the campesino to the rule of rural proprietors, a daily struggle did in fact go on in the countryside. Campesinos challenged the extensive political meaning of property in rural land individually and through ad hoc strike committees or grievance committees organized to defend their interests. They confronted landowners by rejecting proprietary claims to unilateral determination of conditions of labor and land use.

The period 1932-1936 is important in this regard because it precedes the systematic reintervention of urban-centered labor movements into the countryside. Rural labor movements lacked coordination, ideological orientation, or monetary and organizational inputs from their class and ideological allies.[41] Nevertheless, campesino resistance to hacendado authority persisted —an indication of the continuity of organized efforts by campesinos in particular haciendas to make claims against the hacendados apart from legally recognized unions and the coordination of a national labor movement.

The resistance consisted of pilferage, sabotage, strikes, work slowdowns, or individual acts of violence, which are nowhere systematically recorded. It is necessary, therefore, to use cases to illustrate the type and quality of resistance which did occur and the reaction of the hacendados to this resistance. The effort here is to indicate the quality and content of rural labor's challenge to proprietary authority. Further, it is exceedingly difficult, if not impossible, to know the extent of resistance expressed in low labor productivity, that is, in the refusal of campesinos to produce beyond a minimal level for their respective hacendados. This was perhaps the most widespread, if least dramatic, form of resistance to proprietary authority. The high proportion of administrative and supervisory personnel in the haciendas is one indication of the costs of maintaining discipline and production in the latifundio,[42] but the magnitude of depressed productivity can still not be precisely measured.

More explicit challenges to rural proprietors—strikes, labor

petitions, sabotage—generally had as their objectives the assertion of three types of demands: (1) reestablishment of customary prerogatives or conditions of work which had deteriorated
because of unilateral decisions on the part of the landowner,
such as decrease in pasture rights, land allotments, or increase
in labor obligations; (2) demands that the landowner comply
with existing obligations, for example, pay salaries owed or
obey labor legislation;[43] (3) demands for improvements in existing conditions, including requests for higher wages, decreased
labor obligations, larger land allotments, and participation in
management of the fundo or in the profits.

The first two types of demands are typical of a reactive labor movement, one on the defensive or concerned with implementation of existing legislation instead of further innovation.[44] This was generally the position of rural labor in Chile
during the period 1932-1936. The third type, demands for
improvements in existing conditions or participation in proprietary decision making and a greater share of the surplus,
indicates a rural labor movement which has forced rural proprietors to react to worker offensives. Naturally, the first two
types may sometimes escalate into the third. All these demands,
however, even those requesting higher wages or an increase in
pasture rights, represented a contest over proprietary authority.
Whereas campesinos did not seek expropriation of farms, nor
did they rebel en masse, they did seek to participate in decision
making which concerned the terms of the labor contract and
conditions of farm management. Their activity did not reach
the level of armed revolt or occupation of farms, yet it constituted a challenge to the existing concepts and prerogatives of
proprietorship. The following cases are illustrative.

San Cayetano, Botacura, and Tabontinaja, 1932

In September 1932 the campesinos in fundos San Cayetano,
Botacura, and Tabontinaja (located in the province of Linares
in the area around San Javier) came in mass to the labor inspector's office and claimed that the proprietor of the three fundos
owed them two to three months' salary and that food rations
were insufficient. The workers asked to be paid, to have food
rations increased, and to have salaries raised. They informed the
labor inspector that they and the rest of the work force of 300

workers would not work until the landowner met their demands. The inspector told the workers he could not accept an
illegal strike but would attempt to settle the problem within
twenty-four hours if they went back to work. The inspector
telephoned the absentee landowner, explained the threat of a
strike, and the next day the landowner arrived with money to
pay the back salaries. In the presence of the labor inspector the
complaints of individual campesinos were dealt with, and the
landowner agreed to raise food rations by one-third, raise salaries by 40 percent, and, over a period of time, repair some of
the inquilinos' housing. The labor inspector, acting in accord
with the Labor Code, ordered 108 labor contracts to be prepared. The workers, according to the inspector, returned to
work and thanked him for his intervention.[45]

This case illustrates both the successful mediation of a bureaucratic intervenor between rural labor and landowner and
the modified proprietary discretion of the landowners in a situation where activist workers could bring to bear the provisions
of the Labor Code to delimit the authority of rural proprietors.
It also illustrates the basically reactive nature of such activism
(demands for back salaries), which escalated into demands for
improved living and working conditions. No formal workers'
organization existed. The source of the conflict was the landowners' failure to fulfill certain legal obligations. There is no
record of further collective action on the part of the workers to
institutionalize the ad hoc organization after the conflict was
over. Yet the campesinos were able, through collective confrontation with the hacendado, to obtain short-term victories and
to challenge the unilateral decision making of the landowner.[46]

Fundo El Durazno, 1933

In Peumo in 1933 the owner of Fundo El Durazno decided
to require workers to brand any of their animals that grazed in
the hacienda. Seemingly an effort to control the number of
animals that each inquilino grazed in the farm, the landowner's
decision represented the imposition of effective limits on the inquilinos' ability to capitalize themselves through livestock husbandry and, in this sense, entailed a deterioration of existing
conditions and customary perquisites on the fundo. The inquilinos refused to have their animals branded and were notified

to leave the fundo within fifteen days. The dismissal was illegal, since the Labor Code specified that inquilinos be given two months notice, except under certain particular conditions. In a letter to the Labor Department, the inquilinos accused the landowner of attempting to "put an inappropriate brand on our cattle." The campesinos refused to leave the fundo. The local labor inspector mediated the incident and the landowner agreed to revoke the dismissal of workers, but the animals were to be branded or removed from the fundo. The inquilinos' resistance in this case proved unsuccessful because the landowner was judged to be within his proprietary authority, but the workers had managed to organize a short-term collective reaction to the landowner's unilateral decision to revise existing arrangements by reference to formal stipulations.[47]

Hacienda Canteras, 1935

In early 1935 a collective conflict developed between the workers in Hacienda Canteras and the administration of the enterprise. This fundo, located in the province of Bío Bío, belonged to the Social Security Administration (and previously to the Caja de Colonización Agrícola). The conflict originated with the farm administrator's introduction of interest charges on seed which had been loaned to the inquilinos for planting in their tenancies and sharecrops. This act represented an innovation in customary relationships that was detrimental to the workers. As in the cases cited above, the workers reacted to deteriorating conditions by collectively challenging the proprietor's initiative. They presented a labor petition and threatened to strike if their demands were not met. In addition to elimination of the interest charges, the petition demanded a raise in wages, permission to leave the hacienda through gates which normally remained locked, and the right to return the loaned seed prior to distribution of the harvest (from the undivided crop instead of out of the inquilino's share).

Police went to the farm to maintain order. The regional chief of the Service of Investigations, Julio Gutiérrez, also appeared at the hacienda. The labor inspector, whose intervention was requested by the workers, reported as follows:

> From the outset I was informed that the movement had a subversive character, but I found that the workers only sought a small

economic improvement and the elimination of the 17 percent tax for cleaning and selecting seed.

The workers withdrew their demands for a raise in salary since they obtained a raise of 50 centavos in December. Over the second point the administrator agreed to consult the Caja Central del Seguro since this is not stipulated in the contracts nor does there exist any document which justifies payment of 17 percent by the inquilinos.

The other points were settled to the satisfaction of the workers and the administration. . . .[48]

Temporary worker mobilization for collective action in reaction to landowner efforts to alter customary arrangements and to noncompliance with contractual relations escalated slightly into demands for higher wages. Through the intervention of the labor inspector, the workers attained partial success in their resistance, though they dropped demands for salary increases. No permanent rural union existed in the hacienda. Yet the workers were able to respond collectively to landowner-initiated action that threatened their well-being.

Many such cases, however, ended in less satisfactory resolutions for the workers involved. The legality of labor petitions in the countryside did not signify their passive acceptance by the hacendados. Still uncommon, such collective action on the part of rural labor was most often viewed as subversive—a concrete threat to the existing order. In the absence of permanent unions, landowners could gradually eliminate "troublemakers" and otherwise sanction rebellious laborers, as the following case illustrates.

Lo Prado and Santa Elvira, 1933

In late December 1933, the workers in fundos Lo Prado and Santa Elvira in the province of Santiago presented a labor petition to the landowner of the two properties in accordance with the provisions of the Labor Code. For inquilinos, the petitions requested a salary of four pesos, improved food rations, improved land allotments and pasture rights, two hours' rest at the noonday meal, and strict compliance with the Labor Code, especially in regard to labor contracts and housing conditions. For voluntarios, the petition requested a salary of five pesos a day, improved food rations, a clean place to sleep, and two hours' rest at the noonday meal. For milkmaids, the petition requested forty centavos per can of milk in the summer and sixty centavos in the winter.[49] The workers requested that the landowner answer their petition within five days. At the end of the five days, the signers of the petition were taken as prisoners to the public jail. They were accused of disobeying the Labor Code and threatening the property of the fundo. When they were brought before the court, the judge released the workers, "since a legal labor petition existed, no reason existed for their detention." The next Saturday the landowner refused to pay the workers who had participated in presenting the petition; he then ordered them out of the fundo. The order meant eviction from their homes and dismissal from their employment.

At this point, Emilio Zapata, Trotskyist deputy (Izquierda Comunista) for the district, went to the fundo to inquire into the matter so as "to make the incident known in the Congress."[50] A police lieutenant arrived at the fundo and came to the house in which Zapata was conversing with some inquilinos. The lieutenant asked Zapata to identify himself. He identified himself as a deputy and showed his congressional identity card (*carnet de diputado*). The police officer informed Zapata that he was under arrest. Insisting that a deputy had immunity (*fuero*), Zapata refused to accompany the carabinero and then shut the door in the lieutenant's face. The police broke down the door, seized Zapata, and pulled him onto the road. The carabineros dragged Zapata, biting, kicking, and screaming insults, from the fundo all the way to Barrancas.[51] Zapata was incarcerated until 9:45 that evening, when Manuel Hidalgo, Trotskyist senator, arrived at the jail and helped to obtain his release, along with that of the workers. (Zapata had refused to leave the jail if the campesinos were not also released.) Recalling this occasion, Zapata declared: "The police were at the entire disposition of the *terratenientes*. They were their servants, to warn them that campesinos were gathering and to assist in repressing them. When a labor petition was presented, they accused the workers of stealing a chicken or a sack of beans to justify throwing them out of their houses and off the fundo."[52]

Without permanent organizations to defend their interests and obtain law enforcement through labor inspectors, the campesino resistance to rural proprietors could be harshly repressed. In late 1935, Emilio Zapata Díaz became the first politician-labor leader to attempt to organize rural labor on a national scale in order to overcome the political domination of the countryside by the hacendados. While insisting that "only the Proletarian Revolution can destroy the capitalist system of exploitation,"[53] Zapata created a national organization of campesinos based on short-term material incentives to its members by using tactics appropriate to the existing formal democracy of Chile during the 1930s. Not proletarian revolution but manipulation of the existing parliamentary and administrative apparatus served as a tool in challenging the traditional authority of rural proprietors.

Emilio Zapata and the Liga Nacional de Defensa de Campesinos Pobres

By 1935, when Emilio Zapata founded the Liga Nacional de Defensa de Campesinos Pobres, he had already had an active political career. Member of the Partido Obrero Socialista (POS) and then of the Communist party, Zapata suffered the repression of the Ibáñez regime with political exile to Isla Más Afuera. Because of ill health, he was sent back to the mainland, where he persisted in antigovernmental activity. Again he was returned to Isla Más Afuera and again the prison doctor sent him back to the mainland for reasons of health. In 1927 he served as president of the Liga Nacional de Arrendatarios de Chile, participating in the *tribunales de la vivienda*, which had been created to deal with tenant-landlord conflict. From a working-class background ("I was a housepainter like my grandfather"), Zapata was socially and ideologically linked to the working-class movement which grew up in the first two decades of the twentieth century.

Zapata's initial contact with rural proselytizing and conflict came just prior to 1920, when a workers' cultural center (Centro del Despertar) in which he participated established a school in Peñaflor. Zapata had friends among the smallholders and inquilinos in the region, especially in the Fundo Pelvin.[54] On Sundays Zapata would go to the public plaza and "give talks protesting the bestial treatment the administrator meted out to the laborers and the miserable conditions in which the campesinos lived."[55] In one of those meetings the crowd in the plaza was attacked by twenty to thirty overseers from the fundos in the area, who rode on horseback through the crowd in front of the church on the plaza. Zapata remembers:

They tried to take me prisoner. I had to run. I ran until I came to the house of a friend, a shoemaker, named José Mella. He hid me in his house and went to talk to the subdelegado of Peñaflor, a Radical with Socialist background. The subdelegado informed the intendente and he in turn the minister of interior. As things stood I was trapped by the agents of the landowners [aquellos que huasqueaban a los campesinos] who had staked out the escape routes. Fortunately, the minister of interior took the necessary measures. He ordered a police officer from Santiago to Peñaflor so that I could leave the town.[56]

In 1920 Zapata attempted unsuccessfully to organize rural laborers in Peñaflor. He then became a leader in the anti-alcoholism movement directed by Carlos Fernández Peña, Doctora Ernestina Pérez, and Carlos Alberto Martínez. He always maintained contacts, however, with the campesinos in Peñaflor. In 1932 he was elected deputy for the second district of Santiago. Breaking with the Communist party, he followed Manuel Hidalgo into the Trotskyist Izquierda Comunista. Until 1937, when he joined the Socialist party, Zapata remained one of the small minority of serious, committed Trotskyists and eventually served as the editor and publisher of the Trotskyist organ, Izquierda.

Zapata's intervention in rural labor conflicts and union organizing stemmed from his ideological convictions and his determination to destroy the existing system of property and power in Chile and to replace it with a socialist one.[57] His election as deputy afforded him the opportunity to combine his ideological commitment with participation in the "bourgeois parliament," employing the tactical opportunities which the Congress provided to mobilize rural workers and, where possible, defend them against exploitation by the landowners.

Zapata developed a strategy by which to focus attention on violators of the Labor Code, and to support campesino demands. His strategy included his letters to the Labor Department denouncing supposed code violations and demanding an investigation. Acting on these complaints the Labor Department sent inspectors to the haciendas involved and required formal reports of the visits. The visits caused embarrassment and legal problems for the landowners. Zapata, previously informed of the conditions in the fundo he denounced through personal contacts or visits to the property, sometimes even paid out of his pocket for chemical analysis of food rations in order to determine their quality and to better document his complaints to the Labor Department.

In the first months of 1934 Zapata denounced landowners in a number of fundos, including Polpaico (José Luis Lecaros), El Mirador (Deputy Mario Urrutia), La Quinta de Maipo (Juan Benoit), Ongolmo (Ventura Matte B.), and La Rinconada de Maipú (owned by the government). In July 1934 the Labor Department prepared a special report in response to Zapata's various denunciations of landowners.[58] In many cases Zapata's complaints led to improvement of the campesinos' situation and to short-term material gain. Still, no systematic effort was made to formally organize the workers in the haciendas.

In February of 1935 *Izquierda* published an article in which an agrarian program was put forward.[59] The program included the organization of associations of campesinos, smallholders, colonos, and sharecroppers, the organization of committees in each hacienda or fundo, and the establishment of relations between class organizations of the industrial proletariat and the campesino. The program formulated such immediate demands as minimum salaries of ten pesos a day; a six-hour work day; double time for work at night; payment in cash; freedom of commerce for workers and access of small merchants and peddlers to the haciendas; fifteen days paid vacation a year; freedom of movement, association, and the right to strike; unimpeded circulation of the worker press; elimination of child labor; and equality of wages for men and women. For smallholders, renters, sharecroppers, and colonos the program called for prohibition of eviction for debts; preferential access to credit through the Caja de Crédito Agrario; creation of machine-tractor stations to service, at low cost, the campesino enterprises; formation of cooperatives (consumer, production, and commercialization); control over access and delivery of land, legal use, and location through associations of colonos and smallholders; immediate reduction of rents, interest, and amortization payments; and free use of irrigation water.

The program was simply a proclamation by an ideological organ of a small Marxist party, but Zapata was building a clientele in the countryside through his active intervention on behalf of the campesinos in the Congress and before various bureaucratic agencies. A weather disaster, however, rather than a preplanned organizational drive, precipitated the creation of Chile's first national campesino organization—the Liga Nacional de Defensa de Campesinos Pobres.

In October and November 1934 frost and bad weather seriously damaged agricultural crops. In much of Chile, including parts of the province of Santiago, farmers suffered nearly a total loss of crops. In January 1935 the Chilean Congress passed Law 5.558 to provide monetary compensation for farmers who suffered significant losses because of the frost. The reglamento for this law called for written documentation of losses, indicating farm location, proprietary status of claimant (*mediero, arrendatario*, and so forth), crops affected, and assessed value of crop and land. The law charged local committees (*juntas*) with receiving these claims and dispensing compensation. Local politicians manipulated the local juntas and there was much corruption. People without crop losses, and some without farms, received compensation. The thirty-day time limit stipulated for filing claims was short and meant that many smallholders or inquilinos never found out about the compensation program, whereas friends or compadres of local junta members were well informed and able to take advantage of the available benefits.

On August 14, 1935 Zapata moved in the Congress to extend the period for making claims under Law 5.558.[60] Next he denounced the corruption that had occurred and demanded a full investigation. On September 11, 1935, under the headline "The Defense of the Small Campesino Sustained by Zapata in the Congress," *Izquierda* reported a meeting which had taken place on the preceding Sunday:

> In the house of the workers of the commune of Quinta Normal, Walker Martinez 102 . . . a gathering of farmers affected by the frosts of last year convened; and among them were smallholders, renters, sharecroppers and parceleros from the communes of Renca, Perejil, Barrancas, Quilicura, Conchali, Lampa, and others.
>
> Our Comrade Deputy Emilio Zapata, who made a long exposition of the problems facing those who cultivate the soil, attended this important meeting. The assembly made the following resolutions:
>
> (1) to organize a league of small farmers [*pequeños agricultores*] with committees in each commune, into which will enter the different strata of campesinos. . . .

(2) to support the denunciations formulated by Zapata in the parliament, soliciting that the Minister of Agriculture incorporate a representative of the committees in each commune to collaborate in the investigation of irregularities and to form part of communal organization to dispense aid to those affected by the frosts.

(3) to request that the Minister of Agriculture ... extend the time period for applying for the benefits of Law 5.558. ...

(4) to issue a call to all the agricultural workers to organize themselves in each rural commune, according to the formula which will be made known Sunday, September 15.

Such was the beginning of the Liga Nacional de Defensa de Campesinos Pobres. Mobilized around the concrete benefits flowing from existing legislation, its origin was not in a revolutionary attack on rural proprietors but in governmental compensation for crop damages. Its initial appeal excluded agricultural wage laborers, although inquilinos were also included, since as producers they were, in principle, eligible for the benefits provided by Law 5.558.

The campaign led by Zapata to extend the benefits of Law 5.558 to excluded elements of the rural population continued through September 1935. On September 18 *Izquierda* headlined "The Liga de Defensa de los Campesinos Pobres Is Organized." The first ligas were organized in Renca, Colina, Lampa, Quilicura, Maipú, Peñaflor, Curacaví, Quinta Normal, and Talagante—all in the province of Santiago. In its beginning stages, the Liga was national in name only.

By October 1935, however, the Liga had largely escaped its narrow functional origins and proclaimed a general program for the countryside which included reduction of rents and taxes on sharecrop land; permanent legislation to protect campesinos against the risks of weather; representation for the Liga in the Caja de Crédito Agrario, Junta de Exportación Agricola, and Caja de Seguro, as well as in all other organizations related to agricultural production; reform of the rigged auctions at municipal markets and establishment of open markets to eliminate the middleman between farmer and consumer; prohibition of grazing land in haciendas in close proximity to the cities; protection against eviction; governmental low-cost rentals of farm machinery to campesinos; electrification of the countryside; and improvement in diet and housing for the campesinos.[61]

By November 1935 various communal Ligas had requested that Zapata intervene to solve problems involving educational facilities, transportation and communication difficulties, and electrification of small rural towns, in addition to the usual labor problems of their membership.

On November 6, 1935, the Chilean Congress agreed to send legislation to the president of Chile for extension of the benefits of Law 5.558 to the previously excluded campesinos. Thus, the initial campaign resulted in victory. From 1936 to 1939 the Liga Nacional de Defensa de Campesinos Pobres expanded its membership throughout Chile. The initial narrow appeal was extended to include a frontal attack on the hacienda system. By 1936 the political alignment of the Liga—to the left of the emerging Popular Front coalition and in competition with the Communist party's rural organizational efforts—also became clear. In May 1936, at a congress of the campesinos pobres in which Oscar Schnake, Marmaduke Grove, and Zapata all participated, Communist Deputy Escobar sought to enlist the Liga "in representation of the Popular Front."[62] The leadership of the Liga, including Zapata and Bernardo Yuras, expressed reservations. But in late 1936 to early 1937, with the Trotskyist party experiencing little growth, Zapata and his companions joined the Socialist party, to which Zapata brought the Liga. The struggle in the countryside between Trotskyists and Communists was thus transferred to the Socialist party.

Organization and Finances of the Liga

The Liga Nacional de Defensa de Campesinos Pobres never had a truly national organization. An executive committee in Santiago, essentially Zapata, Bernardo Yuras, and Carlos Acuña, prepared the Liga's propaganda, bulletins, rubber stamps, and statutes which were sent, on request, to campesinos or Socialist party cadres who wrote to Zapata expressing interest in forming a new liga. In some cases Socialist party militants helped to organize local ligas. In others, campesinos wrote to Zapata at the Congress to request instructions as to how to constitute a local liga or to call to his attention abuses by landowners, which Zapata then denounced in the sessions of the Congress, asking for Labor Department intervention. When the latter occurred Zapata also brought to the campesinos' attention the need to organize with the Liga Nacional in order to defend their interests. In either situation, the operation was centralized in Zapata's small, unpaid staff in Santiago, which eventually included several lawyers and law students who handled legal claims of Liga members in the labor courts and ordinary tribunals.[63] The Liga Nacional never had a paid staff or regional offices and thus remained an extremely fragile organization highly dependent on Zapata's personal direction and inspiration.

Once organized, the local ligas sent reports of their problems to Zapata or the Santiago office. Zapata did his best to see that governmental agencies attended to the claims of liga members, which could range from illegal or unjust dismissals to inequitable distribution of irrigation water to inquilinos and smallholders. The activities of the local ligas, especially those outside the Santiago-Valparaíso area, were practically autonomous from the national Liga. Financing depended on local dues, whose amount each local liga determined. Zapata's handling of complaints and petitions, his speeches in the Congress, and his trips around the country to meet with local ligas held the loosely organized Liga Nacional together after the initial impetus of the benefits of Law 5.558.

Zapata also fought for the enactment of Law 6.290 (later called "Ley Zapata"), which provided funds for loans to campesinos through the Caja de Crédito Agrario. He skillfully played the parliamentary game, using his leverage on committees to bargain for legislation of benefit to campesinos. Law 6.290 provided new material benefits which the Liga could extend to its membership.[64] In addition, Zapata made efforts to obtain clear legal titles for smallholders with tenuous tenure status and to have governmental properties on the outskirts of towns parceled for the benefits of workers. Less concretely, the Liga offered psychological liberation from the domination of the landowners and occasional assistance in preparing labor petitions or processing formal complaints before the Labor Department. Still, by 1939, the Liga Nacional de Defensa de Campesinos Pobres remained an underfinanced collection of local ligas with little of a national organization except the Executive Committee. As Zapata put it: "We did not have the necessary resources. Perhaps with more perseverance we could have done more."[65]

The Executive Committee obtained no financial support
from the Socialist party. In order to finance a "congreso de
campesinos" in March 1939, Zapata secretly obtained 30,000
pesos from President Aguirre Cerda. In effect, the Popular
Front government subsidized the First National Congress of
Chilean Campesinos.[66] Zapata remarked in this regard: "We
tried to link the actions of the ligas to the Party despite the
fact they were not afforded their due importance. The Party
didn't provide a cent [*Ni dieron una chaucha*]. Everything was
at our expense. We obtained from the minister of industry free
transportation on the trains. I already had this right as Deputy,
but not the other compañeros. In the Liga there was never a
single paid functionary."[67]

By the beginning of 1939 the Liga Nacional had local ligas
from Coquimbo to Puerto Montt. A newly installed Popular
Front government seemed to provide hope for better conditions
for rural labor. While the Liga's leadership initially praised President Pedro Aguirre Cerda, Bernardo Yuras cautioned: "The
campesinos have their eyes on the new leader and hope that
his government will end the regime of latifundio. . . . Chile . . .
will finish the labor of independence by eliminating this class
[of hacendados]."[68] The Liga also demanded legal recognition
by the government and "authentic representation in all the state
institutions in order that the voice of the campesino pobre be
heard."[69] Thus, by 1939, at the zenith of its national influence
after the congress in Santiago, the Liga demanded a role in the
Popular Front government and posts for its members or representatives in key governmental agencies.

But the Liga did not represent a threat only to the hacendados. Within the coalition of Marxist and center parties that
formed the Popular Front government, intense competition
took place for control of the national labor movement. In this
struggle Zapata's Liga challenged the Communist party for control of rural labor. Communist efforts to displace the ligas at the
local level, and to eliminate Zapata's influence in the countryside, divided the rural labor movement at a time when unified
action was essential in order to resist the landowners' repression
of rural labor.

The Liga and the Communist Party

The Communist party, since the days of Recabarren and FOCH's initial intervention in the rural sector, had an ideological commitment to organize the rural labor force and create a worker-campesino alliance in a national class organization. From the outset the Party had designated *encargados* (literally "in charge of") for the countryside, but not until the Popular Front period (after 1936) did the Communist party systematically engage in rural labor organization on a national scale. In 1937, at the conclusion of a "national campesino congress" in Santiago, Juan Chacón Corona, eventual chief of the Party's Departamento Agrario, was named secretary-general of a newly created Federación Nacional Agraria.[70] For the electoral campaign of Aguirre Cerda the Party named Chacón "Encargado Nacional Agrario," and Communist functionaries went into the countryside to rally support for the Popular Front candidate, linking his candidacy to the agrarian question.[71] After the elections the Party committed itself to work on a national scale with functionaries in the countryside. From 1938 onward the Communist party fostered the establishment of legal unions as well as union committees and "free unions" (*sindicatos libres*) and assisted campesinos in the presentation of labor petitions and the organization of strikes. Juan Chacón Corona claimed in his report to the Eleventh National Congress of the Communist Party (1939) that over 400 unions with approximately 60,000 members had been organized during this period. Labor Department records and press reports confirm creation of more than 200 campesino unions in 1939, but membership totals are not systematically reported.[72]

While the Liga organized by Zapata had opted for commune-wide associations, the Communists attempted in many cases to conform with the formal stipulations of the Labor Code: "sindicatos industriales" in each fundo and "sindicatos profesionales" by commune, department, or region to link together the individual unions. When enough unions had been created in a region, the Party attempted to organize a federation, "unión provincial" or "comité coordinador." All these organizations were in turn affiliated with the CTCH. For example,

the Federación de Sindicatos de Asalariados Agrícolas de Re-
quinoa encompassed the Sindicato Profesional Agrícola de Re-
quinoa and the individual unions organized in fundos Santa
Amalia, Los Perales, Las Mercedes, Pimpinela, Totihue, Chu-
maco, Aurora, Los Lirios, California, and El Trigal. All, in turn,
were organizationally affiliated with the CTCH.

The Communists had ideological and historical grievances
against Zapata. From 1932 to 1936, after Zapata left the Party,
the Trotskyist newspaper he directed systematically attacked
the "Stalinists." As late as 1968 Zapata's resistance to the Party
was not forgotten, as these comments in Jose Miguel Varas'
biography of Chacón indicate:

> From 1915 on a "leftist" group, counterrevolutionaries disguised
> as militant revolutionaries [*dinamiteros*], held positions of leadership
> in the POS. These bandits, headed by Pablo Lopez and Emilio Zapata,
> waged an internal struggle against the position of Recabarren. After
> the founding of the Communist party, Lopez and Zapata took advan-
> tage of the lack of understanding of Marxism by the majority of leaders,
> and continued within the Party as its worst problems. Later they took
> Trotskyite positions until they received the kick in the ass they de-
> served [*hasta recibir, finalmente, la patada en el culo que merecían*].[73]

More important, the Liga Nacional threatened the Communist
desire for hegemony over the rural labor movement and control
of the CTCH. Thus, while the campesinos carried on the struggle against the hacendados, the Communists attempted to liquidate the Liga's local organizations and to form unions in the
fundos where the ligas existed. Zapata, understating the case,
observed in 1971: "Relationships with Chacón were strained.
Chacón Corona wanted the Communists to have exclusive control over the organization of the campesinos. There was a real
competition. They tried to take away our people."[74]

Particularly strong competition between the Liga Nacional
and the Communists took place in the Valley of Choapa, where
the Liga was initially quite strong. The Communists sent Cipriano Pontigo—later deputy for the district—to combat the Liga
and create unions. Pontigo began in Tranquilla and then moved
to Coirón. Gradually, the Communists dominated campesino
organizations in several of the Choapa fundos. But even when
the Liga Nacional practically disappeared after 1942, remnants
of the Liga in the valley remained militants of the Socialist

party, thus preventing monolithic control by the Communists of the rural labor organizations in the valley.[75]

At the first national congress of the CTCH in July 1939, the competitive struggle between the Liga and the Communist rural labor organizations came to a head. In April 1939 the Liga Nacional had sponsored what was billed as the First National Congress of Chilean Campesinos (see p. 158). It sent out a circular to unions and workers' organizations, asking their cooperation in the preparation of the coming congress and rejecting the temporary suspension of rural unionization decreed by the Popular Front government—which had been agreed to by the CTCH, the Communists, and the Socialists. Several weeks before the scheduled congress (April 2, 1939), Liga representative Bernardo Yuras spoke before a group of campesinos from the local ligas in San Bernardo. Yuras' words and the tone of his presentation were an indictment of Aguirre Cerda, the Communists, and other elements who had agreed to halt rural unionization and lower the level of conflict in the countryside. Yuras declared, in part: "You must unite . . . and agitate for economic improvements and begin the conquest to which every Chilean campesino aspires—the end of the latifundio regime. The land should belong to he who works it. . . . Comrade campesinos, the solution to the problem [is] to take the land and distribute it among the workers—in production cooperatives or through the Caja de Colonización Agrícola. . . ."[76] At a time when the Popular Front government sought to lower the pressure of conflict in the countryside, the representative of the Liga Nacional called for more agitation and intensification of the struggle against the proprietors of rural land.

Three weeks later, the Liga Nacional carried out the Primer Congreso Nacional del Campesinado Chileno. During this meeting Zapata severely criticized the government, which was secretly funding the congreso, for the temporary suspension of rural unionization. He was "elected" Lider del Campesinado— titular head of the new Federación Nacional del Campesinado (the Liga Nacional plus rural unions and committees controlled by the Socialist party). The Federación Nacional del Campesinado called for the immediate revocation of the ministerial order that had suspended rural unionization. The Congress of Campesinos ended with a declaration that "the right of unionization for the campesinos is inalienable; the congress is determined to defend this right; the recognition of this right and its exercise is necessary for the maintenance of social peace."[77] Remembering the situation of 1939, Zapata remarked in 1971:

> What Aguirre Cerda had to do was tell the patrones that they couldn't use lockouts or sabotage production, and that they couldn't throw people off the land in political reprisal.
>
> I suggested to Aguirre Cerda that he requisition the fundos under the terms of the comisariat, rather than maintain a passive policy toward the class enemies. I told him that his Government had begun its administration without opening a "new book."
>
> Neither Aguirre Cerda nor his Ministers were responsive. They were walls without ears. The Party didn't discipline me because they knew I was right.
>
> Although they possessed the legal means to prevent it, they did nothing while the terratenientes threw the campesinos "into the street" for the crime of voting for Aguirre Cerda or for associating themselves in ligas or unions.[78]

Zapata advocated direct confrontation of the landowners through available *legal* means—which would have permitted requisitioning a large number of fundos. Such a tactic went beyond the intentions of Aguirre Cerda and the Popular Front coalition.

In July 1939, just prior to the National Congress of the CTCH in which control of Chile's national labor confederation would be decided between Communists and Socialists, the Communists sponsored the "First National Congress of Rural Unions." This congress, presided over by Juan Chacón Corona, was a clear prelude to the electoral struggle within the CTCH. The internal organ of the central committee of the Communist party declared on July 25, 1939:

> One of the fundamental objectives of a true Marxist program in Chile consists in forging . . . the worker-campesino alliance.
>
> Those who attempt, like some Trotzkyites, to penetrate the Congress of the CTCH with delegations of so-called campesinos pobres with the exclusive objective of winning votes, are recurring to repugnant politics [*politiquería*].
>
> The effort to create conflict in the Congress between the proletarian delegations and the delegations of campesinos pobres is nothing more nor less than a valuable service which the fifth column [provides] the reactionaries and fascists.[79]

This attack was clearly aimed at Zapata and the Liga Nacional de Defensa de Campesinos Pobres. In the CTCH congress, Communist delegates challenged the credentials of the Liga delegations. After an internal struggle resulted in the acceptance of the Liga representatives, the Liga votes provided the margin of victory for Socialist Bernardo Ibáñez over his Communist rival for the position of secretary general (Salvador Ocampo).

Zapata won only a temporary victory. In 1940, unable to tolerate the Popular Front's "temporary" suspension of rural unionization and the Socialist party's compliance in this "treason to the campesinos," Zapata left the Socialist party and formed part of the Partido Socialista de los Trabajadores (PST). Unwilling to follow other PST politicos into the Communist party, Zapata soon lost his seat in Congress and disappeared from national politics. Zapata's ideological commitment and class consciousness would no longer allow him to collaborate with a government in which Arturo Olavarría would eventually be named minister of interior, prohibit strikes during the harvest, and put into practice the system of "final judgment" (el juicio final) to deal with labor conflicts in the countryside. As Olavarría himself described the juicio final:

> . . . a group of carabineros would arrive at a fundo accompanied by a convoy of trucks. When the inquilinos were assembled in the area, the carabinero officer would order those who wished to continue the strike to stand on his left. The officer would then order that the strikers gather their families, cats, dogs, chickens and belongings and get in the trucks to be evicted. . . . This tactic I converted into a system. General Oscar Reeves Leiva, Director General of Carabineros called it . . . el juicio final, as the good ones went on the right and the bad ones on the left, as it is hoped will occur one day in the valley of Josafat. Of course, I didn't have to use the juicio final many times. . . . [80]

Zapata lost his congressional seat to his opponent amid rumors he had been given a fundo and had sold out to the Right. His defeat marked the final decline of the Liga Nacional de Defensa de Campesinos Pobres. Earlier, Bernardo Yuras, the only member of the Executive Committee of rural background (his father was a Yugoslav peasant immigrant) had resigned because of a personal conflict with Carlos Acuña, the nominal secretary general of the Liga Nacional.[81] After 1940 the Liga passed into the hands of the Socialist party, where it died a quiet death despite feeble efforts, including those of Marmaduke Grove, to maintain at least some semblance of Liga activity. The Liga's weak organizational structure could not be sustained without Zapata.

The Popular Front in the Countryside

While the struggle within the Popular Front government and within the CTCH persisted, with the campesinos in the middle, the rural labor force suffered the consequences of landowner retaliation for organization of the Liga and unions and for labor petitions or strikes. Despite the National Agricultural Society's agreement to influence its members to avoid massive dismissals if the Popular Front parties halted rural unionization, the landowners widely violated the agreement. Landowners joined together in throwing union organizers, persons signing labor petitions, and participants in other forms of resistance off the land. From all over Chile campesinos flooded the Labor Department with letters, complaints, and pleas to defend them against the concerted action of the landowners. In some cases rural proprietors attempted to form "yellow unions" to squeeze out the recently formed workers' organizations in their fundos.[82] More commonly, however, they sought to discredit the unions and dismiss active members. Sometimes they used violence against the workers, and destruction of crops and homes; blacklisting to prevent future employment was routine. The pattern established in the early FOCH rural conflicts recurred as the landowners acted to protect their proprietary interests.

Despite their own retaliatory measures, landowners frantically insisted on rigorous governmental action to repress the legal unionization of campesinos, as the following letter shows:

Your Excellency, President of the Republic:

The undersigned landowners of the commune of Pirque wish to inform Your Excellency of the delicate situation in which agricultural activity finds itself in this region, social peace being broken by propaganda directed against the authority and prestige of the proprietors by "outside agitators" [elementos sin vinculación alguna en la comuna]....

[Formation of rural unions in several fundos] incites the people to rebellion and social indiscipline. They even told them that the current government favors the division of land among the workers, and in order to achieve this the workers must strongly unite themselves. . . . the agitators then directed their campaign to fundo Lo Arcaya . . . with such underhanded procedures as nocturnal visits to the inquilinos until they convinced them to cooperate in this labor of social dissolution.

. . . all the unions were immediately registered in the books of the Socialist party. . . . Next the propaganda was directed to the fundos of Señores Astoreca, Hunneus and Viál, where mass meetings of the workers took place on the bridge of the River Clarillo, and where they told the campesinos that the Right was plotting a Revolution; that it was indispensable to be organized and that all should arm themselves as they were able, with rifles, shotguns, revolvers and knives, etc. . . . Saturday more than 300 workers of these fundos abandoned their labors. . . .

. . . We have in this commune the initial elements of a State of Revolution. . . . All this disorder is produced under the pretext of the right of rural workers to organize.

Your Excellency, we have desired that these facts be known to you . . . to request that you immediately suspend the processing of the requests for rural union organization in this commune.[83]

Once rural unionization was suspended (see chapter 4), the landowners moved to destroy the nascent campesino organizations and castigate the workers who had participated in the "subversive" threat to proprietary authority. The Intendente of Curicó (in one of many similar communications)[84] informed the minister of interior and the minister of labor in April 1939 that

Because of the unionization of agricultural workers and the labor petitions which they have presented to their patrones, the patrones are preparing to dismiss their workers—a large part of them [the workers] have already been notified. It is necessary to call to your attention the injustice of this matter, since with their labor and the labor of their ancestors they have contributed to the wealth of the patrones. Nevertheless, they don't have enough to provide food for their family if they miss a day's work.[85]

The rural labor force had no remedy for this sort of landowner retaliation. On the national level, the Popular Front government remained willing to use the police power of the state to defend the proprietary authority of rural landowners. Thus, strikers were met with tactics like the juicio final or with simple physical abuse. National police enforced court orders for evictions of campesinos. The government provided the coercive means necessary for the hacendados to retain control of the countryside.

Contrarily, the government had administratively suspended the rights of rural labor. This meant that the power of rural proprietors extended well past the legal delimitation contained in the Labor Code. The campesinos faced, thus, a situation in which the government supported the landowners' demands for order without reference to the correlative rights of the rural labor force. It was order without law. The landowners correctly viewed the exercise of existing legal rights by rural labor as the "initial elements of a state of Revolution." In a literal sense, respect for the formal rights of campesinos would have entailed revolutionary change for the countryside and the broader political community. Faced with the massive reaction of landowners to rural unionization and labor conflict—but deprived of the protection of legal unions—the campesinos were tyrannized by the rural proprietors.[86]

The CTCH, including as it did both Communists and Socialists (and from 1939 to 1941 the Liga Nacional de Defensa de Campesinos Pobres), attempted to defend the campesinos from landowner repression. The National Secretariat and local consejos pressured the various ministries and the president of Chile to protect rural labor's rights according to the Labor Code and to repeal the order against unionization. The CTCH also repeatedly denounced the massive evictions that the landowners were carrying out and the violence to which they subjected campesinos. Labor inspectors who did not respond favorably to rural workers were also denounced.[87] The national CTCH leadership forwarded complaints from individual workers, rural unions, and the local consejos to the Labor Department and demanded that appropriate action be taken.[88] The CTCH also sought, unsuccessfully, the right to represent rural laborers in the labor courts, juntas de conciliación (which handled the labor petitions), and individual conciliations (*comparendo*) with labor inspectors. Since the CTCH did not have legal recognition, this right was denied by the Labor Department. Informal participation of CTCH representatives was often accepted, at the discretion of labor inspectors, if such intervention did not "make difficult the correct application of the laws and neither prejudice nor perturb the reaching of a just and harmonious solution to the conflict."[89] The CTCH also frequently requested the creation of Labor Department inspectorates or labor courts where these did not exist, in order to better process labor conflicts.[90] In November 1940, the CTCH (like Zapata earlier) insisted on the simple application of the unionization provisions of the Labor Code in the countryside and proposed a reglamento for the Code's application in this sector. The CTCH's demands were ignored. The "temporary" suspension of rural unionization was maintained.

Sometimes, however, the CTCH was able to force landowners and the Labor Department to rectify illegal actions against the campesinos.[91] Organized publicity campaigns in the leftist press against particular landowners or against labor inspectors who did not defend the rights of the workers could produce positive results. In the province of Santiago, where the Unión Provincial de Sindicatos Agrícolas was active, the Communist party newspaper *El Siglo* often published attacks on landowners and Labor Department personnel who acted against the workers' interests.[92] Luis Coray, Communist party functionary and leader of the Unión Provincial de Sindicatos Agrícolas, was so disliked for his belligerence and "meddling" by Labor Department officials that eventually the department refused to allow him to represent workers in official proceedings.[93]

But even the limited number of victories won by CTCH-affiliated rural labor organizations and individual campesinos tended to be quite short-term. Labor petitions, once resolved, could be followed by dismissals. If the labor petitions were ruled illegal, as they often were because of procedural errors or omissions, workers could be dismissed immediately.

San Luis de Quilicura, 1940

An illustrative case from the period 1940-1941 is the strike in San Luis de Quilicura.[94] The strike followed a labor petition presented by the workers on November 4, 1940, to the landowner's agent in the fundo. The workers belonged to a union which sought legal status but was unable to obtain legal personality because of the temporary suspension of rural unionization initiated in early 1939. The union was affiliated with the CTCH and advised by Luis Coray, president of the Unión Provincial de Sindicatos Agrícolas. The Junta de Conciliación dealt with the labor petition in several sessions and eventually ruled the petition illegal because only sixty-two workers had signed it instead of the seventy-two that should have signed to meet the legal minimum requirement of 55 percent of the work force.

The landowner gave notice to various workers and proposed compensation for their unharvested crops and pasture rights as well as a special five hundred peso indemnity for each campesino evicted. The workers refused the landowner's offer, and Luis Coray, representing the workers, made a counteroffer. The landowner rejected Coray's intervention.

The Labor Department sought to intervene and resolve the conflict. After initial contacts, the landowner's agents wrote to the Labor Department as follows:

> The strike initiated in the middle of November by sixty-two signers of a second labor petition was declared illegal.
>
> As soon as the Labor Department was advised of the termination of the respective labor contracts, the sixty-two signers of this petition were, in accord with the law, "outside the fundo."
>
> . . . of the sixty-two signers of the last labor petition, four left the fundo of their own accord . . . twenty-two are still working for the fundo, and of the remaining thirty-six we have dismissed and obtained the corresponding eviction order for seven inquilinos, seven voluntarios and four milkmaids, whose behavior had been incompatible with the discipline and respect indispensable in the management of a fundo.
>
> In regard to the eighteen [persons] subject to eviction, voluntarily and for reasons of equity, I have made offers of indemnity through the Labor Department, on the condition that they leave the fundo in a reasonable amount of time. As these proposals have not been accepted, we now revoke them and will not make others, following from here on the relevant legal stipulations.
>
> Since the striking workers no longer have any relationships with the fundo we have nothing to talk about with them and still less with representatives of the CTCH. . . .[95]

The legal rights of rural proprietors were still extensive enough, combined with the de-legalization of rural unions, to repress rural labor and retain political control of the countryside.

From 1940 until 1946 rural unions and committees of rural workers continued to present labor petitions and to call strikes. In 1941 an attempt to carry out a general strike of campesinos failed.[96] Governmental belligerence toward rural labor increased. Yet, in the same year, President Aguirre Cerda vetoed a congressional measure that would have outlawed the Communist party. The measure was a rightist reaction to labor conflict, especially in the countryside. Aguirre Cerda's willingness to defend the Communist party's legal status, however, did not affect his commitment to maintain the political basis for the Popular Front's program of modernization—repression of rural labor. Cooperation in Congress from important sectors of the president's own Radical party as well as from the Right remained contingent on preserving the political domination of the hacendados in the rural sector.

The Ríos Administration, 1942-1946

In late 1941 Aguirre Cerda died. Elections in 1942 replaced him with Juan Antonio Ríos, a Radical politician with avowedly anti-Communist tendencies. Ríos, a member of the more conservative wing of the Radical party, had made clear his dislike for the "extremist" elements collaborating with Aguirre Cerda. Ríos' administration (1942-1946) was characterized by a continuation of Aguirre Cerda's developmentalist program of industrialization and modernization of agricultural production. The program emphasized close cooperation with producers, creation of new services and technical subsidies to the hacendados, and continued repression of rural labor.

La Higuera, 1942

Indicative of the milieu in the countryside from 1942 to 1946 were the developments in Hacienda La Higuera owned by Enrique Döll. Labor conflicts on this farm dated from FOCH penetration after World War I (see chapter 2). In July 1942 workers presented a labor petition to the landowner, who was also the mayor (*alcalde*) of the commune of La Ligua. After various delays (the landowner representatives simply failed to attend the sessions of the Junta de Conciliación) Döll dismissed various workers and evicted the leaders of the union from the hacienda. As the landowner, he had insisted that he would give the orders in his hacienda; the workers could obey or they could leave. He admitted illegal actions such as requiring the workers to sell their crops to him (specifically prohibited in the Labor Code). The governmental officials involved took no action against Döll but instead criticized the "communist agitators who incited the workers to form unions and make exaggerated demands that could not be met."[97]

Slowly the large number of unions organized from 1939 to 1940 diminished. By 1944 there remained in the province of Santiago only thirty-four effectively operating unions (still not legally recognized of course) out of some fifty-five formed in the wave of unionization in 1939.[98] In other provinces even more severe declines occurred. Many organizations survived until 1943-1944; most, however, succumbed after five years of "temporary suspension" of the possibility of gaining legal status—and of resisting the retaliation of landowners.[99]

In 1946 President Ríos died in office. The Radical party still dominated the left-center electoral coalition but this time nominated an ostensibly more leftist politician as its presidential candidate, Gabriel González Videla. González Videla's electoral campaign, carried out in frank cooperation with the Communist party, promised the repeal of the administrative order that prevented rural unionization. The campaign and the subsequent ministerial participation by the Communists in González Videla's cabinet brought renewed efforts by Socialists and Communists in the countryside and produced a wave of rural unionization and labor conflicts more massive than that which had occurred from 1939 to 1940.[100]

In January 1946 the Communists and some Socialists again began to make systematic efforts to obtain the repeal of the ministerial order which had suspended rural unionization. In Fundo San Antonio de Naltagua (Melipilla, Santiago Province) the workers called upon the labor inspector of Melipilla to formally constitute an agricultural union, knowing full well that the temporary suspension remained in effect. When the inspector denied the request, the CTCH appealed to the minister of labor to intervene.[101] This request also was denied. But with renewed penetration of union organizers and electoral agents into the countryside, the dormant rural unions and workers' organizations began again to come alive to overtly challenge the power of rural proprietors.

Massive Mobilization of Rural Labor and Renewed Repression

González Videla's campaign promise to rescind the temporary suspension of rural unionization provided added impetus

TABLE 5   DECLINE IN RURAL UNIONS, 1939 AND 1945

Province	Unions Formed, 1939	Unions Reported Active by Labor Department, 1945
Coquimbo	12	"algunos sindicatos libres en Copiapó y Ovalle"
Aconcagua	46	1
Valparaíso	15	2
Santiago	55	34 (1944)
O'Higgins	21	0
Colchagua	11	1
Curicó	17	0
Talca	14	0
Linares	5	0
Concepción	1	0
Bío Bío	2	No data
Malleco	3	"
Cautín	3	"
Valdivia	4	"
Osorno	1	"
Chiloé	2	"
Puerto Montt	1	"

SOURCE: Figures (for 1939) are from Brian Loveman, *Antecedentes para el estudio del movimiento campesino chileno: Pliegos de peticiones, huelgas y sindicatos agrícolas, 1932-1966* vol. 1 (Santiago: ICIRA, 1971). The Labor Department figures for 1945 underestimate union activity and fail to report on some provinces, but the decline, if less intense, did occur; see Oficio 8185, 31 agosto 1945, "Informa sobre número aproximado obreros de los sindicatos agrícolas que se indican," *Oficios* 29, 1945, 8101-8400.

to rural mobilization. Juan Chacón Corona, again the Communist party's chief rural functionary, headed the electoral effort in the countryside and then, upon González Videla's victory, became chief of the Instituto de Economía Agrícola (the agency responsible for setting agricultural prices). For the first six months of González Videla's presidency the rural labor movement, especially those organizations given impetus by the Communist party, made a frontal attack on the Chilean hacienda system in the most massive threat to property in rural land experienced in Chile to that time. Campesinos presented approximately 656 labor petitions to landowners from late 1946 to early 1947. Once the government lifted the suspension of rural unionization, rural workers formed over 300 unions, most of them in accord with the provisions of the Labor Code.[102] With Communist party functionaries in governmental positions, the nationally organized, Party-sponsored campesino organizations experienced a resurgence. The Federación Industrial Nacional de Trabajadores Agrícolas, under the leadership of Juan Ahumado Trigo, called for the expropriation of fundos,[103] and the committees which were formed among smallholders, sharecroppers, and agricultural workers exerted pressure at the grass roots. The Asociación Nacional de Agricultores de Chile, another rural organization supported by the Communist party, attempted to organize the nonhacienda rural labor force, especially smallholders, tenants, colonos, and sharecroppers. This organization also pressed for expropriation of rural land. For example, the president of the campesino committee in Fundo Ñanco (Collipulli, province of Malleco) wrote to the minister of labor in March 1947 to request the minister's cooperation in the expropriation of the fundo and protection of the workers, inquilinos, and sharecroppers facing dismissal or eviction.[104] The labor inspector who investigated the case reported that the landowner declared that "the only difficulties and problems are those created by Lorenzo Medina with his Communist propaganda among the workers, which is causing alarm among the landowners. . . ."[105]

This new wave of rural activism and unionization which challenged the Chilean landowners in 1947 was met, initially, with much the same tactics as in the period 1939-1941. Initial economic gains through collective action by the workers brought retaliation by the landowners. Union leaders were particular targets for dismissal and eviction, but other workers were also persecuted. As usual, landowners could almost always find "legal" cause for dismissals. Illustrative is a report from the department of Maipo (Buin) in the province of Santiago in April 1947. In 19 haciendas and fundos, 118 workers, among them 26 union leaders, were thrown out of work and off the land.[106] All over Chile landowners reacted in like manner to "extirpate the Communist threat."[107]

Once again landowners and landowner associations appealed directly to the president to stop the drive against their customary proprietary authority and the menace to political stability. Telegrams and letters to the Labor Department, such as the one reproduced below, arrived from all over Chile.[108]

> Agricultores [in this] province are justly alarmed [by the] formation of rural unions with intervention [of] representatives of [the] Communist party who introduce themselves into fundos against the will of owners. Political unions, organized in this fashion, constitute constant danger [to the] tranquility [of the] countryside. Will impede development [of] production. Therefore we direct ourselves respectfully [to] Your Excellency.... We ask that you give instructions to labor inspectors to abstain from facilitating [the] formation of rural unions of agricultural workers and principally at [the] request [of] agents [of the] Communist party. Ernesto Aguirre, Pres. Sociedad Agrícola.[109]

At first on the defensive, landowners recovered quickly and reacted in unity to the threat to rural proprietorship. Repression by landowners was followed by González Videla's turn toward the Right, persecution of the Communists, and, as pointed out in the previous chapter, adoption of Law 8.811 to "de-legalize" the hundreds of unions which had been formed. Finally, the Law for the Permanent Defense of Democracy outlawed the Communist party and served as a pretext for the repression of the labor movement, especially in the countryside. In 1948 the number of labor petitions presented by rural workers dropped from almost four hundred (1947) to twenty-four.[110] The decline continued for the next three years, reaching its nadir in 1951, when rural workers presented only eleven labor petitions in all of Chile.[111]

For the most part, the workers who did present labor petitions in the countryside during these years were close to urban
areas or to concentrations of unionized workers or miners. Examples were the unions in the vineyards of Puente Alto, supported by Socialist *político* and later *alcalde* Manuel Muñoz as
well as by Socialist senator Carlos Alberto Martínez; workers
in the fundos near Lota and Colcura, linked to the coal miners;
El Ñilhue in Catemu, San Vicente de Naltagua, and the unions
in the Valley of Choapa also remained active centers of rural
labor conflict. Some publicly owned fundos also maintained de
facto workers' organizations. These fundos, especially those of
the Health Service, like those in Choapa, Hacienda Hospital, or
El Peral, had been organized by Socialists during Salvador Allende's tenure as minister of health and the Socialist-Liga Nacional de Defensa de Campesinos Pobres' penetration into these
enterprises.

During the period 1948-1951 rural labor and Marxist or leftist labor in general went underground. At best, leaders acted
covertly. When the elections of 1952 returned Carlos Ibáñez
to the presidency, an initial coalition with a majority faction
of the Socialist party brought minimum-wage legislation to the
campesinos. Quickly, however, Ibáñez's antiparty, personalist,
and basically conservative orientations drove the Socialists out
of the coalition and, by 1956, into an opposition alliance with
the Communists. During this period the national labor movement reunified, forming the Confederación Única de Trabajadores (CUTCH). Severe economic difficulties and mounting
inflation brought increasing worker militancy. Ibáñez, making
use of the Law for the Permanent Defense of Democracy, acted
to repress the Marxist labor movement. Sporadic repression under the terms of existing anti-Communist legislation was cause
enough (until 1955) for the Communist party to issue instructions to leaders and functionaries not to make themselves targets for arrest through activism in the countryside.[112] As late
as 1956, the Ibáñez government sent Juan Chacón Corona and
various members of the Party's central committee to detention
camps in Pisagua because of a general strike effort. As usual,
the weakest link in the Party-union network, campesino organizations, were the first to feel the effects of repression.

After 1952, however, a new force made itself felt in the

countryside to compete with Marxist labor movements and parties in challenging the traditional prerogatives of rural proprietors: the Catholic Left. From 1952 to 1964 the rural labor movement would be more heterogeneous and would represent a more diverse ideological and political challenge to the power of landowners in the countryside than before. The attack on the hacienda system was now to be justified not only in traditional Marxist language but as a goal of Catholic exponents of social justice. Not only Marx but also the Pope would serve as ideological basis for the campesino's struggle against the political domination of proprietors of rural land.

For the campesino, however, who bore the brunt of the struggle, the reaction of landowners to "Catholic" labor petitions and strikes was not to be markedly different than their reaction had been to "Marxist" labor petitions and strikes. The issue remained the political domination of rural labor by the hacendado and the challenge of an organized labor force to the extensive scope and domain of authority of the rural proprietors.

ASICH and the Federación Sindical Cristiana de la Tierra

Catholic social doctrine in the late nineteenth and twentieth centuries has provided the basis for a variety of Christian political and syndical movements.[113] In Chile, prior to 1953, Catholic-oriented labor leaders or worker organizations had played a very minor role in the rural sector. In 1938, at the suggestion of Oscar Larson, the Catholic Church created the Secretariado Nacional Económico Social, among whose objectives was to "procure . . . the economic well-being of the campesino."[114] A Unión de Campesinos was organized as part of the activities of this Secretariado, and by 1941 the Unión de Campesinos had about three hundred members in twelve fundos.[115] According to Landsberger and Canitrot, Larson and Emilio Tagle also assisted the campesinos in the preparation of a labor petition in Fundo Huelquén (Buin).[116] The landowner, who was a deputy from the Conservative party, attacked the clerics who had participated in this action, suggesting they leave determination of the workers' salary to God and the conscience of the patrón.[117]

At another level this conflict represented the growing rift between the Conservative party and its youth organization, which split off to become the Falanje Nacional (and eventually the Chilean Christian Democratic party). Soon the landowners began to complain about falanjista lawyers and priests who assisted the campesinos in their claims against the hacendados: "these falanjistas are worse than the Communists, since we know how to defend ourselves against the Communists, but not so against the falanjistas who have incited the workers in the fundo."[118] The Conservative party, traditional ally of the Church in Chile, demanded that the efforts of Larson and his colleagues be stopped and that the Unión de Campesinos be disbanded. The Church accepted the demand and sent Larson on missions out of Chile.[119]

Catholic-oriented rural workers' organizations were practically nonexistent from this time until the creation of the Federación Sindical Cristiana de la Tierra in 1952. This organization, led by Emilio Lorenzini, took form in the vineyard region of Molina in the province of Talca. Lorenzini began his work in the countryside of Talca as a Falanje politician. Eventually he linked his activities to the bishopric of Talca and through the bishop to the Catholic labor organization, Acción Sindical Chilena (ASICH).[120] Interestingly, the Federación Sindical Cristiana de la Tierra grew out of Viña San Pedro, one of the first rural properties in which legal rural unions had been created, then broken up in 1932. In addition, the Molina region had been a target of FOCH-oriented rural labor conflicts during the 1920s and saw renewed unionization drives in the 1939-40 and 1946-7 waves of rural unionization.[121] As recently as 1947 strikes had occurred in the area. In this sense the Catholic labor organizers, despite their seeming unawareness of this history, were not working in virgin territory.

The landowners reacted to the organizational efforts of Lorenzini and ASICH in essentially the same way they had previously dealt with other campesino organizations. The threat to proprietary authority was no more acceptable from Catholic organizers than it had been from Communists or Socialists. The landowners viewed Lorenzini as an agitator, and the landowner association in Lontué protested his activities to the minister of interior.[122] In addition, they dismissed labor leaders and members of worker committees in the farms.

The police, as agents of proprietary interests, maintained order by harrassing Lorenzini and other leaders when they violated "private property" to meet with agricultural workers.

Gradually Lorenzini connected his activities with ASICH's national office in Santiago. He cemented the relationship in 1953 by sending an ASICH-sponsored delegation of campesinos to the Congress of the Central Única de Trabajadores (CUTCH) in Santiago.[123]

ASICH-Federación Sindical Cristiana de la Tierra performed services for the campesinos similar to those of other nationally linked rural labor organizations: legal advice and assistance in labor conflicts and in the labor courts, preparation of labor petitions, and publicity campaigns denouncing abuses of rural proprietors. But ASICH also provided literacy training, labor education, and spiritual guidance.[124] The campesino leaders trained in ASICH's syndical school would later become leaders in the national rural labor organizations created after 1960, especially the Unión de Campesinos Cristianos.[125] These campesino leadership cadres represented, in the long run, the most important contribution of ASICH and Lorenzini to the rural labor movement. In the short run, however, the drama of large-scale labor conflicts in the rural areas clouded the importance of cadre formation.

In October 1953 Lorenzini organized the Primer Congreso Sindical de los Obreros Campesinos de Molina, at which the workers decided on the content of labor petitions to be presented in the vineyards and fundos in November. Once the petitions were presented, the landowners sought grounds in the Junta de Conciliación for declaring them illegal under the terms of Law 8.811. Such grounds were not difficult to find, given the restrictiveness of legislation governing rural labor conflicts. Under Lorenzini's direction the workers then threatened to strike. The workers made good on the strike threat and the movement led eventually to a campesino march on Santiago which was widely publicized in the Santiago press. The Molina strike is generally cited as the most important rural labor conflict in Chile prior to 1964, for both the numbers of campesinos involved and its psychological impact in the national capital. The eventual victory won by the campesinos included the release from prison of Lorenzini and other rural labor leaders who had been arrested under the provisions of the Law for the Permanent Defense of Democracy.[126]

From 1953 to 1957 ASICH maintained its role in the countryside around Molina but had less success in expanding the movement outside the region. Labor petitions and strikes, in gradually decreasing numbers, were repeated for the grape harvests of 1954 through 1957. Complaints were registered with labor inspectors, and enforcement of existing labor legislation was requested.[127] Even in 1955, however, before the organization had seriously declined, landowners could still successfully resist much of ASICH's pressure, and they retaliated against the rural labor force. When the Labor Department declared labor petitions illegal because of omissions or errors, ASICH, like the Marxist labor organizations, could not prevent landowners from using any of a variety of pretexts to legally dismiss the campesinos who had signed the labor petition.

The Labor Department's agricultural inspector on a special assignment to the zone of Molina in 1955 reported as follows:

> The vineyards in the region of Molina are in a state of a continuous tension between two forces, one the Asociación de Agricultores of Molina and the other ASICH (Asociación Sindical Chilena) which, on its own initiative, has taken on the representation of the workers . . . about 70 percent of the labor force in the properties of this region.
> . . . in the constant struggle between ASICH and the landowners, it is the workers who are injured, those who have direct relations with this organization [ASICH] being dismissed. . . .
> Friday the 25th of the past month there was a meeting in the Gobernación of Molina. The meeting had to be held in two sessions. First the named authorities [met] with the Asociación de Agricultores and afterwards with ASICH, since the former refuse to come to a meeting in which ASICH participated.[128]

The legitimacy of ASICH and of associations of rural labor were still generally unrecognized by Chilean landowners. At times forced to concede short-term gains to organized rural labor, the landowners retained the capability to retaliate shortly thereafter and, in most cases, to break the campesino unions.

The threat of ASICH to rural proprietors in the Molina region declined after 1955 as the organization's strength decreased and Lorenzini left Molina.[129] Landsberger and Canitrot conclude that it was a movement whose time had not yet come, a "false spring; the delicate shoots came out because of a few temperate

days, but then comes the first freeze and they perish."[130] While
the authors are correct that "unionization [of the rural labor
force], like agrarian reform, is part of a brusque change in the
distribution of social power,"[131] it would be a mistake to view
the movement in Molina as a "false spring" instead of part of
a recurring pattern of rural labor conflicts (especially in the
zone of Molina) followed by government and landowner repression of the campesinos. The ASICH-Lorenzini-led movement
formed part of a larger challenge to the political meaning of
property in rural land.

ASICH was explicitly in competition with Communist labor
organizers in the countryside. Active in a period when the Communists were still outlawed, ASICH, through its journal *Tierra
y Libertad*, carried out a systematic anti-Communist campaign.
Typical of this attitude was the commentary of March 1954:
"We won in Molina, and as long as we campesinos are not fools
and do not put up with [*no le aguantemos la pará*] the Partido
Communista or Frente del Pueblo as it calls itself now, we shall
win everywhere we are united."[132]

ASICH's ideological and religious commitment to the campesinos must be seen as a Catholic alternative to Marxist concepts of property and society. In this respect, also, the movement in Molina formed part of a wider struggle within the
Chilean polity between varying concepts of a new order which
might replace the capitalist system of exploitation. For the
landowners, the challenge to property in rural land became
more diverse and sought legitimacy in a changing Catholic
church, which now propagated "radical" social doctrine. For
the campesinos, entrance of the Catholic Left into the countryside meant the possibility of additional allies in the struggle
against the hacendado.

In 1960 ASICH formed the Unión de Campesinos Cristianos
(UCC) to unite the isolated rural unions and farm committees
and to expand the activity of rural labor. The UCC, led initially
by urban elements, including Lorenzini,[133] dedicated itself to
stimulating syndical organizations—grouping all classes of rural
labor and small proprietors, promoting the "integral social, economic, technical and moral development of the campesinos,"
creating services for its members, and supporting an agrarian
reform program "that guaranteed the active participation of

organized campesinos in its formulation and implementation. . . ."[134] From 1961 to 1964 UCC carried on the struggle
in the vineyard region of Molina, founded consumer cooperatives, intensified leadership training efforts, and maintained
regular publication of *Tierra y Libertad*. UCC also continued
the tradition of legal services for members and increased efforts
to secure governmental regulation of the hacendados through
the enforcement of existing labor law and the enactment of
more favorable legislation. Activities ceased to be predomi-
nantly local (Molina) as organizational and service operations
were extended from Aconcagua to Linares and then outside
the central valley.

Finally, in 1964 the UCC endorsed the presidential candidacy of Christian Democrat Eduardo Frei in *Tierra y Libertad*.
Mass meetings and quickie leadership training courses mobilized
rural support for the Christian Democratic candidate. After the
election *Tierra y Libertad* declared that the "campesinos gave
victory to the Christian Revolution."[135] From the localistic organizational efforts of Lorenzini and ASICH had been created
a national Catholic rural labor organization which stimulated
labor conflicts, demanded agrarian reform, and supported the
newly installed Christian Democratic government.

Parallel Catholic Rural Labor Organization

Parallel to the efforts of ASICH, the Church hierarchy gave
a new emphasis to rural activity after 1953. In 1952 the National Council of Bishops made the decision to create Acción
Católica Rural (ACR). Later, this basically apostolic organization gave rise to the Instituto de Educación Rural.[136] The first
rural activity of ACR was carried out by Humberto Muñoz in
the district of Maipú (Santiago Province) in 1953. To a great
extent, the ACR represented a counterthrust to Protestant penetration of the countryside. Initial emphasis was on training
local leaders (*militantes*) "who would work permanently in the
rural apostolate."[137]

In March 1955 the Church, with the assistance of progressive
landowners, created the Institute of Rural Education (IER).
The IER functioned as a technical-doctrinal educational institution, supporting the work of ACR. The IER formed *centros
campesinos* within fundos, in agreement with the hacendados,

because "the solution to the social and economic problems of the countryside require the cooperation of the patrones in projects of community development."[138] The IER, thus, maintained a much less militant line in regard to agrarian reform than did ASICH. Further, the IER emphasized the need for labor and capital to cooperate in the agricultural sector.

The increasing militancy of other rural labor organizations from 1958 to 1961 created tactical and moral dilemmas for campesinos trained in the IER centers. In 1962 some leaders within the IER proposed the formation of a syndical department to defend the rights of rural labor in a more vigorous fashion.[139] By uniting the centros campesinos and cooperatives that the IER had spawned, these leaders created the Asociación Nacional de Organizaciones Campesinos (ANOC). ANOC was specifically defined as "an association of organizations, not of persons. This association must be apolitical and neutral in matters of religion."[140] By apolitical ANOC meant that party politics should not intrude in the local organizations. The national organization nevertheless declared: "In the future the Congressmen should listen to campesino leaders before dispatching laws that affect [the campesinos]."[141] It also called for direct representation of ANOC in national institutions like CORFO, the Banco Central, and private banks and corporations because "up to now only the large property owners have received assistance from [these institutions]."[142]

ANOC, extending its activities from Coquimbo to Valdivia, spread its resources thinner than did UCC. While retaining a somewhat more conservative orientation than did UCC, by 1964 ANOC also prepared labor petitions and stimulated strikes in the countryside. The IER continued to support ANOC activity, paying the salaries of ANOC leaders, training leaders, and preparing as well as propagating "radio-school" courses. In 1962 ANOC, along with the UCC and the syndical department of the Christian Democratic party, sent delegates to the national congress of the CUT. In a fashion quite similar to the reaction of the Communists in 1939 to Zapata's Ligas de Campesinos Pobres, but this time with success, the Catholic rural labor leaders were denied participation in the national labor confederation because they represented "nonsyndical" organizations. Fearful of losing control of the CUT, the

Marxists successfully prevented incorporation of the Catholic rural labor movement into the CUT. The rejection explicitly defined the Marxist-Catholic split which was to characterize the rural labor movement for the next decade.

ANOC, UCC, and the smaller groups proceeded to carry out their own congress—Primer Congreso Nacional de Campesinos Libres. A decision to create a coordinating committee between UCC and ANOC "to give impulse to a campaign to realize the aspirations of the campesinos as revealed in this congress" fore-shadowed the later unification of ANOC and UCC in the Confederación Nacional Campesina.

Like the UCC, ANOC gave special attention to training leadership cadres. From 1962 to 1965 ANOC carried out three national training courses for campesino leaders. ANOC emphasized that it was "formed by authentic campesinos . . . year after year these men have the duty to orient, advise and represent the rural masses. . . . They must continue to study the manner to prevail against the egotism of the latifundists and, on the other hand, against the . . . politicians who desire to take advantage of the campesino's ignorance."[143] To this end ANOC sponsored (1962-1965) 29 provincial and 50 commune-level leadership courses. During the same years ANOC assisted campesinos in 131 labor conflicts and made 175 formal complaints to the Labor Department against rural proprietors.[144]

By 1964 the two major groups of Catholic rural labor organizations represented an important challenge to landowners in rural Chile. Adopting tactics of labor conflict which, with the exception of land occupations or "recuperation," were identical to Marxist rural organizations, the Catholic rural labor movement provided an alternative syndical umbrella for non-Marxist campesino organizations.

Resurgence of Marxist Organizations in the Countryside

The presidential elections of 1953 had once again sent leftist political organizers to the countryside. The Socialist party, which supported the candidacy of ex-dictator Carlos Ibáñez, combined with the personalist Agrarian Labor party in forming committees against vote-buying (*cohecho*) in efforts to win rural votes from the traditionally patrón-controlled rural labor force. Minimum-wage legislation, backed by the Socialist participants in the Ibáñez regime, somewhat upgraded the conditions of rural labor. But the Socialist party soon withdrew from the Ibáñez cabinet, and the regime gradually moved toward the right of the political spectrum.

The Communist party, slowly recovering from the repression of the González Videla period, was able by 1954 to re-activate the Federación Industrial de Trabajadores Agrícolas (FINTA), shortening the name to Federación Nacional de Trabajadores Agrícolas. Juan Ahumada Trigo, who remained in charge of this organization, was assisted by another Communist functionary-politico by the name of César Cerda. The Federación Nacional de Trabajadores attempted to protect campesinos from dismissals and evictions as retaliation by the landowners for efforts to organize rural labor unions, and to secure compliance with labor law by registering formal complaints with the Labor Department.[145] The Federación urged an extensive agrarian reform program, investment in rural education, improved medical services in the rural sector, and the repeal of Law 8.811 to be followed by application of the Labor Code's unionization provisions in the countryside. The Federación also requested that the number of labor inspectors be increased and that they be provided transportation for making visits to the fundos when complaints were registered.

In short, the Communist-dominated Federación Nacional de Trabajadores Agricolas had a program for the countryside—something lacking even in the case of ASICH. It also had groups of workers organized into committees or *sindicatos libres* in fundos all over Chile. Some of these fundos had first been organized by FOCH, then again in the 1939-1940 wave of unionization, and for a third time in the 1946-1947 mobilization in the countryside. In other fundos the organizational efforts went back only to 1947 or to the election campaign of 1953. Nevertheless, in 1953 (and outside Molina) the Federación Nacional de Trabajadores Agricolas was the only activist class organization which challenged the authority of rural proprietors on a national scale.

After Carlos Ibáñez's election as president of Chile in 1953, the Federación Nacional de Trabajadores Agrícolas adopted a systematic tactical plan for organizing rural labor. The basic effort comprised making operational the slogan "worker-campesino alliance." Explaining this tactic to a group of Marxist experts on the agrarian question in Cuba in 1962, Juan Ahumada stated:

> For a long time now the Federación de Trabajadores Agrícolas has relied on the unions of industrial workers and miners and the consejos of the Central Única de Trabajadores, soliciting their aid, which takes many forms. One of the most effective has been that in which an industrial union resolves to take charge of the assistance and attention to a rural union or committee of campesinos. We have called this APADRINAMIENTO. The industrial union becomes a sort of godfather [padrino] of the campesinos. In this fashion we have industrial workers who go to the countryside and commit themselves to the attention of campesinos or agricultural workers; providing, from the industrial unions, medical attention and legal assistance in the case of labor claims or collective labor conflicts which are not legal. . . .
>
> Another manner of helping is that in which industrial unions designate one or two members to participate in the Federación de Trabajadores Agrícolas as activists and in this capacity go out to the countryside and attend to rural organization.[146]

The Federación Nacional de Trabajadores Agricolas, through Communist party officials, functionaries, urban union leaders, and campesino cadres, organized hundreds of *comités campesinos* (in fundos with fewer than twenty-five workers) and sindicatos libres. These organizations transmitted complaints to the national organization or to the local CUT consejo and were assisted in dealing with the landowners and Labor Department bureaucrats. Thus, like all Chilean rural labor organizations before and after, the Federación served the important function of mediating between campesinos and governmental agencies, especially in presenting complaints against rural proprietors.[147] The intensity of activity of the Federación reached a peak in the period 1955-1956, but continued into 1958. Public demonstrations, propaganda campaigns, and especially the activism of leftist deputies and local politicians accompanied numerous formal complaints to the Labor Department against individual landowners for violations of the law. In many cases the Federación obtained visits by labor inspectors to fundos where their members worked in order to insist on compliance with labor legislation. Given the lack of resources and small number of rural inspections carried out by the Labor Department, pressure by organized campesinos, represented at the national level by

Juan Ahumada, meant that selective benefits in the form of legal compliance could be provided for the Federación membership.

Because retaliation by the landowner was, as usual, directed
against participants in "subversive" organizations or activities,
campesinos often held meetings at night in out-of-the-way loca-
tions. Membership was not always acknowledged. In this sense
the activity of the Federación was less overt than that during
the periods of massive rural mobilization and efforts to constitute rural unions. Legal labor petitions being difficult to present, the campesinos had recourse to other tactics which also
decreased, somewhat, the vulnerability of campesinos whom
the law required to sign labor petitions.

Legal petitions were not, however, completely neglected.
Still, the difficulties of presenting such a petition successfully
and complying with all the provisions of Law 8.811 made this
tactic less common. The difficulties are well illustrated by a
case in Viña La Finca (Buin) in 1955. The workers presented
a labor petition and the landowner objected on the grounds
that the fundo was harvesting—harvesting grass. The Labor Department agreed that while the grape harvest had not yet begun, "The vineyards in the zone not only cultivate vines, but
also animal feed (*pasto*) and corn in a continuous cycle from
January until the end of March." Thus, the petition was illegal
because it was presented in time of harvest. Still, the workers
received a 15 peso per day raise in pay (from 140 to 155 pesos)
as a result of the "illegal" petition.[148]

The resurgence of rural labor activism combined with "free
union" organization formed part of a planned programmatic
decision by the Communist party to renew the struggle in the
countryside to coincide with a more general offensive against
the Ibáñez regime.[149] On the national level this decision
brought increased and more vigorous enforcement of the Law
for the Permanent Defense of Democracy and sent various
party officials to detention camps in Pisagua.[150] The minister
of interior, in a circular of September 20, 1955, reminded gobernadores and intendentes that it was their duty to prevent
Communist participation in union leadership. Labor Department personnel also received these instructions, along with
the threat of severe sanctions for those who were not diligent

in preventing "Communists or members of other antidemocratic factions or movements" from occupying leadership posts in unions.[151]

The Ibáñez government, however, did not have consistent policies on this issue. At the same time that the government ordered repression of Communists, the Labor Department formally invited the Federación Nacional de Trabajadores Agrícolas (along with ASICH and SNA) to send representatives to participate in the department's "Advisory Commission on Agricultural Labor."[152] The Federación named César Cerda C. and Juan Ahumada Trigo—individuals about whose long-time Party affiliation there was no doubt. Yet they worked within the commission and were annually thanked by the Labor Department for their participation.[153]

Throughout the period 1953-1958 the Federación Nacional de Trabajadores Agrícolas remained active in the countryside. In many cases the Federación's intervention forced landowners to pay back wages, reevaluate regalías, rescind dismissals, update (or introduce) labor contracts, or otherwise respond to campesino demands. In addition, the Federación maintained a center in Santiago to train campesino leadership cadres. The Federación's newspaper, *El Surco,* as well as the Communist party paper *El Siglo*, publicized the campesino's situation and forced remedial action by the government.[154] The Asociación Nacional de Agricultores (smallholders, colonos, sharecroppers) and the Asociación Nacional de Indígenas (Indians, especially those in the southern provinces from Arauco to Valdivia) were also revitalized. These organizations re-activated the struggle for a "real agrarian reform which would provide land for the tiller" and the return of ancestral lands to the Mapuche in southern Chile.

Despite the national scope of the Federación, in each province or rural district its members were isolated on individual fundos. The Federación lacked organizational infrastructure. Provincial federations or regional associations to link the fundos did not exist. Contacts with national headquarters were through Party functionaries, industrial workers and miners, or individual campesino leaders. The movement remained, in this respect, fragile—a skeleton to be fleshed out if a viable national organization was to be constructed. Still, by the presidential election of 1958 the extent of this organization in the countryside—

underestimated by the traditional political parties—became apparent as the Socialist-Communist (FRAP) candidate, Salvador Allende, fell only about 35,000 votes short of gaining a plurality (over Jorge Alessandri), with significant vote totals in the rural communes.

Prelude to the "Revolution in Liberty"

The Federación Nacional de Trabajadores Agrícolas and ASICH remained active in the countryside. Neither represented the great mass of rural labor, but their activity in regional and local centers maintained sporadic pressure on rural proprietors. Both were extensions of national political movements, as had been most rural labor organizations before them. As in 1919, the struggle of the campesinos against the landowners was linked to broader questions of national politics. The political power of the hacendados in the countryside remained extensive, as did their capability to influence the policy of the national government in matters connected to their position in the countryside. But by 1958 the challenge to this capability had grown serious. As one of the last acts of his presidency, Ibáñez arranged for the repeal of the legislation which had outlawed the Communist party in 1948. The 1958 presidential campaign thus became the first in a decade in which the Communists could overtly participate. The Communist-Socialist (FRAP) coalition, through the dispersed organizational contacts of the Federación Nacional de Trabajadores Agrícolas and the smaller asociaciones, made great electoral gains in rural areas. Only the 41,000 votes received by a "radical" priest from Aconcagua (the so-called *cura de catapilco*) prevented the FRAP candidate from winning.

During this campaign, the Communists distributed an agrarian reform proposal as part of FRAP electoral propaganda,[155] and the agrarian question once again came to the forefront of national attention. Shortly after Jorge Alessandri occupied the presidency in 1958, Fidel Castro was victorious in Cuba. Land reform became an issue of principal concern throughout Latin America. Chile was no exception.

Throughout the Alessandri presidency the Marxist-oriented rural labor organizations increased pressure on the government and rural proprietors through labor petitions, strikes, and land occupations. At the same time, ASICH and the Christian Democrats made large commitments in the countryside. The rural sector became the center of a national political struggle between the Christian Democrats and the FRAP coalition. Competition between these groups was reflected in efforts to organize rural labor and to put pressure on the incumbent government. By 1961 the principal Communist and Socialist rural labor organizations joined under the banner of the Federación Nacional Campesina e Indígena. José Campusano, long time Communist party functionary and activist, headed this organization.[156]

From 1960 until 1964 the competition between the Catholic rural labor movement and the Marxist federation placed increasing pressure on the authority of rural proprietors.[157] Both Marxist and Catholic organizers opted for illegal tactics and "free unions" or rural committees. Where legal unions still managed to survive, however, the same old struggle between landowners and organized campesinos continued. Likewise, the same pattern of campesino complaints or petitions and landowner retaliation—dismissals, evictions, "changes in modes of production for purely commercial reasons"—placed even the legal unions (given the restrictiveness of Law 8.811) on the defensive. While the Marxist organizations attempted to link rural organizations to urban and mining unions, ASICH maintained strength in the Talca-Curicó region. By 1962 the Labor Department was simply unable to deal with the mass of complaints coming from newly founded campesino committees, leftist and Christian Democratic politicians, and the national rural labor organizations. Both Marxists and the Christian Democrats began to rally rural labor behind the slogan of agrarian reform, in addition to focusing on landowner violations of labor law.

The competition between Marxists and Christian Democrats in the countryside provided the campesinos new allies at the same time that pressure on landowners and the government increased.[158] The upcoming electoral struggle of 1964 provided, once again, a critical role for rural labor in the national political arena. As had been the case since the first rural unionization efforts, the fate of rural activism and rural unions depended upon the resolution of political struggle at the national level.

6

Urbanization, Party Politics, and Rural Labor

What the hacendado lost in the first half of this century was the Seignorial quality of his power. He no longer controlled the governmental authorities or local political leaders.

Andrés Pascal, 1968

The government of the Terratenientes of our country has had to recognize, much to its regret, a fact that we Communists have been insisting upon for many years: The necessity of carrying out an Agrarian Reform in Chile that liquidates the latifundio.

César Cerda and Juan Ahumada, 1962

The struggle of rural labor against the hacendados' dominance in the countryside from 1919 to 1964 accompanied a broader social and economic transformation of Chilean society. This transformation entailed an opening of the countryside to urban influences. The expansion of road networks brought merchants, middlemen, itinerant peddlers, truckers, and missionaries to rural areas. Buses took rural laborers on more frequent trips to nearby towns and cities. Campesinos read newspapers and magazines and listened to transistor radios. Urban mass culture penetrated the countryside.

Urbanization of the countryside began in Chile in the late nineteenth century. From 1930 to 1960 it intensified. By 1960 very few hacendados could properly be considered local or regional sovereigns even on a de facto basis. And while within the hacienda the rural proprietor retained extensive scope and domain of authority, even here existed clear differences from the situation in 1930.

It is not possible in the present context to analyze in its entirety the multifaceted process of urbanization of the countryside. Even if data were available, an assessment of the impact of peddlers, evangelists, truckers, schoolteachers, postal clerks, and

189

other urban agents on the transformation of the Chilean countryside would require a study of equal or greater length than the present one.[1] The lack of existing studies, however, puts this enterprise, for the moment, out of the question. For instance, there can be little doubt that road construction was a critical variable in the economic development and political transformation of particular rural zones, yet no descriptive treatment of this phenomenon exists nor has the political process through which policymakers made road-construction decisions been investigated.[2] Perhaps influential hacendados obtained public-works investments in roads and bridges which eventually served to undermine their own monopoly control over the rural labor force. In any case, in the absence of empirical studies of these questions, discussion in this chapter is limited to three principal aspects of the urbanization of the countryside which heavily contributed to the declining power of rural proprietors: (1) expanded penetration of governmental authorities into the countryside; (2) the multifront attack on the legitimacy of the proprietary authority of the hacendado accompanied by the demand for redefinition of property rights in rural land; and (3) the intervention of urban-based political parties in the countryside. First, however, brief mention must be made of the importance of such other urban-related influences on the hacienda system as increased urban markets, mechanization of the agricultural enterprise, and rural-urban migration.

As the network of interactions between rural and urban residents expanded, the insularity of the hacienda community was progressively eroded. Labor conflict and a desire to modernize farm production induced rural proprietors to rely less and less on inquilinos and resident labor. The disruptive influence of temporary labor—migrants as well as seasonal workers who lived in towns or cities—united rural labor with urban workers who were unwilling to accept the traditional, extensive authority of the hacendado. Intersectoral labor mobility particularly threatened the customary relationship between hacendado and rural labor. Hugo Zemelman has argued that it was precisely the campesino who migrated to urban centers and returned to work as a wage laborer in the countryside who played the most dynamic role in resisting the customary prerogatives of rural proprietors:

> We sustain the idea that the most dynamic group is constituted by
> those who have had urban experiences through migration, since they
> have broken their [traditional] relations and experienced a real change
> of position within the agrarian structure in a most profound manner.
> . . . They will demonstrate a more favorable disposition to participate
> actively in syndical organizations because their change of position
> within the system of production prepares them to have a more global
> view of its structure.[3]

Without entering into the controversy over which group of
campesinos is most militant or revolutionary,[4] we may note
substantial evidence in the Chilean case that nonresident rural
laborers returning from the nitrate fields, coal mines, or urban
employment have played an important part in some rural labor
conflicts. The periodic crises in the nitrate fields between 1919
and 1931 brought waves of unemployed workers back to the
countryside. With their experience in union organization in the
nitrate fields, these workers represented an important source of
resistance to patronal authority. As early as 1921 landowners
in some areas rejected returning nitrate workers even during
the harvest season. The Labor Department, which served as an
employment office for the hacendados, received many letters
like the following:

> In answer to the telegrams you have sent me concerning workers, I
> can tell you that I need [them] as long as they are families; I will give
> them a good position and pay each of them two pesos a day. "By the
> job" [a trato] they can earn more. If they know how to plow with a
> horse in the vineyard they can earn up to four pesos a day. I will not
> accept single workers from the north.[5]

Not only the returned nitrate workers but also other unemployed or seasonal workers living in towns or *albergues* (temporary quarters for large numbers of unemployed) incited labor
conflicts in the countryside.[6] The *afuerino* (nonresident rural
workers; literally "outsider") became an increasingly more important element of rural labor during the period 1930-1960
and an increasingly significant source of rural labor conflict.
Through these workers urban and mining worker-culture came
into the countryside and was juxtaposed to the traditional authority of the hacendado.[7]

The nitrate fields and other mining enterprises influenced
the hacienda not only through the returned workers, however,
but also through the workers who were recruited from the rural

sector by labor recruitors (*enganchadores*). Chilean landowners had complained since the last part of the nineteenth century about seasonal labor shortages. From 1919 on the sectoral competition for summer labor became severe between agricultural and mining interests. The landowners attempted to exercise their influence to regulate the timing of labor recruiting (*enganches*) for the nitrate fields and other mines so that they would not coincide with the critical periods of agricultural labor. Government officials added their voices on this matter, as illustrated by the following letter from the Intendente of Curicó in 1926:

> The enormous flow of workers toward the north and the continuous enganches of people to the mines and the nitrate fields is removing [the young people] from the countryside. . . . Actually there are many fields unreaped for lack of hands despite wages of 80 to 100 pesos per cuadra . . . which two years ago was paid at 25-30 pesos.
>
> The fundos, in general, cannot extend their cultivation. . . .
>
> . . . the Government would do a great service to these central provinces, essentially agricultural, if enganches were impeded in the months of harvest and planting each year, that is to say from December to May of each year.[8]

The interdependence through the labor market of the sectors of the Chilean economy thus reduced the insulated situation of the hacendado and also induced agricultural mechanization in an effort to eliminate the risks of labor shortage at the harvest.[9] Movements of nonresident agricultural labor were relatively large. The Labor Department commonly received requests for five hundred to one thousand workers for a particular region during harvest seasons.[10] On the other hand, in years when the nitrate fields slowed production or faced economic crisis, floods of unemployed returned to the countryside. Under these conditions the landowners refused to pay the transportation costs required by the Labor Department and insisted that employing the workers was a "favor." Provincial or departmental authorities requested free passes for the workers on the government-owned railroad. In some cases, the Labor Department intervened to obtain these passes; in others, the department refused to subsidize the hacendados beyond certain limits.[11]

Unfortunately there exists no systematic study of the national labor market during this period. We can only say that labor mobility increased, that professional labor recruiters roamed the countryside promising campesinos great rewards in the nitrate fields or copper mines, and that unemployed nitrate workers and other town-living seasonal workers played an increasingly important role in the urbanization of the countryside by promoting resistance to the traditional authority of rural proprietors. Rural-urban migration, as well as intersectoral and seasonal migration, was thus an important part of the transformation of the rural sector from 1919 onward. The remainder of the present chapter, however, emphasizes three phenomena which can be more directly linked to the redefinition of proprietary authority in the countryside: (1) expanded governmental penetration into the countryside; (2) declining legitimacy of the hacienda system; and (3) party politics in the rural sector.

Expanded Governmental Penetration into the Countryside

In the period 1919-1964 (and especially after 1931), expanded governmental penetration into the countryside in the form of rural schools, health clinics, post offices and telegraph lines, civil registers, and inspectors from the Social Security, Labor and Health departments contributed to the development of numerous small towns and villages. Semi-urban service and commercial centers which housed the offices of one or more governmental agencies provided new sources of goods and services to the rural population and dispersed the previously monocentric patron-client relationship between campesinos and hacendado. The appearance of governmental bureaucrats altered the political structure of the countryside. The Socialist postal clerk or doctor, the Radical or Communist schoolteacher, the urban, middle-class police lieutenant temporarily stationed in the rural locality at an early stage in a career he hoped would end in Santiago, Valparaíso, or Concepción—all represented threats to the hegemony of the hacendado. Thus, in 1934, after the events at Ranquíl (the uprising of smallholders and the ensuing massacre), the official organ of the SNA suggested:

> . . . taking into consideration . . . that in some rural schools there are teachers with frankly disturbing tendencies [*tendencias disociadoras*] . . . the Directive Council considers it necessary that every member of the agricultural societies report to our institution, with the facts of the case, all the subversive activities or communist teachings in which rural teachers engage, so that appropriate measures can be taken to put an end to such activities.[12]

The introduction of relatively autonomous urban agents into the countryside entailed the creation of alternative structures of authority, both material and ideological, in the rural sector. Even the frequently exercised capability of dominant landowners to have "difficult" or "uncooperative" bureaucrats transferred did not prevent the eventual autonomization, partial or total, of some bureaucratic agencies from the hacendado's influence. Schoolteachers occupied particularly strategic positions. Where Marxist or populist primary teachers could establish good personal contacts in rural zones, the SNA's fears of "subversion" became reality. In the period 1930-1964 schoolteachers often led campesino challenges to landowner authority. Illustrative is a strike in Fundo Cuatro Alamos de lo Espejo (Santiago Province) in 1946. The labor inspector handling the case reported as follows:

> For months now elements of the Communist party have bombarded this property with a sustained campaign of agitation among the workers. The leaders of this group of "activists" is a schoolteacher [*profesora primaria*] in Lo Espejo who is also a leader in the local CTCH. . . . The product of this agitation was a labor conflict beginning on September 6, 1946, two days after the presidential election . . . ending in a settlement favorable to the workers. . . .[13]

But this role was not limited to teachers. Railroad clerks, social security officials, labor inspectors, post office personnel—in short, almost any sort of governmental official who might obtain work through party patronage—could threaten the authority of the hacendado by subtle influences on the rural work force as well as by deliberate efforts to assist in the formation of campesino class organizations.

In some rural areas, in exceptional cases, public officials even took management-labor relations in the countryside into their own hands, ending the essentially unilateral determination of working conditions typical in most of the rural sector. Especially from 1939 to 1942, and again in the period 1946-1947, these officials could sometimes use as leverage the radical challenge of an organized and active rural labor movement. Still, the case of the gobernador in Molina in 1939 is extraordinary. Preceding by fourteen years the famous Molina strike,[14] the gobernador arranged for a region-wide (*departamento*) labor agreement "in consultation" with the region's principal landowners.

Acting as intermediary between the landowners and a mobilized
labor force, the gobernador obtained the hacendados' formal
agreement to do as follows:

(1) Raise salaries for workers and inquilinos. (Minimum salary 6
pesos for non-resident labor.)

(2) Improve food rations. (Galleta of 300 grams. Three for nonresident workers, two for inquilinos. After the grape harvest, meat once a
week and coffee every day.)

(3) Improve and sanitize existing housing.

(4) Increase the land allotments of the inquilinos.

(5) Provide medical attention. Support the installation of emergency
aid stations in which the workers could receive medical and pharmaceu-
tical services covered by Law 4.054.

(6) Provide primary instruction; avoid employing minors in agricultural labors and to effect a census of school-age children in the fundos;
facilitate the creation of schools.

No agreement could be reached on revocation of notices of
dismissal already issued by the landowners; the hacendados insisted on leaving the matter to the appropriate courts.[15] Although the agreement was never completely put into effect,
there existed an enormous difference between formal governmental intervention and mediation in this case and the events
less than twenty years before in rural labor conflicts (see chapter 2). No longer did landowners insist that such matters were
"merely of personal concern." In exchange for governmental
support the landowners gradually had to accept limits on their
authority and on their political power in the countryside.

This divestiture of traditional proprietary prerogatives to multiple governmental agents did not necessarily imply, however,
an immediate and radical loss of the hacendado's power. A gradual transition occurred, especially in cases where the sanctity of
private property was threatened. Well into the 1950s the national police force commonly repressed those workers who resisted the landowner's mandates or sought to organize rural
unions in order to alter the scope and domain of the proprietor's intraproperty authority. Whereas the police did not generally respond directly to the landowner's commands, the national regime acted to uphold proprietary authority. But even
so, the authority of the hacendado was now contingent on the
behavior of bureaucrats, policemen, and other governmental officials. The response to the landowner's demands became less

automatic. Particularly in cases involving evictions of campesinos (the legal right of proprietors to force uncooperative or organized workers out of their homes while at the same time eliminating their access to land, pasture, and the minimal guarantees of the hacienda environment), the transformation subordinated the hacendado's power to decision makers in provincial offices or in Santiago. *Desalojos con fuerza pública* ("evictions with police intervention") became matters for ministerial attention rather than for hacendado discretion:

> Mr. Minister:
>
> Saturday the 11th [of May] approximately seventy workers, accompanied by Alfredo Navarrete, Regional Secretary of the CTCH, appeared at my office.
>
> These workers told me that their patrones had notified them that they must abandon their houses. . . . They said if they did not retire they would be expelled by the police [*fuerza pública*].
>
> . . . I cited the patrones [who confirmed the workers' presentation].
>
> I urged them to desist in their purposes . . . [and] in deference to me as Intendente, [the patrones] agreed to allow the workers to stay in the fundos until the 31st of this month.
>
> . . . There is also pending in this Intendencia an oficio of fuerza pública from the labor court, dated 9 May in which is ordered the eviction of two inquilinos in Fundo "El Guaico" of Fernando Zañartu. This gentleman, called by the Intendencia in order to avoid the eviction, has given the workers until the 20th of this month to leave the houses. I have knowledge that the affected inquilinos will not leave on the day indicated, and therefore request that you indicate to me if I should enforce these judicial orders.[16]

What once would have been an almost automatic response to protect private property now sometimes required ministerial orders. No longer could the hacendados expect unconditional support by public authorities. Thus, while the proprietor's discretion in farm management, land use or nonuse, alienation, or other resource-related decisions remained intact, intervention of national and bureaucratic authority gradually eroded the authority of rural proprietors in reference to the labor force. By 1960, although generally supportive of private property, the Chilean national regime recognized a much more delimited private property, and the hacendado depended more than ever on national authority to maintain order and discipline in the countryside.

Declining Legitimacy of the Hacienda System

As the authority of the landowner gradually eroded, the services he provided the rural population also declined. Agricultural production did not keep pace with population growth. Real wages of rural labor declined by approximately one-third from 1953 to 1959.[17] By 1960 the landowner stood exposed in the public mind as an inefficient producer who exploited rural labor but retained vestiges of a seignorial authority within his property. In short, the proprietary authority of the hacendado was losing its legitimacy, and without the extensive control over national institutions which the landowners had exercised as late as 1950 there no longer existed a guaranteed coercive capability to maintain the integrity of the hacendado's proprietary role.

A never-ending ideological and "technical" challenge to the legitimacy of proprietary authority as vested in the hacendado accompanied the penetration of bureaucratic authority into the countryside in the period 1930-1960. The frequent proposals for land reform after World War I, from sources as diverse as the aristocratic President Sanfuentes (1919) and the Marxist Luis Recabarren, had in common a rejection of the existing system of property in rural land. The underlying sense of agreement within the Chilean polity by 1960 that some alteration of the system of rural property in land was necessary provided the impetus, along with the Alliance for Progress, rural labor activism, and party competition, for the ultimate redefinition of rural proprietorship and the move to experiment with new proprietary arrangements.

Poor Economic Performance

From 1949 until 1962 the value of Chile's agricultural imports exceeded that of her agricultural exports.[18] By 1964 the negative balance came to 120 million dollars, of which 85 million corresponded to products which potentially could be produced in the Chilean countryside.[19] At the same time, about 40 percent of the land in Chile's fertile central valley (Aconcagua to Ñuble) remained uncultivated, that is, in natural pastures. In addition, approximately 40 percent of the irrigated land from Aconcagua to Cautín was also in natural pastures.[20] Whereas the agricultural sector had not been a key sector in overall terms since the late nineteenth century, its growth from 1931 to 1960 failed to keep pace even with population growth.[21]

Efforts to explain the poor performance in the agricultural sector cited various causes. Landowners insisted that the principal cause could be found in low government-fixed prices for commodities and the increasing costs of labor and agricultural inputs.[22] Critics focused on the land tenure system, particularly the inefficiency of the hacienda system. In any case, by 1960 Chileans were in general agreement that the agricultural sector was a drag on the national economy and that its poor economic performance and inability to meet domestic food needs contributed to the inflationary process. What this meant was that by 1960 most Chileans accepted the idea that some type of reform of the rural property system was desirable from an economic standpoint. Some critics favored reform through taxation, thereby forcing nonproductive units onto the market through the tax structure. Others argued for regional planning, agricultural subsidies (through tariff policy or credits), a more favorable pricing policy for agricultural commodities, or land distribution. Almost all agreed that a solution required more governmental intervention and that proprietary authority had to be redefined either directly (for example, mandatory crop zones, expropriation of abandoned or poorly exploited land) or indirectly (for example, taxation, investment policy, labor legislation). Whatever the particulars of the critics' charges, a general consensus was that property in rural land was not "a matter of merely private concern." The traditional, extensive definition of rural proprietorship was, from an economic standpoint, no longer acceptable.

Exploitation of Rural Labor: Critiques by the
Marxists and the Catholic Left

Since 1919 Marxist politicians and intellectuals had focused on the injustice, inefficiency, and exploitative nature of the hacienda system as a particularly malevolent form of capitalist exploitation of labor. A constant barrage of muckraking by the worker press (except when it was itself repressed during certain periods) carried accounts of the hacendados' violations of the law and maltreatment of rural labor. The persistent attack on the hacendados made good political propaganda in the urban areas and enabled the Communist and Socialist politicians to give widespread circulation to their parliamentary interventions and public speeches. Second, appeals directly to the campesinos enhanced the prestige of the Marxist groups in the countryside as they attempted to organize the rural workers to oppose the hacendado class and restructure the Chilean polity. The image of the landowner as arbitrary, willfully noncompliant with legal obligations, and exploiting the labor force was persistently and widely broadcast by Marxist politicians and intellectuals through the popular press, in the universities, in the parliament, and in the countryside.

In contrast to the Marxists, Catholic social action in the countryside became prominent only after 1953,[23] but some Catholic political groups had focused on the need for land reform in the mid-1940s.[24] In 1945 Eduardo Frei, as minister of public works, sent to Congress a message which dealt with the agrarian problem. The project, however, was never debated and represented merely the position of the then-falanjista deputies.[25] In 1952 Ignacio Palma V., then minister of lands, also presented a project for agrarian reform intended to modify the Caja de Colonización and the law of Huertos Obreros in order to bring the agricultural sector out of economic stagnation. From 1953 onward the Catholic Left maintained land reform as a principal ideological tenet in order to replace capitalism with a more humane, "communitarian" society.

The Catholic reformers based their efforts in the social doctrine of progressive elements within the Chilean Church, including Padre Hurtado and Bishop-to-be Larraín. By 1953 Larraín was publicly espousing the virtues of agrarian reform: "Accession of the greatest possible number to landed property is one of the social objectives that the Church constantly supports. . . . To the Marxist cry of 'No proprietor' we contrast the Christian 'Everyone a proprietor'."[26]

The progressive elements within the Chilean church allied themselves with Catholic politicians and intellectuals in attacking the evils of the hacienda system. Citing Pope John XXIII's *Mater et Magistra* ("It is not enough to assert the natural character of the right of private property, but the effective distribution among all social classes is to be insisted upon")[27] the Church began formal experiments in land reform prior to the 1962 land reform program of the Chilean government. In the period 1960-1962 some Church lands became the focii for rural labor conflicts which involved Marxist unions. In response, the Church formed INPROA (Instituto de Promoción Agraria) and initiated experimental land reform projects on Church lands.[28]

The move by the Church to support some kind of land reform coincided with the populist vote-getting efforts in the country-side of the Christian Democratic party and the efforts of the Catholic rural labor movement. Like the landowners' traditional antagonists, the Marxists, important elements within the Church and the Catholic lay community came to see reform or elimination of the hacienda system as essential. This point of view weakened a traditional prop of the hacienda system—the alliance between the Catholic church and the Conservative party. The Church gave important moral support to the Christian Democrats in their calls for land reform, support which served to further remove the legitimacy from the existing system of property in rural land.

Party Politics and Rural Labor

Delegitimation of the hacienda system, rural labor activism, and increased bureaucratic penetration of the countryside—all threatened the maintenance of the traditional hacienda system. But until 1961 the Chilean landowners retained a trump card —veto power in Congress over rural unionization and agrarian reform legislation. Manipulation of elections in the countryside was an important source of the landowners' national political power. In 1958, however, an electoral reform played a key role in the complex struggle in the countryside. Political parties and the electoral process, once bulwarks of the rural property system, became agents in the transformation of the political meaning of property in rural land.

From 1932 until September 11, 1973, Chile was the only Latin American nation in which competitive party politics determined, without the intervention of the military or revolutionary movements, the occupants of the presidency, Congress, and higher policymaking positions in the national bureaucracy.[29] The same parties which competed at the national level also vied for control of local governmental institutions as well as for influence in national and regional student federations, labor unions, and other community and class organizations.[30] Not

only the durability but the scope and penetration of the party
system made political parties a key element in the national political system.

The party spectrum from 1932 to 1964 was essentially uni-
dimensional, a left-to-right dimension based on ideological differences concerning the role of the state in society and the
"social question." The existence of some "red zones" reflected the location of mines or industrial enterprises with
organized workers rather than regionalism per se. Ethnic and
religious minorities divided their allegiance among various
parties; no exclusively ethnic or religious movements became
political parties.

The Chilean system combined multiparty politics with presidential government. Governments did not fall; presidents
served six-year terms, during which various ministerial coalitions
or ministries of "technicians" or even of personal friends developed. Whatever happened in elections, the president, with the
substantial powers vested in him by the Constitution of 1925
and the subsequent amendments, remained in charge.

The polarized multiparty system, however, provided a difficult context for presidential dominance. Typically, Chilean presidents were even unable to maintain the total support of their
own parties during their six-year terms.[31] Since the presidential
electoral platforms generally contained more leftist or populist
planks than the Congress would accept, the growing frustration
of leftist members of presidential coalitions led to the eventual
decomposition of these arrangements and to a gradual rightward
drift during the course of the president's term of office. This
trend prevailed universally from 1932 on.

The Chilean Congress, thus, provided the political Right with
an opportunity to constrain the activity of presidential coalitions, even if the rightists could not elect presidents. As Petras
has pointed out, "though the traditional oligarchy did not 'rule'
Chile between 1938 to 1958, it did limit the scope of action of
the left-center coalitions that elected the president."[32]

The Basis of Stability

The success of the Chilean party system rested to great extent
on a growing pride of most Chileans in their formal democracy.
No open political system, especially a system that encapsulated

as much conflict as the Chilean polity from 1932 to 1964, could survive without a supportive political culture. But a supportive political culture is not enough, particularly where large segments of the population experience economic and social deprivations that provide daily contradictions to the system's formal commitments to equality, decent living conditions, and social mobility.

Control of the votes of rural labor provided the Conservative and Liberal parties, as well as some Radicals, with enough parliamentary seats to retain important veto capabilities. The stability of the system depended upon continued dominance of the hacienda system in the countryside in exchange for approval of governmental programs of industrialization and modernization in the urban areas. In practice, the rightist parties also exacted benefits from the urban and industrial development programs by participating in government-supported private enterprises and channeling governmental credit into "desirable" areas.

Underlying this superficial arrangement were important contradictions. The electoral clientele of Socialists, Communists, Radicals, and even the Liberals consisted mainly of urban dwellers. A most important element in maintaining this support, especially for the Radicals, Democrats, and Socialist participants in presidential coalitions, was the struggle to keep basic food prices, controlled by governmental decree, within reasonable limits. Throughout this period the issue of inflation, reflected in the price of flour, bread, cooking oil, sugar, and other staples, was a dominant theme in every election except the presidential election of 1964, which focused on the "danger of communism." After the onset of the Depression (1929-1930), the Chilean government began to fix minimum prices for agricultural commodities to defend producers. When the Depression ended, the government began to fix maximum prices for a variety of wholesale and retail commodities. This development created a conflict between urban politicians and landowners. The growing militancy of the urban and industrial labor movement made it inevitable that increases in agricultural prices would reverberate to some extent in pressure for higher wages. In addition,

> a direct confrontation with the workers would have entailed a loss of electoral support by the reformist bourgeois parties. In these conditions the bourgeoisie decided again and again to oppose increases in agricultural prices. . . . The bourgeoisie was disposed to find ways to compen-

sate the landowners. The nature of these measures depended upon
political exigencies but there was one means which was almost always
constant: repression of the rural union movement.[33]

It must be added that the Marxist parties, with the exception
of the Trotskyist wing of the Socialists, periodically colluded in
this repression. Coalition governments headed by Radicals from
1938 to 1952 repeatedly sacrificed the rural labor movement in
order to maintain the internal viability of governmental coalitions and to save programs in Congress, where the political Right
continued to exercise important veto capabilities. Repression of
rural labor combined with nonenforcement of labor law, housing
codes, and noncollection of social security and health insurance
payments represented the most important governmental "subsidy" to rural proprietors from 1932 to 1964. Farmers were
thus compensated for the relatively low prices of agricultural
commodities.[34] Indeed, the real income of rural labor experienced a secular decline from 1940 to 1964.[35] Thus, the basis of
the equilibrium among the parties, that is, the legal participation
of the antisystem parties, was that they did not intervene in the
countryside to challenge the hacendados' domination of the
rural labor force and thereby destroy the sectoral trade-offs
that united the rural and urban elites. Maintenance of the hacienda system provided the essential trade-off for the stability
of the party system which, in turn, prevented radical transformations of the Chilean polity and economy.

For that very reason, the limits of tolerance in the system
coincided with the intervention of the nonrightist parties into
the countryside. Bernardo Yuras perceptively described these
relationships in a letter to the Socialist party in 1938 in which
he requested greater support for the Liga Nacional de Defensa
de Campesinos Pobres:

> For many years the campesinos have been the electoral reserve and
> base of domination for the landowners. Presently, and with even less
> intensive operations than would have been possible with the decided
> support of the Socialist party, they [the landowners] understand that
> this electoral control is escaping their hands, and for this reason they
> combat—and they will combat—all penetration into their fundos.
> This is the reason why they oppose unionization or any form of
> campesino organizations. This is the truth concerning all the complaints
> [alharacas] raised in regard to supposed revolutionary agitation, disor-
> ganization of production, strikes carried out by professional agitators

... and the problems which have alarmed some popular front leaders, naturally those with linkages to the hacendados.

But we will not cede even an inch in the race to organize the campesinos in efforts at total penetration. We know that some Rightist sectors have proposed to allow campesino organizations as long as they are given guarantees that there will be no party influence, that is, no influence from leftist parties and especially the Socialist Party. This tactic is clear: They don't want any political penetration other than the 'politics of the priest' and vote-buying or, many times, the simple obligation to vote for the candidate that the patrón specifies.[36]

From 1938 onward middle-class and, especially, Marxist parties challenged the hacendados' control of rural votes. But from 1938 to 1958 the major thrust of the Marxist parties in the countryside was not electoral politics. Stimulation of class organizations and labor conflicts, agitation for enforcement of labor law, and ideological penetration took precedence over the electoral struggle. Even during the most difficult periods for the Marxist parties and their agents in the rural labor movement, including the outlawing of "communists" from 1948 to 1958, some party-linked rural labor organizations survived and served as focii of permanent resistance to hacendado domination. The existence of these organizations provided leftist or populist parties with potential for creating situations of conflict, embarrassing incumbent governments, agitating for improved conditions for rural labor, and directly challenging landed proprietors.

In part, the Marxists' nonelectoral emphasis derived from a realistic assessment of the continued capability of landowners to control rural voters through bribes, particularistic perquisites, or coercion. Even in the cities bribery (*cohecho*) still played an important part in Chilean elections.[37] In the countryside, the campesino traded his vote for needed income or favors. Failure to vote for the patrón's candidate could also bring retribution. For example, the Sindicato Industrial Agrícola in Fundo Miraflores, Cerrillos (Santiago province) complained in 1940:

[The owner] requires the workers to register in the Partido Nacionalista. If they refuse he dismisses them ... and brings in other workers to replace them.

They are preparing for the elections of 1941 ... demanding that the heads of family throw their sons out of the houses so that the youth cannot organize nor make electoral propaganda favorable to the

Popular Front government. At the same time, they dismiss these workers, other landowners are warned not to hire them.[38]

This did not mean that the Marxist parties ignored the potential voter gains in the rural areas, but for the Communists, in
particular, electoral activity supplemented other patterns of
penetration into the countryside. As José Campusano commented in 1971: "We simply did not have good possibilities of
electing deputies in most areas. Our task was one of ideological
penetration [adoctrinamiento], political education and organization—not the quest for votes. Until recently, we did little electoral work; indeed that may be considered a defect of ours."[39]

Campusano's statement is somewhat misleading. Union activity and political education could assist local politicos in electoral matters. In the period 1938-1947 Socialist and Communist
councilmen (regidores) or would-be councilmen relied on rural
and town workers' organizations for voting support. For example, in Quilicura and Quinta Normal (Santiago Province) Socialist regidores Carlos Cortés, R. Sepulveda, and José Muñoz had
close contacts with the local Ligas de Campesinos Pobres. Communists also used the position of regidor to support rural unions
and used the rural unions to elect regidores.[40]

The interdependence of union organization, labor conflicts,
and electoral competition was not lost upon the Marxists nor
even on the middle-class Radical party. The Radicals, especially
during the Popular Front period—and at the local level— cooperated with Popular Front committees and union organizations.
Demands for the enforcement of labor law and defense of the
campesinos often included the official stamp of the local Radical party organization.[41] But despite this electoral activity, the
main focus of party activity in the countryside, prior to 1958,
and especially of the Marxist parties, remained in nonelectoral
efforts to loosen the hold of the landowners on the rural labor
force. Until 1958 the electoral potential of rural votes remained
a principal resource of the political Right and the landowners.

Patterns of Party Activity in the Countryside, 1932-1958

From 1932 to 1958 various center and leftist political parties made sporadic interventions into the countryside. Only
the Communists maintained a constant presence. Even the

Communists, however, failed to create an important rural party organization on a national scale. The Communists, like all Chilean parties, maintained essentially an urban organization; rural activities represented high-risk, high-exposure attacks on the bastion of the Chilean oligarchy.

Yet even this limited and sporadic penetration threatened rural proprietors in a variety of ways. In the first place, the recognized legitimacy of party organizations and local party office holders allowed party politicians so inclined to point out the gap between the requirements of labor law, housing codes, and social security provisions and landowner performance. In some areas, party politicians could pressure bureaucrats to enforce laws and secure respect for the campesinos' legal rights. Parties and party members served as mediators among campesinos, bureaucrats, and rural proprietors by registering complaints regarding noncompliance with existing labor legislation. These efforts introduced into the hacienda enterprise external (bureaucratic) authority, which tended to debilitate the legitimacy and effectiveness of the customary authority of rural proprietors over the rural labor force.

The pattern of activity had two basic variants: complaints registered by local or national party organizations, and complaints registered by local or national elected officials (regidor, deputy, senator). Supplementing these two basic strategies, parliamentary committees of one party or a group of parties sometimes lodged complaints with the appropriate ministers or department heads and demanded remedial action. On other occasions, party leaders attempted to intervene directly to assist workers at the office of the labor inspector, labor court, social security office, or health clinic. They accompanied the campesinos to the respective governmental office and helped them to get attention and fill out the official forms, or smoothed their way by demanding preferential attention for their clients.

For some bureaucrats the strategy represented an annoyance or a deviation from official procedures. During the Popular Front period, the expansion of this sort of activity by the Popular Front parties caused some bureaucrats to register their official displeasure at serving as leverage for populist or Marxist clientele-building. For example, the labor inspector in San Felipe

(Aconcagua Province) complained that "unfortunately, Democrat, Socialist, and Communist politicians are coming to represent the workers. I find this unacceptable and I don't permit it because it . . . means that the functionary serves, indirectly, as an instrument of people desiring to gain political strength from the working masses on the foundation of our efforts [as functionaries in the public service]."[42] The inspector's comments accurately reflected the political context of the situation: political parties made efforts to assure bureaucratic responsiveness to campesino demands. If successful, the parties could make electoral, ideological, and organizational gains. But this opportunity for the parties existed only because without party intervention, or intervention of other external agents, the bureaucrats did not generally respond adequately to the campesinos' needs or demands.

Middle-class and populist parties (Democrat party, Radical party, Agrarian Labor party, and others) as well as the Marxist parties made intermittent interventions in the countryside throughout the period 1932-1958. Only rarely did the non-Marxist parties get involved in labor conflicts or union organizing.[43] In contrast, the parallel operations of the Marxists' local party organizations and the local sections of the national labor confederation (CTCH) gave the Marxist parties advantageous access to information about labor conflicts or the problems of individual workers. Many times party headquarters and the local CTCH office occupied the same building or even the same room.

To some extent, however, the party affiliation of bureaucrats also played a role in political entrepreneurship. In the Health Service, doctors assigned to local hospitals or the clerks who distributed numbers to ration the doctors' time among patients occupied strategic roles. Not infrequently local doctors also became regidores. In the Social Security Administration, the processing of applications for pensions, welfare, or medical benefits offered other opportunities for party activists to recruit clientele. Where they could place bureaucrats through patronage, the parties added leverage; where they could not, applying pressure on the bureaucrats made the campesinos aware that at least some political party organizations intervened on their behalf. For the middle-class parties this awareness could mean votes. For the Marxists, in addition to votes, it could mean the initial bridge between clientelism and ideological penetration. For the campesinos, intervention of the parties on their behalf, whatever the motivation, increased the public exposure of bureaucrats who generally failed to handle adequately the campesino demands.

The second variant of party intervention might be labeled "casework." Casework consisted of written, telephoned, or personal requests by deputies or senators for bureaucratic attention to particular campesino demands. Casework took place in regard to various governmental agencies. A deputy might send a note (*recomendación*) to a doctor at the health service to obtain better service for his clients; requests could be made for the prompt processing of applications for pensions; labor problems might bring the congressman's suggestion that a labor inspector visit a particular farm or pay special attention to the problems of particular workers who registered their complaints at the inspectorate. This type of casework is common in American politics; in Chile it became common in relation to rural clientele after 1958.

In an effort to detail systematically the casework activity in regard to rural labor problems, the letters, telegrams, and telephone calls from congressmen (deputies and senators) recorded by the Labor Department have been collected. No doubt some loss of material has occurred over the years. Some telephone calls were never recorded; some telegrams may have been lost. There is no reason to believe, however, that any systematic loss of material has occurred, that is, that the Labor Department archivists have excluded letters from deputies or senators of particular parties or that in particular years letters were destroyed. In collecting the materials there is also the possibility that some inadvertent omissions have occurred. The cases were collected by a complete search of the Labor Archive volumes from 1931 to 1968; it is nevertheless possible that some cases have been overlooked. Again, however, no systematic bias exists.

The data (see figures 1-3) show that before 1961, with the exception of the deviant case of 1955, very few parliamentarians did casework on behalf of campesinos. In no year, again with the exception of 1955, did the number of congressmen doing such work exceed six. A partial explanation of the deviant case can be found in the planned campaign of agitation by the Marx-

FIGURE 1   RURAL CASEWORK BY CONGRESSMEN (DEPUTIES
AND SENATORS) 1930-1968

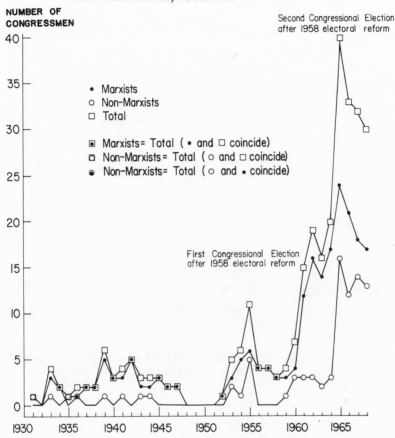

ists against the Ibáñez government in 1955. Marxist deputies
employed casework as part of a deliberate offensive against the
regime, which resulted in the reestablishment of detention centers in Pisagua to take agitators out of circulation under the
terms of the Law for the Permanent Defense of Democracy.
Communist leaders headed the list of detainees. In 1956 casework declined and only one Communist and three Socialists
were involved in rural labor casework.

Of further interest is the distribution of casework by party
for the period 1931-1968. The data are presented in two categories, "Marxist" and "Non-Marxist," and then further broken
down by party in the cases of Communists, Socialists, and Chris-

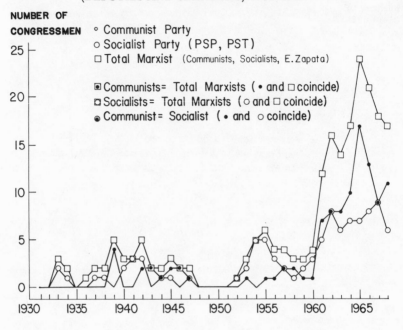

FIGURE 2   RURAL CASEWORK BY MARXIST CONGRESSMEN
            (DEPUTIES AND SENATORS) 1930-1968

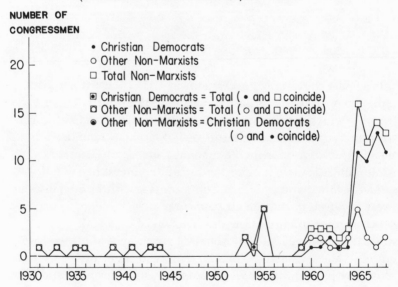

FIGURE 3   RURAL CASEWORK BY NON-MARXIST CONGRESSMEN
            (DEPUTIES AND SENATORS) 1930-1968

tian Democrats. A special category has been created for Emilio Zapata. The label "Zapata" could be changed to Partido Izquierda Comunista (1932-1936), and Zapata's efforts after 1937 added to the Socialists. But the special nature of Zapata's contribution to campesino organization justifies handling his activities as a separate category. During this entire period only one instance of casework on behalf of rural labor by a member of the Conservative or Liberal parties was encountered; the category "other non-Marxist" refers, therefore, to middle-class or populist parties like the Democrat party, Democratic party, Radical party, National Democratic party (PADENA), or Agrarian Labor party. In any case, with the exception of the one member of the Partido Democrático, two interventions by members of the Partido Demócrata (1933, 1936), and four by Radical deputies (1939, 1941, 1943, 1944), all such casework prior to 1953 originated with Marxist politicians.

Indicative of the fact that intervention by the Marxist parties (especially Communists) and Emilio Zapata's Liga in the rural sector were motivated only partially by electoral ambitions is the relatively greater propensity of these politicians to do casework outside their own electoral districts. Table 6 classifies the cases by party and then divides them into two subcategories: cases in which the congressman or senator intervened in his own electoral district and cases where the intervention was external to his election district, including cases in which intervention consisted of raising national or regional problems of rural workers with the Labor Department or minister of labor. As can be seen, Christian Democrats show a marked tendency to concentrate on their own electoral domains, while Socialists and Communists tended to pay less exclusive concern to their own electoral districts. The data on other non-Marxists, adjusted for one deputy who accounted for 44 percent of all cases, suggest that the small number of other non-Marxists who did rural casework from 1931 to 1968—a total of 27 congressmen—intervened in cases outside their own electoral districts to approximately the same extent as did Socialists. But casework by members of these parties, which dominated the Chilean Congress until 1965, accounted for only 6 percent of all such interventions documented in the Labor Department Archive from 1931 to 1968 (again adjusted for the deputy who by himself accounted for 44 percent

TABLE 6 CONGRESSMEN'S CASEWORK IN THE COUNTRYSIDE, 1932-1968

Party	Casework		Total	Percentage in Electoral District
	In Electoral District	Out of Electoral District[a]		
Falanje-Christian Democrats	88 (54)[b]	18 (13)[b]	106 (67)[b]	83 (81)[b]
Other non-Marxists	47 (21)[c]	14 (13)[c]	61 (34)[c]	77 (62)[c]
Socialists[f]	127 (77)[d]	48 (44)[d]	175 (121)[d]	73 (64)[d]
Communists	113 (79)[e]	70 (55)[e]	183 (134)[e]	62 (59)[e]
Zapata[g]	13	19	32	41
Total	388 (244)	169 (144)	557 (388)	70 (63)

SOURCE: Data compiled by author from materials in Chilean Labor Department Archive.

NOTE: In order to reduce the contribution of extreme cases, deputies whose share of their party's total reached 10 percent have been excluded in calculating an adjusted score (shown in parentheses). The effect, in each case, has been to reduce the percentage of casework within the intervening congressmen's own electoral districts. This adjustment procedure significantly alters the score for "Other non-Marxists," where one highly electoral-oriented deputy accounted for 44 percent of all cases, and the score for "Socialists," where three deputies accounted for 29 percent of all cases.

[a] Includes cases in which congressmen intervened on behalf of campesinos both within and outside their own electoral districts.

[b] Adjusted for 3 deputies = 39 cases.

[c] Adjusted for 1 deputy = 27 cases.

[d] Adjusted for 3 deputies = 50 cases.

[e] Adjusted for 2 deputies = 49 cases.

[f] Does not include four deputies who co-signed letters sent by Zapata in 1940 but did no casework on their own.

[g] If the cases handled by Emilio Zapata after 1937 are assigned to the Socialist party (before 1937 Zapata was a member of the Trotskyist Izquierda Comunista), the Socialist raw score is reduced to 69 percent and adjusted score to 60 percent.

of all interventions by other non-Marxists). Emilio Zapata's ideological commitment to altering the national political order in part through national organization of the rural workers is indicated by the relatively low proportion of his casework in his own electoral district—less than 50 percent.

Parliamentary casework normally began with a letter, telegram, or conversation in which a parliamentarian made known a complaint to officials of the Labor Department. Letters might come directly from the congressmen or from the respective body of the Congress at the request of a particular congressman or group of congressmen, for example, as follows:

> Mr. Minister of Labor:
>
> In the session of the 16th of the present month Deputy Zapata requested that a letter [*oficio*] be sent to you, urging that you order an inspector of your Service to visit Fundo La Cé in Talagante in order to check the housing which, according to information in the Deputy's possession, is in ruinous and unhealthy condition.[44]

Upon reception of a letter of this sort the minister of labor or the director of the Labor Department generally ordered an inspection visit. In the case of the above letter, an inspector visited the farm on January 25, 1940, approximately two months after the deputy made the complaint, and left formal instructions ordering the landowner to provide the workers with potable water and sanitary housing. The proprietor received a sixty-day time limit in which to comply or pay a fine of 5,000 pesos for each violation.[45]

Casework disrupted routine violations of law or landowner abuses and confronted the landowner with bureaucratic authority. Campesinos saw that the landowner's power and authority had limits. But very practical limits existed for this sort of casework. Because of the lack of personnel, vehicles, and funds of the Labor Department, parliamentarians could not effectively insist on systematic or massive programs of inspection in the countryside (see chapter 3). When small numbers of politicians used the tactics of casework, some landowners were forced to alter existing arrangements to the benefit of selected campesinos; when such activity expanded after the electoral reform of 1958—and especially prior to the congressional election of 1961 —the inefficacy of the Labor Department made labor inspectors scapegoats for demagoguery by both Marxist and non-Marxist

politicians seeking votes in the countryside. In the province of
Colchagua, perhaps the zone most affected by the expanded
activity of parliamentarians during the post-1961 period, the
intendente complained to the director of the Labor Department
in July 1962:

> We are at the mercy of Senator [Salamón] Corbalán and his satellites.
> He arrives in a town where his leaders have previously massed the work-
> ers. He asks if they have any complaints to make. Rapidly he sends a
> note to the Minister, creating a scandal. Then comes an order to the lo-
> cal labor inspector "Go as quickly as possible to such and such a fundo
> to investigate such and such a complaint made by Senator Corbalán. In-
> form immediately of the measures adopted, etc. etc."
>
> The inspector has no means to transport himself and since he usually
> is ordered to go to distant fundos . . . he can't get there.
>
> . . . This means that the inspector must use the vehicle of the inten-
> dencia in order to stop, at least in part, this action of FRAP [the Com-
> munist-Socialist coalition] that is intended only to embarrass the Au-
> thorities.
>
> . . . They try to bring on conflicts for which there is no solution.
> Then they can shout in the streets and the plazas of the towns that in
> Chile there is no justice, that the authorities are incompetent, and that
> they do not concern themselves with the exploitation of the workers by
> the landowners.[46]

The Intendente finished his letter by requesting a vehicle and an
additional six functionaries for the Labor Department in Colchagua that "are neither socialists nor communists like the ones
you tried to send me last November."[47] The Labor Department
informed the intendente that efforts would be made to provide
one or two additional inspectors but that the department had
no vehicles of its own in all of the country.[48] Under these conditions casework by politicians on a massive scale served to
point out the gap between legal norms and compliance in the
countryside, embarrass the authorities, and publicize the abuses
of the landowners. It could not bring effective enforcement on
any wide scale. As an electoral and propaganda tactic it well
served the Marxist and middle-class parties. In a small number of
farms it could improve conditions for rural labor. But only an
adequate budget for the Labor Department could make casework a tactic for bringing generalized compliance with labor
legislation in the countryside and defending campesinos against
abuses of landowner authority.

Another type of party activity in the countryside, which more seriously and immediately threatened rural proprietors, involved the stimulation of class organization, labor conflicts, and class consciousness among the campesinos. From 1919 onward, Marxist cadres intervened in the countryside to organize rural syndical organizations (see chapter 5). With the exception of weak Falanje party efforts from 1938 to 1941, rural labor organizations prior to 1953 owed their origins to the deliberate intervention of Marxists in the countryside. Communists operated through local cells, paid Party organizers, the national labor organizations, and Party members in local governmental offices or as teachers in rural schools. Until 1938 even the Communist party did not have an operational rural section (*departamento agrario*), although *"encargados agrarios"* did do Party work in the countryside. These activists were not paid functionaries. As José Campusano put it, *"El activista se arreglaba por su cuenta"* ("The activist looked out for himself").[49] After 1938, however, Communist party organizations consolidated. Rural organizational efforts intensified and "free unions," organized in the countryside by Communists, increased in number. Under the direction of Juan Chacón Corona the Party put together a coordinated rural effort.

Socialist efforts were much more disjointed and personalistic. No evidence exists to indicate that the Socialist party or any of its various fragments employed paid functionaries in the countryside. In 1940 the Liga de Defensa de Campesinos Pobres became the major base organization of a loosely organized agrarian department within the Party (Acción Campesina).[50] This department, understaffed, underfinanced, and largely ignored by most national leaders within the Party, played an ineffective role in rural organization until 1962, although it made sporadic efforts at casework and syndical organization. Socialist rural strength remained in the unions and committees in governmental and semipublic farms. These farms had been organized in the Popular Front years when Salvador Allende, as minister of health, provided Party organizers access to the large estates of the Health Service, and Socialist officials in other governmental agencies had access to fundos owned by public or semipublic enterprises like Hacienda Lipingue in Valdivia.

Typical of the personalistic and localistic tendencies of the

Socialist party's rural penetration into the private farm sector
was the group of "committees of syndical unity" in the Santiago
area headed by Manuel Muñoz Bahamondes. Muñoz occupied
the post of councilman (*regidor*) in Puente Alto. In letters from
the committees of syndical unity which focused on the labor
problems in the vineyards of Puente Alto, Muñoz called himself the "legal representative" (*apoderado legal*) of the campesino unions in various local vineyards. In the Puente Alto area
the rural unions maintained a constant struggle against the hacendados, and Muñoz acted as political and legal adviser to the
unions. His efforts, however, were personal; no organizational
commitment by the Socialist party kept the union activities
alive.[51] As late as 1962 Pedro Correa, head of the Party's Departamento Nacional de Acción Campesina, complained that
the Party "has not developed cadres with knowledge of the
campesinos' problems. We have not been able, for this reason,
to . . . take on in decisive form the great task of organizing the
campesinos as a pillar of the Chilean Revolution."[52] Correa
requested that the Party "grant adequate economic resources to
provide for the needs of the Departamento Nacional de Acción
Campesina."[53] Nevertheless, Socialist rural activity from 1938
to 1961 added support to campesino unions in isolated regions
and, because of its strength in publicly owned farms, frequently
embarrassed the incumbent government.

For all practical purposes middle-class parties generally limited their activities in the countryside to casework and clientelistic favors. The Radical party retained its historical influence
in the large rural-workers and meatpacking union in Magallanes
but played no role in class organizations and rural labor conflicts in other areas. The Christian Democrats became interested
in the countryside only after 1958; even then the Catholic union
movement remained independent of the Party. Unlike the Marxists, the Christian Democratic party intervened in the formation of union organizations and rural labor conflicts only on a
minor scale prior to 1964. After 1964 the Party used the state
apparatus, particularly INDAP, to create a union movement
parallel to the independent Catholic unions and to the Marxist
FCI (see chapter 8).

Prior to 1958, thus, with the local exception of Molina and
the efforts of ASICH, campesino unions were a product of

Marxist and, particularly, Communist penetration into the countryside. The two most important periods of rural labor conflicts and unionization coincided with Marxist participation in coalition governments and with the end to the "tolerance" and "stability" of the Chilean multiparty system. In 1941, after two years of widespread rural labor conflicts, the Chilean Congress voted to outlaw the Communist party. President Aguirre Cerda vetoed the measure. In 1948, after an even more massive period of labor conflicts and rural unionization efforts combined with parallel strikes in mining and industry, the Chilean Congress outlawed the Communist party at the request of President González Videla.[54] In both instances the Communists combined demands for land reform at the national level with conflicts in the countryside.

Some Communist-inspired labor conflicts made expropriation of rural estates an explicit issue. Illustrative is a conflict in the Villarica region of Cautín Province (Hacienda Trancura) in mid-1946. After listing a number of abuses to which the landowner had subjected them during a lengthy labor conflict (ten months), the campesinos ended a letter to the minister of lands and colonization by declaring: "For this reason the undersigned inquilinos request expropriation of the Hacienda for subsequent subdivision among the inquilinos and sharecroppers. We would also like to tell you, Mr. Minister, that we have requested expropriation of this Hacienda on three previous occasions without favorable results."[55] To support this petition, Bernardo Araya Zuleta, secretary general of the Communist splinter of the CTCH and deputy in the Chilean Chamber of Deputies, also sent a letter to the minister of labor to request that the Labor Department force the landowner to pay ten months' back salaries which the workers claimed was owed to them. Combining local conflicts with a national campaign against the hacienda system, the Communists attacked both the power and the legitimacy of the large landowners.

From 1939 to 1947 the national and provincial federations and committees of rural syndicates, with the exception of Zapata's Liga and the small Falanje-supported campesino organization in Santiago Province, were headed by Communist party functionaries. Party militants like Juan Chacón, Luis Coray, José Valenzuela, and Juan Ahumada Trigo played prominent roles; Chacón Corona and Ahumada Trigo both later became Communist deputies in the Congress. Because the overwhelming Communist domination of rural labor organizations after 1941, until the formation of ASICH's rural section in the Molina area, often confused the agrarian question with the tactical and strategic goals of the Communist party, land reform meant Communism to many landowners.

Party-induced labor conflicts forced landowners to bare the foundations of rural proprietorship: coercion and the state police. The legitimacy of paternalistic authority disappeared. Campesinos recognized that collective action could bring victories if the instruments of coercion at the disposal of the government could be wrested from the landowners. Thus, the electoral arena became even more relevant. Ultimately, if the landowners lost control of Congress, they could prevent neither land reform legislation nor liberalized conditions for rural unionization. At the margin the electoral struggle and rural labor organization complemented one another and combined to threaten the existence of the hacienda system in Chile.

From Electoral Reform to Land Reform:
The Role of Carlos Ibáñez in Chilean Democracy

From 1927 to 1931 Carlos Ibáñez ruled Chile in an authoritarian, quasidictatorial fashion. His government repressed the leftist political parties and labor movement. But this interruption of oligarchic parliamentary rule brought a transition to middle-class coalition politics in which the center party (Radicals) dominated presidential coalitions from 1938 to 1952. In addition to the break with the parliamentary system, Ibáñez left as a legacy Chile's first agrarian reform law and a labor code. Ibáñez's hostility to politics separated him from the party system; he governed Chile personally, relying on parties to support him where he could obtain such support but never subordinating his government to the party regime. Unrestrained by a commitment to the organizational infrastructure of the existing order, Ibáñez's authoritarianism brutalized working-class organizations but also disparaged the traditional political parties.

In his second presidency, twenty years later (1952-1958), Ibáñez was elected on a program symbolized by a broom—to sweep the corruption of party politics from government. Paradoxically, his campaign and initial ministerial coalition relied on a combination of numerous "mushroom" parties and movements in addition to the main body of a splintered Socialist party and the Agrarian Labor party. Shortly thereafter the Socialists withdrew from the coalition and Ibáñez again moved against the labor movement. Using the provisions of the Law for the Permanent Defense of Democracy, he eventually sent Communists and other leaders in labor conflicts to detention camps in Pisagua (1956). Rampant inflation left Ibáñez without any solid party support; again he governed Chile personally. His noncommitment to the party system again made it possible, however, for Ibáñez to leave important political reforms as a legacy. At the end of his term of office, when he no longer would have to deal with labor conflicts, Ibáñez kept his campaign promise of 1952 to repeal the Law for the Permanent Defense of Democracy. This act assured that in the presidential elections of 1958 the Communist party could again participate openly.

With the support of the left and center parties, Ibáñez also pushed through an electoral law written by Falanje deputy Jorge Rogers Sotomayor. This electoral reform introduced an Australian ballot and increased penalties for electoral fraud and bribery. The introduction of a public ballot meant that landowners could no longer effectively control the votes of rural labor. The electoral hegemony of the Right in the countryside thus gave way to forces that advocated social change in the rural areas, particularly the FRAP (Socialists and Communists) and the Christian Democrats.[56] In 1958 the performance of the FRAP candidate in rural districts left little doubt that landowners' control over rural votes had considerably declined.[57]

The electoral success of the FRAP candidate in rural districts in 1958 reinforced and stimulated renewed syndical efforts as well as further electoral efforts. Intensified organizational efforts in the rural sector by the Marxists as well as leftist electoral gains made the countryside a focus for the upcoming parliamentary elections of 1961. In these elections the Right (Conservatives and Liberals) failed to gain one-third of the seats in Congress for the first time in the twentieth century. FRAP obtained more votes than any other single party and now controlled 27.5 percent of the seats in the Chamber of Deputies

(40) and elected 13 senators (of a total of 45). The Christian Democrats for the first time received more votes than the Conservatives. The outcome of the election left the incumbent government dependent upon the centrist Radical party; in exchange for their parliamentary support the Radicals demanded ministerial participation and "hoping to gain popular backing to win the presidency in 1964 the Radicals were now sponsoring several reforms, including an agrarian reform bill."[58] The availability of the campesino vote contributed to reevaluation of the rural work force by the middle-class parties and, therefore, to the reemergence of the agrarian question as a central issue in national politics. Thus, the party system and the electoral system which had served as the basis for landowner dominance in the countryside as well as in national politics became, after 1958, principal instruments in the eventual destruction of the existing system of property in rural land.

At the same time that the political Right lost control of Congress, increased campesino labor militancy, the growing influence of the Cuban Revolution, and the counterrevolutionary drive of United States foreign policy (Alliance for Progress)[59] reinforced the renewed salience of the agrarian question. In response to the international pressures for land reform and to the internal political situation, the Alessandri government proposed a land reform law to the Chilean Congress after extensive debates within the governmental coalition.[60] The law which finally passed (Law 15.020) eventually served as the basis for larger-scale expropriations carried out after 1964 by the Christian Democratic government of Eduardo Frei, despite the limited implementation of the law from 1962 to 1964. Thus the electoral reform of 1958 and renewed mobilization of rural labor led shortly thereafter to land reform—and to the erosion of the hacienda system which was a cornerstone of Chilean formal democracy.

3
A Decade of Agrarian Reform

7

The Alessandri Land Reform

If the large properties show themselves economically inefficient, their lands will be subdivided—and given to those who want plots and can work them. Compensation [will be given] to the existing owners according to the law which has been on our books for some time. We desire to increase the number of small farmers and thus provide a social basis for political democracy.

Pedro Aguirre Cerda, November 5, 1938

The Alessandri Agrarian Reform arose as an imposition by North American Imperialism, as a condition for conceding loans to the Chilean Government and, at the same time, as an effort by the reactionary classes to drown campesino insurgency.

José González, *Principios*, March-April 1964

Someone has to lose with Agrarian Reform. The campesino now has nothing left to lose; so it's the landowner's turn. He may not consider agrarian reform "good business," but when they put a shotgun against his chest, he will consider it preferable to losing his life.

Lay representative of Bishop Manuel Larraín, 1962

Chileans of diverse ideological persuasions had long advocated land reform as a means to prevent social revolution, modernize the agricultural economy, and provide justice for the rural labor force. Although land reform legislation was inevitably rationalized in terms of the latter of these objectives, only the first of these goals induced Chilean governments to put land reform programs into operation. The Alessandri land reform law of 1962 was the last in a series of anti-Marxist, counterrevolutionary land reform laws which sought to pacify leftist political movements and campesino activists without altering the political dominance of the hacendado in the countryside.

Major land reform laws in Chile prior to 1962 coincided with immediately preceding crises of legitimacy and threats to the

223

maintenance of the existing regime. The first, the law creating the Caja de Colonización Agrícola in December 1928 (Law 4.496), followed seven years of constitutional crisis and the establishment of a personalist-military government which abolished the effective role of the traditional political parties and the Congress for almost five years (see chapter 2). The two other major land reform laws prior to 1962 followed periods of campesino violence, strikes, labor petitions, and union organization. Law 5.604 (1935), a revision of the 1928 legislation, followed shortly after the tragic events at Ranquíl and the first efforts at legal unionization in the countryside. The other land reform legislation of significance prior to 1962 (Law 7.747 of 1943) followed four years of campesino militancy in the countryside. These laws established programs of colonization in the frontier region and sought to take pressure off the hacienda system in the central valley.

Almost from its inception, lack of funding crippled the program of the Caja de Colonización Agrícola. Without exercising its authority to expropriate land, the Caja could have purchased large quantities of land on the open market in the period 1929-1940 for purposes of subdivision and establishment of family farms or slightly larger commercial farms. The problem of the Caja was never lack of land for sale. As Ellsworth noted, in the period 1939-1940 "some 971,000 hectares were available for purchase, or seven times the 138,000 hectares actually acquired."[1]

After 1944 the Caja essentially ceased to operate because of a lack of financial resources. Inflation destroyed the value of (nonreadjustable) amortization payments made by the small number of land reform beneficiaries. Lack of funding along with the devaluation of these payments emasculated the Caja's operations. From 1928 to 1960 the Caja de Colonización Agrícola established 94 colonies (*colonias*) and distributed land to 3,392 settlers (*colonos*).[2] In 1960 these land reform beneficiaries represented less than 1 percent of the families directly dependent for employment on the agricultural sector.[3] Throughout these years the Chilean elite well understood the symbolic uses of land reform legislation to pacify reformers and militant campesinos with the illusion of rural proprietorship through colonization.

In light of the rightist electoral setback in 1961,[4] the influence of the Cuban Revolution, the counterthrust of the Alliance for Progress,[5] and the pressure of rural labor conflicts, the Alessandri government followed the advice of those who urged a land reform that would establish a new group of rural proprietors which would "constitute a middle class of campesinos indispensable to a greater social stability."[6] But while many saw the land reform law as a potentially counterrevolutionary measure, the principles it embodied, in contrast to its implementation from 1962 to 1964, represented a radical departure from the traditional meaning of property in rural land.

Law 15.020: The Legal Framework

Law 15.020[7] specified that land reform in Chile was necessary in order to permit access to property in land to those who worked it,[8] to improve the living conditions of the campesino population, and to increase agrarian production. Formally, land reform consisted of redistribution of property rights in rural land to provide better living conditions for the rural labor force and to improve agricultural production through technological modernization.

Redefinition of Legal Rights and Obligations of Rural Proprietors

The first article of Law 15.020 reaffirmed the provisions of the Constitution of 1925 in declaring that "The exercise of the right of property in rural land is subject to the limitations required for the maintenance and progress of the social order." The article continued: "Every agricultural proprietor is obligated to cultivate the land, increase its productivity and fertility, conserve the other natural resources and to effect the investments necessary to better its exploitation . . . and the conditions of life of those working on it, in accord with technical advances." Rural proprietors acquired the legal obligation to cultivate the land in a fashion which increased productivity and fertility. Property in rural land no longer legally included the discretionary authority not to cultivate. This provision, by itself, represented an important legal transformation in the authority of the hacendados. Taken as a whole, Article 1 of Law 15.020 was a legislative affirmation that property in rural land entailed obligations to the Chilean political community at large and to the rural labor force in particular. In great part, the law explicitly redefined private property as a matter of public interest. (Recall the landowner's remarks in the labor conflict in Aculeo cited in chapter 2 to the effect that what he did within the domain of his private property was a matter "*meramente privativa de él.*" Law 15.020 explicitly rejected this ample definition of private property.)

Article 46 of the law and the Decreto Reglamentario No. 2 of February 7, 1963, contained a further limit on the legal definition of proprietary authority. These regulations prohibited landowners from entering into farm rental agreements of less than six years (excluding sharecroppers, and land upon which truck crops were grown). Likewise, the land reform law required that the landlord invest 5 percent of earnings in housing on the fundo and 10 percent in improvement of the soil, irrigation systems, and fencing. While difficulties existed in the enforcement of these provisions, the imposition of formal investment obligations on farm operators represented a radical departure from previous proprietary discretion.[9] Enforcement of this legislation or extension of the principle contained in this section of the law to deal with other areas of farm investment and management policy could have dramatically altered the nature of decision making concerning agricultural enterprises. The principle contained in this section of the law—that is, mandatory investment requirements in specifically identified projects or budget categories—is potentially as dramatic as the principle of income taxes. Once the principle is accepted, the rate (or percentage of profits to be reinvested) can be adjusted so that private proprietors make decisions regarding the investment of decreasingly small shares of total investment in the agricultural sector. Although implications of this provision were not pursued by the Alessandri government, they did provide the legal basis for a fundamental redistribution of proprietary authority from the private to the public sector.

In addition, Law 15.020 introduced a new concept in property in rural land, the so-called *unidad económica*, which consisted of "the land area necessary, given the quality of soil, location, topography, climate, and other characteristics, which, worked by the parcelero and his family, permits the family group to live and prosper with the product of its rational management . . . " (Article 12b). This new type of property was to be legally indivisible and subject to limits on mortgage and alienation established by the land reform agency (Corporación de Reforma Agraria). These economic units could be declared "family farms" (*propiedad agrícola familiar*) by presidential decree, thereby entitling the owner to certain tax exemptions as well as to preferential access to technical assistance and agricultural credit. Credit was to be extended by the Banco del Estado, Corporación de Fomento de la Producción (CORFO), and the Corporación de la Vivienda (CORVI).

The law prohibited these new proprietors from purchasing other such properties if they already owned rural properties which, conjointly, were assessed at a value exceeding the value of the propiedad agrícola familiar to be purchased. Qualification of the prohibition allowed each smallholder to purchase an additional propiedad agrícola familiar for each three children. Any land transfers which violated these norms became null and void (Article 35). Article 62 further prohibited private subdivision of rural properties into parcels of less than 15 hectares of irrigated land and 50 hectares of unirrigated land.

Land Subject to Expropriation[10]

Article 15 of Law 15.020 stated the following:

For the purpose of agrarian reform, authority is granted to expropriate the following types of rural properties which are hereby declared to be of public utility:

1. Abandoned properties, as well as those that are notoriously poorly exploited and below adequate levels of productivity in relation to the predominant economic conditions for similar land in the region;

2. Up to half of the land that is irrigated by public works constructed by the State, as long as the property is larger than one unidad económica, and that this is not damaged by expropriation;

3. Those [properties] that have been put up for public auction due to unpaid debts and assigned to credit institutions;

4. Properties that belong to public or private corporations and are not exploited directly by them;

5. Rented properties that do not comply with the provisions of Article 46 of the present law;

6. Properties that the Corporación de Reforma Agraria judges to be indispensable to acquire in order to complete a particular program of subdivision and that have been offered for sale, or that belong to some

of the institutions referred to in D.F.L. 49 of 1959, when there are grave defects in legal title;

7. Swamp and lowlands that are permanently flooded or salt lands susceptible to drainage and improvement, as well as those that have been seriously damaged by erosion or the formation of dunes. In this case expropriation will require a previous report by the Ministry of Agriculture;

8. Properties declared minifundios by the Ministry of Agriculture, for the sole purpose of consolidation and redistribution with preference to the ex-proprietors if they should desire to receive new unidades;

9. Land occupied in the zone of application of the Ley de la Propiedad Austral where questions of legal title have arisen;

10. Land containing [particular types of natural forests] and lands situated up to one kilometer from the edge of lakes that constitute national property of public use in which it is indispensable to protect natural vegetation.[11]

Article 16 of the law added those properties which were not included in the above enumeration but whose expropriation was agreed upon in order to carry out a regional development plan drawn up by the Consejo Superior de Fomento Agropecuario (CONSFA), if the properties could be subdivided or were necessary in order to complement the subdivision of another property. Such expropriations could be effected only the year after publication of the respective decree which approved the regional development plan. The exceptions stipulated in Article 20 (Predios Rústicos No Expropriables) moderated the relatively flexible provisions of Articles 15 and 16. Exempted from expropriation were all those rural properties which

> should be destined preferentially to reforestation or that are principally dedicated to the production of fruit or wine; those whose principal production serves as an essential input to an industry existing when this law enters into effect and which belong to the same owner; the parcels of unidades constituted previously through the Caja de Colonización Agrícola, CORA, or other land sold by the State ... which doesn't exceed one unidad económica and the properties declared propiedad agrícola familiar.

In addition, proprietors who dedicated dry lands to artificial pastures and were declared "cooperators" with the national livestock development plan received exemptions from expropriation. This provision, along with the exemption for fruit growers and vineyards, protected a number of Chile's most valuable agricultural properties from expropriation.

Authority to expropriate individual properties was assigned to the Corporación de Reforma Agraria (CORA).[12] The decision to expropriate designated rural estates required approval by a two-thirds vote of the members in attendance at special sessions of CORA's consejo in a session called explicitly for that purpose. Proprietors expropriated under the provisions of Article 16 acquired the right to retain a "reserve" of about 80 hectares or a "reasonable area in relation to his productive activities and the conditions of the region." In no case could the reserve exceed an equivalent of a determined number of unidades económicas to be specified by the president of the republic. (This number was eventually set at twenty unidades económicas.)

Payment for Expropriated Land

Departing from the stipulations of the 1925 Constitution (subsequently amended to make operative this article of the land reform law),[13] Law 15.020 allowed CORA to pay for some types of expropriated property with no more than 20 percent cash, and the balance over a minimum of ten years, at 4 percent interest plus annual readjustments for inflation equal to the adjustment made on the price of parcels which resulted from the subdivision. At the discretion of the CORA consejo, with a two-thirds vote of members present at a special session called for that purpose, different terms of payment than those stipulated in this article could be agreed upon.

Provisions in the law for payment of expropriated land was a critical concern. Requirement for full payment in cash, as the existing constitutional provision demanded, would have seriously limited the amount of land that might have been purchased. As passed, the law allowed deferred payments only in the case of poorly cultivated or abandoned properties.

Tribunales Especiales de Expropriaciones Agrarias

Article 29 of Law 15.020 provided for the creation of special courts to hear complaints by landowners about expropriation procedures or terms of expropriation in their individual cases. Career judges (Ministro de la Corte de Apelaciones) presided over these courts, which included the regional agronomist of the Dirección de Agricultura y Pesca of the Ministry of Agriculture.

Also included on the court was a representative of the regional agricultural society.[14] Proceedings of the special agrarian courts were subject to the provisions of the Civil Code. The law also permitted subsequent appeals to the regular courts. Whereas special courts in which they participated protected the landowners, the law made no provision for the participation of rural labor organizations in this aspect of the land reform process.

Rural Labor and Law 15.020

The land reform law and its subsequent reglamentos provided certain marginal benefits to the rural labor force in the form of additional rural labor legislation. R.R.A. No. 21 eliminated the existing provincial commissions which yearly, since 1953, established the agricultural minimum wage. Instead, the agricultural minimum wage was to be readjusted annually in a percentage equivalent to the rise in the government-controlled consumer price index.

Second, the decree reaffirmed the right to pay part of the minimum wage in kind but required express written agreement of the worker who accepted the assessment of the individual regalías in the labor contract. The worker could also opt for total payment in cash.[15] For the period 1963-1964 a minimum of 35 percent of the agricultural wage had to be paid in cash, increased after May 1, 1964, to 50 percent. These provisions legally eliminated the landowners' authority to unilaterally assess the value of firewood, pasture rights, housing, and other regalías, thereby evading the minimum-wage laws.

Third, the decree reaffirmed the requirement that the monthly rental value of the worker's house could not be discounted from his wage unless the housing met government specified standards. The law required compliance with the new housing standards adopted in 1960.[16]

Likewise, R.R.A. No. 23[17] established a special procedure to handle campesino complaints concerning the family allowances specified in Law 8.811 of 1947. Nonpayment of family allowances had long been a scandal in the countryside and a focus of publicity campaigns by the leftist press as well as by rural labor petitions. Article 45 of the land reform law stipulated that the president of the republic could decree special regulations concerning agricultural salaries and family allowances, and establish special procedures to insure that rural workers received the allowances to which they were entitled by law. R.R.A. No. 23 attempted to provide for a "simple, agile, serious and efficient procedure to register and resolve the complaints of agricultural workers concerning lack of payment or frauds in the payment of family allowances to which they have a right."[18] The provision was necessary because

> there existed a "black legend" about what was called the robbery of the family allowances of the campesinos which had its origin in irregularities of unscrupulous patrones who cheated their workers. These isolated incidents caused not only great damage to the workers involved . . . but also created an ambience of mistrust in the entire agricultural sector and constituted a gratuitous offense to those patrones who correctly complied with their social obligations. There existed a tendency for this ambience of mistrust to be generalized with the evident purpose of political and social agitation among the campesinos.[19]

Finally, Article 47 of the law, as regulated by the relevant reglamentos, provided that workers who had been employed for one year or more in a public or semipublic farm expropriated by CORA for subdivision had a right to an indemnity.[20]

Despite provisions which should have tended to favor resident workers in the redistribution of rural properties,[21] land reform as conceived by the Alessandri government often brought unemployment to rural labor.[22] The case of Fundo Santa Elena illustrates the negative effects of land reform for some sectors of rural labor.

Fundo Santa Elena in the province of O'Higgins was owned by the National Health Service (SNS). In accord with the dispositions that ordered public and semipublic agencies to dispose of properties which they did not directly manage, the SNS proceeded to sell this property to the Caja de Colonización Agrícola for subsequent subdivision.[23] On February 5, 1960, the Caja established a merit system to assure more equitable selection of land reform beneficiaries. The adopted point system favored those with agricultural work experience, specialized agricultural training, professional degrees related to agriculture, and funds deposited in a "colonization" account.[24] The system was biased against agricultural laborers and even inquilinos in most cases. When the Caja acted to parcel Santa Elena to new proprietors (colonos), the labor inspector in the province of O'Higgins reported:

... This fundo will be turned over to the Caja de Colonización Agrícola on May 1, 1961, in order that this organization subdivide it and turn it over to parceleros or "aspirantes a colonos," who must meet the requirements demanded by the Caja according to ... D.F.L. 49 of the Minister of Hacienda. ...

In fact, the Caja de Colonización has almost made material delivery of the property, lacking only the authorization to the Health Service to collectively dismiss, due to permanent termination of labors, ... its empleados and workers.[25]

This termination affects 27 inquilinos (including 3 mayordomos); 55 voluntarios ... without taking into account the afuerinos, seasonal workers and 4 *empleados particulares*.

... Unquestionably, because this is now an accomplished fact, ordered by law and agreed to by the Consejo of the National Health Service ... it cannot be stopped nor said that it is unjustified. But the facts are that it will produce unemployment. ... The majority of fundos [in this zone] do not have the capacity to absorb the unemployed workers that will soon be produced.[26]

These results were not inherent in the provisions of Law 15.020. Exclusion of agricultural workers as beneficiaries in favor of urban elements or agricultural administrators necessitated the application of the provisions for compensation to workers forced off the land through "land reform."[27]

Organizational Infrastructure Created by Law 15.020

The land reform law established three executory agencies: Corporación de Reforma Agraria (CORA), Instituto de Desarrollo Agropecuario (INDAP), and the Consejo Superior de Fomento Agropecuario (CONSFA). Three agencies were deemed necessary so that each of the parties in the governmental coalition could control aspects of the reform program and provide employment for supporters. CORA was to be under the control of the Conservative party, INDAP of the Radical party, and CONSFA of the Liberal party.

CONSFA

In the land reform law CONSFA was defined as a planning and coordinating agency in the agrarian sector. Its functions included formulation of general and regional plans for the division, consolidation and recovery of land, and improvement of the condition of life of the campesino population (Article 5). Article 5 of law 15.020 detailed the standards for regional plans of agricultural development (which if developed would have allowed expropriations on a regional basis). Second, CONSFA was to "promote and coordinate the action of the diverse organizations, institutions and enterprises in the public sector for the better completion and development of these regional development plans." Third, the agency was authorized to "carry out studies and promote the application of better systems of land tenure, rural property and agricultural exploitation." In addition, CONSFA could authorize CORA to create "special centers of agricultural production in zones of land division or consolidation of minifundio" and to "propose the norms under which agricultural credit should be available in the country, to whom and in what amounts, amortization periods, and interest rates. . . ."

Formally, CONSFA had authority to alter dramatically the terms of agricultural production and to authorize the establishment, at least experimentally, of different types of proprietary arrangements in the rural sector. The authority to establish different types of land tenure and proprietary arrangements was a fundamental requirement in altering traditional property systems in the Chilean countryside. While the Alessandri government did not make significant use of this authority, it would be the basis for the creation of new types of property in rural land in the subsequent government of Christian Democratic President Eduardo Frei.

CORA

Law 15.020 converted the Caja de Colonización Agrícola into the Corporación de Reforma Agraria, an autonomous legal corporation (*empresa autónoma del estado*). CORA's function was to "promote and effect the division of rural property, in accord with the economic necessities of the country and each region, consolidate minifundio, form *villorios agrícolas* and *centros de huertos familiares*; create *centros especiales de producción agropecuaria*, promote and effect colonization of new lands, provide to its *parceleros* and *asignatarios* and to the cooperatives formed by them the needed credit and technical assistance, during the time necessary to assure their good results . . .[Article 11]."

The land reform law provided that CORA could purchase land for its "rational division" or for management by cooper-

atives (Article 11). Given Chile's lack of experience with agricultural cooperatives on any wide scale, these provisions, along
with authority to create new types of ambiguously defined agricultural units—for example, "centro especial de producción
agropecuaria"—provided great potential flexibility in establishing new types of agricultural properties. After 1964 the terms
of the law allowed establishment of a variety of agricultural cooperatives and collectively worked *asentamientos* (which became "agrarian reform cooperatives" after the transitional
asentamiento period). CORA had the authority necessary, in
cooperation with CONSFA, to alter radically the structure of
the rural property system in Chile. Again, for all its restrictions,
Law 15.020 provided a good deal of leverage for the executory
agencies of the land reform legislation.

INDAP

The Consejo de Fomento e Investigación Agrícola was re-
named Instituto de Desarrollo Agropecuario and converted into
an autonomous state corporation like CORA. Among the principal functions assigned to INDAP by Law 15.020 were the
following:

(a) to provide free technical assistance and reasonable credit to smallholders and medium-sized farms, including minifundio and Indian
farmers and their respective cooperatives, as well as stimulate the
activity of artisans and small industries in rural zones.
(b) provide credit to owners of minifundios and propiedades familiares
agrícolas or indivisible smallholds in order to facilitate the redistribution of land to the benefit of the tiller in cases of liquidation of
inheritances or comunidades or to transform minifundios into unidades
económicas. . . .
(c) administer in common or in a coordinated fashion minifundio and
small agricultural properties with the agreement of the interested
parties.
(d) promote the organization of cooperatives whose activities are directly related to production, industrialization or commercialization of agricultural, forest or fish products or with the betterment
of rural life in any of its aspects.
(e) extend credit and technical assistance to the parceleros installed by
CORA, when so determined by CONSFA.

Under the rubric of technical assistance and promotion of the
improvement of life in the rural sector, INDAP had great latitude

in carrying out rural education programs. R.R.A. 18 of March 22, 1963, defined INDAP's authority to include any activities "related to agricultural production and derivative industries, education, and community development." After 1964 this mandate was stretched to its legal limits (and sometimes beyond), by INDAP personnel as the agency helped organize rural unions and present labor petitions as well as assist in rural strikes. In the period 1962-1964, however, INDAP basically limited itself to the provision of credit, technical assistance to smallholders, and feeble efforts to form agricultural cooperatives.

The combined organizational infrastructure of INDAP, CORA, and CONSFA and the legal authority vested in these agencies by Law 15.020 provided important instruments through which to effect fundamental alterations in the system of land tenure and rural proprietorship. Essentially conservative instruments during the Alessandri period, it would take the following government only a very short time to convert these governmental agencies into organizational weapons against the hacendados and into sources of mobilizational efforts among the campesinos.

Implementation of Law 15.020: 1962-1964

The Alessandri land reform program was called by the opposition parties in Chile *reforma de macetero*, or "flowerpot reform." In a narrow sense the characterization is probably accurate. Of approximately 60,000 hectares affected by the land reform, 40,000 pertained to a single, publicly owned hacienda (Hacienda Mariposas) in San Clemente, Talca,[28] which accounted for about two-thirds of land affected and approximately 45 percent of land reform beneficiaries in the period 1962-1964.[29] Almost 70 percent of the land subdivided by the Alessandri government belonged to governmental or semi-public agencies. The government acquired only about 18,000 hectares from private owners. CORA did not employ the expropriation provisions of the law, nor were any regional development plans made operative. The "reform" consisted of geographically isolated, high-cost showcase colonies (*colonias*).

While the recipients of land (*parceleros, huerteros*) were defined as the reform's beneficiaries, governmental functionaries working for the land reform agencies seem to have been the real beneficiaries of the law's limited implementation. By 1964 CORA had ten functionaries for every sixteen colonos. Colonos earned from the land they received, on the average, about 18 percent of what each of the CORA bureaucrats received in salaries.[30]

The land reform effected by the Alessandri regime instituted a system of mixed private properties within the subdivided fundos. Some of the properties were larger than unidades económicas (*hijuelas* or *lotes*). Most were supposedly equivalent to unidades económicas. In addition, the program created less-than-subsistence plots (huertos) upon which CORA settled inquilinos or voluntarios with fewer merit points. This mixed system quickly produced a pattern of wage labor and even disguised inquilinaje on the parcelas, whose owners often used the huerteros as hired hands. The huertos were new minifundios. The parcelas, at best, became small commercial farms which exploited the labor of the landless or the huertero.

As had occurred throughout the history of the Caja de Colonización Agrícola, some of the land reform beneficiaries attempted to reproduce on a small scale the hacendado-inquilino pattern of farm management.[31] The CIDA report on Chile observed in the case of Colonia Arturo Lyon as follows:

> A disguised form of inquilinaje exists, although this type of worker is not mentioned by name. However, these workers reside permanently on the property and have many characteristics of the inquilino system, such as regalías of housing, obligated labor, etc. In relation to the colonos these workers appear in a patrón-inquilino situation.
>
> Also, despite the legal prohibition, sharecropping exists within the colonia.[32]

In this fashion the land reform carried out by the Alessandri regime seemed to reproduce in miniature the traditional system of rural proprietorship and patrón-worker relationships.

The limited accomplishments of CORA during the Alessandri period can be explained in part by the delay between passage of Law 15.020 and promulgation of the necessary reglamentos for each part of the Land Reform Law. In addition, Congress did not until July 1963 enact the constitutional amendment making possible deferred payments for land purchased by CORA. From 1963 to 1964 CORA had planned to establish 12,347 smallholders (parceleros and huerteros); in fact, the agency installed only 1,066 new proprietors on parcelas and huertos.[33] The government purchased land for this purpose from public or semipublic agencies or from private landowners who offered their land for sale to CORA. The latter generally received good prices for their land and relatively favorable terms of payment. Juan Carlos Collarte estimates that CORA paid between 2 and 22 times the assessed value of the land. Collarte points out that the figure would be still higher if we take into account that infrastructure and farm buildings represented between 75 and 95 percent of assessed value, and were frequently not transferred to CORA. The same author suggests that by paying for the farms at assessed value (a policy adopted by the Christian Democrats after 1964) and with 10 percent cash—instead of 20— CORA could have purchased about twenty times the amount of land acquired with the same investment.[34] (See Table 7 for the data on which Collarte based his estimates.)

In accord with Law 15.020 and the subsequent constitutional amendment, land could have been purchased for 10 percent cash and the balance over ten years. Instead, with the exception of two publicly owned properties, the government paid for farms with 20 percent cash and the remainder in less than three years.[35] This purchasing policy seriously limited the amount of land which could be acquired with the budgeted funds and was, regardless of the nominal size of the land-acquisition budget, a relatively less effective instrument for redistributing property in rural land than a policy which maximized acquisitions through low cash payments and long-term amortizations.

In short, Law 15.020, despite its conservative orientation, contained a much more radical potential impact than the flower pot reform carried out by the Alessandri government. As a transitional legal redefinition of property in rural land, Law 15.020 placed various new restrictions upon rural proprietors, perhaps the most important being the basing of proprietorship itself on conditions of economic performance and modernization of the agricultural enterprise. That CORA did not implement this aspect of the law during the remaining year of the Alessandri government does not lessen the significance of this legal redefinition of rural proprietary authority. The introduction of deferred-payment provisions for land acquisitions (in a constitutional amendment) through expropriation of "abandoned or notoriously poorly exploited land" opened the door

TABLE 7 PROPERTIES ACQUIRED BY CORA, 1962-1964

Colony	Province	Area in Hectares	Asking* Price	Sale* Price	Sale Price as Percentage of Asking Price	Assessed* Value	Sale Price as Percentage of Assessed Value
Alfalfares	O'Higgins	732.75	500,000	370,510	77.8%	96,317	385%
John F. Kennedy	Santiago	3,308.75	–	1,459,124	–	**	–
Santa Elena (sector San Nicolás)	O'Higgins	1,341.80	280,000	151,149	72.4%	**	–
San Antonio de Chimbarongo	Colchagua	566.90	500,000	265,125	70.4%	135,490	196%
Peumo Negro	Talca	672.20	699,000	344,880	59.4%	54,100	638%
Ranquilemito	Talca	770.00	381,000	326,293	88.5%	33,856	964%
Mariposas	Talca	40,027.00	–	2,132,833	–	**	–
Enrique Zañartu Prieto	Concepción	2,354.10	500,000	336,744	77.3%	51,660	652%
San Antonio de Duqueco	Bío Bío	892.60	180,000	121,270	81.0%	17,720	684%
Santa Amelia	Bío Bío	1,058.60	520,000	292,300	62.1%	39,382	742%
R. Ester Rodríquez (1st sector)	Arauco	2,523.40	372,450	218,355	80.9%	12,875	1,700%
R. Ester Rodríquez (2d sector)	Arauco	3,657.30	559,500	308,105	76.7%	21,140	1,458%
R. Ester Rodríquez (3d sector)	Arauco	1,505.80	223,978	136,649	80.2%	5,902	2,308%
Federico Pena Cereceda	Arauco	3,395.50	538,390	395,106	80.1%	24,601	1,606%

SOURCE: Juan Carlos Collarte, Ph.D. diss. (draft), chapter 7; and CIDA, *Chile: Tenencia de la tierra y desarrollo socio-económico del sector agrícola* (Santiago: ICIRA, 1966), pp. 365-68.

*In escudos of each year.

**Government land.

for technical criteria of poor exploitation consistent with the vision of a modernized agriculture of any future government and amenable to the political pressures developing from campesino organizations for a broader program of land redistribution.

On the other hand, Law 15.020 offered landowners a good deal of legal support in their effort to resist a massive land reform program. The delaying potential inherent in the series of judicial appeals possible on any particular expropriation decision by CORA gave landowners particularly important leverage in resisting implementation of a land reform program. Likewise, the limitations of deferred payment to abandoned or poorly exploited farms meant that large-scale reforms would involve sums of money unavailable to the Chilean government.

Many landowners reacted to the terms of Law 15.020 and the increasing pressure of rural labor organizations by subdividing their fundos in order to exempt themselves from expropriation procedures. Formal subdivisions, with de facto maintenance of existing production and administrative units, increased to such an extent that the Christian Democratic government (1964-1970) eventually proposed legislation to forbid the subdivision of any agricultural property over 80 hectares without prior approval of CORA.

Despite its provisions which restricted a massive redistribution of property in rural land, Law 15.020 represented a transitional break with the customary extensive authority of rural landowners. Above all, it based proprietorship on the conditions of productive efficiency, compliance with social legislation, and compatibility with national agrarian planning. This meant a formal end to the Civil Code's concept of proprietorship and a potentially increased role of governmental authority in rural proprietorship through regional planning, national land policies, and bureaucratic-technical criteria for efficient farm management. The law also allowed governmental experiments in collective, cooperative, and state production units while it created a corps of agrarian bureaucracies through which to devise and implement rural development programs. The language of the law went well beyond the intentions or actions of the Alessandri government in all of these areas but nevertheless provided a legal basis for innovation in the agricultural sector which might seriously affect the political capabilities of the large landowners and offer new opportunities to rural labor. Authorization to extend credit, marketing assistance, technical services, and organizational assistance to campesino associations provided a broad framework within which substantial redistribution of access to governmental services might redefine the political meaning of property for the hacendado and the campesino proprietor.

Prior to its replacement by the Christian Democratic agrarian reform law, Law 15.020 allowed the succeeding government to expropriate almost 500 farms with a settled population of over 8,000 campesino families.[36] The fear of worse terms of expropriation upon enactment of the new legislation proposed by the Frei government assisted CORA in overcoming to some extent the potential for landowner resistance within the framework of Law 15.020. With this legal basis the Christian Democrats operated until late 1967, when the moderate redefinition of property in rural land contained in Law 15.020 gave way to the radical alteration of the legal basis of rural proprietorship of Law 16.640 and the "Revolution in Liberty" in the countryside.

8

The Revolution in Liberty and Property in Rural Land

When President Frei talked with the humble campesinos he never tired of repeating a phrase that constituted his greatest goal: 'I want, that in the future, it be said of me that I was the President of the campesino.' . . . To accomplish this goal all means were employed, whether constitutional or not, whether legal or not, whether moral or not. The question was to fulfill this great goal without delay.

Arturo Olavarría Bravo

The road to power is organization. The crisis consists of the fact that the majority of our people are not organized.

Eduardo Frei

Victorious in the presidential elections of 1964, the Christian Democrats labeled their program "Revolution in Liberty."[1] Revolutionary change, according to the Christian Democrats, would be accomplished by establishing numerous intermediate organizations which linked campesinos and urban workers to national centers of political power and by introducing innovative legislative and administrative measures which benefited the popular classes. Respect for legal procedures and the content of existing law was central to the notion of Revolution in Liberty. In fact, however, the Christian Democratic government frequently neglected or deliberately violated existing law in carrying out its national program, particularly in the countryside.

At stake was the capability of rural proprietors to demand that the police power of the state enforce property rights in the face of illegal campesino pressure. The restrictive nature of existing labor legislation, and the extensive scope and domain of proprietary authority, did not allow the government to act within the law to carry out a revolution in the countryside. Respect for law meant that police had to be used when campesinos refused to carry on the struggle with landowners within the

241

framework of existing legal norms. The support for existing proprietors, insofar as it occurred, disillusioned activist campesinos who had taken electoral propaganda literally and expected a rapid, massive redistribution of property in rural land. At the same time, it provided fuel for the Marxist press, which proclaimed that the Revolution in Liberty meant the same old repression of rural labor.

The dilemma posed by a commitment to both revolution and legality was not the only problem for the Christian Democratic agrarian program. Fundamental disagreements existed within the Christian Democratic government on the nature of land reform and its role in the Revolution in Liberty. For some Christian Democrats land reform was an essential part of a broader effort to redefine and redistribute property in Chile. Rejecting capitalism and socialism, these Christian Democrats advocated rapid introduction of "communitarian" property to eliminate the class antagonisms implied in a social system which separates labor and capital. Communitarian property would unite capital and labor and give rise to an integrated, harmonious social order—a "Christian" alternative to the evils of capitalism and Marxist socialism. While these leftist Christian Democrats never precisely defined the legal and organizational attributes of communitarian property in rural land, they seemed to offer a government-assisted "workers' enterprise" that combined a generalized collective proprietorship of farms with small individual usufruct within the estate.

The insistence by some elements within the Christian Democratic party and government on communitarian property was strongly rejected by others who favored redistributing property rights to the benefit of selected campesinos while maintaining or only marginally modifying existing proprietary arrangements. This conflict within the party and government—at times the two overlapped—was presaged in 1963 by Jacques Chonchol in *Mensaje*. Chonchol emphasized the need for a mixed system of rural property with a limited role for individual or family farms. Chonchol argued that "the communitarian association can take on distinct forms but . . . the essential thing is that those who work in it are the same ones who possess the land and the capital and who decide in an organized and responsible manner the use to be made of the fruits of the enterprise."[2] The editors of the journal in which the article appeared felt it necessary to respond with a lengthy editors' note, which declared in part: "The editors believe that in the majority of circumstances . . . the solution will be family properties supported to a greater or lesser degree by cooperatives, according to the entrepreneurial capabilities of the campesinos. That family property is the ideal proclaimed by the Social Doctrine of the Church seems to us beyond question. . . ."[3]

Within the Christian Democratic party and government, ideological and programmatic conflict over the type of rural property to be established as well as over the extent of redistribution of property rights that ought to occur continued (1964-1967). Almost a full year passed before President Frei actually sent a land reform proposal to the Congress. The Christian Democratic agrarian program, thus, involved a great deal of improvisation and pragmatic juggling of ideological concerns to conform with local necessity and political pressure. At the end of its first year of government (1965), the Christian Democrats still walked a tightrope between land reform (individual smallholds) and land reform (communitarian property).

When the Christian Democratic land reform law finally emerged from the Congress in 1967, ambiguity remained: the law specified three different types of rural property and left the issue to be resolved, concretely, in the case of each asentamiento at the termination of the transitional period. The issue could not be definitively resolved within the party or the government, and so, at least formally, the campesinos themselves were called upon to decide the type of proprietorship they preferred after the transitional stage of asentamiento. In practice, the advocates of communitarian property used the resources and influence of INDAP and CORA to prepare the campesinos for various forms of collective proprietorship.

Not until 1967, however, could the Christian Democrats push land reform and rural unionization laws through the Congress. In the period 1964-1967, caught between their own mobilizational efforts, those of the Marxist parties and rural labor movement, and the constraints of existing legal norms, the Christian Democrats carried out a mixed program of legal and administrative innovation and mobilizational activity in the countryside. Their program consisted of (1) legislative acts and administrative reforms to improve the position of rural labor while further delimiting the authority of rural proprietors, (2) intensified enforcement of labor law, (3) stepped-up use of the provisions of the Alessandri land reform law along with further modification of existing property rights, (4) establishment of a transitional form of rural property for use in the lands acquired for land reform, and (5) mobilization of rural labor in legally recognized unions, cooperatives, and committees, and in illegal associations which employed both legal and illegal tactics in confronting the landowners. In practice these measures were interdependent. Effective enforcement of labor law and increased "willingness" of landowners to sell their rural estates to CORA depended in great part on mobilized campesino pressure. Governmental legislation which protected workers from dismissal, increased Labor Department responsiveness to campesinos' demands, and the material benefits directly and indirectly provided by the government to those campesinos who joined government-sponsored (especially by INDAP) organizations facilitated rural mobilization. In turn, campesino mobilization brought landowner response as it had historically in the Chilean countryside. Mass dismissal of workers, subdivision of properties in order to avoid the terms of the proposed land reform law, and persecution of labor leaders gave urgency and justification to governmental legislation which dealt with these immediate problems.

By 1967, prior to either the land reform law or the rural unionization law, the political meaning of property in rural land had been greatly altered. Because, in a sense, the laws that finally passed were a product and extension of the political struggle from 1964 to 1967, it is necessary to review the pre-1967 period before discussing the radical, formal redefinition of rural proprietorship contained in the rural unionization law (16.625) and the land reform law itself (16.640).

Administrative and Legislative Reforms, 1964-1967

The Revolution in Liberty began rather unobtrusively in the countryside. In late February 1965, the government modified Article 7 of Decree 261 (1948)—administrative procedures for rural unionization—in a fashion intended to reduce procedural delays and administrative harrassment of rural unions.[4] Next the Labor Department moved to develop model bylaws for rural unions. Instead of a lengthy process involving numerous corrections of wording and punctuation in the documents submitted by the unions-in-formation, union organizers could fill in the appropriate blanks on mimeographed forms provided by the Labor Department. While procedural difficulties continued to hinder formation of rural unions, the initial thrust of the Labor Department under the Christian Democratic regime was to simplify and speed up the procedure.[5] From this rather innocuous beginning, the government moved rapidly to improve the conditions of rural labor and restrict still further the authority of rural proprietors.

On April 21, 1965, Law 16.250 introduced a number of significant innovations in the rural sector. The law made the agricultural minimum wage equivalent to that in other sectors of the economy. The law further required that 75 percent of the minimum agricultural wage be paid in cash. Neither housing nor the customary non-cash benefits could be discounted from the worker's cash wage.[6] Since rural proprietors could not legally reduce perquisites or in-kind payments already enjoyed by the workers in order to meet the 75 percent cash requirement, the workers obtained an even greater real wage increase. The agricultural work day was limited to eight hours, with overtime rates to be paid for additional labor (provisions allowed longer days in peak periods, compensated for by shorter days in slow periods). In combination these provisions broke the traditional system of inquilinaje (see chapter 2) at the same time that they guaranteed the campesinos more income for less work.

Along with innovations in campesino-patrón relationships, Law 16.250 (as amended in Law 16.270) provided immunity from dismissal for all workers during the formation of a union. Shortly thereafter, Law 16.455 established a complex system to protect workers against arbitrary termination of employment. While the law did not guarantee workers their jobs, it could make arbitrary dismissals or retaliation for union activity costly to the proprietor.[7] In a limited sense, the campesino had a legal right to his job. He could be dismissed only "for cause."

The initial reaction of some landowners was to resist or circumvent the law in order to eliminate agitators or union leaders and to recover the costs imposed by the benefits which the new laws provided to rural labor. Illustrative is the following letter from a group of campesinos in mid-1965:

> ... we are workers in Fundo Los Hornos in Buin, administered by Jorge Solo Saldivar.
>
> With the establishment of new salaries this señor immediately began to retaliate against us and to take away the in-kind payments which we enjoy in order to compensate for his added costs. In April of this year he insisted that we provide two workers daily to the fundo [a deterioration of existing conditions]. We complained to the Labor Department and ... the Provincial Inspector put things in their place. In order to dismiss us Solo Saldivar decided to accuse us of stealing firewood—an effort to get around the "ley de inamovilidad." An inquilino has been accused at the Buin court of stealing firewood. Another measure which he has taken against us is to require inquilinos (even those more than seventy years old) to fulfill their "obligación" personally, instead of through their sons (as is customary).[8]

The reactions of landowners and their agents were consistent with the historical experience of rural labor in Chile. Gains won in labor legislation or through labor conflicts had almost always been eroded through hacendado reprisals. Unless the Christian Democrats could enforce the new norms in the countryside, the conditions of campesinos would be little improved.[9] To this end, the government initiated the most intensive and systematic program for enforcement of labor law in the rural sector in Chilean history.

Intensified Enforcement of Labor Law

In late 1965 the Labor Department estimated that there were approximately 75,000 agricultural units larger than 10 hectares where code enforcement was probably necessary.[10] In order to visit the 75,000 enterprises larger than 10 hectares the department estimated a necessary input of 58,050 work days. (The department calculated that an inspector could, on an average, handle 1.3 fundos per day.) To inspect them all in a year would have required, according to the department, 234 inspectors (see Table 8).[11] Based on these estimates the Labor Department concluded: "If you consider these hard facts in relation to the obligation of this Service to inspect every enterprise subject to regulation at least once each year, without even considering the respective return visits to confirm compliance, it is clear that fulfillment of this obligation with the actual number of inspectors is impossible."[12]

In light of the economic infeasibility of a national program the Labor Department had already decided, in late 1964, to launch an experimental program of labor law enforcement in the two nearest provinces south of Santiago—O'Higgins and Colchagua. The program was intended to develop teams of inspectors from the Labor Department and Social Security Administration which could systematically and exhaustively visit the rural sector to force compliance with labor law.

In early May 1965 the first joint team of inspectors (Comisión Especial de Fiscalización Agrícola, or CEFA), headed by Pedro Donoso,[13] met in Rancagua with Carlos Espinosa M. (Director of the Department of Inspection), Arturo Figueroa Penroz (Director of Agricultural Inspection), and Enrique Arias (Zone Director of Social Security). In this meeting the objectives of the pilot program were reviewed: to inspect every agricultural unit in O'Higgins and Colchagua that employed agricultural labor on a permanent basis (about 3,400 farms). The inspectors were instructed to be systematic and thorough in their work (literally, as Donoso put it, *"Había que barrer"*). Implementation of the program began in the department of Caupolicán. The CEFA's labors continued from May 1965 until March 5, 1967.

In the first year, the inspection team visited 1,202 agricultural units, and the system proved so successful that the Labor Department created additional CEFA teams for other regions while the original team still operated in O'Higgins and Colchagua. The department gave the new inspection teams more autonomy from headquarters, allowing them to work out of provincial or departmental offices.

In each enterprise visited, the team of inspectors filled out a detailed administrative form which included, in addition to a list of violations, a census of the farm workers, individual conditions of work, regalías, length of residence or employment in the fundo, and any unique arrangements in the farm, for example, systems of worker participation in profits, compensation for regalías in cash, or *ración cosechada*.[14] For each proprietor, the inspectors left a set of instructions that listed violations and established a time limit for compliance.[15] Where compliance

TABLE 8 DISTRIBUTION OF AGRICULTURAL UNITS, AREA, WORKERS, INSPECTORATES, AND LABOR DEPARTMENT PERSONNEL, 1965

Province	Agricultural Area (1000 hectares)	Agricultural Units (10 hectares or larger)	Number of Workers	Labor Department Offices	Number of Inspectors	Inspectors Needed Exclusively for Agriculture
Tarapacá	235	465	790	2	6	2
Antofagasta	3	74	467	4	6	1
Atacama	85	335	2,666	3	5	1
Coquimbo	1,980	1,567	14,275	5	10	5
Aconcagua	628	606	10,901	3	6	2
Valparaíso	341	1,057	12,591	5	22	3
Santiago	1,342	2,816	39,229	12	82	9
O'Higgins	342	1,339	22,691	4	6	4
Colchagua	596	2,005	17,162	2	4	6
Curicó	326	1,310	10,742	2	3	4
Talca	602	2,047	23,418	2	6	6
Maule	413	3,130	5,202	2	4	10
Linares	536	2,655	20,215	3	4	8

Ñuble	1,092	7,139	28,970	4	7	22
Concepción	447	3,690	12,383	5	13	11
Arauco	385	1,859	4,313	4	3	6
Bío Bío	806	3,350	15,861	3	3	10
Malleco	1,081	4,919	11,029	5	3	15
Cautín	1,322	11,437	20,921	5	10	36
Valdivia	1,490	5,692	22,332	3	5	18
Osorno	697	2,896	12,215	2	3	9
Llanquihue	937	6,058	9,582	3	5	19
Chiloé	675	6,503	5,791	2	1	20
Aisén	1,298	1,868	2,045	2	3	6
Magallanes	3,977	638	4,913	2	5	2
Total	21,363	75,465	330,722	89	225	235

SOURCE: Labor Department, Oficio 7905, October 30, 1965.

was not forthcoming, heavy fines were levied.[16] In some extreme cases the fines approached the commercial value of the agricultural properties.[17] The inspectors proceeded particularly harshly with violations of Law 16.250 (as amended by laws 16.270 and 16.455) in regard to unjustified dismissals of workers.[18] Most fines, however, were not confiscatory but still large enough to persuade landowners that the Labor Department was now serious about code enforcement in the rural sector.[19]

Intensified enforcement of labor law and the application of fines for violations put rural proprietors on the defensive. It also increased campesino confidence in the government and in their own improving situation. A letter from a union which was being formed in Hacienda Pullally during this period captures the campesino reaction to the Labor Department's new militancy in enforcing labor law.

> . . . the agricultural union in formation in Pullally, with 130 workers, brings to your attention that for the first time in the history of Chile, and thanks to a government which we totally support . . . justice is being done and the law is being applied to those accustomed to evading it.[20]

For the first time in Chilean history the authority of the hacendados was being effectively, if not universally, regulated.

Application of Law 15.020 and Further Modification of Property Law

The government accompanied intensified enforcement of labor law with a serious effort to expropriate rural properties under the terms of Law 15.020. Some rural proprietors, fearing less favorable terms in the land reform legislation proposed in late 1965 by the Christian Democratic government, became willing to dispose of their land before the new law could be passed and put into operation. Other landowners responded by formally subdividing their properties in order to avoid the 80-hectare limit in the proposed legislation. This action involved a division of legal title to the property but not necessarily of farm management. Formal subdivision, in addition to protecting the landowners from expropriation, also served to destroy rural unions by leaving less than twenty permanent workers in each new property, twenty being the minimum number of workers required to maintain a legal union. Proprietors often continued to operate the subdivided units as a single enterprise.

In response to the threat to both the agrarian reform program and to the existing legal unions, the government pushed through Congress Law 16.465 (April 26, 1966), which prohibited the subdivision of all rural properties larger than 80 hectares without prior authorization from CORA.[21] In addition to restrictions on subdivision, Law 16.465 also limited proprietary authority in regard to land rentals by extending the provisions of Article 46 of Law 15.020 to truck cropping (*chacarería*) and sharecropping (*mediería*). Thus, all existing contracts were extended to the six-year minimum specified in the 1962 law. Inquilinos, inquilino-medieros, sharecroppers, and truck croppers (*chacareros*), previously having only a tenuous access to land, were now guaranteed a minimum six-year contract when landowners entered into rental arrangements. These provisions also protected campesinos from reprisals when they joined unions, made formal complaints to the Labor Department, or pressured CORA to expropriate the farms on which they worked.

Finally, in January 1967 the Chilean Congress adopted a constitutional amendment which paved the way for approval later in 1967 of the Christian Democratic agrarian reform law. The amendment substantially redefined the rights of proprietors in general and of rural proprietors in particular. Significant sections of the new constitutional provisions read as follows:

> When the interest of the national community should require, the law shall be empowered to reserve in the State the exclusive dominion of natural resources, productive goods, or others which might be declared of preeminent importance for the economic, social or cultural life of the country. It will also favor the proper distribution of property and the establishment of family property.
> No one shall be deprived of his property except by virtue of the general or special law which authorizes expropriation for the cause of public utility or social interest declared by the Legislator. He who is expropriated shall have a right to indemnization. . . .
> As to the expropriation of landed estates, the indemnity shall be equivalent to the current assessment for the territorial tax, plus the value of improvements not included in the assessment, and may be paid part in cash and the balance in payments not to exceed 30 years, all in the form and condition determined by the law.[22]

The amendment effectively terminated the extensive Civil Code interpretation of private property in Chile. For rural proprietors it also constitutionally fixed indemnity at assessed value for tax purposes. Since commercial values of land generally exceeded substantially valuation for taxation purposes, this stipulation represented a serious financial blow to landowners. By the beginning of 1967, thus, the Christian Democratic government, with the legislative support of the Marxist parties, had significantly redefined the legal attributes of proprietorship in Chile.

The Asentamiento

The legal constriction of proprietary authority contained in the various legislative acts mentioned above accompanied the initiation of expropriation of rural properties under the terms of Law 15.020. From 1965 to 1967 the government expropriated for purposes of land reform 495 properties with a total of approximately 1,200,000 hectares.[23] In these expropriated properties the government began to introduce a new type of rural proprietorship—the *asentamiento*.

The asentamiento (literally "settlement"), a transitional form of proprietorship intended to allow rural laborers to acquire gradually the management and technical skills to become independent proprietors, emerged from immediate political realities rather than ideological or technical design. Perhaps the epitome of the improvisation and eclectic pragmatism characteristic of the Christian Democratic experience in the rural sector, the asentamiento took shape in the course of political struggle between the Christian Democratic government and the campesino unions in the valley of Choapa in the province of Coquimbo.

The National Health Service (SNS) and its predecessor, the Beneficencia, had controlled farms in the valley of Choapa for over one hundred years. During these years the SNS periodically rented the farms to private proprietors who dealt, in turn, with the rural labor force. From 1940 to 1965, however, employees of the SNS managed the farms. Since the early 1920s, these properties had been the focii of a Marxist rural labor movement. The organizations were renovated and strengthened during the Popular Front period (1938-1941), when Salvador Allende served as minister of health and provided access to governmental farms for Socialist labor organizers. Whereas the unions never obtained legal recognition, they persistently struggled to improve the conditions of work and access to land for the farms' labor force.

From 1941 until 1964, subdivision of the Choapa farms was periodically considered and then dropped. After passage of Law 15.020 the Alessandri government determined that many government-owned rural properties would be subdivided. The government set April 1964 as the date for transfer of the SNS farms in the Choapa Valley to CORA. The SNS agreed to pay severance benefits to the workers, and CORA took on the responsibility for subdivision.[24] The unions called a strike. Salaries and regalías were improved, and transfer of the land was postponed for a year. Subdivision in the valley of Choapa thus became a problem for the Christian Democrats when they took office.

The Christian Democrats were well aware of the strength of the Socialists and Communists in the valley. In a report by CORFO (February 1965) the government concluded: "It is obvious that the political parties control the activity of the unions and, therefore, the conflicts and relations between workers and proprietor in the Hacienda."[25] Thus, in what seems to have been a deliberate effort to eliminate the Marxist unions and replace them with new worker committees susceptible to control by the government through CORA, the Christian Democratic government chose initially to bypass the unions in programming the land reform in the valley.

Until April 1965, the government had not yet determined the type of units to be created by the land reform program. Pressure from the Choapa unions forced the government into action. As an interim measure, CORA offered to rent the fundos to the campesinos grouped in "committees." The unions rejected the offer.[26] The Federación de Campesinos e Indígenas, with which the unions were affiliated, proposed transfer of the farms to the unions, but with freedom for each union to determine the type of property system, collective or individual, to be established in the farms. CORA refused simply to turn the farms over to the unions and negotiations were temporarily stalemated.

In the meantime, governmental officials, technical advisers at ICIRA, and Marxist intellectuals (e.g., David Baytelman who later became the first director of CORA under President Salvador Allende in 1970) sought a compromise solution. As worked out in negotiations between union representatives and governmental officials, the agreement contained the following principal features:

(1)   All residents in each fundo are to be registered by CORA, with the cooperation of the workers.

(2)   From the workers in each fundo a committee of five will be selected. In this election each head of family has voting rights. Union leaders may serve on the committee.

(3)   The committee will serve one year and must assemble the workers fifteen days prior to expiration of this period to elect a new committee. A quorum of two-thirds of the heads of families are necessary in order to carry out this election. If this number is not attained, a second meeting will be held and those attending can elect the committee.

(4)   The committee represents all of the registered workers in the farm; all workers are bound by the agreements it makes.

(5)   The committee will enter into agreements with CORA to exploit the fundo while studies are carried out concerning subdivision of the farm.

The workers in each farm entered into a contract with CORA to form a Sociedad Agrícola de Reforma Agraria (SARA). During an initial period, CORA, as owner of the land and water rights, provided these resources to the SARA. The campesinos contributed their labor. In addition, CORA agreed to provide the necessary agricultural inputs as well as the operating capital and technical assistance required to farm the land. The value of these inputs was to be returned to CORA at the end of the contract year. The SARA agreement assigned to CORA from 5 to 20 percent of the enterprise's income (*entradas*) with the obligation to reinvest it in the farm. The remainder of any surplus produced belonged to the campesinos for distribution as stipulated in the reglamento (bylaws) of the SARA. The reglamento provided for a management council (Consejo de Administración) composed of the five members of the campesino committee and two CORA functionaries (Asentamiento Director and Projects Director) to manage the internal administration of the enterprise.[27]

Theoretically, the consejo managed almost every aspect of asentamiento business. It prepared an annual work plan to be approved by the CORA zonal director and funded from CORA's Santiago headquarters. Each month it distributed wage advances (*anticipos*) to the workers against their shares of the surplus at the end of the year. In addition, the consejo paid wages, social security taxes, and family allowances corresponding to the asentados and hired wage labor.

Discipline within the asentamiento was also the concern of the consejo. Loss of privileges, fines, and in extreme cases, expulsion from the farm could be used to deal with those who didn't cooperate. Appeals in such an event would be heard by CORA's zonal director. The reglamento, valid for one year but subject to modification as needed by the consejo, also gave the consejo authority to act in "any areas unforeseen in this reglamento" (with the quorum of three campesino members and a CORA official). Importantly, however, the decision as to what type of production units would emerge from the asentamiento had been left open. This deferral was clearly a product of the struggle by the unions in Choapa.[28]

Despite the limited victory of the unions in Choapa in resisting total domination by CORA, however, the SARA arrangement was still highly paternalistic, leaving the campesinos subject to CORA's whims in many areas of farm management and internal policymaking. Where strong campesino organizations existed, pressure could be placed on CORA to restrain its not-always benevolent tutelage. But since the asentamiento originated in the struggle between the governmental policymakers and the Marxist labor unions, the extension of the asentamiento concept to other regions of Chile as the only transitional form of property in the Christian Democratic land reform did not in any way guarantee that campesinos in other zones could deal with CORA as militantly or as effectively as had the unions in Choapa. In fact, as the asentamiento was extended to other provinces, CORA, rather than the campesinos, became the dominant proprietary influence in the SARA.

Since the reglamento made clear that the land and water rights belonged to CORA (which "provides it for use by the Sociedad"), the campesinos remained landless until CORA assigned the property to them at the end of the tutelary period. Great variation existed from asentamiento to asentamiento in the quality and extent of campesino participation in farm management (and in obtaining expropriation in the first place).[29] In Choapa, for example, the existing unions retained de facto control over the campesino committees. In other asentamientos, the committee rarely met independently of the consejo, that is, without CORA participation. In small asentamientos the asamblea was confused in practice with the campesino committee and the entire membership met in the consejo de administración.[30]

Where previous campesino organizations were weak or nonexistent, the asentamiento became a tutelary institution extremely dependent on CORA. Production and investment decisions, and accounting and commercial transactions were all CORA-performed functions. Centralized in provincial or national headquarters, CORA failed to make explicit assignments of responsibility for individual asentamientos to particular functionaries. This failure tended to produce a pattern of collective irresponsibility as the CORA officials evaded determination of culpability for inadequate performance of the rural production units.

The workers had a new, if temporary, patrón. Insecure in regard to the length of the tutelary period, to their own status within the asentamiento, and to the type of proprietary arrangement ultimately to emerge, the asentados found that the asentamiento left much to be desired in providing incentives for intensive labor inputs. As might have been expected, some workers decided to maximize the time spent on their small land allotments and to minimize the time and effort spent in the larger enterprise. Given the uncertainty surrounding the eventual subdivision of the property—and if it should occur, which land parcel the individual campesino would occupy—such individualistic strategy was predictable. In other asentamientos, however, collective exploitation was more immediately successful. In such cases, prior union organization and strong campesino leadership seem to have played important roles.[31]

By mid-1967 the Christian Democratic government had expropriated almost 500 properties and established approximately 150 asentamientos. In almost all these asentamientos, tension existed concerning the type of proprietorship which would be established when the asentamiento period ended. Internal ambiguities were compounded by attacks from the political Right, which appealed to the undeniable desire of many campesinos for a private holding free from CORA's tutelage. The rightists accused the governmental program of obvious Marxist-inspiration and suggested that the program sought to create collective farms all over Chile. The Marxist parties, on the other hand, attacked the asentamiento as a paternalistic device through which the government sought to create a large clientele in the countryside and gain the votes of rural labor.

Mobilization of Rural Labor

A final and most important aspect of the period 1964-1967 in the countryside was the massive mobilization of rural labor by governmental agencies and by Marxist (FCI) and Catholic (UCC, ANOC, and MCI) labor organizations.[32] The multi-pronged attack on the hacienda system produced not only the largest number of legal and illegal rural labor conflicts in Chilean history, but it also left the institutional channels for handling the conflicts overwhelmed. Labor Department personnel were soon unable to communicate properly even the existence of labor disputes to Santiago headquarters as required.[33]

Rural proprietors found the massiveness of the rural labor mobilization even more disturbing because governmental personnel as well as the labor organizers from campesino unions commonly employed illegal labor petitions, illegal strikes, and illegal land occupations to press their demands.[34] Legal petitions were employed where possible, but Law 8.811, by prohibiting rural unions from operating on more than one farm, from presenting labor petitions during the harvest, and from striking, precluded an activist, legal rural labor movement. At the same time that campesinos organized legal farm unions, illegal commune-wide and even regional federations also appeared.[35] The organizations presented commune-wide labor petitions representing workers on various farms in a commune, and strikes occurred in up to seventy farms at a time. In many cases, governmental personnel from the agrarian bureaucracies (especially INDAP and to a lesser extent CORA) supported the labor conflicts and even assisted in the preparation of labor petitions.

CORA and INDAP personnel also smothered the Labor Department with complaints concerning landowner noncompliance with labor law.[36] INDAP personnel "acted in anticipation of the norms of the rural unionization law" to form illegal unions. Frequent appearances by INDAP organizers (*promotores*) at Labor Department offices in representation of campesino groups brought a ruling from the Labor Department: "The functionaries . . . of the Instituto de Desarrollo Agropecuario . . . do not have the legal right to intervene in the presentation of labor petitions and in the process of negotiation of labor conflicts in the agricultural sector."[37] In response, INDAP personnel received instructions to act only "informally" when stimulating or supporting labor petitions.[38]

The wave of labor conflicts continued. Pressure on the landowners from the campesinos and the government increased.[39] In defense of their proprietary authority, landowners could only invoke the law and hope that the government—no longer under their control and barely subject to their veto—would enforce it.[40] Consistent with the ambiguity which characterized the Christian Democrats in this area, the government sometimes did, and sometimes did not, enforce the law. In some farms police squelched illegal strikes and the government ordered the workers to resume their labors.[41] In other cases, however, the government used the existence of labor conflicts as a pretext to place a governmental representative (*interventor*) in the farm and begin

TABLE 9   LABOR PETITIONS AND STRIKES IN THE COUNTRYSIDE, 1963-1966

Year	Labor Petitions	Strikes
1963	33	13
1964	49	45
1965	646[a]	155
1966	752[a]	457[b]

SOURCE: Brian Loveman, *Antecedentes para el estudio del movimiento campesino chileno: Pliegos de peticiones, huelgas y sindicatos agrícolas, 1932-1966* (Santiago: ICIRA, 1971).

[a] The figures on labor petitions were arrived at by combining the petitions reported by Almino Affonso et al., *Movimiento campesino chileno* (Santiago: ICIRA, 1970) with those I substantiated in the Labor Department Archive and which the above authors had not reported. The inability of the Labor Department to process the large amount of information on conflicts during this period means that both the data reported by Affonso et al. and that reported here are subject to error in the form of (1) missing data and (2) repetition when conflicts in the same farm are reported for different dates but in reality represent only one labor conflict. This problem is further complicated because it was not uncommon for a settlement to be reached in a farm followed shortly thereafter by a second (or more) labor petition—thus a "new" labor conflict.

[b] Affonso et al. report 586 strikes for this year by counting each farm involved as one strike. I have reported strikes involving more than one farm as only one strike.

organizing the campesinos for expropriation of the property. While the government sought to reassure the landowners that only inefficient farms would be expropriated, and also to provide improved prices for agricultural commodities in order to stimulate agricultural production, the Christian Democrats could not control the demands of even the Catholic labor organizations.

In this context the Congress finally acted on the Christian Democratic legislation on rural unions and land reform. After almost three years of land reform through improvisation, the Congress adopted a formalized redefinition of rural proprietorship. The first of these laws (Law 16.625) replaced the restrictive unionization provisions of Law 8.811 with a new concept in rural unions.

Law 16.625: The Legal Framework

In late April 1967, the obstacles to rural unionization contained in Law 8.811 disappeared with passage by Congress of Law 16.625.[42] This new union legislation guaranteed the right of all rural workers, including those employed by governmental agencies, to join unions. These unions, except in special cases, "must be formed by a minimum of 100 persons who work either in the same or separate farms, enterprises or properties" (Article 1).[43] In turn, unions could form federations and confederations. The law established the commune as the territorial base for rural unions. Within the commune, union committees on each organized farm formed the base organization of the union structure. The reglamento designated the province as the territorial base for federations of communal unions, whereas national associations which integrated provincial federations formed confederations (Reg., Article 2).[44]

Unions acquired legal personality by registering the act of constitution and internal bylaws with the Labor Department office of jurisdiction. The law required the presence of a Labor Department official or other impartial third party (*ministro de fé*)—any one of various governmental officials—at the act of constitution (Article 4). These provisions entirely eliminated the bureaucratic delays involved in obtaining legal personality and the possibility that Labor Department orders could prevent unionization, as had occurred in 1933 and from 1939 to 1946.

Within a commune any number of rural unions could be formed, and workers in a single farm could belong to different unions. The law supported the campesinos' right to drop membership in one union and join another or to belong to no union at all. In each farm, the settlement reached by the employer with the "most representative" union applied to all the workers in that farm. These provisions, along with those for financing the unions, created the conditions for competition for membership among unions. Marxist labor organizers criticized the law for allowing multiple unions (*paralelismo*), arguing that this provision constituted a serious threat to the solidarity of the working class.

Law 16.625 also insured a basic financial solvency for the newly founded unions. Requirements that every rural worker contribute 2 percent of his or her taxable income to either (1) a union designated by the worker or (2) the Fondo de Educación y Extensión Sindical of the Labor Department guaranteed obligatory worker support of unions—whether or not the workers actually became members. In addition, the law obligated rural proprietors to pay an additional 2 percent of the taxable wage of each worker to the local Labor Department office. The Fondo de Educación y Extensión Sindical received half of this tax revenue, the other 50 percent going on a proportional basis, according to registered membership, to the union federations and confederations. Article 4 of the law stipulated further that employers could be required by the unions to deduct union dues from the workers' wages,[45] providing the unions with a base income and allowing the establishment of provincial and national union bureaucracies.[46]

The law also provided important protection to rural workers in the organization of unions. Candidates for union offices, including those of federations and confederations, received immunity from dismissal (*inamovilidad*) by employers from the time of their nomination to the day of the election (not to exceed two months). Elected union officers acquired permanent immunity from dismissal, which lasted for six months after leaving union office. Five workers in each union, plus two for every one hundred members, could legally enjoy immunity. In addition, all members of unions-in-formation were extended immunity until the union received notification of its legal constitution

(Article 8). Every farm where a union had at least five members elected a farm delegate (*delegado*), who also received protection from dismissal.

For those rural proprietors who employed more than ten workers, the law imposed the obligation to provide a permanent locale for union meetings and an office for the union officers. The reglamento specified minimum standards for these facilities to insure that landowners did not offer the workers an abandoned chicken coop (Article 41). In farms with more than 150 level hectares and twenty-five workers the law further required the landowner to make available a minimum of 1½ hectares for a sports field.

By providing that "any person can visit the workers in their houses or in the union locale without permission from the proprietor," Law 16.625 ended the authority of rural proprietors to regulate entry and exit into their properties. The "privateness" of private property deteriorated accordingly.[47]

Section III of Law 16.625 introduced a new system for managing rural labor conflicts. Conciliation remained mandatory after workers presented labor petitions to the individual rural proprietors. But the petitions could now be presented by zone, province, or even nationally. If conciliation failed and the parties did not agree on arbitration, the workers could legally strike.[48] During a legal strike the law prohibited the proprietor from removing farm animals, machinery, or other products, with the exception of perishables.[49] In some types of conflicts the government could by decree extend the settlements reached to determined zones or to the entire country (Article 130).

Development of regional and national rural labor organizations made processing of conflicts by individual employers a difficult problem. In order to solve the problem, Law 16.625 provided for the establishment of employers' unions,[50] which could be formed with a minimum of ten rural proprietors who employed agricultural workers. Article 103 of the reglamento required that a payment of 1 percent of the taxable income of agricultural workers in each property be paid to the corresponding employers' unions.

The employers' unions took on the specific task of representing rural proprietors in negotiations with campesino organizations. Once nationally organized, the employers' unions shifted the burden of assisting landowners in labor conflicts from the SNA to specific syndical organizations. Although the unions did not eliminate the SNA as a voice of the landowners, they did coordinate landowner action in labor conflicts at the local level in a manner previously unknown. As Sergio Gómez points out:

> Law 16.625 . . . created and gave expression to a union movement among rural proprietors previously nonexistent at the local level. Until then, the SNA and other less important institutions like the Southern Agricultural Society (CAS) included relatively few members. While they effectively represented the interests of large landowners at the national level and in the parliament, there did not exist coordinated local action.[51]

In this regard Law 16.625 provided impetus for a nation-wide intensification of relationships among previously loosely organized rural proprietors in order to defend their collective interest vis-à-vis rural labor. Instead of limited-membership, quasi-aristocratic associations like the old "Liga Agraria" or local chapters of the SNA, which protected large landowners, employers' unions served to articulate the interests and represent a heterogeneous mix of rural proprietors. The unionization law created the legal conditions for a united employer class, linked together in local employers' unions, regional federations, and a national confederation.

Law 16.625: Implementation

Rural labor organizations took little time to comply massively with Law 16.625 by organizing legal communal unions and presenting legal labor petitions. For example, only one day after the law appeared in the Diario Oficial, campesinos in Melipilla presented a mimeographed labor petition, signed by the workers in thirty-four farms, to the respective rural proprietors.[52]

Labor Department officials still had no instructions on how to handle commune-wide petitions. In Melipilla the departmental inspector wrote to headquarters: "Could you please send instructions concerning the procedure to follow in this type of petition."[53] Not until May 24, 1967, did Labor Department personnel receive instructions:

> Until the Reglamento for Law 16.625 is available, regional and provincial labor petitions will continue to be accepted. Inspectors should

receive the petitions presented by the workers and in cooperation with Intendentes and Gobernadores attempt to establish the appropriate conciliatory machinery in accord with Article 26 of the law. . . .[54]

Labor Department confusion on the appropriate implementation of the law gave rise to a series of interpretive memoranda during 1967.[55] Without the required administrative reglamento, the department had no guidelines to follow in constituting the unions. April 29, 1967, the day the law went into effect, the Labor Department instructed personnel to delay forming unions until the reglamento appeared.[56] The department reiterated these instructions on June 1, 1967, ordering labor inspectors to return any documents concerning constitution of unions presented to them.[57]

In the meantime, efforts by INDAP, FCI, ANOC, UCC, and other, smaller labor organizations to organize unions in compliance with the law created a problem for department personnel unable to cooperate in constituting unions. In early June 1967 the director of the Labor Department, Guillermo Videla Vial, informed the Minister of Labor of the bottleneck in the following terms:

> At this time the Service under my direction faces a grave problem. One month and a half after promulgation of the law we cannot apply it for lack of the Reglamento. This has caused serious criticisms and complaints about the Department which compromise its image. . . .
> For this reason I request that the definitive Reglamento be written and processed as quickly as possible.[58]

Under this pressure the Department finally began to apply the law without the reglamento. On June 17, 1967, the department instructed personnel, "from this date Law 16.625 will be applied. The dispositions of Article 9 will be applied and you will receive Acts of Constitution and By-Laws. Observations [requiring revision] on the bylaws will be made after the Reglamento is available."[59]

From 1967 to 1970 the unions expanded in number and in membership. By June 1970, 488 unions existed with a combined membership of 127,688 members.[60] The unions, most of which were grouped in three national confederations,[61] persistently pressured rural proprietors for better wages, improved regalías, and, ultimately, expropriation of land. Soon after passage of Law 16.625, Labor Department functionaries

TABLE 10 RURAL UNIONS AND UNION MEMBERSHIP, DECEMBER 1967

Province	Campesino Unions	Number of Federations*	Number of Members	Employers' Unions	Number of Members
Atacama	4	--	418	--	--
Coquimbo	14	1 (10)	3,409	2	50
Aconcagua	14	1 (10)	1,940	4	92
Valparaíso	8	--	1,587	4	53
Santiago	36	3 (23)	5,403	9	169
O'Higgins	23	3 (22)	5,100	12	194
Colchagua	16	1 (4)	2,996	9	154
Curicó	15	2 (8)	3,859	5	69
Talca	19	1 (8)	7,755	7	109
Maule	2	--	452	1	29
Linares	17	1 (5)	2,622	1	34
Ñuble	20	1 (5)	3,436	2	52
Concepción	9	2 (6)	1,223	5	89

Arauco	--	--	--	1	23
Bío Bío	9	--	2,006	7	93
Malleco	5	--	1,202	4	80
Cautín	13	1 (10)	1,697	9	149
Valdivia	22	3 (18)	3,025	6	163
Osorno	7	1 (7)	1,134	5	85
Llanquihue	9	--	1,148	7	398
Total	262	21 (136)	50,309	100	2,005

SOURCE: Oficio 2833, 2 mayo 1968.

*( ) indicates number of unions affiliated with Federations.

began to make inspection visits at the request (and in the company) of campesino leaders. Union leaders assisted in the preparation of inspection programs. The department processed literally thousands of campesino complaints against individual proprietors.

The Christian Democratic government sought to maintain a semblance of order by more frequently using police against campesino movements that exceeded legal norms.[62] Campesinos increasingly employed land occupations (*tomas*) as a tactical instrument in labor disputes. Marxist parties, seeking to exploit the conflict within the governmental party over how much "Revolution" and how much "Liberty" (Law) should characterize the rural program, used the rural labor movement to focus on the contradictions of the Christian Democratic program. The emergence of the Movimiento de Izquierda Revolucionario (MIR) as a significant force in the countryside placed even the relatively conservative tactics of the Communists and Socialists into question.

The extent of the mobilization of the campesinos originally induced by the government exceeded in magnitude and intensity the government's ability to control it. The government rejected systematic repression; yet it also refused to allow illegality to become the institutionalized pattern of agrarian reform. The campesino movement magnified the internal contradictions within the governmental party and left the original dilemma— how to carry out a revolution within a viable legal order—more pronounced.[63]

Another dilemma, the type of agricultural units that the agrarian reform should establish in Chile, further exacerbated the internal divisions within the governmental party after passage of the land reform law in 1967. Combined with increasing campesino pressure, the pace and quality of the implementation of land redistribution also became difficult problems for a government committed to Revolution in Liberty.

Law 16.640: The Legal Framework

After almost two years of discussion, debate, and revision, the Chilean Congress produced a lengthy and complex agrarian reform law.[64] Shortly thereafter, ICIRA published a volume of over 300 pages explaining the law's provisions.[65] Whereas a complete review of the law is impossible in the present context, a brief overview follows, with emphasis on the redefinition of rural proprietorship. The law first stipulated:

A property will be considered "poorly exploited" [thus subject to expropriation] if the proprietor has committed any of the following violations more than twice during the last two years before expropriation:

Appropriation of family allowances, dismissal of workers without just cause as specified in Law 16.455, nonpayment of salaries or regalías owed to workers or nonpayment of social security taxes. . . .

The burden of demonstrating compliance with these provisions rests with the proprietor. (Article 1)

Thus the law embodied the principle that no right to property exists where the proprietor does not comply with existing labor legislation and norms of justice in dealing with rural labor.

Land Subject to Expropriation

Law 16.640 declared the following types of properties to be of "public utility" and subject to total or partial expropriation:

(1) All privately held farms that exceed 80 basic hectares of irrigated land (80 BIH) with the land held by married persons considered as a single unit.[66]

(2) Abandoned and poorly exploited land (not to be applied in the case of properties less than 80 BIH for three years).

(3) Properties resulting from the subdivision of farms larger than 80 BIH since November 4, 1964, unless physical subdivision has taken place and the land is worked personally by the owner. Proof of compliance corresponds to the owner. (Farms could *only* be expropriated under this clause during the first three years following passage of the law.)

(4) Corporate and government farms, except those of campesino cooperatives and CORA.[67]

(5) Rented farms, land given in sharecrop or land otherwise not directly exploited by its owner if the legislation regulating such arrangements is violated.

(6) Commonly held properties not meeting the stipulations of the law.

(7) Properties in the zone of application of the Law of Southern Property [under specified circumstances]. (Article 9)

(8) Properties necessary for the agrarian reform program offered by their owners to CORA.

(9) Minifundios, for the sole purpose of consolidation and reassignment (with preference to ex-proprietors).

(10) Properties located in a zone where the state undertakes public works to rehabilitate the land for agricultural production.

(11) Properties in an area where the state plans irrigation projects or areas designated "irrigation zones."

Privately held properties of less than 80 BIH remained legally unexpropriable unless classified as "abandoned" or "poorly exploited" (after three years) or if they were in an irrigation zone. Legally, the right to maintain minifundio also disappeared if the government chose to apply this section of the law. The law also removed the legal basis for private corporate farms.

It should be noted, however, that expropriability did not apply to agricultural machinery, livestock, tools, or other movables. Also, the expropriation clause lacked the mandatory "shall be expropriated." The law established categories of expropriable land. The decision to carry out expropriation remained discretionary.

The Right to "Reserve"

Expropriated proprietors, with the exception of those expropriated under the "abandoned" or "poorly exploited" clause, retained a right to 80 hectares (BIH). The right could be extended under very special circumstances to 320 hectares (BIH), but in practice this never occurred. To exercise the right, the law required the proprietor to petition CORA in writing within thirty days of notification of expropriation. Unless the proprietor rented or otherwise allowed indirect exploitation of the farm, the law allowed him to choose the land to compose the "reserve," qualified by the provision that the shape, location, and quality of the reserve did not impede rational exploitation of the expropriated land and water supply. The law also declared that the reserve should include the proprietor's house and that the proprietor be given preference in locating farm buildings and installations in the reserve. This provision created great difficulties in the expropriated farms and caused CORA to make large initial investments in farm infrastructure.

Expropriation and Compensation

The law stipulated that the authority to expropriate any particular property resided in CORA's consejo. The decision to expropriate, thus, was administrative.[68] If proprietors objected to the expropriation, or questioned its legality or the clause under which CORA acted, provincial agrarian tribunals heard appeals.

The law required CORA to pay the owner the tax-assessed value of the property (not the commercial value), plus the value of improvements not included in the last assessment. All improvements made since November 4, 1964, had to be paid for in cash (as per value assessed by CORA). If the proprietor objected to CORA's assessment, appeals could be taken to the appropriate agrarian tribunal. Compensation combined a down payment of from 1 to 10 percent (depending upon the reason for expropriation) and the remainder in bonds amortized in twenty-five to thirty years (Articles 42-55).

From the time that CORA's consejo decided to expropriate a farm, CORA had a full year to deposit the down payment with the departmental court (Juez de Letras de Mayor Cuantía del Departamento). If CORA failed to fulfill this obligation, the proprietor could petition the court to cancel the expropriation and the inscription of the property in title to CORA. CORA could not again expropriate the property for the same reason for three years. Prior to depositing the down payment and registering the property in its name, CORA could not take material possession of the property. In practice, a shortage of personnel and funds delayed "taking of possession" of many farms for almost a year, although delaying payment of a fixed cost in the Chilean case (inflation of 25 percent per year and up) did not produce a totally negative result for CORA.

The Agrarian Tribunals (Articles 136-138)

The drafters of Law 16.640 made an effort to limit the legal conflicts over expropriation and compensation to the newly created agrarian tribunals. The law provided for one tribunal in each province and ten agrarian tribunals of appeal. These tribunals exercised exclusive jurisdiction in agrarian reform cases and their verdicts were final. Since legal procedural delays before these tribunals made landowner victories possible, CORA tended to favor grounds of expropriation not subject to appeal (for example, excess size and voluntary transfers).

The agrarian tribunals conformed to the Christian Democratic commitment to an orderly, legal reform. To leftist critics of the government the tribunals were simply another example of the governments's lack of commitment to the "real" revolution which wouldn't allow the existing legal order to interfere in a rapid, massive, and complete elimination of privately held agricultural properties larger than a family farm. To the landowners, the agrarian tribunals represented an important legal channel for slowing down or stopping governmental expropriations.

New Types of Rural Property

"Upon taking possession of the expropriated property, CORA shall install a campesino asentamiento" (Article 66). The law established a three-year minimum for the period of asentamiento, extendable to five years in special cases. As a general rule, the law provided that at the end of this transitional period the land would be subdivided and assigned to individual campesinos (Article 67). But it also provided that when, in the judgment of CORA, individual parcels were not desirable, CORA could assign the land in communitarian properties. For legal purposes communitarian properties included those "that belong in common to all those who work it, or a cooperative formed by these, constituting a human and economic community. Each member contributes with his personal work to the common labor and participates in the product obtained in relation to the nature and amount of labor he realizes" (Article 1). The law specifically listed campesino cooperatives, agrarian reform cooperatives, communal properties (*co-propiedad a campesinos*), and mixed communitarian (co-propiedad of a campesino cooperative or an agrarian reform cooperative) as acceptable communitarian properties. The law authorized CORA to assign property in communitarian form in several cases, including (1) when technical necessities indicated it and (2) when the asentados requested it. The law also allowed mixed assignments of land, which combined individual parcels with communal property and membership in a cooperative. It is important to reiterate, however, that the law required that preference be given to assignment of land in private parcels to individual campesinos.

On receiving possession of the land the new proprietor remained obligated to (1) pay for the land, (2) work the land personally, (3) live in a place compatible with personal exploitation of the land, and (4) belong to an agrarian reform cooperative, if CORA so determined (Article 75). Unlike other proprietors, the land reform beneficiary could not (1) alienate the land or the rights assigned in co-propiedad without authorization of CORA, (2) subdivide the land, (3) rent the land or provide it in any fashion for indirect exploitation without the authorization of CORA and the agrarian reform cooperative, and (4) mortgage the land. These prohibitions, with the exception of subdivision, lasted only until the land was paid for (Articles 76 and 77). The law sought to stimulate agricultural cooperatives and other forms of communitarian property even when individual campesinos received the land.[69]

An Overlooked Provision of Law 16.640

Article 171 of the land reform law specified that in cases of lock-outs or illegal strikes in rural properties, the president of the republic could order the workers back to work by decree. A governmental official (*interventor*), assisted by police if necessary, could then take over management of the farm until the conflict could be settled. Any illegal strike in a rural property was cause for such intervention under the terms of Article 171. The provision became particularly significant after 1970, when the Allende government assigned "interventores" in hundreds of farms in response to workers' strikes—not to deal with the strikes but as a means to gradually divest proprietors of their rural properties. As written, Article 171 provided the basis either for governmental repression of the labor movement or for worker-pressured governmental take-overs of private properties. As eventually employed, it provided a quasilegal alternative to expropriation according to the generic provisions of Law 16.640, of which it formed a part (see chapter 9).

Law 16.640: Implementation

By July 14, 1970, CORA organized 910 asentamientos on 1,319 expropriated properties.[70] Table 11 illustrates the legal causes of expropriation most frequently invoked by CORA. After the publication of Reglamento 281 of May 15, 1968, which set up a point system for judging the efficiency of exploitation of rural properties, expropriations of "poorly exploited" farms gradually increased.[71] Prior to this time CORA relied heavily on voluntary transfers and excess-size expropriations. The ability to apply the "poorly exploited" or "abandoned" clause reduced the initial cash outlay by CORA from 10 percent of assessed value to 5 or 1 percent. The less money invested in downpayments, the more land could be acquired. Table 12 shows the cumulative process of expropriation from 1965 to July 14, 1970.

By July 1970, CORA had expropriated approximately 18 percent of the country's irrigated land and 12 percent of the nonirrigated agricultural land. Until August 1, 1970, CORA made 98 definitive land assignments to the benefit of 5,668 families. Another 23,471 campesino families still remained in legally constituted asentamientos.[72] Ninety percent of these land assignments were made to communitarian enterprises. In practice, CORA "found it technically necessary to stimulate communitarian assignments of land."[73] In this regard, CORA overtly defied the legislative intent of Law 16.640 as defined by its framers. CORA imposed the communitarian solution as a technical necessity in a clear victory for the leftist sectors of the governmental party. CORA justified this development, stating as follows:

> Cooperative tenancy . . . permits a much greater flexibility and adaptability than a traditional, rigid, individual system in which personal interest takes priority over that of the community.
>
> This system of land tenure greatly facilitates the creation of regional production cooperatives and commercialization, so useful and necessary in Chile.
>
> Other reasons which support this decision are that the cooperative system allows great economy in the management of machinery, water, pastures, and, generally, the indirectly productive infrastructure like warehouses, silos, corrals, etc.
>
> . . . The exploitation of a property in cooperative tenancy signifies that the campesino community that owns the property freely decides by the common accord of its members the form in which the land is exploited, deciding that each campesino works individual parcels or exploiting sections in common.[74]

Asentamiento Proprietorship and the Agrarian Reform Cooperatives

Economic performance of the asentamientos varied greatly.[75] So too did the relationship between CORA and individual asentamientos. In many cases, CORA failed both to provide necessary technical assistance and to adequately prepare the campesinos to carry out functions of management, accounting, and

TABLE 11   LEGAL CAUSE FOR EXPROPRIATIONS EFFECTED,
            1965-JULY 14, 1970

	Number	Percentage
Abandoned or poorly exploited	604	45.7
Voluntary transfers	392	29.8
Excess size	171	13.0
Corporate farms	41	3.1
Properties of 80 BIH resulting from division of larger properties from November 21, 1965 to July 26, 1967	88	6.7
Properties resulting from the division of properties larger than 80 BIH after November 4, 1964 whose material subdivision did not effectively take place	23	1.7
Total	1319	100.0

SOURCE: CORA, *Reforma agraria chilena, 1965-1970* (Santiago: CORA, 1970), p. 38.

TABLE 12   EXPROPRIATIONS, 1965-JULY 14, 1970

Year	Number of Properties[a]	Area in Hectares		Total
		Irrigated	Unirrigated	
1965	99	41,260.1	499,923.0	541,183.1
1966	265	57,877.4	468,326.0	526,203.4
1967 (Law 15.020)	131	20,141.8	115,155.4	136,297.2
1967 (Law 16.640)	86	30,443.1	119,285.4	149,728.5
1968	223	44,681.1	612,566.3	657,247.4
1969	314	54,478.8	807,361.8	861,840.6
1970 (to July 14)	201	30,986.6	604,181.5	635,168.1[b]
Total	1,319	279,868.9	3,128,919.4	3,408,788.3

SOURCE: CORA, *Reforma agraria chilena, 1965-1970* (Santiago: CORA, 1970), p. 36.

[a]Some asentamientos are formed by combining two or more properties.

[b]Error in original reads 535,163.1

commercialization on the farm.[76] In other asentamientos, however, campesinos, determined to run their own affairs, literally prohibited unwanted CORA officials from entering into their enterprises.

General agreement exists that the members of the asentamientos increased their real wages from two to ten times.[77] Gross production on the asentamientos also increased.[78] But full membership rights (and eventual assignment of land) were limited to heads of households and in some cases to ex-inquilinos. This limitation meant that within the asentamiento proprietorship was unequally distributed among the residents from the outset. The tendency to employ wage labor rather than to add new members to the asentamiento group intensified the emerging restratification of the rural labor force within the farms. As the farms became more mechanized, these wage hands, lacking full membership rights in the asentamiento, suffered from unemployment.[79]

By 1970, rather systematic critiques of the asentamiento system and the resulting agrarian reform cooperatives existed. The political Right insisted that the asentados

> did not become proprietors of land since they could not freely manage it. . . . it was prohibited to rent the land and to mortgage it. They had to exploit it in accord with the plans of the Minister of Agriculture and CORA, having little initiative in deciding what crops were most convenient to cultivate. And most surprising, abusive and absurd, any problem that occurred had to be submitted for arbitration by CORA, without possibility of appeal. In addition, those assigned land had to put up with the inspection visits of CORA functionaries.
>
> All these limitations and impositions violated and altered substantially the definition of property [dominio] in Article 582 of the Civil Code . . . "the real right in a corporal entity to enjoy and dispose of it arbitrarily."
>
> How can you enjoy and dispose of a thing submitted to so many limitations and prohibitions?[80]

For those insisting on a traditional, extensive concept of property in rural land, the land reform beneficiaries were not proprietors but rather "inquilinos of the State."[81] To other critics, however, the asentados represented a new privileged class in the countryside which acted as a brake on the campesino movement:[82]

> The organization of asentamientos has been realized property by property, in most cases respecting the boundaries of the expropriated property. This has prevented regional planning for homogeneous or interdependent zones. . . .
>
> This policy has meant that the inquilinos of the expropriated properties benefitted, almost exclusively, by receiving land and capital, while the smallholders, minifundistas, and wage workers were excluded.[83]

For these critics, the asentamiento damaged the utopian vision of a classless society with no privileged propertied class in the countryside. In addition, the asentamiento maintained many of the aspects of the traditional enterprise, for example, the regalías of the individual workers. By "maintaining an individualistic spirit and economic stratification among the asentados," the organization of "truly" communitarian enterprises was hindered.[84]

Both the conservative and the leftist critics agreed that "[CORA] makes the fundamental decisions in reference to planning, investment, credit, commercialization, inputs, etc. . . . campesino participation is quite limited. . . . CORA impedes the campesinos from acquiring knowledge of the market and of financial and commercial institutions."[85] The administrative paternalism of CORA dominated the asentamiento system.

Campesino Cooperatives in the Nonreformed Sector

INDAP accompanied CORA's land reform with a program destined to alter the situation of campesino proprietors (smallholders, sharecroppers, minifundistas). INDAP defined its goals in this area as (1) promotion of a campesino movement as an instrument through which campesinos could participate in a new social and economic structure, (2) creation of a modern, noncapitalist campesino economy, and (3) promotion of a change in the traditional social and cultural values among the campesinos.[86] To stimulate a modern, noncapitalist campesino economy, INDAP promoted the organization of campesino cooperatives, committees, and pre-cooperatives as well as communitarian enterprises (essentially limited partnerships subsidized by INDAP). In order to induce the creation of these organizations, INDAP channeled agricultural credit, consumer goods, and technical assistance through campesino organizations. In practice, this meant that the campesinos had to belong to some type of INDAP organization in order to receive assistance. Many cooperatives and committees, thus, had little organizational life except as a conduit for INDAP or other governmental agencies' inputs. Nevertheless, the creation of campesino cooperatives greatly expanded the contacts among campesino proprietors in various regions and, eventually, through federations of cooperatives, province-wide. The growth of the cooperative movement in the campesino sector is illustrated in Table 13.

The cooperatives, along with the campesino committees, received INDAP credits and agricultural inputs in addition to political-organizational orientation in INDAP extension centers (Centrales de Capacitación). *Quiubo Compadre*, INDAP's house journal, carried INDAP's message to thousands of campesinos. Most of the cooperatives provided consumer goods, commercialization services, and credit to members. The "empresa comunitaria," cooperative management and land tenure, occurred only rarely. And most campesino cooperatives, unsuccessful as business enterprises, depended heavily on INDAP subsidies and services. Without these, few cooperatives would have been established, and fewer still maintained.[87] Since the loss of state support meant the probable demise of the vast majority of these cooperatives, they remained fragile organizations.

By 1970, however, approximately 100,000 smallholders and resident laborers had been organized into cooperatives, precooperatives, and campesino committees. A structure of regional marketing and processing cooperatives began to emerge.[88] INDAP's promotional work left the campesinos highly organized for political action in the interests of the small proprietor. Less success accrued to INDAP's efforts to establish a "modern, noncapitalist campesino economy." The nonreformed campesino economy remained individualistic, with the rare exceptions of scattered communitarian enterprises specializing in hog or chicken production.[89]

Rural Proprietorship in 1970: An Overview

In 1970 the countryside still contained 3,000 to 4,000 private farms over 80 hectares (BIH). The minifundios and comunidades remained untouched. Some 1,300 expropriated properties passed into the hands of campesino "land reform beneficiaries" to be exploited as asentamientos during a three- to five-year transitional period and then to be converted into agrarian

TABLE 13   CAMPESINO COOPERATIVES WITH LEGAL PERSONALITY, 1965-1970

Year	Number	Members	Federations	Cooperatives Affiliated	Confederations	Federations Affiliated
1964	24	1,718				
1965	43	3,204				
1966	84	7,802				
1967	123	11,452				
1968	171	18,456				
1969	222	30,034	7	51		
1970[a]	250	37,675	9[b]	81	1	9

SOURCE: INDAP, 1964/1970, n.p.

[a]To October 22.

[b]Does not include five federations in formation which would include 45 affiliated cooperatives.

reform cooperatives. In the nonreformed campesino economy, the smallholders (*pequeños propietarios*) continued, for the most part, to work their farms individually, although a system of cooperatives linked over 50,000 of these campesinos together to provide a variety of inputs and services. The Christian Democratic program had created a variety of new interest groups in the countryside by establishing new forms of rural property.

The Christian Democratic experience not only altered the legal attributes of proprietorship but also seriously modified the distribution of rural proprietary authority in Chile. Almost 20 percent of the country's irrigated land passed from the control of individual proprietors to that of newly instituted communitarian proprietorships. Within the private farm sector, many decisions previously within the exclusive sphere of the landowner now required the participation of rural unions. The state also acquired large proprietary responsibilities in the rural sector. CORA claimed that the role of the state was temporary; however, many elements in the agrarian bureaucracy, and the leftist critics of the Christian Democrats, desired to enlarge the proprietary role of the state and completely eliminate the private commercial farm sector.

After six years of drastic change in the countryside, the mix of rural proprietorship was extensive. The situation remained elastic as national presidential elections approached. All Chileans knew that the transformation of the countryside had not been completed. The direction of future alterations hinged on the outcome of the upcoming presidential contest of 1970. Rafael Moreno, CORA director during the Christian Democratic years, proclaimed that because of the Christian Democratic reforms "the road is open." Open to what, Moreno did not make clear, but the high degree of campesino involvement in class organizations meant that the incoming regime would have much less flexibility in imposing solutions on the rural labor force than did the Christian Democrats.

In a bitterly contested election, the Marxist candidate gained a narrow victory. The Christian Democrats soon found that the road was open much further than they had suspected. In the rural sector, the new government moved rapidly to redefine and redistribute property in rural land.

9

Unidad Popular
in the Countryside

We did what the Comrade Campesinos asked us to do. The only way to accelerate the process of Agrarian Reform is to pressure CORA by "occupying" the Fundo.

MIR spokesman, 1971

CORA will not accept pressure for expropriation through illegal land occupations on the part of the workers.

CORA spokesman, 1971

The Chilean situation is not being decided in the parliament nor in the capital; it will not be resolved with more speeches or less speeches, nor with constitutional accusations or televised polemics. [The issues] will be defined in the direct social confrontation that is occurring between the dispossessed and the displacing classes. Chonchol has understood this and he is acting quickly and audaciously, delivering destructive blows against the landowner oligarchy.

Clarín editorial, 1971

The confirmation of Salvador Allende as president of Chile triggered a wave of panic in the private sector of the Chilean economy.[1] Some Chileans sold all they owned and left the country to flee "communism." In the short run the black-market money exchange devalued the Chilean *escudo* from 300 to 500 percent. Pledged to eliminate the hacienda system, nationalize foreign mining interests, and expropriate Chile's largest industrial and commercial enterprises, Allende symbolized the end of the existing system of property and the political regime for which it provided the foundation. Rafael Moreno had declared that "the road is open." Allende announced that the road led to the establishment of a socialist society to replace the existing formal democracy and exploitative capitalist economy. During the first two years of the Allende government, political conflict focused on the preliminary redefinition and redistribution of property in the transition to socialism.

In the countryside the Allende government committed itself preferentially to the final destruction of the hacienda system.[2] This meant, in the first instance, expropriation of all rural properties larger than 80 hectares (BIH). Allende appointed Jacques Chonchol, the ousted director of INDAP in the Frei government, minister of agriculture. Chonchol proceeded immediately to carry out his earlier recommendations for a "massive, rapid and drastic" agrarian reform. In Allende's first year of government CORA expropriated almost as many properties as had the Christian Democrats in six years (over 1300). Chonchol promised to expropriate all farms over 80 hectares (BIH) before the end of 1972. The government had essentially fulfilled this promise by mid-1972, by adding some 3000 farms to those expropriated by the Christian Democrats.

Despite intensification of the land reform process, unresolved issues plagued the Unidad Popular (Popular Unity) government as they had the Christian Democrats. Allende, like Frei, proclaimed his intentions to operate within the law and the constitution until the existing "bourgeois institutions" could be legally replaced with a peoples' assembly (*asamblea del pueblo*) and peoples' courts. Lacking control over the armed forces, which seemingly decided to forego intervention in politics unless Allende exceeded constitutional norms, Allende's tactics corresponded to a realistic interpretation of the limits of his power given the existing balance of forces at the national level. The Popular Unity coalition controlled the presidency and the several thousand administrative appointments which Chilean presidents could make to the policymaking positions of the national bureaucracies. The Congress remained in control of the opposition parties. The court system and the controlaría remained effective constraints on mobilizational politics so long as the governmental coalition lacked the strength to overtly defy its commitment to legality.

Elements within the governmental coalition (especially left-Socialists and MAPU) and the Movimiento de Izquierda Revolucionaria (MIR) rejected the coalition's commitment to operate within the framework of existing legal norms.[3] The leftist critics argued that existing laws and institutions served only to retard the transition to socialism and to protect monopoly capitalists, landowners, and the agrarian bourgeoisie. In the countryside these groups resorted to land occupations, illegal strikes, and confrontations between campesinos and landowners.[4] In the harvest which followed Allende's inauguration (November 1970 to March 1971) the most dramatic confrontations took place in the province of Cautín, where MIR's rural section, Movimiento Campesino Revolucionario (MCR), supported numerous efforts by Indian campesinos to recover ancestral lands.[5] These movements also received support from Socialist and MAPU militants, and within the first year resulted in several deaths.[6] From the start, the government lost the initiative to leftist critics and was forced to react to militant campesino movements. Chonchol temporarily moved the Ministry of Agriculture to Cautín to deal with the first challenge to the government's claim to represent the vanguard of the revolution.[7]

The Problem of Lawful Revolution in the Countryside

Allende, like Frei, faced the dilemma of maintaining some semblance of order and authority while carrying out a proclaimed revolutionary program. Again, in concrete terms, the issue turned on the use of police against campesinos in order to uphold the existing property rights of landowners. Much less willing to use the police against worker movements than had been the Christian Democrats, Allende and his minister of interior nevertheless repeatedly and publicly condemned land occupations, urging the campesinos to allow the government to proceed with its program of expropriation without the daily pressure of armed confrontations and the negative implications for production of permanent conflict in the countryside.[8]

While maintaining a symbolic commitment to law, the Allende government moved even further than had the Christian Democrats in removing private proprietorship from the protection of the state. Infrequent use of the police to uphold private property rights did nothing to convince rural proprietors of the government's willingness to apply legal sanctions against campesino movements which dispossessed the landowners. In the first eighteen months of the Allende government campesinos temporarily or permanently occupied some 1700 rural properties.[9] Landowners responded with vigilante groups to retake the properties, while at the same time pleading with the government to enforce the law.[10]

Under the provisions of Article 171 of the agrarian reform law, the government used the numerous "labor conflicts" as grounds for covertly transferring rural properties from the control of their owners to government "interventors" and the campesinos. Article 171 provided that "In the case of lock-out or illegal work stoppage that, for any reason, suspends exploitation of a rural enterprise, the President of the Republic can order resumption of labors [*reanudación de faenas*] with the intervention of the civil authority . . . and the support of the police (if necessary). The 'interventor' will have all the prerogatives necessary to continue operation of the enterprise."

Some governmental personnel and members of governmental coalition parties began to encourage campesino land occupations, since work stoppage "for any reason" could legally bring governmental intervention and, in special circumstances, governmental administration of the enterprise. This procedure avoided the bureaucratic-judicial routine of expropriation and legally introduced governmental administrators into private farms. Flexible use of this provision provided an alternative means for carrying out the process of expropriation and effective transfer of proprietorship to agents of the state or to campesino organizations.[11] In fact, the tactic was used in so many farms that the government soon ran out of party loyalists within the agrarian bureaucracies from which "interventors" had to be selected. (The Controlaría ruled that interventors in farms had to be natural persons, who were public officials; the Ministry of Labor initially insisted that interventors come from the agrarian bureaucracies, ostensibly to insure some competence in rural administration.)

Intervention provided the Popular Unity government with a legal tool to speed up the program of expropriation.[12] The use of this tool, however, depended upon mobilization of campesinos for direct action. The government still faced the dilemma of controlling militant campesino movements, which used illegal confrontation tactics, without deploying police while at the same time maintaining the myth of respect for law. The Popular Unity government never resolved this dilemma. Campesino militancy showed every sign of increasing, both to the left of the government under MIR, MAPU, and left-Socialist tutelage and to the right of the government from the Christian Democratic and "independent" campesino organizations which resisted the government's agrarian program.

The Design of Production Units for "Socialist Agriculture"

The Popular Unity government faced a second and even more serious problem in the countryside. Like the Christian Democrats, the Allende government came to power with a commitment to eliminate the hacienda system but without a concrete program for an alternative system of rural proprietorship and agricultural production. Highly critical of the asentamiento and the resultant agrarian reform cooperatives, intellectuals and party leaders within the governmental coalition did not agree upon the structural foundations for a "socialist agriculture" in Chile. The government's massive expropriation of large farms during the first year was unaccompanied by a program for reorganization of the rural sector. Some new asentamientos were created, but the government soon (May 1971) announced publicly that no new asentamientos would be formed.[13] Instead, some sort of regional campesino enterprise would take its place.[14]

Intense debate ensued within the coalition government over the nature of the basic production units for a Chilean socialist agriculture. Some Socialists favored state farms (*haciendas del estado*).[15] Other Socialists and the Communist party proposed large cooperative farms with campesinos assigned private rights to garden plots and housing.[16] Members of MAPU supported both haciendas del estado and commune-wide enterprises with ownership of the land, in the latter case, vested in "all the campesinos in the commune."[17] In general, the governmental parties favored increasing the size of agricultural units, destroying the campesinos' localist identification with the existing hacienda or fundo, and preventing the type of stratification or "kulakization" of the countryside, which they believed they saw in the asentamiento. But these general orientations provided no program for reorganization of the rural sector.

The Popular Unity government's failure to define the production unit that would serve as the building block for socialist agriculture created a sense of disorder in the countryside. Attacks on the asentamiento system and the asentados as a new privileged class brought the resistance of the Federation of

Asentamientos, the already established agrarian reform cooperatives, and many campesinos living in pre-asentamientos when
the Allende government took over. The rapid expropriation of
some 1300 farms without any concrete plans for reorganization
added to the initial disarray.

Campesino Organizations and Governmental Agrarian Policy

A third source of difficulty for the Popular Unity government derived from the fragmentation of the campesino movement into unions, asentamientos, cooperatives, committees,
and unorganized day workers (afuerinos) and migrants as well
as from the traditional smallholder communities and the Mapuche Indian groups in southern Chile. Intellectually committed
to a participatory role for campesinos in policymaking, the government found that this intellectual commitment was inconsis-
tent with a parallel commitment to national planning and imposition of a new property system alien to all previous campesino
experience. In short, many campesinos simply did not have the
same vision of the countryside as the intellectual leaders within
the government. The tension between effective participation
for campesinos in governmental decision-making and the policymakers' efforts to introduce their own program for a new Chilean agriculture became particularly acute when the government
moved to introduce institutional innovations into the countryside in the form of (1) Consejos Comunales Campesinos and
(2) the Centro de Reforma Agraria (CERA), the new form of
proprietorship which the government sought to substitute for
the asentamiento.

These two institutional innovations were the major reforms
of the Popular Unity government in the countryside during the
first two years of government. While the Allende government
successfully expropriated the remaining haciendas, pressured
landowners to accept reserves smaller than the potential 80 hectares established in Law 16.640, nationalized much of agricultural credit and the exportation of agricultural commodities (in
SOCORA),[18] the Consejos Campesinos and the CERA were the
intended building blocks in a new structure for Chilean agriculture. Recognizing that the government gave top priority to
elimination of the latifundio, it is nevertheless appropriate to
evaluate the Allende government's rural program with special

reference to these new institutions because they represented the government's efforts to redefine and redistribute property in rural land.

The Consejos Comunales Campesinos

On January 11, 1971, the Popular Unity government decreed the creation of the National Campesino Council (*Consejo Nacional Campesino*). Promised as one of the "20 points" in the government's electoral program for the countryside, the government proclaimed that the Consejo Nacional Campesino, supplemented by communal and provincial consejos, would provide a participatory role for campesino organizations in the policy-making process related to the rural sector. Campesino representatives would also replace the landowners within the governmental agencies and semifiscal services like CORFO, INDAP, ECA, CORA, and the Central Bank.

Creation of the Consejo Nacional Campesino was a clear effort on the part of Jacques Chonchol to put together the representatives of diverse campesino organizations in a single national organization with the hope of legitimizing governmental policy through formal campesino participation. Despite Chonchol's often repeated commitment to a participatory role for the campesinos in the agrarian reform process, he rejected the wording of the decree that established the Consejo Nacional Campesino as proposed by some campesinos in favor of a more restrictive interpretation. Instead of declaring that "the Consejo Nacional Campesino will be charged with working with the government in all agricultural matters," Chonchol insisted that the decree read as follows:

The C.N.C. (Consejo Nacional Campesino) will be charged with transmitting the opinion of the campesinos to the Government in regard to agricultural matters and especially in those matters related to

(a) national plans of rural development, rural production and agrarian reform.

(b) policies on price, credit, commercialization and taxation, and others related to development, production and agrarian reform.

(c) programs and budgets of public and semi-public agencies in the rural sector.

(d) general policies related to the social and economic conditions of rural labor.

The decree also provided that "all plans, programs, budgets, and policies will be examined and reported upon by the Consejo Nacional Campesino prior to adoption by the Minister of Agriculture or President of the Republic."[19] The advisory role, instead of a formally determinative role, apparently corresponded to Chonchol's notion that "the State, as representative of the majority of the nation, cannot renounce its right to decide to initiate its plans to fulfill the program of the Popular Unity Government."[20]

Membership in the Consejo Nacional Campesino was limited to representatives of campesino organizations. Two representatives each from the confederations of unions—El Triunfo Campesino, Ranquíl, and Libertad—the Confederation of Asentamientos, the Confederation of Campesino Cooperatives and of a national organization of smallholders (still to be formed) composed the Consejo Nacional. The decree excluded two small organizations, Provincias Agrarias Unidas (generally labeled a "yellow," or employer-dominated, organization) and the federation Sargento Candelaria (the former Movimiento Campesino Independiente). Further, the Consejo Nacional Campesino contained no representation of unorganized campesinos, migrant workers, or Indians. The campesino organizations retained the authority to change their representatives whenever they desired; normal terms of office lasted two years. The decree gave the campesino organizations thirty days in which to constitute the Consejo, after which time the minister of agriculture might constitute the Consejo with the representatives of those organizations that had designated participants.

The decree further stipulated that in each province two representatives of each legally recognized campesino federation would form the Consejo Provincial Campesino. The base organization in the consejo system, organized at the level of the commune, consisted of representatives of "all the campesino organizations existing in the commune and those represented in the Consejo Provincial" (Article XIV). The minister of agriculture was to name a representative to each provincial and communal consejo. The decree left the manner of constitution of the provincial and communal consejos to the discretion of the Consejo Nacional.

In practice, government organizers attempted to form communal and provincial consejos prior to the establishment of any norms by the Consejo Nacional. Seeking to preempt opposition groups, governmental officials from different agrarian bureaucracies organized consejos and deliberately excluded opposition organizations.[21] The dominance of Christian Democrats in many areas led the governmental agents to adopt a modified form of consejo communal which included the possibility of at-large representation for unorganized campesinos. The government later legalized the modified form of consejo after reaching an informal agreement in February 1971 with campesino groups in Cautín, where Mapuche Indians formed directly elected consejos and demanded governmental recognition. Whereas the original reglamento of the decree that created consejos campesinos stipulated that communal consejos include one representative from each unionized farm, one representative from each asentamiento, and one representative for every fifty members of campesino cooperatives in the commune, the revised decree of February 1971 also included up to fifteen directly elected members to provide representation for the unorganized campesinos. In November 1971 the government tacitly moved to accept consejos formed totally by representatives directly elected in special assemblies.

Even with all this maneuvering, many consejos remained in the hands of the opposition. Within the consejos, conflicting interests among asentados, smallholders and workers in small commercial farms, and migrants, combined with the intromission of party competition, disrupted the government's efforts to create a national instrument for coordinated control of rural labor. In some areas the consejos played an important role in selecting farms for expropriation,[22] channeling INDAP credit, and pressuring the agrarian bureaucracy. But the unions, cooperatives, and asentamientos generally refused to be subordinated to the new government-induced institutions. The government, predictably, worked with those consejos which supported its program (and were dominated by members of governmental parties) and refused to work with consejos which demanded veto power over governmental policy or formulation of governmental objectives. Conceptualized as institutional arrangements potentially responsible for commune-wide rural planning (with some degree of campesino participation in policymaking), in the short run the consejos campesinos became merely another arena in which the government and opposition forces contested for the control and support of rural labor.[23]

The inability of the Allende government to dominate the consejo system nationally limited the governmental coalition's willingness to extend a uniformly participatory role to the consejos in policymaking and administration of rural programs. By maintaining the advisory role of the consejos, the government remained free to work through those organizations controlled by sympathetic campesino elements and to reject the recommendations of consejos dominated by relatively independent worker organizations or those clearly under the control of the opposition parties, especially the Christian Democrats. In October of 1971, the Consejo Nacional Campesino, in accepting the modified local consejos, declared also that "the Consejos Comunales will be planning and linkage [relacionadores] agencies, not executory, and therefore, cannot subordinate the other campesino organizations" (cooperatives, unions, asentamientos, committees).[24] This left the role of the consejos ambiguous, and assured that the existing campesino unions, asentamientos, and cooperatives retained a more significant place in the daily life of most of the rural population.

For the government the problem rested in the ambiguous role assigned to rural unions in the socialist agriculture it sought to create, the control of most asentamientos by organizations hostile to the government, especially after Chonchol's frontal attack on the asentados as a new privileged class, and the clearly capitalist orientation of most of the campesino cooperatives.

In the first year of the Popular Unity government, great efforts were made to increase membership in unions affiliated with or sympathetic to parties in the Popular Unity coalition. Membership drives focused on taking members from the existing unions and organizing those rural workers left out of the union movement from 1964 to 1970, particularly migrant workers, day laborers (afuerinos), and owners of minifundio plots. When left-wing Christian Democrats left the party in late 1971 to form the Izquierda Cristiana, a similar split took place in El Triunfo Campesino, the union confederation fostered by INDAP (Chonchol) during the Christian Democratic government. Most of these unions formed a new organization called

Unidad Obrero Campesino, dominated by MAPU and Izquierda Cristiana elements.

The resources of government provided the Allende coalition, as it had earlier provided the Christian Democrats, with the basis for attracting campesinos to unions favored by governmental largesse. A year after the Popular Unity government took office, the number of rural workers affiliated with unions had increased from 140,000 to 210,000; of these almost two-thirds now belonged to unions oriented toward the governmental parties, exactly reversing the situation in 1970 when opposition unions contained almost two-thirds of organized campesinos.

In response, the Christian Democrats and other opposition groups formed a new Central Única, uniting the majority of El Triunfo Campesino unions, Provincias Agrarias Unidas, and the Confederation of Asentamientos. The Confederation Libertad, grouping the unions created by the UCC and ANOC, maintained a militantly independent Christian stance. It rejected cooperation with the political Right and insisted on campesino rather than bureaucratic control over rural policy (see Table 14).

In the case of the asentamientos, the Popular Unity government decided on a policy of benign neglect. Unwilling to pay the price necessary to disestablish them, the government nevertheless remained temporarily noncommittal on the fate of the asentamientos. Until the government officially announced its plan for the creation of new production units in agriculture, Christian Democratic leaders insisted that the government intended to create *haciendas del estado* (state farms) to replace the asentamiento; only in September 1971, under intense pressure from the opposition, did Chonchol categorically declare that asentamientos created during the period 1964-1970 would be respected.[25]

For many campesinos the asentamiento *was* the agrarian reform. For the government, on the other hand, the asentamiento represented a deficient rural enterprise, an obstacle to social justice in the countryside, a source of new class cleavages, a basis for a "kulak" class, and perhaps most important, an opposition stronghold in the countryside. Though some asentamientos contained elements loyal to the Allende government (asentamientos like "9 de julio" in San Esteban, where socialist unions had a long organizational history in the farms prior to expropri-

TABLE 14 UNION AFFILIATION OF RURAL WORKERS, 1968-1971

Confederation	Number of Members				Percentage Change		
	1968	1969	1970	1971	1969/1968	1970/1969	1971/1970
El Triunfo Campesino	39,288	47,609	64,003	43,402	21.2	34.4	-32.2
Libertad	17,421	23,024	29,132	32,749	32.2	26.5	12.4
Ranquil	18,253	30,912	43,867	97,782	69.4	41.9	122.9
Unidad Obrero-Campesino				32,445			
Provincias Agrarias Unidas		355	1,686	513		374.9	-204.2
Subtotal	74,962	101,900	138,688	206,851	35.9	36.1	49.2
Federación Provincial "Sargento Candelaria"	1,394	1,743	1,604	2,080			
Total	76,356	103,643	140,293	208,971	36.3	35.4	49.0

SOURCE: FEES, "Descripción numérica de la Organización Sindical Campesina Chilena, 1968-1969"; and FEES, "Afiliación sindical por federaciones y provincias," mimeo, 1971 and 1972, cited in C. Kay, "La participación campesina en el gobierno de la Unidad Popular," typescript (Santiago, 1972).

ation), the leadership of the federations of asentamientos and the national confederation maintained close alliances with the Christian Democrats. The asentamiento represented, thus, a multiple challenge to the Popular Unity government. As a model for rural proprietorship it had largely been accepted by the campesinos; the government sought not only to delegitimate it but also to substitute a more complex, large-scale rural enterprise.

In August 1971 Chonchol announced to the press that "the government has decided to adopt a new transitional form [of rural proprietorship] in order to avoid the defects of the actual system. . . . This new transitional organization is called Centro de Reforma Agraria . . . and will be created by uniting two or more neighboring farms to form a sizable enterprise that can be managed by the campesinos."[26] The newspaper also reported that the minister had delivered to the campesino leaders (Consejo Nacional Campesino) a document in which the organization of these Centros de Reforma Agraria was already fully elaborated.[27] The asentamiento owed its origin to conflict between campesino unions and governmental policymakers. The Centro de Reforma Agraria originated in the minds of several Chilean and foreign intellectuals and was modified by discussion among the leadership of the Popular Unity governmental parties; campesino participation in determining the formal structure of rural proprietorship introduced by the Allende government was notably absent. Campesino resistance to the government's proposals, however, indicated that bureaucratic imposition of a particular sort of socialist agriculture would be no easier for Allende than had been the efforts of the Christian Democrats to ignore the unions in the valley of Choapa in the first stages of their agrarian reform efforts.

The Centros de Reforma Agraria

The internal debate within the government concerning the nature of rural production units which would form the building blocks of a socialist agriculture resulted in a provisional solution that satisfied no one. Unable to resolve the ideological and practical differences between the various coalition parties, the government found itself obliged to introduce some alternative to the asentamiento, which it had scathingly denounced. What emerged, the Centro de Reforma Agraria (CERA), represented a highly innovative, complex, and untried regional production unit which also took on some aspects of a territorial government for purposes of economic planning and administration of programs of regional development.

Defined as a "transitional form of property," as had been the asentamiento, the Centro de Reforma Agraria took its name from clauses in the agrarian reform law which gave CORA the exclusive authority to "create, direct and administer . . . centros de reforma agraria. . . . " Completely undefined in the law, this wording provided the opportunity for the Allende government to introduce a totally new concept of rural property while claiming to be operating within the context of existing law. Again, as in the use of administrative intervention as a means to speed up expropriation, the elastic application of existing law allowed the Popular Unity government to avoid efforts to enact new legislation, which the opposition-controlled Congress would have rejected, or the need to act illegally in carrying out its agrarian reform program. The government's initial description of the centros de reforma agraria, however, produced immediate charges by the opposition and by many campesino organizations that centro de reforma agraria was merely another name for state farm—or at best a government-controlled production unit in which the campesinos would enjoy little effective decision-making capability.

Coinciding with Chonchol's announcement that the government intended to create centros de reforma agraria, ICIRA's Santiago office circulated an explanation of the centros.[28] This document declared that the centros de reforma agraria would be transitional economic and social organizations which would replace the asentamientos in order to (1) promote class solidarity, (2) eliminate the campesinos localist orientation [mentalidad predial] which had been instilled by the latifundio system, (3) create larger economic units, (4) facilitate commune-wide planning and administration of production, and (5) improve cultivation and management of the farms. Most important, the CERA would replace the asentamiento since "[the asentamiento] divides the campesinos because it does not give land to all but only a small minority . . . giving the few many privileges and to the majority much misery."[29] The new production unit, the CERA, aimed not only at replacing the asentamiento with a larger-scale enterprise but at creating a classless society in the countryside. The CERAs were not only production units but also societal units and governmental units; this definition of the CERA explicitly linked the problem of agricultural production to the problem of establishing a classless society. Consistent with the government's declared intentions to create a socialist society, the CERA concept sought to deal simultaneously with the complex interrelationships between property systems, production, social justice, and a democratic polity. Unfortunately, the CERA concept originated more in immediate political expediency and compromise between the political parties of the governmental coalition than in critical, analytical efforts to evaluate the economic, technical, and political feasibility of alternative production units along with their implications for social justice in a socialist society.

Minor criticisms of the CERA regarding restrictions on individual land allotments and pasture rights, participation of women and teenagers in the assembly and as officers, and the ambiguity of the campesinos' individual rights within the CERA accompanied the major source of opposition to the CERA—belief that the CERA was a barely disguised effort to introduce state and collective farms. Opposition occurred despite the government's announcement that state farms (haciendas del estado, centros de producción) indeed would be created in special cases, but that they differed fundamentally from the CERA.

With the plans for the CERA in the open, the Christian Democrats and the National party reinforced the campaign against the government's agrarian reform plans that had been waged through the pages of *La Prensa* and *El Mercurio* during the first nine months of the Popular Unity government. Led by Rafael Moreno (director of CORA during the Frei presidency) and Andrés Aylwin, the Christian Democrats made every effort to support the campesinos' rights to private farms and the maintenance of the asentamiento system. Quoting the government's justification for the CERA,[30] the Christian Democrats declared that "in creating the centros de reforma agraria the government does not intend to make campesinos owners of the land—because according to CORA this would be to create a privilege."[31] Subsequently, the Consejo Nacional Campesino rejected the

CERA as defined by the government, insisting that "property in rural land should be assigned to the campesinos in cooperatives with the campesinos' house and a garden plot of two hectares assigned as private property." (The Consejo Nacional Campesino had not participated in the formulation of the CERA concept—a silent commentary on the Popular Unity government's willingness to allow effective campesino decision making on fundamental questions of rural policy.)

Resistance to the CERA became intense almost immediately. By June 1972 the government claimed to have constituted only 150 (most of which departed from the original model) while leaving several thousand expropriated farms without any formal organization. In some farms campesinos independently established asentamientos in open violation of governmental policy which denied recognition to newly created asentamientos. Several national campesino organizations (El Triunfo Campesino, the Confederation of Asentamientos, Provincias Agrarias Unidas) supported this tactic in order to resist imposition of the CERA model. The president of El Triunfo Campesino announced that the tactic would be employed by campesinos on a national scale when confronted by CORA's refusal to form asentamientos as required by law.[32]

In response, the Popular Unity government reassured the campesinos that workers would be granted private titles to their own houses and garden plots, while the remainder of the enterprise would belong collectively to the campesino membership. Simultaneously, Chonchol sped up assignment of land titles to campesino cooperatives emerging from the asentamiento period. This move provided some confirmation of governmental intentions to comply with promises made to the existing asentamientos but did nothing to clarify how the confirmation of "kulaks" in their property rights could be made consistent with the eventual establishment of a classless society in the countryside through creation of "a single class of campesinos with equal rights and obligations," dependent upon the CERA for daily social and economic relationships.

The government itself defined the CERA as a transitional form of property in the rural sector, a preliminary stage in the creation of a socialist agriculture. The overwhelming majority of farms expropriated by the Allende government remained organized in pre-CERA committees on the individual farms. The CERA, at least as originally conceived, presented organizational difficulties and problems of administration which were difficult to justify except in reference to utopian social goals—establishment of a classless society—which would not likely have resulted even if the CERA had been successfully organized on a wide scale. The Popular Unity government's initial definition of the CERA, contrary to the declarations of some coalition ideologues, did not eliminate proprietorship and, therefore, privilege; it merely transferred more prerogatives of proprietorship to bureaucrats while removing from the individual enterprise or group of campesino enterprises control over the surplus generated in the rural sector. The establishment of communal, provincial, and national capitalization funds to which, in principle, the CERA were to turn over 90 percent of profits, despite the intended control of these funds by campesino organizations for purposes of redistribution, could only have served to lessen the power of individual campesinos and campesino organizations vis-à-vis a growing state bureaucracy.

To introduce such an organizational scheme as a transitional form of rural proprietorship while still leaving undefined the permanent building block of a Chilean socialist agriculture seems to have been a serious tactical and political error on the part of the Allende government in the countryside. Even as a permanent reorganization of Chilean political boundaries and of agricultural production, the CERA would have involved costs which may have outweighed any theoretical benefits of scale or class solidarity; as a transitional institution the costs greatly outweighed the supposed benefits. As Jacques Chonchol had insisted:

> The fundamental problem . . . is to create campesino enterprises of scale that permit a relatively specialized agriculture . . . the productive land must be organized cooperatively, not in individual properties. Within the framework we must give a large participatory role to the campesino in the direction of the enterprise. The assistance of the State must be just that, assistance, and not a directive role. We must look for a system of planning that begins with the locality, because one of the great flaws that socialist planning has had in the rural sector has been overly centralized planning. In our country, such planning will be imperfect and will always fail. [33]

But the intellectuals and politicians within the Popular Unity government adopted a paternalistic role toward the campesinos, as had the Christian Democrats. Chonchol's own recognition of the flaws of central planning and of bureaucratic mismanagement could not overcome a long Chilean tradition of bureaucratic centralism and of glorification of the people, or the campesinos, in the abstract accompanied by a profound mistrust of *effective* popular participation in decision making. Even Chonchol's intellectual commitment to a participatory role for campesino organizations was sometimes tempered by political expediency and the ideological utopianism of some sectors of the Popular Unity government.

In the case of the CERA it appears that campesino input into the decision-making process which produced the CERA concept would have saved the government from its more utopian element. It would also have engendered a simpler system of rural proprietorship which could have met Chonchol's basic criteria for communitarian-socialist or cooperative farms (with private rights to housing and garden plots) without the controversial untested features of the commune-wide CERA-territorial government. Insofar as governmental policy in operation departed from Chonchol's cogent analysis of the situation in the rural sector, Chonchol's own predictions of failure were borne out:

> Active participation of the workers is more important in the countryside than in industry because many problems must be resolved from day to day. The agricultural process is, besides, much more conditioned by natural factors than the industrial process . . . planning cannot be imposed from above. A capability for active participation and response at the base must be recognized. For the process to be efficient the campesinos must feel commited [*comprometido*].[34]

The CERA simply did not provide the campesinos with this kind of participatory role, nor did it provide them with the types of incentives necessary to stimulate a productive system of rural enterprise. The government was forced to revert to ambiguously defined "campesino committees" on more or less the same scale as the traditional rural enterprise. These committees bore marked resemblance to the asentamientos but lacked the legal status of the asentamiento as stipulated in the agrarian reform law.[35]

Two Years on the Road to Socialism in the Countryside

By the end of 1972, for the first time in Chilean history, the countryside no longer featured a physical concentration of property in rural land in large haciendas or latifundios. The elimination of the traditional hacienda system represented the major accomplishment of the Popular Unity government's rural program from 1970 to 1972. In eliminating the hacienda system, the Allende government created both an opportunity to restructure the rural sector and a challenge to the ingenuity, pragmatism, and political skill of governmental policymakers, to which it did not successfully respond. Both major institutional innovations introduced by the government into the rural sector, the Consejos Campesinos and the CERA, failed to take into account the diversity of campesino interests and preferences precisely because campesino participation in developing the legal and administrative framework for these institutions was nonexistent. The government accompanied rhetoric affirming the need for campesino participation in decision making with bureaucratic imposition of elite-intellectual-generated programs. This led, in addition, to serious production problems in the rural sector.[36]

Thus, despite the government's view of the president of the National Confederation of Asentamientos as a spokesman for the opposition and especially the Christian Democrats, Juan Chacon's opinions represented those of many campesinos and campesino organizations:[37]

> [The government] speaks of collective farms or State farms without consulting with the campesinos. . . . We have engaged in a struggle . . . to liberate ourselves from the yoke of the patrón. . . . We believe that the land should belong to the campesinos and we want a Chilean agrarian reform planned in conjunction with the campesinos.[38]

In some cases the government even failed to honor its pledge to respect the existing asentamientos when, for "technical reasons," particular properties were needed to fill out specialized haciendas del estado. One such case, Asentamiento Arquilhue in Valdivia, led to a temporary campesino occupation of the CORA headquarters in the zone. Eventually, however, the government incorporated the asentamiento into the "Complejo Forestal y Maderero del Estado Panguipulli," after confrontations between different campesino groups supported by the

Christian Democrats and the government. The government allowed those campesinos from the asentamiento who did not wish to remain in the newly created state enterprise to seek openings in other asentamientos.[39] In a joint declaration by various campesino organizations in Valdivia which opposed governmental policy, the workers declared: "the asentamiento was integrated into the Complejo overnight without the knowledge or participation of the campesinos who categorically reject the implementation of State-owned property in agriculture."[40]

The government itself added fuel to the conflict surrounding rural property when a spokesman (*subsecretario de economía*) announced that the government generally opposed workers' enterprises (*empresas de trabajadores*) "because workers' enterprises are the last bastion of capitalism since they cause the workers to lose their solidarity and unity and create in them a capitalist mentality oriented toward competition and markets."[41] This declaration gave credibility to the Christian Democrats' claims that the CERA represented an ill-disguised transition to collectives and state farms.

Emilio Lorenzini, the Christian Democratic deputy who led the Molina strike in 1953 (see chapter 5), responded by noting the intellectual sterility and political implications of the government's rigid concept of property and proprietorship. Recognizing, as suggested in the first chapter of this book, that property and proprietorship take on importance as decision-making capabilities rather than as absolute or holistic assignments of ownership, Lorenzini remarked:

> The government does not understand workers' enterprises because it begins with an antiquated concept of property. . . . We believe that property in the means of production can be divested of the abusive privileges conferred in it by traditional capitalism and neo State-capitalism. . . .
>
> The government has been unable to understand that in a new world in which the rules of the game experience revolutionary change, it does not matter who is the owner of capital, but rather who has the power to decide, to obtain the fruits of the enterprise, and to orient national production.
>
> We achieve nothing if we merely change the group which exploits the workers in the capitalist system for . . . an 'interventor' designated by bureaucrats. . . . That is, those who control State property—the bureaucrats—control the management of production, receive the fruits

of production and orient production to serve the political party of the government.

The workers continue to sell their labor to those who control the capital. . . . Before they were stockholders, now they are bureaucrats.[42]

Lorenzini's comments focus precisely on the ambiguities and contradictions of the Popular Unity government's agrarian program: How can a theoretical commitment to social justice, political democracy, and rising production be operationalized in a socialist agriculture which recognizes effective worker participation with proprietary interests while limiting the bureaucratization and overbearing paternalism or authoritarianism of the state?

There can be no doubt that the leading policymaker for the rural sector during the first two years of Popular Unity government recognized and understood the dilemma. Jacques Chonchol did not advocate massive or even widespread adoption of state farms. He remained committed to relatively large-scale, modernized campesino cooperatives. Because of the historical development of the rural union movement in Chile and the emphasis of the campesinos on improvements in land allotments and other perquisites, Chonchol also accepted, if somewhat reluctantly, the principle of private rights to housing and a garden plot. His reluctance was not due to any overriding ideological concerns but rather to the world-wide and Chilean experience that private plots within collective enterprises give rise to competing demands for labor in the collective and private enterprises which the campesinos often resolve in favor of the private plots. Selling private produce provides direct and immediate income whereas labor on the collective enterprise assumes distribution of a surplus at the end of the harvest season. Where appropriate incentive systems are lacking, or where poor management, corruption, or bad luck make the worker's share of the collective surplus less attractive than the immediate benefits derived from a private plot, then the private enterprise within the collective enterprise operates as a drag on the collective economy. In the asentamientos this was a notorious problem.

In some asentamientos, for example in Aconcagua, asentados earned three to four times as much on one-half or one cuadra than their total income from the collective enterprise for a year.

Early tomatoes, industrial crops like hemp, and export crops grown on private plots in this area make possible very good incomes on small, intensively worked plots. Willing to dedicate the collective enterprise to more extensive cultivation and even to essentially traditional livestock husbandry, the campesinos maximized private money income and minimized collective labor investment.

This problem must be solved if any type of collective enterprise is to function successfully in the agricultural sector. The general prescription, to make work in the collective enterprise an attractive alternative to labor on the private plots, can only be applied in practice on each farm depending upon production patterns, traditional regalías, and access to markets. One possibility may be for the collective enterprise to guarantee the members a ración cosechada for allowing their plots to be exploited as part of the collective domain. This solution, already accepted in many private farms, would provide the campesino with guaranteed private benefits, yet make his income dependent upon performance in the collective enterprise, especially if the quantity of ración cosechada depended upon average yield in land of similar quality throughout the farm.[43] Under these circumstances, the higher the level of production on the farm, the greater the share of the individual campesino—in kind—to be sold privately if he so desires or marketed cooperatively if that option proves itself, according to the campesino's judgment, more desirable.

Despite Chonchol's general understanding of the problems facing the agrarian sector, his influence was limited. Within the governmental coalition there existed strong ideological currents favoring the abolition of all private property in rural land. Without a strong party to support him (Chonchol seems to have relied on the Communist party to moderate the influence of left-Socialists and Mapucistas), he never secured control over the agrarian bureaucracy. His staying power in the ministry during a period of intense conflict within the government and of heavy criticism from the opposition was a tribute to his prestige. But as agricultural production declined and the CERA proved unsatisfactory, Chonchol provided an obvious scapegoat. In November 1972 Allende accepted Chonchol's resignation, despite the protests of the Left-Christian party (Izquierda Cristiana).[44]

Again, the question came back to the definition and distribution of property in rural land and to the relationship between the resolution of these two issues and agricultural production, social justice, and political democracy. Until mid-1973 the Popular Unity government was unable to find a satisfactory, or even workable, solution to these problems. The chaotic situation in the countryside contributed to the political polarization and declining productivity that led to the military coup of September 1973. The basic question "on the road to socialism" remained the same old social question, still focused, as in 1919, on the proper relationship between labor, property rights, and governmental authority. For the campesino the issue still turned on the political meaning of property in rural land.

10

From Revolution in Liberty to Military Rule

The agrarian policies adopted by Chile's Popular Unity government had much in common with socialist agrarian reforms carried out earlier in the Soviet Union, Eastern Europe, and Cuba. The Allende government moved relatively rapidly to destroy the existing system of large, private rural estates and to transform them into cooperatives or collective farms. Pressure also developed to reduce the size or totally eliminate the sector of middle-sized private commercial farms, and the extent of state management and regulation of the agricultural economy dramatically increased.

But the Chilean political situation provided a radically different context for socialist agrarian reforms than had the revolutionary environment of the Soviet Union, Eastern Europe, or Cuba at the time of agrarian reforms in those countries. In these earlier twentieth-century socialist revolutions, initial redistribution and redefinition of property in rural land aimed at gaining the support of an important peasant and rural worker population for a revolutionary political movement. Land reform mobilized mass support for new regimes at a time when existing legal norms were shattered and an alternative politico-legal order had yet to be created. Destruction of the existing property system, including property in rural land, preceded institutionalization of new political regimes. Collectivization of rural property generally followed consolidation of power by the revolutionary regime. Furthermore, this pattern occurred in national economies having dominant agricultural sectors or, at least, agricultural sectors that employed a large proportion of the labor force and contributed heavily to the value of national exports.[1]

Unlike the Soviet, Eastern European, and Cuban cases, large-scale agrarian reform efforts began in Chile (1964) well after the majority of the labor force had moved into the nonagricultural sector. By that time agriculture also represented a relatively insignificant component of the national economy in terms of its share of domestic production and as an earner of foreign exchange. Stagnation over a period of almost three decades most saliently characterized the agricultural sector and produced for Chile a growing negative trade balance in agricultural products.[2]

Instead of a frankly revolutionary process, the initial land reforms in 1964 formed part of a national reformist program that included a commitment to the maintenance of an important private sector in agriculture as well as an array of cooperative and "communitarian" production units. The subsequent election of a Communist-Socialist-controlled coalition government *after* an effective land reform program had been instituted had no parallel in Latin America, Europe, or other parts of the Third World.

The Marxist-dominated coalition government lacked a revolutionary army or militias to support its program and publicly committed itself to making the transition to socialism while respecting constitutional norms, including maintenance of the multiparty system and electoral politics until the government could alter these institutions through legal reform. In this context the government relied heavily on the extensive executive authority granted by the Chilean constitution to the president of the republic and minimized the role of the Congress and the courts, still controlled by opposition parties and career functionaries. This strategy represented a conventional approach, in Chilean politics, for a president without a congressional majority.

Yet in the nine years of Christian Democratic and Popular Unity reforms, rural proprietors faced a principal dilemma of property owners in a revolutionary environment: refusal by the state to enforce the legal prerogatives of proprietorship. In 1965 the Christian Democrats determined through their policies that rural proprietors could no longer confidently depend upon the national police to guarantee the exercise of property rights in land. Gradually, labor conflicts and temporary land occupations became almost synonymous. Workers, in addition to refusing to work, controlled access to the rural estates and prohibited the owners from moving goods or materials from the farms. Still, the Christian Democrats occasionally used police to uphold pro-

prietary claims and to enforce govenmental back-to-work decrees (*reanudación de faenas*).

The Allende government went one step further by ordering
police not to intervene to support property rights against workers' movements or trespassers without specific orders from the
Ministry of Interior. Guaranteeing the legal exercise of proprietary authority by reference to the coercive capability of the
state became an exception rather than the rule. In August 1972
the conservative daily *El Mercurio* editorialized: "The government systematically refuses to send police to remove those who
invade private property. The Executive, who boasts of his respect for the judiciary, in this fashion undermines its independence and legal power. The orders issued by the judges are not
carried out."[3] In practice, force alone determined the status of
many proprietors as land occupations and labor conflicts transferred proprietary decision making from the legal owners to
campesinos and governmental bureaucrats. In the latter case,
the government intervened under the terms of the agrarian reform law to take over the administration of the rural enterprise.

By the end of 1973 the leaders of the military regime that
ousted Allende reported that the Chilean state had legal possession of 60.84 percent of all the irrigated farmlands in the country and also held title to 31.78 percent of all nonirrigated but
arable rural land. Through expropriation, intervention, and
other administrative devices, CORA controlled some ten million
hectares.[4] While these figures are no doubt approximations, the
impressive transfer of landed estates out of the private sector
and into various cooperatives, state farms, and collectives—all
highly dependent upon the state for operation—was indicative
of the rapid pace of the Popular Unity government on the road
to socialism in the countryside.

The rapid pace and organizational chaos of the Popular Unity
government's rural program never permitted clarification or
even definition of the distribution of proprietary authority en-
visioned for Chile's socialist agriculture. Increasingly vocal hostility to private property, including cooperatives and workers'
enterprises, by the more militant sectors of the Marxist left and
MAPU presaged a more focused emphasis on state farms (under
a variety of names) along with intensified attacks on the private
commercial farm sector.

The military government that deposed Allende promised to reverse entirely this process of socialization, and even seemed bent on dismantling some of the cooperatives and asentamiento enterprises introduced by the Christian Democrats. Returning to a model of land reform based on subdivision of farms into private parcels, the military and its advisers "temporarily"prohibited strikes and labor petitions, and disbanded Marxist-oriented unions in both the rural sector and the urban areas. These acts, in turn, must inevitably lead to decreased vigilance in application of labor law for, historically, labor petitions and union activism have been prerequisites for any sort of systematic enforcement of workers' rights in the countryside.

The military made clear that production in the rural sector by private enterprise formed the foundation of their transitional rural program. While rejecting any return to the traditional hacienda system, the military junta seemed to adopt as its own the policy orientations of the SNA: depolitization of agriculture, support for efficient producers, and work incentives and profit-sharing plans for rural labor—but intolerance of class-conscious workers' organizations' pressing demands against rural employers.

When the military took over, the legal status of thousands of farms was ambiguous. The junta announced that the state would guarantee all rural properties of less than 40 hectares (BIH) against expropriation and that farms larger than that would not be expropriated for a number of years. The military also declared that some farms, where the military decided that land had been illegally taken, would be returned to their previous owners. In addition, some former hacendados were to be allowed to buy land from the Chilean state with bonds they received in compensation for expropriated farms.[5] All in all, the military's initial program looked like the Chilean version of the Stolypin reforms combined with some elements of the counter-revolution in Guatemala after 1954.[6]

In any case, the dramatic dead-end on the Chilean road to socialism makes somewhat difficult the determination of the distribution of property in rural land and the political meaning of property in rural land in Chile in 1975. Nevertheless, a preliminary assessment of the effects of the Popular Unity government's rural program and the "counterreforms"[7] of the military government is the subject of this concluding chapter.

The Legal Authority of Rural Proprietors

The legal prerogatives of rural proprietors can be outlined formally while recognizing the tenuousness of the landowners' effective proprietorship. Individual proprietors are bound by the Agrarian Reform Law of 1967, the subsequent amendments and reglamentos of this law, and the extensive labor legislation of the years 1964-1973. These delimitations subject private property in agricultural land to proprietary intervention of both the state and of rural labor. Of particular importance was Reglamento 281 of May 15, 1968, which made nonexpropriation of private holdings dependent upon compliance with technical criteria of farm and land management. For example, Reglamento 281 considered poorly exploited and subject to expropriation any farm that devoted less than 80 percent of irrigated land to annual and permanent crops, orchards, and artificial pastures. Analagous legal criteria applied to other types of land. In addition, the rural unionization law and other labor legislation assigned proprietary initiatives to rural labor.

From 1965 until 1973 rural labor conflicts allowed some campesinos to gain further proprietary participation or, if the workers so chose, force the landowners to turn their farms over to CORA. The military government's "temporary" suspension of labor conflicts and strikes restored the limitation on rural workers in force prior to 1931. Whatever the intent of this measure, in effect it returned to farm operators a breadth of discretion unknown—legally—in the countryside for over forty years. How long the "restoration" will last cannot be presently known. The permanent de-legalization of rural labor movements and its enforcement by police or military units would leave rural workers again without remedy in their struggle to force landowners to comply with labor law, to improve work conditions, and to pay wages that permit an increase in the welfare of the campesino work force.

In the reformed sector of Chilean agriculture and in the case of agricultural cooperatives, reglamentos or "decrees with force of law" regulated campesino proprietorship. Legal recognition of these enterprises depended upon ministerial or CORA's approval of the by-laws followed by a decree that formalized their legal status. The reglamentos defined the terms and conditions of membership, management, administration, and distribution of the surplus.[8] Some provisions, such as supervision of accounting procedures and periodic governmental audits, provided useful external checks on corrupt or oligarchic tendencies within campesino enterprises. But the detailed specification of the constitutional charter of the production units by administrative regulations underlined the paternalistic-statist orientation of the entire agrarian reform program in Chile after 1964. The imposition of administratively designed charters on the campesino enterprises prevented the development of a consensual institutional framework for rural enterprises in the reformed sector. Although governmental policy in the rural sector must be related to broader economic and political objectives, the lack of participation by rural workers in the design and implementation of innovative production and management arrangements produced disadvantageous results for the macroeconomy as well as for the rural sector.

The military government's initial "solution" to these problems seemed to be a return to the private smallhold and the discouragement or even dissolution of cooperatives and workers' enterprises where land was worked collectively. When some campesinos resist these policies, as inevitably they will, it remains to be seen if the military or their civilian advisers can be any more successful than the Popular Unity government in establishing innovative, functioning collectives or cooperatives, or allowing the campesinos to do so themselves. This most radical of all solutions would require a faith in the campesinos that neither the Christian Democrats nor the Popular Unity politicians exhibited.

Despite the fact that all rural proprietors, whether in the reformed sector or in the "unreformed" private sector, came under extensive legal regulation in the management of their land during the years from 1965 to 1973, important entrepreneurial and managerial authority remained in private hands. Private proprietors and coproprietors determined the daily work routine within the production units, decided which crops to grow, what

inputs to use, and, within limits, where and when to market
their products.

From 1970 to 1973 expanded state control over the availability and distribution of inputs, imports of machinery, marketing,
and credit meant the gradual de facto elimination of these prerogatives. This led many asentados and proprietors of other
farms to protest the inefficiency of the agrarian bureaucracy
and the growing concentration of proprietary authority in the
hands of the state. Campesino union confederations—Triunfo
Campesino, Libertad, and the Confederation of Asentamientos
and Cooperatives of Agrarian Reform—joined a nationwide
strike of opposition elements against the policies of the Allende
government in late 1972 and demanded an end to state monop-
olies in marketing and exports, respect for the right to strike by
producers as well as by workers, security of tenure for smallholders against land occupations and illegal labor conflicts, and
efficient provision of the necessary inputs for agricultural production.[9] These demands entailed the state's return of proprietary authority to rural proprietors, merchants, and private enterprise.

In January 1973 the Popular Unity government attempted to
establish a governmental monopoly on the marketing of wheat
in order to guarantee adequate levels of consumption in urban
areas. Producers were required to sell their wheat to the governmental buying agency, Empresa de Comercio Agrícola (ECA).
Many believed that the price set for wheat by the governmental
monopoly (*estanco del trigo*) was inadequate.[10] The landowner
associations (SNA, regional associations, and employers' unions)
and the asentados rejected the terms of the government's decrees. The SNA president characterized the measure as "reactionary" and compared it to the manner in which feudal lords
appropriated the produce of serfs.[11] Landowners claimed that
efforts to create an estanco del trigo merely demonstrated the
extent of the government-induced decline in agricultural production. In various provinces the asentados announced their in-
tention to resist the governmental measure. They claimed that
the government had threatened to cut off all state assistance,
foreclose on loans, and repossess machinery bought from CORA
or CORFO if the asentados did not turn their wheat over to the

government at the state-set price.[12] *El Mercurio* quoted leaders from the provincial federation of asentados in Curicó: "We as campesinos are not disposed to deliver even one grain of wheat under these conditions. We will not deliver our wheat until they take into account the costs of producing this commodity so that we can protect our income [*salario*] and not have to be in hock to the State Bank [*y no tener que estar practicamente vendidos al Banco del Estado*]."[13] The proprietary authority of rural landowners, in the reformed and nonreformed sector, faced the possibility of being reduced to a point of losing the prerogative of not selling the products of their labor or even of determining how much to leave for their own consumption.

In sum, the cumulative effect of the transformations of rural proprietorship since 1964 substantially restricted the legal authority of proprietors to manage the physical and natural resources claimed as property. State authority for macroeconomic planning and regulation placed individual and cooperative rural enterprises in the private sector in a permanently vulnerable position vis-à-vis short-run governmental policies and the performance of the agrarian-related bureaucracies. A reversal of this trend seemed to be high on the agenda of the military regime from 1973-1975.

Legal and Customary
Territorial Jursidiction of Rural Proprietors

By the time the Allende government was violently deposed by the Chilean military, only isolated relics of the traditional hacienda system remained. Landowners exercised neither legal nor customary territorial jurisdiction over resident workers or even trespassers. In this respect the combination of rural unions, labor law, and a government ill-disposed to defend the prerogatives of private property dealt a death blow to the hacienda as *patria chica* and to the rural proprietor as master of his domain. The military government immediately made known its hostility to the old hacienda system, but the broad interpretation of private property held by some military personnel and especially by their civilian advisers may portend a return of the days when workers had to ask permission of the patrón to receive visitors in their houses. While no such case has yet arisen the implications of the current policies do not preclude such a partial restoration of the role of hacendado as lord of his domain.

Legal and Customary Obligations
of Rural Proprietors toward Rural Labor

The combined stipulations of the new rural labor legislation, the 1967 unionization law, and the agrarian reform law left rural proprietors with more extensive legal obligations toward the labor force than those which industrialists had toward the urban worker (see chapters 3 and 8). Intensified enforcement efforts by the Labor Department, noncompliance with regulations as grounds for expropriation, and militant action by rural unions all tended to solidify the transition from paternalism, benign or otherwise, to a system of formal contractual relations between employer and worker. As in any human relationship, room remained for personal arrangements to circumvent or improve upon formal ones. But the obligations of employers toward rural workers contained a legislated institutionalization of customary perquisites in addition to more typical forms of modern social legislation such as an eight-hour work day. Other obligations, like part payment for days not worked because of bad weather, represented new guarantees to rural workers. Likewise, the dispositions of labor law and the agrarian reform law that required landowners to set aside land for recreational purposes, union halls, and schools forced landowners to provide collective goods and services that in most circumstances are the responsibility of governmental authorities.

Precisely because repression of rural labor and nonenforcement of labor law could no longer be the basis of national political alliances between urban middle-class interests and the old landowner class, the increased legal obligations of rural proprietors toward rural labor resulted in intensified sectoral clashes over the relative price of agricultural and industrial goods. The increasing cost of labor could not be financed by rural proprietors at the same time that governmental pricing policy discriminated against the agricultural sector. No matter what the character of the national regime in power, if industrialization policies depend upon protective tariffs and discriminate against agriculture in order to maintain lower-than-market prices for urban consumers, then the agricultural sector cannot be expected to finance legislated welfare gains for rural labor. Yet the sudden introduction of "efficiency prices" for agricultural commodities, or even prices that reflected a somewhat more reliable estimate of demand, was (before the coup of 1973) viewed as unacceptable in an urban society that took for granted governmental price-fixing and habitually blamed the incumbent politicians for inflation. The military government attempted to reverse this trend by instituting an initial policy of a less-regulated market for agricultural commodities. As an incentive to production the policy seemed quite plausible; its political viability in the long run will depend upon the response of farmers to market conditions and their faith (converted into investments in agriculture) in the ability of the government to effectively enforce its guarantees to private producers.

In part, of course, the credibility of the government depends upon repression of any militant rural labor movements, the destruction of Marxist-oriented campesino organizations, and the ability of landowners to enforce discipline on their farms. It seemed inevitable that the protection of laws that provided campesinos due process in dismissals and shielded labor leaders from persecution and eviction would be denied to many rural workers. Many of the obligations of the landowners toward the rural labor force seemed destined to become again merely symbolic obligations under a government that was more concerned with production than with legality and above all with restoration of the sacredness of private property.

Exclusive Legal and Customary Perquisites of Proprietors of Rural Land

The agrarian reform process from 1964 to 1973 provided important selective benefits to some rural proprietors—especially the new proprietors in the asentamientos and some members of campesino organizations serviced by INDAP. Credit, technical assistance, organizational training, marketing assistance, preferential pricing of and access to consumer goods, new housing, and other subsidies became available to the clientele of the agrarian bureaucracies. CORA claimed to have constructed 7,406 new houses and repaired 1,300 others from 1965 to July 1970, while making available potable water and electricity to

many campesino families.[14] The agrarian reform also provided
other infrastructure—including farm buildings, fencing, social-
service centers (*equipamiento comunitario*), irrigation works,
and roads—to the new proprietors as well as to their neighbors.
Rafael Menjivar estimated that from 1965 to 1968, the public
investment in agrarian reform, narrowly defined as the operation of CORA and creation of the asentamientos, reached $US
117,547,000 or approximately $US 13,252 per family settled
in asentamientos.[15] By excluding administration and miscella-
neous costs, the total can be reduced to $US 11,662 per settled
family.[16] A later estimate by Solon Barraclough for the period
1964 to September 1970 suggested that a cash outlay of six to
ten thousand dollars per family was made to cover investments
in land, improvements, working capital, and administration and
to finance annual operating costs. Barraclough further noted
that many of these outlays consisted of short-term credits that
beneficiaries partially repaid during the same year, although
CORA lost nearly 40 percent of these short-term credits largely
because of inflation.[17]

Even partially accepting the idea that some of the investment
"can hardly be attributed to agrarian reform as [it] merely represented a diversion to reform beneficiaries of investments necessary for Chile's agricultural development,"[18] the programs
provided selective benefits to a relatively small number of campesinos and new proprietors. In this sense the Allende government correctly observed that the Frei agrarian reform created a
new privileged class in the countryside. As an exclusive prerogative of their status as new proprietors, the asentados received
preferential treatment from governmental agencies that markedly improved their income and standard of living to the exclusion, and sometimes at the expense of, rural workers who
did not become members of asentamientos.

In the nonreformed campesino economy certain other proprietors also obtained new access to governmental services and
credit as a selective benefit to members of government-sponsored cooperatives and campesino committees. These campesinos, serviced in most cases by INDAP, increased in number
from 20,000 in 1964 to an average of over 45,000 between
1965 and 1970. For them benefits resulted from their membership in particular types of producers' associations or unions

rather than as a result of proprietorship per se. But the vast majority of smallholders and minifundistas still lived with the lowest income levels, poorest health conditions, highest rates of illiteracy, and worst housing of all rural workers. They did not belong to campesino organizations and failed to benefit from agrarian reform. Indeed, some lost opportunities previously available to supplement their incomes through part-time or seasonal employment in the haciendas.

Before 1970 the new opportunities for rural labor did not come at the expense of the majority of large estate owners. The dual strategy of the Christian Democrats allowed an important role for private commercial agriculture. Large landowners continued to capture the lion's share of agricultural credit furnished by the State Bank and CORFO as well as that available from the private credit markets. But other exclusive prerogatives of the hacendados (see chapter 2) gradually disappeared. The agrarian reform process from 1964 to 1970 all but liquidated the political dominance of the estate owners in the rural locality as well as in the national political system. Landowners no longer automatically controlled the votes of campesinos or appointments to the public administration in their regions.

From 1970 to 1973 the Allende government sought to remove the privileged status from the asentados and to eliminate all large landholdings. It thus ended the possibility that hacendados, by virtue of their property in rural land, might command legal or customary access to goods or services from the campesinos or the state. The government successfully destroyed the traditional hacienda component of the agrarian sector. The asentados, however, vigorously defended their newly won gains, claiming that the government was legally obligated to continue the formation of asentamientos in expropriated properties and to provide the needed subsidies to make the enterprises going concerns. The new proprietors struggled, as did the hacendados in the past, to secure and retain selective provision of governmental goods and services as a perquisite of property in rural land.

The military government's initial focus on private, individual parcels may presage a decline in the asentamiento system. The new government stressed creation of a "free market in land." If the inalienability of the asentamiento land is removed, through subdivisions or otherwise, re-creation of large private farms through real estate transactions will certainly occur in some regions. But the military's notions concerning private commercial agriculture do not include a restoration of the inefficient traditional hacienda system. SNA president Alfonso Márquez de la Plata confirmed that, "The concept of the hacienda of the last century is totally gone. The SNA is aware of the need for justice and will not support those who would restore the whip. But I believe that after the lesson of Marxism it would be crazy to think of things of that nature [restoration of the hacienda system]."[19]

The Distribution of Property in Rural Land

At the beginning of 1973 the reformed sector—that is, all of the properties expropriated under the Frei and Allende governments—accounted for a little under one-half of the total area in irrigated land and about one-third of the land in basic hectares (BIH).[20] The campesinos in the reformed sector represented about 18 percent of the rural labor force. The other new component in the agrarian structure included the former hacendados who now held reserves of up to 80 hectares (BIH). Although precise data was not available, the number of these proprietors probably did not exceed 1600. While no studies have been published to indicate recent changes in the patterns of ownership or subdivision of land in the private rural economy, preliminary findings of a current study determined that extensive illegal subdivision of rural properties took place between 1965 and 1970.[21] At the end of 1972 Solon Barraclough and Almino Affonso reported that rural land was distributed broadly, as shown in Table 15.

In addition to eliminating the haciendas and creating the reformed sector, the land reform process from 1964 to 1973 increased the number of middle-sized private commercial farms through subdivision and the establishment of the landowner reserves. Table 16 offers a comparative view of the land tenure situation by property size in 1965 and 1972.

Whereas agrarian reform destroyed the traditional hacienda systems, it did not substantially reduce the physical concentration of land into a relatively small number of properties. In the final month of 1972, 6.1 percent of all rural properties

TABLE 15 APPROXIMATE DISTRIBUTION OF LAND AND LABOR IN AGRICULTURE, 1972 (AS PERCENTAGE OF TOTAL)

	Land in Hectares (BIH)	Permanent and Temporary Workers (includes unemployed)	Value of Gross Production	Value of Marketed Production	Proportion of Production Marketed
Reformed sector (asentamientos, CERAS, comités, centros de producción, etc.)	36	18	29	29	(80)
Small properties (minifundios and farms of 20 hectares [BIH] or less)	22	60	28	15	(45)
Middle and large size-farms, including "reserves," farms of 20 to 80 hectares (BIH) and 3% of land in properties over 80 hectares (BIH)	42	22	43	56	(95)
	100	100	100	100	(76)

SOURCE: Solon Barraclough and Almino Affonso, "Diagnóstico de la reforma agraria," ICIRA (December 1972), p. 5.

TABLE 16   APPROXIMATE DISTRIBUTION OF LAND IN AGRI-
CULTURE, 1965 AND 1972 (By Size of Units)

Size of Properties (in Hectares BIH)	Number of Units		Percentage of Land Area		Number of Units
	1965%	1972%	1965%	1972%	
Less than 5 hectares	81.4	79.3	9.7	9.7	189,500
5 - 20	11.5	11.3	12.7	13.0	26,900
20 - 40	3.0	3.3	9.5	11.6	8,900
40 - 60	1.3	2.5	7.1	14.5	5,200
60 - 80	0.8	1.6	5.7	12.8	3,800
80 -	2.0	0.1	55.3	2.9	200
Reformed sector	0.0	1.9	0.0	35.5	4,700
	100.0	100.0	100.0	100.0	

SOURCE: ICIRA, "Avance del proceso de reforma agraria, 1972," cited
in "La Batalla contra el Latifundio," in *Chile Hoy*, Suplemento Agrario
(1 diciembre 1972), p. 8; and "El Paro de los Conchenchos," ibid., p. 2.

contained 65.7 percent of agricultural land (BIH). At the other
end of the spectrum, 90.6 percent of agricultural properties contained only 22.4 percent of the land in farms (BIH). Other than
the reformed sector, the most important growth in the proportional share of land in particular property categories took place
among farms of from 40 to 80 hectares (BIH); their area in hectares (BIH) increased from 12.8 to 27.3 percent. These shifts in
the locus of proprietary claims in rural land from hacendados to
cooperative enterprises and commercial farmers entailed a dispersion of decision-making capabilities in the rural sector despite
the maintenance of a relatively high degree of physical concentration of land in a small number of properties. If the military
actively pursues its policy of parcelization in the countryside,
property in rural land could be highly dispersed within a two- to
three-year period.

Internal Distribution of Proprietary Authority:
The Reformed Sector

The disorganization of the reformed sector in agriculture, as
observed in 1973, made it extremely difficult to generalize

about the location of even formal proprietary discretion within the enterprises that occupied about 36 to 40 percent of Chile's agricultural land (BIH). In the asentamientos a common organizational pattern existed that assigned managerial and entrepreneurial functions to an elected management committee, subject to the constraints of the authority of the general assembly of asentados. But until the asentados received title to the rural property CORA retained a large amount of proprietary authority in the individual farm units and exercised considerable influence in farm management. Where the asentados completed the transitional period and gained legal independence, including title to the land as a mixed or collective enterprise, private accountants sometimes took the place of the CORA functionaries as management "consultants" to the asentamientos. The accountants generally had more widespread urban contacts than the campesinos and thus replaced the governmental bureaucrats as intermediaries between campesinos and factor markets or buyers. Unlike the public officials, however, the accountants could be dismissed if the campesinos found their performance unsatisfactory.

Despite their defects, including the tendency in some asentamientos toward domination by an obligarchic clique or even by an inept, paternalistic president who merely took on the role of the ex-hacendado in "providing" for "his" campesinos, the asentamientos served to broadly redistribute property in rural land among a group of favored rural laborers. Each asentado retained (or acquired) a private garden plot as well as voting rights within the asentamiento. But the asentamientos still to a considerable degree employed wage labor, and the asentados attempted to limit the number of full members of the enterprise. The sons and daughters of asentados and other workers living or working on the farm did not participate as equal members. This situation implied continuing management-labor conflicts and domination of the enterprise by the middle-aged heads of family to the exclusion of the often better-educated younger generation. A slowly growing rural labor force and the propensity of the asentados themselves to mechanize farm operations offered no long-term prospects for a general solution to the employment problems in agriculture through extension of the asentamiento system to the entire reformed sector.

The Allende government officially halted constitution of new asentamientos late in 1971. With the failure of the CERA concept, introduced to replace the asentamiento, the government began to call the expropriated properties in the reformed sector —except for the state farms—*comités campesinos*. That the legal and organizational status of these comités remained unclear provided the military government with the option of simply subdividing large properties and creating a large class of peasant proprietors instead of consolidating the cooperative and collective farm sector.

The Nonreformed Sector[22]

It may be the irony of the Chilean land reform process that a growing emphasis on collective enterprises produced ever more efficient private farms in which the rural labor force obtained an increasingly important share of income in the rural enterprise. Ringlein's sample of private farms showed that in the period 1963-64 to 1968-69 farm workers' real wages, including payments in kind, nearly doubled.[23] At the same time, the strength of rural unions, the threat of expropriation, and the obligations imposed by labor law implied a shift in proprietary authority within the private farm sector.

In some cases, the changes even induced workers to oppose governmental expropriation of particular properties. Campesinos obtained little success in preventing expropriation, but such resistance by the workers indicated their perception that at least in some areas they were relatively well off when compared with workers in nearby asentamientos—despite the governmental subsidies to the reformed units. Some landowners deliberately opted for extended sharecropping, systems of profit sharing, or other devices to compete with the lure of land reform and to attempt to block governmental expropriation of their farms. The overall effect of these tactics was to improve markedly the conditions of rural workers and to vest them with limited proprietary interests within properties in the private farm sector.

In other cases, after expropriation occurred, cooperative relationships developed between the landowner (now confined on his reserve) and the asentados. While conflicts between the asentados and the ex-hacendados over assessment of the farm's value, location of the reserve, unpaid salaries, or other grievances were common, renting of farm machinery, provision of credit to individual campesinos or to the asentamiento, and even managerial assistance often linked the asentados with their ex-patrón. This relationship provided the campesinos with alternatives to bureaucratic purveyors of goods and services and provided the ex-hacendados with occasional workers, commercial clients, and some political leverage in dealing with the campesinos.

The Allende government's efforts to limit the number of reserves and to decrease their average size was designed to prevent further evolution of the new relationship between campesinos and the ex-hacendados. For the Popular Unity coalition the landowner reserves represented a bastion of capitalism in the countryside and a potential linkage between the campesinos and the "social base of reaction." Sixty percent of the expropriated hacendados retained reserves during the years 1964 to 1970. The Allende government managed to reduce this figure to 10 percent between 1970 and 1972. The size of reserves was also reduced from 80 to 40 hectares through narrow interpretation of the 1967 Agrarian Reform Law.[24]

As the private commercial sector and the campesinos in the reformed sector faced common problems vis-à-vis governmental policies, weather, crop and animal disease, and so on, the likelihood of cooperative relationships tended to increase despite public efforts to keep the ex-hacendados in quarantine. The increased productivity of the private commercial sector and the improved position of rural labor within these enterprises might, with appropriate public incentives to agriculture more generally, offer an alternative model of agrarian reform to the campesino enterprises. In a mixed agricultural sector such an alternative might provide mutually competitive inducements for continued innovation in production and management to the benefit of rural workers, the cooperatives and individually-owned firms, and the national economy.

For a socialist regime, of course, this alternative was neither desirable nor feasible. Elimination of the landlord class represented a political goal of the Popular Unity government and was given short-term priority over economic problems such as production in the rural sector. From 1970 to 1973 various officials in the government expressed their willingness to sacrifice short-run production in order to eliminate, once and for all, the hacienda system and the hacendados from the countryside. This short-term commitment, especially after 1971 when the political power of the hacendados was quite limited, played a significant role in the deterioration of agricultural production and the eventual coup that ousted the Popular Unity government.

In contrast, if the restoration of private enterprise to respectability can only be accomplished through military repression of the rural labor movement, then the campesinos will have traded the scorn for their intelligence manifested by many Popular Unity officials for a loss of those proprietary interests in the private farm sector gained since 1965. In either case, coerced workers are not productive workers; without appropriate incentive systems—that is, incentives that have concrete meaning for rural workers—neither socialist nor capitalist agriculture can succeed with a labor-intensive production unit. Where employment alternatives are not widely available, increased productivity through mechanization which pushes workers from the rural to urban areas can be a very costly political and economic strategy. This is the question any Chilean government must resolve: How can increasing welfare for rural workers be combined with increased productivity through labor-intensive technologies? The answer, as always, depends in great part on the distribution of property in rural land.

Linkages among Rural Proprietors

From 1964 to 1967 differences over the best manner to negotiate with the Christian Democratic government about the proposed agrarian reform law divided the major landowner organizations in Chile. Kaufman claims that until the summer of 1967, when the agrarian reform bill was finally passed, the moderation of the SNA leadership and the relative flexibility of the rightist politicians tended to be the predominant theme in the overall opposition to the land reform.[25] After 1967, Kaufman suggests, moderation declined and more solid resistance to the Christian Democratic program developed.[26] But even within the SNA, hardline resistance had its advocates in the period 1964-1967, and regional agricultural societies opposed the Frei program vigorously from the beginning. The Coordinating Committee of Agricultural Associations, formed in October 1965, persistently opposed "moderate" tactics by the SNA prior to 1967; with the passage of the Agrarian Reform Law the moderate leadership in the SNA lost credibility, and the organization returned to a more hardline position and a closer alliance with the new National party, an amalgamation of the Conservatives and Liberals.

Whatever the initial division among the large landowners, the net result of the agrarian reform process was an impressive expansion of membership in the existing agricultural societies and the creation of numerous employers' unions in the countryside. As suggested in chapter 1, as private property in land came itself to be the focus of governmental hostility, the rural proprietors solidified their opposition and responded with class action against the government and rural labor. From April 1968 to December 1969, the number of members of employers' unions increased from 1,917 to 9,803, while the number of landowners affiliated with the SNA increased (1965-1969) by 2,666, reaching a total of 4,500 members.[27]

In 1967 rural proprietors formed the Confederation of Agricultural Employers' Unions (CONSEMACH). Under the terms of the Rural Unionization Law of 1967, employers' unions acquired an important role in rural labor conflicts. Formed on a commune-wide basis, the employers' unions provided an expanded context for dealing with common interests among rural proprietors. The unions recruited many farmers never before related to the previously "aristocratic" SNA or the producers' associations which attracted representatives of specialized and relatively more modern enterprises. As Gonzalo Arroyo and Sergio Gómez have written, a new sector of rural entrepreneurs (*grupo empresarial*) "seems to have arisen as an indirect, and perhaps unexpected, result of the process of agrarian reform and of the political weakness of the Christian Democratic and current [Allende] government."[28] These new interest groups and syndical organizations took on the task of sectoral representation. They argued that it was necessary to unite workers with employers in order to protect the agricultural sector against discrimination by public officials and urban interests. The employers' unions emphasized the importance of sectoral solidarity; they attempted to de-emphasize intrasectoral class differences.

The Allende government's rural programs intensified the resistance of rural proprietors to the agrarian reform and tended to increase the solidarity of the members of the employers' unions as well as of the traditional landowner associations. Producer strikes, vigilante groups (to protect or recover occupied farms) and mass media campaigns which publicized the government's "lawlessness" and bungling administration in agriculture replaced the parliamentary negotiations emphasized by the SNA from 1964 to 1967 as principal tactics to deal with governmental rural programs.

The sectoral thesis advanced by the rural proprietors increasingly, after 1970, offered the possibility of further linkages among different types of rural proprietors and the opportunity to expand the social base of opposition to the Allende government's programs. Transformed from rural workers into rural proprietors in large-scale cooperative enterprises (and with the persistence of their intrafarm private plots), the asentados often perceived a convergence of their interests with those of the private commercial sector. Likewise, the numerous small proprietors linked together in a variety of cooperatives and producer committees during the period 1964-1970 shared some basic interests with other rural proprietors. The statement by a spokesman for the National Confederation of Asentamientos and Agrarian Reform Cooperatives, reported in *El Mercurio* (October 27, 1972), indicated the changed incentive structure for the new proprietors:

> The income of the campesinos in the reformed sector does not depend upon wages but upon produce from the land. We are, therefore, concerned with the prices fixed for [agricultural] products.
>
> We consider it urgent that a study be carried out concerning agricultural commodities so that prices be set at a level which creates a stimulus for production by our national producers—to avoid spending the foreign exchange of the country on food produced by farmers in other nations.
>
> . . . In selling our produce we see our freedom increasingly limited and our dependence upon the State greatly mounting. . . .[29]

In addition to basic questions of prices for agricultural commodities, inputs, and relative prices, the perception of an increasing insecurity of tenure for even the owners of small rural properties, derived from the numerous land occupations from

1970 to 1972, tended to increase the membership and solidarity of employers' associations. By the beginning of 1973, thus, rural employers' organizations had more members, a broader social base, and offered a more militant resistance to the incumbent government than at any other time in Chilean history.

With the military coup, formal consolidation of the rural employers' organizations which represented large and small farms further strengthened the sectoral unity of rural proprietors. Pushing for constitutional guarantees against expropriation of all farms of less than 40 hectares (BIH) (and informal guarantees for those farms larger than this size but "efficiently managed"), the private farm sector looked to the military to restore protection to capitalist agriculture and private property in rural land. The military government's initial policies toward agriculture, including quite favorable credit and price policy, and even a move toward reducing some tariffs on manufactured goods, won the praise of both the traditional landowner interests (SNA) and the leaders of the asentados and small farmer associations. Indeed, a preliminary adoption of economic tactics that emphasized comparative advantage and the elimination of inefficient industries represented such a radical departure from policies pursued over the last forty years that effective implementation is sure to produce a most intense sectoral clash between agriculture, competitive industry, and mining, on the one hand, and the numbers of industries in Chile that can survive only under the umbrella of high tariff barriers built up over the years of import substitution-oriented industrialization. Such a policy orientation would strengthen the linkages among all groups of farmers, but the cost would seem to be substantial dislocations and unemployment in the industrial sector.

Even policies quite favorable to farmers in general, however, will only marginally affect a large number of rural workers and smallholders that remain outside class organizations or interest groups. With almost 40,000 campesinos in the nonreformed sector organized in cooperatives, and another 50,000 in INDAP-supported campesino producer committees (comités), more than 50 percent of smallholders still belonged to no producer organization.[30] The minifundistas in particular failed to receive the benefits purveyed by the public agencies during the Frei years and continued unaffiliated to producer associations at the time of the coup. To some degree, these figures fail to take into account the participation of smallholders in unions, since many worked part-time or seasonally as agricultural wage laborers. But as farmers per se they remained unorganized. A large number of the minifundistas, including many of the Mapuche, failed to benefit from either the official land reform program or the complementary benefits provided to organized smallholders. The minifundistas remained, along with the poorest migrants, the most depressed elements within the rural sector.[31]

Rural Proprietors and Rural Labor: Linkages to Urban Interests and to National and Regional Governmental Institutions

The agrarian reform program initiated by the Christian Democrats in 1964 broke or weakened most of the channels to high-level governmental decision makers always before available to the large landowners. Shortly after the Christian Democrats came to office Aníbal Correa, the editor of the SNA monthly journal, publicly protested the lack of contact between the landowners and the top officials of the regime. While his letter was also intended to support a "progressive" wing of the SNA against the hardliners, who insisted on firm resistance to the governmental program, Correa's letter accurately depicted the broken communication networks that curtailed the landowners' usual participation in governmental policymaking. Years of formal and informal participation as decision makers or, at the least, as holders of veto capabilities within the public bureaucracy, came to an end:

> ·... the times are different and we, as a pressure group organization, have virtually no communication with the government ... the current directorate is undoubtedly in a situation in which there is no clear and legitimate possibility of an understanding with the government. We know that [agrarian reform] signifies a profound transformation of the present structures, but in the SNA we have not been able to determine, for lack of contacts and information, in what form this step will be aplied or proposed to the Congress.[32]

Years of patronage appointments to the complex of Chilean agrarian reform bureaucracies and other public agencies left many Conservatives, Liberals, and Radicals in important administrative posts. These officials could slow down, alter, or derail aspects of the agrarian reform program in their administration. But at the top levels of the government, landowners no longer could define the parameters of public policy or limit the commitment of the central government to carry out a relatively comprehensive agrarian reform program.

At the same time, the Christian Democrats carefully cultivated industrial proprietors to prevent the formation of a broad coalition of propertied interests against the government. While the industrial capitalists held an underlying mistrust of the Frei government, they did not intervene to defend the agrarian property owners.[33] Despite the industrialists' fears that the principle introduced by the land reform (expropriation of "inefficient" producers) might be extended to other areas of the ecomomy, the Frei government skillfully neutralized them by providing new economic opportunities to domestic firms and emphasizing the potentially positive effects of land reform for the urban economy, for example, cheaper food and larger markets for manufactured goods. Some urban interests benefited immediately from the agrarian reform; governmental contracts to build roads, farm buildings, and housing, and to provide other services to the agencies involved in the land reform process profited a number of private firms, thus mitigating ideological objections to the land reform. The isolation of the landowners from nonrural entrepreneurs, along with the government's insistence that only inefficient operators would be expropriated, left the affected hacendados relatively exposed and without the possibility of mobilizing substantial support from other groups.

Given the quasicorporate nature of relationships between interest groups and Chilean bureaucracies, loss of access to the top levels of administrative decision making was a serious loss to the landowners. Neutralization of their potential urban allies further weakened their position. Nevertheless, until 1970, the large landowners who were not expropriated managed to maintain favorable relationships with governmental credit institutions, private banks, and export-import firms. They also exercised limited veto capabilities in the Congress through the National party and the more conservative elements within the Christian Democratic party. Overall, however, the long-standing pattern in which hacendados exercised vetoes in regard to policies affecting the countryside disappeared. No longer could they

control the extent or content of penetration into the countryside by the agrarian bureaucracies, the Labor Department, or
other governmental agencies. Government- and party-sponsored
proselytization and organization of rural labor, labor conflicts,
strikes, and land occupations destroyed the legitimacy and political basis of the hacienda system. Gradually even the technical services and investment provided by the government to
agriculture shifted their orientations from the large estates to
the new proprietors in the reformed sector and to the small and
middle-sized farm units.

By the end of 1972 the Allende government almost entirely
eliminated all farms containing over 80 hectares (BIH). The hacendado, qua hacendado, passed from the Chilean scene. Nevertheless, the Popular Unity coalition insisted that an important
rural bourgeoisie remained as an obstacle to the creation of a socialist agriculture. In particular, the regime identified those proprietors with 40 to 80 hectares (BIH) who, in aggregate, held
27.3 percent of all agricultural land (BIH) as "a powerful and
active bourgeoisie."[34] But this "powerful" agrarian bourgeoisie
had very limited access to governmental decision makers and no
control over the credit policies of a nationalized banking system. The rural proprietors in this category were not, with the
exception of the ex-hacendados on their reserves, a part of the
old landed aristocracy with social ties among Santiago's elite.
Rather, they were capitalist farmers, highly dependent upon
governmental price policy, availability of agricultural inputs
(also to great extent controlled by the government), and marketing channels (increasingly under governmental control or
regulation). These farmers lacked the urban linkages that had
made the hacendados so powerful a force in Chilean politics
during almost four centuries.

In contrast to the hacendados, the linkages of rural workers,
smallholders, and the new proprietors to urban interests and
governmental institutions dramatically increased from 1964 to
1973. Many campesinos came into almost permanent contact
with political parties, the agrarian bureaucracies, public and private credit institutions, private purveyors of agricultural inputs,
and even large agribusiness firms that contracted for the produce of the campesinos through cooperatives and smallholder
committees. Never before had campesinos participated to this

extent within the national policymaking apparatus. Despite the initial dominance of educated bureaucrats over the campesino representatives in CORA, INDAP, or the labor arbitration boards, campesinos became more vocal and more skilled in their policymaking roles. Indeed, the tendency by Christian Democrats and the Popular Unity officials to praise loudly campesino participation in policymaking while attempting to limit such participation to ratification-legitimation of governmental policies increasingly irritated many campesino leaders. Whereas some campesino leaders themselves became lower-level officials in CORA, INDAP, or even the Labor Department, the campesinos learned by experience that for many bureaucrats and governmental policymakers campesino participation was more a rhetorical than substantive commitment. As the campesinos gained confidence, experience, and a sense of their own increased political power, bureaucratic paternalism and tokenism seemed less acceptable.

The six-year experience from 1964 to 1970 left campesino organizations with legal advisers on permanent retainer and an avowed unwillingness to be dominated by governmental decision makers. The road to socialism pursued by the Popular Unity coalition frequently ran counter to the perceived interests of the asentados, small farmers, and the declared preferences of several rural union confederations. The recently established ties between campesino organizations and the Christian Democractic party, as well as the numerous Christian Democrats still active in the agrarian bureaucracy and other governmental agencies with rural functions, served as channels to mobilize antigovernment movements. In early 1973, when the Allende government attempted to introduce a governmental monopoly in the marketing of wheat, the national leaders of the asentados joined the "agrarian bourgeoisie" and the non-Marxist union confederations in vigorous opposition to the government's unilateral imposition of policies on the rural sector. In particular, leaders of the rural union confederation that originated with ASICH, UCC, and ANOC (Confederación Libertad) proclaimed:

> The Confederation "Libertad" cannot approve of a measure that injures the interests of those workers in the reformed sector and that was adopted behind the backs of the campesino. The celebrated partic-

ipation of which we hear so much has been limited to sporadic communications provided to us by the Ministry of Agriculture. Our organizations have not been given a real and effective decision-making power. It is necessary that all the country know that the estanco was established without the approval of our organizations and that the prices of agricultural products were fixed solely by the Government. . . .

We reaffirm our conviction that Chilean agriculture can only prosper with a real, active and permanent participation of the organized campesinos, exercising decision-making power. . . .

For these reasons our national assembly has agreed not to deliver wheat nor any other product until a just price is set, a price that does not force us to work at a loss. We declare that we will defend the fruit of the campesino's labor, the agricultural products, to the last.[35]

This declaration, affirming the right of campesino organizations to participate in governmental decision making and rejecting the legitimacy of policies made without their participation resembles the historical claims of the SNA on the public-policy process.[36] Only once before in Chilean history had a campesino organization made public demands for such formal participation. In 1939 Emilio Zapata's Liga Nacional de Defensa de Campesinos Pobres demanded formal representation in the Popular Front government. Zapata's demands lacked the firm organizational support necessary to make them credible. In 1972 the alliances between non-Marxist campesino organizations and the Christian Democratic party made the campesino demands an effective restraint on some aspects of governmental policy implementation. The successful rejection of the CERA and the continued insistence on asentamiento or cooperative proprietorship rather than state farms also depended upon the linkages of these campesino organizations to urban political movements and parties.

Likewise, the Marxist dominated campesino organizations depended upon the leftist political parties and governmental agencies to provide benefits for the membership. As in the past, the fragmentation of the Chilean left spilled over into the countryside. Within the Marxist campesino organizations competition between Communists and Socialists divided the loyalties and energies of the campesinos. To the left of the Marxist parties, the MIR, MAPU, and some "deviant" Socialists called for ever more radical land reforms, while employing land occupations of even small or middle-sized farms to dramatize their commitments to an entirely socialized agricultural sector.

The political commitments of the rural labor force, thus, came to reflect, roughly, the divisions in the national polity. Christian Democrats and Marxist parties controlled the majority of organized campesinos just as they controlled the majority of the national electorate. On the right, some campesinos joined with the National party and conservative wing of the Radical party. On the left, MAPU dominated a campesino union confederation that splintered off from Triunfo Campesino (the Confederation formed by INDAP from 1964 to 1970), calling itself Unidad Obrero Campesino. MIR's rural department, Movimiento Campesino Revolucionario, lacked great numerical strength but emphasized dramatic confrontation tactics in dealing with landowners and the government. All the campesino organizations maintained linkages to urban interests and political parties to form part of the complicated multiparty, multiclass conflicts taking place in Chile "on the road to socialism."

Still, many thousands of minifundistas and migrant workers lacked supportive urban and governmental contacts. They continued to sell their products to middlemen or small truckers and to rely on the local country store for credit. Many of these poorest of Chilean campesinos belonged to no class organizations; they remained politically impotent in the wider national context as well as in the countryside. The Allende government made great efforts to involve these campesinos in rural unions, cooperatives, committees, and the consejos campesinos. From the end of 1970 until April 1972, the number of rural workers in unions increased from 140,293 to 253,531, a 70 percent rise in membership.[37] In part, the government's policies in this area were intended to wrest majority control of organized campesinos from the Christian Democrats. The ability to entice members through selective benefits provided by the governmental parties allowed the Popular Unity coalition to use the same types of incentives employed earlier by the Frei government to attract the campesinos to organizations that, at least at the level of national leadership, supported governmental programs. The Allende government also attempted to initiate a program to benefit the Mapuche Indian campesinos in southern Chile.[38] But centuries of segregation and abuse from "Chileans" as well as the institutional racism faced by these Indian campesinos could not be quickly eliminated through legislation, no matter how benign.

By mid-1973 rural labor was more aware of the ongoing national political struggle and better linked to urban interests, political parties, and governmental institutions than at any time before in Chilean history. Rural labor remained a highly stratified group, with varying quality and strength of urban linkages. The economic interests of the elements within the rural labor force varied, as did the campesinos' political party affiliation or preference. Rather than forming a unified campesino class, the rural labor force reflected, in simplified microcosm, the multiplicity of political, economic, and social cleavages characteristic of urban Chile.

As in 1919, the struggle in the countryside in 1973 was part of a broader national political confrontation. Competing interests with alternative visions of a Chile-to-be carried their struggle into the rural areas. Unlike the situation in 1919, the majority of campesinos in 1973 belonged to class organizations, were sympathizers or members of national political parties, and were accustomed to dealing with governmental officials. Large landowners no longer controlled the countryside. Political power in rural areas came to be widely dispersed among rural unions, producer associations, campesino cooperatives, competing political parties, voluntary associations of various sorts (mothers' clubs, juntas de vecinos, campesino committees), and governmental bureaucrats.

Now a new struggle was developing against efforts to recentralize political power nationally and in the countryside. The central government, or at least some members of the Popular Unity coalition, sought to establish a dominant role in rural production, including control over the rural labor market, credit, marketing, and prices, in the hands of the national government. These efforts, justified in the name of "socialism" and a "classless society" were viewed by many campesinos as an effort to liquidate the gains of the years of struggle, to eliminate their private claims to land, to appropriate the products of their labor, and to suppress their autonomous political capabilities vis-à-vis the state and the governmental parties.

Some policymakers in the Popular Unity coalition saw opposition to their programs as reactionary resistance to the development of socialism, inspired by the rightist parties and the ex-hacendados in an effort to stop the process of agrarian reform and the construction of a socialist society. In part, this view was correct. The rightist parties and the SNA attempted to rally campesino support by emphasizing the collectivist-statist orientation of the government's rural programs. To an even greater extent, however, the character of interaction by the governmental bureaucracies with the campesinos aroused resentment and resistance. After the years of struggle which culminated in the asentamientos, large-scale labor organizations, and improved incomes and living conditions for many thousands of campesinos, the Popular Unity coalition began to call the campesinos "kulaks," "new reactionaries" (*momios nuevos*), "agents of the CIA," and a "new privileged class."

Urban functionaries went to the countryside to tell the campesinos that they must sacrifice their newly won gains. Yet these same bureaucrats went on strike to protect their professional privileges or to defend their salaries. Whether Christian Democrat, Socialist, or Communist, the bureaucrats sought to eliminate privilege from the countryside while they defended their own even more privileged status. While this defect cannot be attributed to the Popular Unity coalition solely, bureaucratic noncredibility seriously compromised the government's rural program. When the program required substantial willingness on the part of campesinos to sacrifice short-term interests for a promise of future benefits, most campesinos simply chose not to comply. Appeals to socialism and a new Chile swayed only a minority of campesinos in the face of bureaucratic arrogance, ineptitude, and disorganization.

Still, the question remained: Could the Allende government regain the confidence of the campesinos by de-escalating the immediate demands for collectivization, by reforming the agrarian bureaucracies so that they were made more responsive to the campesinos' needs and preferences, and by allowing campesino organizations, including those which were not controlled by the governmental parties, effective participation in policymaking that affected the rural sector? The military takeover made this question academic but posed a quite different one: Will the gains of the campesinos after 1964 be destroyed and their organizations demobilized by a short-term policy of parcelization of the countryside? Can "Stolypin reforms," combined with renewed repression of rural labor organization, defuse, if only for a short time, the agrarian question in Chile?

Whatever the answer to the question, the definition and distribution of property in rural land remained crucial. Depending
upon the content and structure of redistribution of proprietary
authority in the countryside and the types of production units
established, campesinos may acquire additional instruments for
effective political power and economic improvement, or they
may again be subjugated to the yoke of subsistence farms and
police repression. The outcome will depend upon the relationships that can be established among the campesinos and their
organizations, between them and urban interests and political
parties (if the military cedes to a civilian regime), and the ability
of campesinos, through these relationships, to influence governmental policy in the rural sector. If the campesinos are to be
successful they must trust no government, no party, no coalition, and no caudillo. They must be willing to form temporary
alliances to make temporary gains, to oppose their current allies
when those allies advocate programs that injure their interests,
and to establish themselves in a multiplicity of independent, active, and vigorous organizations locally and nationally. This can
occur only if the abrupt end to constitutional government in
Chile did not portend a restructuring of labor organizations in
Chile on the model of Brazil (1964-1974). For the sake of those
campesinos who saw a half-century of struggle bring fruits from
1964 to 1973, we can only desperately hope that the left-
opposition to Allende was wrong when it claimed that Chile's
only options in 1973 were reduced to Marxist socialism or fas-
cism—for the former option is now foreclosed, and the latter,
while not consolidated, is too real a possibility.

Yet, in retrospect, it is clear that what destroyed Chilean formal democracy was not the military coup of September 1973.
As this study has demonstrated, Chile's formal democracy, as it
developed from 1932 until 1964, rested largely upon the trade-
off between traditional elites, the middle-class political parties,
and Marxist political and labor organizations that allowed repression of rural labor to be the cornerstone of Chilean political
economy. The Revolution in Liberty in the countryside carried
out by the Christian Democrats loosened this cornerstone. With
intensification of the agrarian reform process from 1970 to
1973 the edifice swayed to the left. It was rebalanced briefly

with temporary bracing (the military ministers led by General Prats) and then was toppled to the right by a military coup whose leadership proclaimed in June 1974 that it expected to remain in power for at least five years.

The end of systematic exploitation and repression of rural labor entailed the end of Chilean formal democracy. By 1970, despite Allende's promise to respect democratic norms, the question had become what sort of institutional arrangements would replace the formal democracy that Chile had known since 1932. The Christian Democratic ideologues proposed a communitarian society. The Popular Unity coalition embarked on the "road to socialism." The leaders of the military junta rejected both these visions, along with the pattern of liberal Western pluralism, to which Chilean formal democracy had conformed for forty years. But whatever political structures and style the military sought to impose, it was the radical alteration of the political meaning of property in rural land from 1964 to 1973 that destroyed the foundations of Chilean formal democracy—a democracy that rested heavily on the back of the Chilean campesino.

NOTES

Prefatory Note

1. Preston E. James, *Latin America* (New York: Odyssey Press, 1959), p. 234.

2. Ibid.

3. Ibid.

4. Ibid., p. 244.

5. Ibid. (1950 edition), p. 220.

6. Ibid., p. 262.

7. Ibid., p. 264.

8. Marvin Sternberg, "Chilean Land Tenure and Land Reform" (Ph.D. diss., University of California, 1962).

9. Ibid.

10. Dirección de Estadística y Censos, IV Censo Nacional Agropecuario, Año Agrícola 1964-1965, 1, diciembre 1969.

11. Ibid.

Introduction

1. Roberto P. Echeverría, "The Effect of Agricultural Price Policies on Intersectoral Income Transfers" (Ph.D. diss., Cornell University, 1969), p. 59.

2. Ibid.

3. Jean Borde and Mario Góngora, *Evolución de la propiedad rural en el Valle de Puange*, vol. 1 (Santiago: Editorial Universitaria, 1965), p. 30.

4. Ibid., p. 32.

5. Ibid., pp. 34-37.

6. Ibid.

7. Rafael Baranona, Ximena Aranda, and Roberto Santana, *Valle de Putaendo, estudio de estructura agraria* (Santiago: Editorial Universitaria, 1961).

8. Echeverría, "The Effect of Agricultural Price Policies," p. 61.

9. Cristóbal Kay, "Comparative Development of the European Manorial System and the Latin American Hacienda System: An Approach to a Theory of Agrarian Change for Chile" (Ph.D. diss., University of Sussex [England], 1971), p. 88.

10. Ibid., p. 89, citing S. Sepúlveda, *El trigo chileno en el mercado mundial: Ensayo de geografía histórica* (Santiago: Editorial Universitaria,

336 : NOTES TO PAGES xxvii-xxix

1959), pp. 20-21; and C. Keller, *Revolución en la agricultura* (Santiago: Zig Zag, 1956), pp. 92-93.

11. Kay, "Comparative Development," pp. 92-93.

12. Ibid., p. 94, citing Borde and Góngora, *Evolución de la propiedad rural*, pp. 75-76.

13. Mario Góngora, *Origen de los 'Inquilinos' de Chile Central* (Santiago: Editorial Universitaria, 1960).

14. Kay, "Comparative Development," p. 95.

15. Ibid.; and Góngora, *Origen*, p. 101.

16. See Frederick Pike, "Aspects of Class Relations in Chile, 1850-1960," in J. Petras and M. Zeitlin, eds., *Latin America: Reform or Revolution?* (Greenwich, Conn.: Fawcett, 1968), pp. 202-19.

17. M. Zeitlin, "The Social Determinants of Political Democracy in Chile," in Petras and Zeitlin, eds., *Latin America*, p. 229.

18. "Politics" is to be understood as any effort to manage human interdependence. Politics exists when (1) the behavior of one human being or group of human beings or the choices, opportunities, or constraints available to them depend upon the behavior of other human beings and (2) any of the parties to this system of interdependence seeks to influence the behavior of the person(s) upon whom he depends for specific outcomes or opportunities.

19. This is an adaptation of Tawney's "Power may be defined as the capacity of an individual, or group of individuals, to modify the conduct of other individuals or groups in the manner which he desires. . . ."

20. A similar approach to the problem of control over water resources can be found in Vincent Ostrom and Elinor Ostrom, "The Legal and Political Conditions of Water Resource Development," *Land Economics* 48 (February 1972): 1-14; and Vincent Ostrom, *Institutional Arrangements for Water Resource Development*, PB 207 314 (Springfield, Va.: National Technical Information Service, 1971).

21. Where agriculture depends upon access to water as a scarce resource, perhaps including creation and maintenance of irrigation infrastructure, water rights may be even more important than property in land. In Chile, however, until 1951 the doctrine of riparian rights prevailed in accord with the Napoleonic civil code tradition. See Ludwik A. Teclaff, "What You've Always Wanted To Know About Riparian Rights, But Were Afraid To Ask," *Natural Resources Journal* 12 (January 1972): 30-55.

22. Agrarian reform as a concept has a variety of meanings in social science and journalistic literature. For an overview of different ways in which the concept is used see Armand Mattelart, Carmen Castillo, and Leonardo Castillo, *La ideología de la dominación en una sociedad dependiente* (Buenos Aires: Ediciones Signos, 1970), especially pp. 141-48; Thomas F. Carroll, "The Concept of Land Reform," in Documentation of the FAO Center on Land Problems in Asia and Far East (Bangkok, 1954); Kenneth

Parsons, "The Concept of Land Reform," in Documentation of the FAO Center on Land Problems in the Near East, n.d.; Doreen Warriner, *Land Reform and Development in the Middle East* (London: Royal Institute of International Affairs, 1957); Solon Barraclough, "Qué es una reforma agraria," in Oscar Delgado, ed., *Reformas agrarias en el América Latina* (Mexico City: Fondo de Cultura Económica, 1965), pp. 124-45; A.G. Frank, "The Varieties of Land Reform," in Carlos Fuentes et al., eds., *Whither Latin America?* (New York: Monthly Review Press, 1963), pp. 57-63.; and Elias H. Tumas, *Twenty-Six Centuries of Agrarian Reform* (Berkeley and Los Angeles: University of California Press, 1965), especially chapter 2.

23. John D. Montgomery, "Allocation of Authority in Land Reform Programs: A Comparative Study of Administrative Processes and Outputs," *Administrative Science Quarterly* 17 (March 1972): 62-75.

Chapter 1

1. V.I. Lenin, *State and Revolution* (New York: International Publishers, 1971), p. 73.

2. Milton Friedman, *Capitalism and Freedom* (Chicago: University of Chicago Press, 1962), p. 10.

3. The discussion which follows deliberately avoids the question of the origins of property—an insoluble issue. Property as understood in the present study is continually being created, modified, and destroyed. Its substance and extensiveness are defined by political struggle.

4. These terms as used throughout this study are developed in H. Laswell and A. Kaplan, *Power and Society* (New Haven: Yale University Press, 1950), p. 77. The scope of authority or power refers to "the values whose shaping and enjoyment are controlled," and the domain "consists of persons over whom power [or authority] is exercised."

5. See Kenneth Parsons, "John R. Commons' Point of View," *Journal of Land and Public Utility Economics* 18 (1942): 245-66.

6. M.M. Kelso, "A Critique of Land Tenure Research," *Journal of Land and Public Utility Economics* 10 (1934): 394.

7. This conceptualization follows that of J.R. Commons, *Legal Foundations of Capitalism* (Madison: University of Wisconsin Press, 1959), especially chapters 1, 4, and 6.

8. In the present study, I use the term "rural labor" as an equivalent for the Chilean use of *campesino*—a term which includes tenants, smallholders, croppers, and wage laborers as well as the various specialized workers within the hacienda system. Given the great amount of discussion and disagreement over the use of the terms "peasant" and "peasant class" in anthropolitical literature, I do not employ this term at all.

9. The essential difference between feudalism as a political system and more "modern" political arrangements is the scope and domain of proprietorship in rural land. Perhaps the most important defining characteris-

tic of feudalism, territorial jurisdiction as an attribute of proprietorship, is suggested by Morris R. Cohen, *Law and Social Order: Essays in Legal Philosophy* (New York: Harcourt, Brace and World, 1933), pp. 42-43.

10. To such an extent is this true that Elias H. Tuma's *Twenty-Six Centuries of Agrarian Reform* (Berkeley and Los Angeles: University of California Press, 1965), the concluding chapter of which is entitled "Toward a General Theory of Agrarian Reform," does not even mention labor legislation, rural unions, or syndicates.

11. Interestingly, Doreen Warriner (*Land Reform in Principle and in Practice* [Oxford: Clarendon Press, 1969]), one of the foremost experts on the land reform issue, has defined land reform as "redistribution of property or rights in land for the benefit of small farmers and agricultural laborers," and argues that "this is a narrow definition; it reduces land reform to its simplest element, common to all land reform policies in whatever conditions they are carried out. This is what land reform has meant in practice past and present" (p. xiv). Unfortunately, the redistribution of rights in property or the redefinition of property does not necessarily mean beneficial consequences for small farmers or agricultural laborers. Thus, we would be forced to label land "reforms" that produced negative results for some sectors of rural labor something other than land reform (land reaction?) following Warriner's scheme. Likewise, although Warriner contrasts her "narrow" definition of land reform to the "integral" definition of land reform (which includes credit, extension, taxation policy, and so on), which she associates with "agricultural development policy," the *redefinition* of property has in fact been part of most land reform measures. The difference between collective farms and small-holdings in the Soviet Union became a bloody problem precisely because the question was not a narrow one but, rather, one that concerned the nature of the future society and the distribution of redefined property rights in that society.

12. Ernesto Laclau, "Feudalism and Capitalism in Latin America," *New Left Review* 67 (May-June 1971): 33.

13. See P.T. Ellsworth, *Chile, An Economy in Transition* (New York: Macmillan, 1945), pp. 81-82. For example, in the case of Chile, Decreto Ley 520 of 1932 gave the government authority to intervene, requisition, or expropriate rural land and other productive enterprises if proprietors sought to sabotage production or if there were labor conflicts.

14. For Latin America the continuum from very extensive proprietary jurisdiction to more restrictive scope and domain of authority—in the case of larger rural estates (*"hacienda tradicional"* . . . *"empresa agrícola"*)—is well presented in Aldo E. Solari, *Sociología rural Latino-Americana*, 2d ed. (Buenos Aires: PAIDOS, 1968); see chapter 4 and especially pp. 61-65.

15. In Chile the legal vestiges of nobility linked to land (*mayorazgos*) were not eliminated until the middle of the nineteenth century. The issue seems to have turned on the alienability and divisibility of these estates, however,

and not on their jurisdictional prerogatives. See Ricardo Donoso, *Las ideas políticas en Chile* (México: Fondo de Cultura Económica, 1946), chapter 6.

16. Solari, *Sociología*, pp. 83-84.

Chapter 2

1. For a discussion of this period in English see Frederick M. Nunn, *Chilean Politics 1920-1931* (Albuquerque: University of New Mexico Press, 1970); and Jordan Marten Young, "Chilean Parliamentary Government 1891-1924" (Ph.D. diss., Princeton University, 1953).

2. Frederick Pike, *Chile and the United States 1880-1962* (Notre Dame, Ind.: University of Notre Dame Press, second printing, 1965), pp. 171-72.

3. A discussion of the social question in Chile can be found in James O. Morris, *Elites, Intellectuals and Consensus: A Study of the Social Question and the Industrial Relations System in Chile* (Ithaca: New York State School of Industrial and Labor Relations, Cornell University, 1966), especially chapter 4.

4. Luis Recabarren was the most well-known labor leader and politico of the Marxist Left during this period.

5. Luis Emilio Recabarren, *Obras escogidas*, vol. 1 (Santiago: Editorial Recabarren, 1965), p. 46.

6. Translation after James Beckett, "Land Reform in Chile," *Journal of Inter-American Studies* 5 (April 1963): 182.

7. *Código civil de Chile* (Madrid: Instituto de Cultura Hispánica, 1961).

8. Carlos Andrade Geywitz, *Elementos de derecho constitucional chileno* (Santiago: Editorial Jurídica de Chile, 1962), p. 125.

9. Jose Guillermo Guerra, *La constitución de 1925* (Santiago: Establecimientos Gráficos Balcells, 1929), p. 125.

10. Ibid.

11. Ibid., pp. 130-31.

12. *La tributación agrícola en Chile, 1940-1958* (Santiago: Instituto de Economía, Universidad de Chile, 1960), p. 3.

13. For a brief description of prior colonization projects see Mark Jefferson, *Recent Colonization in Chile* (New York: Oxford University Press, 1921).

14. The Chilean term *utilidad pública* is used to define legally the areas in which the state can exercise the right of eminent domain. Article 10 of the Chilean constitution provides that "No one can be deprived of property under his control, nor any part thereof, except by virtue of a judicial order or through expropriation in accord with a law declaring it to be of 'utilidad pública'."

15. See the *Boletín* of the Sociedad Nacional de Agricultura (August 28, 1928), p. 547, for the landowners' reactions.

16. According to Gene Martin Ellis in the area he studied: "Although the government gave liberal terms to the new owners in regard to total price and length of time to pay, the terms were strict enough to exclude all agricultural laborers from the possibility of obtaining land. Not a single agricultural laborer received property. Only one individual, a mayordomo who had previously lived on the divided land, was able to purchase a parcel." ". . . While all the people who obtained land were supposed to be qualified agriculturists this was not always the case. Army officers, government bureaucrats, and people with special influence in the government obtained land despite their obvious lack of qualifications or need." "Land Division in Central Chile" (Ph.D. diss., Syracuse University, 1955), pp. 38, 42.

17. P.T. Ellsworth (*Chile, An Economy in Transition* [New York: Macmillan Company, 1945], pp. 103-4) reported: "Although it is empowered to expropriate property for the purpose of forming colonies, it has based its program upon the purchase of farm lands (principally large fundos) offered for sale and upon the acquisition of certain government-owned lands. From its foundation in 1929 until midyear of 1940, it had thus taken over 389,714 hectares of private property and 142,714 hectares of government property, most of it (80.6 percent) in the central portion of the country."

18. See the letter from La Central General de las Colonias Agrícolas de Chile to the Labor Department, March 30, 1932, *Providencias* 6, 1932, 1251-1500; Oficio 3101, 16 mayo 1932, "Sobre colonización con empleados y obreros cesantes," *Oficios* 7, 1932, 3001-3500; Oficio 1639, n.d. marzo 1932, "Sobre petición de la Sociedad Ex-Alumnos Escuelas Agrícolas y Agricultores de Chile y Aspirantes a Colonos," *Oficios* 4, 1932, 1501-2000; and Oficio 3478, 8 junio 1932, "Sobre colonización con cesantes," *Oficios* 7, 1932, 3001-3500.

19. There seems to have been some willingness within the Caja de Colonización Agrícola to experiment with collective management and production in the colonies, especially during the short "Socialist Republic" in 1932. See Oficio 3478, 8 junio 1932, ibid.

20. For treatments of the origin and alterations of inquilinaje over time, see Alexander Schejtman Mishkin, *El inquilino de Chile Central* (Santiago: ICIRA, 1971); Mario Góngora, *Orígen de los inquilinos de Chile Central* (Santiago: Editorial Universitaria, 1960); and Rafael Baraona et al., *Valle de Putaendo* (Santiago: Instituto de Geografía, Universidad de Chile, 1961).

21. For an insight into this system of labor recruitment see Andrés Sabella, "El Enganchador," *Antología chilena de la tierra* (Santiago: ICIRA, 1970), pp. 43-50.

22. Letter from Sociedad Vinícola del Sur to the Labor Department, Tomé, 18 noviembre 1914, *Notas recibidas* 1914-1915.

23. Ibid.

24. Of course the "market" was heavily influenced by the quasi-monopo-

listic distribution of land and the nonavailability of alternative employment.

25. In practice *vales* continued to be used despite the decree of 1852 that prohibited their use. See Oficio 482, Secretaría de Bienestar Social, La Serena, 10 marzo 1931, "Uso de fichas, vales, etc., canjeables en pulperías, almacenes, etc.," *Providencias* 11, 1931.

26. See David Weeks, "European Antecedents of Land Tenure and the Agrarian Organization of Hispanic America," *Journal of Law and Public Utility Economics* 23 (1947); Jean Borde and Mario Góngora, *Evolución de la propiedad rural en el valle de Puange*, vol. 1 (Santiago: Editorial Universitaria, 1956), especially chapter 1; Sam Schulman, "The Colono System in Latin America," *Rural Sociology* 20 (March 1955); 34-40; and John Francis Bannon, *Indian Labor in the Spanish Indies* (Boston: D.C. Heath, 1966).

27. "Manual del Hacendado Chileno," *Antología chilena*, pp. 69-70.

28. For copies of internal regulations (*reglamentos internos*) specifying the scope and domain of the landowners' formal authority in the period 1930-1940 see Brian Loveman, "Property, Politics and Rural Labor: Agrarian Reform in Chile, 1919-1972" (Ph.D. diss., Indiana University, 1973), pp. 844-48.

29. George McBride, *Chile: Land and Society* (New York: American Geographical Society, Research Series, No. 19, 1936), p. 162.

30. Sergio Gómez, "Class Organization and Conflict in Rural Chile" (M.A. thesis, University of Essex [England], 1971), pp. 49-50.

31. See Jaime Eyzaguirre, *Chile durante el gobierno de Errázuriz Echaurren, 1896-1901* (Santiago: Zig Zag, 1957), p. 30.

32. On this point see McBride, *Chile*, p. 182.

33. Oficio 245, 21 febrero 1924, *Comunicaciones enviadas*, 1er. Cuatrimestre, 1924.

34. See for example Oficio 149, Chillán, 26 diciembre 1924, *Inspecciones regionales*, 1924. A labor inspector in Chillán suggests aiding workers by "taking from some landowners the judicial power they exercise, even though the police, which they use to serve their ends, remain at their disposition."

35. Oficio 397, Gobernación de la Ligua, 17 agosto 1921, *Inspección regional Valparaíso*, vol. 1, 1921.

36. Letter from Enrique Döll, Fundo La Higuera, to the gobernador of La Ligua, 17 agosto 1921, ibid.

37. Oficio 398, Gobernación de La Ligua, 18 agosto 1921, ibid.

38. Letter from Enrique Döll to the gobernador of La Ligua, 18 agosto 1921, ibid.

39. Transcribed in Oficio 479, 28 febrero 1929, *Providencias* 3, 1930, 259-491, 14 marzo-10 mayo.

40. Oficio 296, Intendencia de Bío Bío, Los Angeles, 25 enero 1929, *Archivo* 1-444, 1929, 2 enero-11 febrero.

41. Letter from Luis Martínez to the minister of interior, 9 mayo 1927, *Comunicaciones recibidas*, mayo 1927.

42. As Ernest Feder has put it ("Societal Opposition to Peasant Movements and Its Effects on Farm People in Latin America," in H. Landsberger, ed., *Latin American Peasant Movements* [Ithaca and London: Cornell University Press, 1969], pp. 403-4: "what makes the power of the estate owner distinctive is its virtual absoluteness and vastness. An estate owner's decisions are orders. Hence the organization of a latifundo is not unlike that of a military organization in which the top command retains the exclusive privilege of making decisions on all matters concerning the soldiers' activities and where delegation of power exists only within certain narrow limits—qualified always by the right to intervene, even arbitrarily."

43. Thus, for example, in March 1931 the owners of the Hacienda Vichiculen complained that the visit of labor inspectors to the farm had left the workers in a state of rebellion (*sublevados*) for several days. See the letter from H. Errázuriz to the Labor Department, 10 marzo 1931, *Providencias* 1451-1760, 1931, 11 marzo-26 marzo.

44. This does not mean it was illegal. Rather, it means that the inquilino's legal status was that of "worker," not "renter." Legally, he received access to land as part of his wage; he did not pay a labor "rent."

45. The intendente of Cautín made precisely this point; see Intendencia de Cautin, Memoria Trimestral, 1929, *Providencias* 3, 1930, 14 marzo-10 mayo, 259-491.

46. Transcribed in Oficio 884, 22 abril 1929, *Providencias* 3, 1930, 259-491, 14 marzo-10 mayo.

47. See for example Gobernación de Traiguen, Oficio 292, 3 junio 1927, "Da cuenta sobre irregularidades cometidas por patrones agrícolas," *Comunicaciones enviadas*, 1927, 2001-2500.

48. Ministerio de Bienestar Social, Circular Número 23, 25-5-1928; copy accompanies Gobernación de Victoria, Oficio 859, 17 julio 1931, "Informa sobre reclamo de Mario Manríquez (7-4-18)," *Providencias* 1931, 4701-5000, 25 agosto-7 septiembre.

49. For example, see the cases from Valdivia and Aconcagua, respectively, in Inspección Regional de Valdivia, Oficio 20, 24 abril 1925, *Varios*, 1925, and Sección Colocaciones, Oficio 2329, 11 agosto 1927, *Comunicaciones enviadas*, 1927, 2001-2500.

50. See Oficio 135, Chillán, 24 enero 1924, *Comunicaciones enviadas cuatrimestre*, 1924, for a description of the locked cattle cars in which rural workers were transported.

51. This reglamento is translated and reproduced in Loveman, "Property, Politics and Rural Labor," pp. 81-83.

52. Secretaría de Bienestar Social Bío Bío, Oficio 241, 23 mayo 1931, "Consulta sobre aplicación, Reglamento No. 1636 enganches agrícolas," *Oficios* 1931, 3161-3530, 22 mayo-9 junio.

53. Oficio 3352, 1 junio 1931, "Se acusa recibo oficios No. 241, de fecha 23 del presente [sic]," *Oficios* 1931, 3161-3530, ibid.

54. Oficio 2194, *Notas enviadas*, 1925, agosto-septiembre.

55. Oficio 3404, 3 junio 1931, "Evacua consulta que se indica," *Oficios* 1931, 22 mayo-9 junio, 3161-3530.

56. Luis Correa, in *Antología chilena*, p. 38. Medical personnel in the Health Service saw the problem differently. The chief doctor at a clinic in San Antonio (Santiago Province) complained to the Labor Department in 1931 that "the owners of fundos do not send the workers to the clinic [because] they do not maintain the libretas up to date. [Because of this] the majority of the service we provide we must do as if we were treating 'indigents' " (Junta Central de Beneficencia, No. 3256, Santiago, 23 marzo 1931, *Providencias*, 1931).

57. See Oficio 974, Rancagua, 4 septiembre 1930, "Consulta sobre aplicación de multa," *Archivo* 1930, 2324-2643, 4 septiembre-23 septiembre.

58. Incomplete data for October 1930, February 1931, and May 1931 indicate 1726, 2171, and 819 "visitas rurales," respectively, made by Labor Department personnel. Data include totals for Atacama, Coquimbo, Aconcagua—Valparaíso, Santiago, Colchagua—(O'Higgins), Curicó (Talca), Maule (Linares), Ñuble, Concepción, Bío Bío, Cautín, Valdivia, Chiloé, and Aysén. Totals are computed by the author from monthly inspection reports in each of these provinces. These monthly reports can be found scattered throughout the Labor Department Archive for the period 1930-1931. Another indication of penetration of labor inspectors into the countryside is the claim by officials in Colchagua that 975 rural visits were made in this jurisdiction in 1930 and over 20,000 libretas issued in the countryside in this area to 1931 (Oficio 975, Rancagua, 5 septiembre 1930, *Providencias* 6, 1930, 913-1296).

59. Secretaría de Bienestar Social de Chiloé, Oficio 1419, Puerto Montt, 17 octubre 1931, "Observaciones a la ley 4054, tendientes a hacer más efectivo su cumplimiento," *Providencias*, 1931, 21 noviembre-9 diciembre, 6951-7300.

60. A similar point was made by the Secretario de Bienestar Social in Linares in March 1931 in Oficio 300, Linares, 19 marzo 1931, *Providencias*, 1931, 1761-2100, 27 marzo-16 abril.

61. The legal section of the Labor Department had already pointed out that this required new legislation: "Bases para un nuevo proyecto de tribunales del trabajo y de aplicación administrativa de las multas por infracciones de las leyes sociales. . . ." Memoria de la Inspección General del Trabajo, Oficio 701, 28 febrero 1929, *Oficios*, 1929, 601-1200, 21 febrero-16 abril.

62. C. Gay, *Historia física y política de Chile*, Agricultura, vol. 1 (Paris: 1862); and Schejtman Mishkin, *El inquilino*.

63. Jefferson, *Recent Colonization*, p. 4.

64. See G.F. Scott Eliot, *Chile* (New York: Scribner's, 1907), p. 283.

65. See Schejtman Mishkin, *El Inquilino*, p. 204.

66. Intendencia de Valdivia, Oficio 170, 14 febrero 1929, *Providencias* 4, 1929, 1-197.

67. Schejtman Mishkin, *El inquilino*, p. 201.

68. See the letter to Alberto Sierralta, Chacra Sierralta, Copiapó, 16 enero 1931, *Providencias* 1931, 20 enero-4 febrero.

69. Oficio 1336, Valparaíso, 6 junio 1938, "Informa providencia No. 1174 sobre denuncio Fundo San Víctor Con Con," *Providencias* 13, 1938.

70. For examples of conditions of labor offered during the harvest in this period see Gobernación de San Vicente, Oficio 750, 9 diciembre 1926.

71. Tancredo Pinochet, "Inquilinos en la Hacienda de su Excelencia," in *Antología chilena*, pp. 83-112.

72. See Armand Mattelart et al., *La ideología de la dominación en una sociedad dependiente* (Buenos Aires: Ediciones Signos, 1970), pp. 67-83.

73. In 1896 the police in the capital of each department were placed under the control of the Ministry of Interior. Municipalities retained parallel police powers, however, which were not eliminated until the Ibáñez years (1927-1931).

74. Until 1925 municipalities organized parliamentary election machinery from the preparation of voter lists to the supervision of electoral procedures. Thus, control over the municipality was a key source of national political power.

75. So integral to the electoral process was bribery and fraud that Arturo Alessandri, a few years later elected president in a populist campaign, had earlier favored elimination of universal suffrage: "Hemos dado el sufragio . . . a un pueblo que no estaba preparado para ejercitar esta altísima función de un pueblo soberano y libre, hemos tenido la verguenza de verla convertida y degenerada en el más indecoroso mercado electoral. . . . Necesitamos restringir el sufragio popular . . . para contener el desborde del cohecho electoral desenfrenado que nos corroe y destruye." Cited in Ricardo Donoso, *Alessandri, agitador y demoledor*, vol. 1 (Fondo de Cultura Económica, 1952), p. 96.

76. For more on electoral corruption see John Reese Stevenson, *The Chilean Popular Front* (Philadelphia: University of Pennsylvania Press, 1942), p. 20.

77. See Manual Rivas Vicuña, *Historia política y parlamentaria de Chile*, vol. 2 (Santiago: Ediciones de la Biblioteca Nacional, 1964), pp. 399-400.

78. Throughout this period agricultural credit represented a selective benefit provided by the state to the hacendado. See *Boletín de la oficina del trabajo* Número 19 (1922): 71.

79. Stevenson, *The Chilean Popular Front*, p. 25.

80. Oficio 11657, 30 diciembre 1937, "Refiérese a salarios pagados en fundo La Mariposa de la Caja de Seguro Obligatorio," *Oficios* 47, 1937, 11601-11800.

81. As Roberto Espinoza points out, "Son ellos (los agricultores) los que han contraído compromisos en los bancos y han negociado deudas hipotecarias que están representados por muchos millones de bonos hipotecarios en circulación. Los deudores hipotecarios tienen que pagar esos bonos y otras deudas en papel moneda, y de ahí su conveniencia en que ese circulante valga lo menos que sea posible" (*Cuestiones financieras de Chile* [Santiago: 1909], cited in Mattelart et al., *La ideología*, pp. 90-91, n. 50.

82. Cited in *Boletín de la oficina del trabajo* Número 19 (1922): 79.

83. This data is used also by McBride, *Chile;* and Guerra, *La constitución de 1925.*

84. McBride, *Chile*, p. 125.

85. McBride (*Chile*) estimated that in 1930 about half the nation's population was fed from the production of the haciendas, whereas the small proprietors "mainly feed their own people and supply the needs of the smaller villages, though they contribute also, in a very limited amount to dwellers in cities and mining centers and export a small quantity" (p. 172).

86. Ibid., p. 141.

87. Ibid.

88. In 1929 official sources estimated that of about 386,290 rural laborers some 130,000 did not live in haciendas (ibid., p. 164).

89. Ellis (*Land Division*, p. 60) estimates for the area he studied in Santiago Province that from 1928 to 1954 the proportion of agricultural land in farms over 250 hectares decreased from 79 percent to 41 percent.

90. Pinochet, "Inquilinos en la Hacienda," *passim.*

91. Cristóbal Kay, "Comparative Development of the European Manorial System and the Latin American Hacienda System: An Approach to a Theory of Agrarian Change for Chile" (Ph.D. diss., University of Sussex [England], 1971), p. 108.

92. See the labor petitions in Brian Loveman, *Struggle in the Countryside: A Documentary Supplement* (Bloomington, Ind.: International Development Research Center, 1976).

93. Schejtman Mishkin (*El inquilino*) and Kay ("Comparative Development") are exceptions to this statement and thus offer important insights into patterns of agrarian change in Chile.

94. *Boletín de la oficina del trabajo* Número 19 (1922): 81-82.

95. Sociedad Nacional de Agricultura, Sociedad Agrícola del Sur (Concepción), Sociedad Agrícola del Norte (La Serena), Sociedad Agrícola e Industrial (Temuco), Sociedad Ganadera e Industrial de Osorno.

96. Letter to presidents of five agricultural associations, 28 noviembre 1928, *Archivo* 2, 2001-2200, 1928.

97. Cited in *Boletín de la oficina del trabajo* (1922): 129-30.

98. This labor petition and the documents mentioned below are reproduced in Loveman, *Struggle in the Countryside: A Documentary Supplement.*

99. On September 13, 1883, the Minister of Hacienda, Pedro Lucio Cuadra, wrote to the SNA to request its "cooperation in promoting an association of industrial development" (*Boletín de la Sociedad de Fomento Fabril* 1 [5 enero 1884]:5).

100. Ibid., p. 96.

101. "It is commonly said that 70% of the Congress is made up of Hacendados" (Circular de la Unión Agraria, No. 1920, El Agricultor [Santiago, noviembre 1920], p. 235, cited in McBride, *Chile*, p. 213, n. 35).

102. Mattelart et al., *La ideología*, pp. 96, 123.

103. McBride, *Chile*, pp. 181-82.

104. Alberto Edwards, *La fronda aristocrática en Chile* (Santiago: Ediciones Ercilla, 1936), pp. 153-54.

105. See Morris, *Elites*, pp. 1-4, for a discussion of the concept "industrial relations system."

Chapter 3

1. See Murray Edelman, *The Symbolic Uses of Politics* (Chicago: University of Illinois Press, 1967), p. 23.

2. On the problems of organization of disadvantaged groups and classes for collective action see Mancur Olson, Jr., *The Logic of Collective Action* (Cambridge, Mass.: Harvard University Press, 1965).

3. An example is the administration of the Sugar Act by the U.S. Department of Agriculture. The American Sugar Cane League has managed to get its representatives appointed to positions carrying with them responsibility for determining minimum wage and living conditions of rural labor in the cane areas. See Peter Schuck, "Tied to the Sugar Lands," *Saturday Review* (May 6, 1972): 36-42.

4. Letter from Alejandro Dussaillant to Inspector Del Trabajo, Lontué, 13 octubre 1932, *Providencias* 21, 1932, 6251-6500.

5. Landowners frequently claimed that many of the generic provisions of the Labor Code, especially those concerning unionization, did not legally apply to rural labor. In light of these claims Mariano Bustos' comments in 1931 in the "Actas de las sesiones de la comisión revisora del Código del Trabajo," marzo y abril 1931, *Oficios* 1932, are of interest: "In this fashion it is intended that no workers be excluded from the regime of labor legislation because of the type of industries in which they work." And in the 5th session (10 marzo 1931): "Señores Escríbar and Bustos manifest

that it is their understanding that all provisions relating to minimum wages will apply to agricultural workers."

6. Sociedad Nacional de Agricultura, *Memoria,* 1931, pp. 18-21.

7. Letter from Demetrio Zañartu to Bernardo Catalán et al., "Firmantes del pliego de peticiones del Fundo Santa Virginia," accompanying Oficio 7591, 1939, *Oficios* 29, 1939, 7401-7700.

8. Oficio 7591, 24 agosto 1939, *Oficios* 29, 1939, 7401-7700.

9. Example taken from the labor conflict in Fundo Abra, July 1939, note sent to José Luis Lecaros, Oficio 321, Rengo, 3 julio 1939, by labor inspector Osvaldo Silva Córdova.

10. I have read the minutes of the sessions of the Junta de Conciliación Agrícola for Santiago Province from 1939 to 1947. Not all labor conflicts came to the Junta since some were solved directly between the parties or with the mediation of labor inspectors or other government officials. For the numerous petitions that were dealt with by the arbitration board, however, landowners often raised questions about the legality of individual labor petitions. But after 1939 the legality of rural labor petitions in general was not raised. Likewise, labor inspectors attempted to enforce Article 509 of the Labor Code, which prohibited dismissals of workers during labor conflicts.

11. Oficio 5028, 26 mayo 1941, *Oficios* 18, 1941, 5001-5300.

12. Oficio 66, 5 enero 1945, "No es aplicable lo dispuesto en la letra B del Art. 27 de la ley 7747 . . . ," *Oficios* 1, 1945, 1-250.

13. Letter from SNA to Director General del Trabajo, 29 abril 1954, signed by Recaredo Ossa, Presidente, and César Sepúlveda, Secretario General, accompanying Oficio 5446, *Oficios* 20, 1954, 5401-5650.

14. See the letter from the SNA to the director of the Labor Department's section on conflicts, salaries, and wages, 30 noviembre 1953, reproduced in Brian Loveman, "Property, Politics and Rural Labor: Agrarian Reform in Chile" (Ph.D. diss., Indiana University, 1973), pp. 705-8.

15. The law itself provided that, in case of doubt whether a laborer worked a full turn, the local labor inspector would resolve the issue subject, as usual, to appeal to the labor courts.

16. Oficio 5446, 18 julio 1954, "El salario mínimo agrícola se paga a los obreros que cumplen jornada completa. . . ," *Oficios* 20, 1954, 5401-5650.

17. Letter from SNA to Director General del Trabajo, 9 septiembre 1961, accompanying Oficio 5439, 1961, *Oficios* 23, 1961, 5301-5500.

18. Servicio de Seguro Social, D.G. No. 405-4, Santiago, 23 mayo 1960, accompanying Labor Department Oficio 5439, 1961, *Oficios* 23, 1961, 5301-5500.

19. Oficio 25, Osorno, 7 enero 1956, "Consulta sobre validez de los 'comodatos' ante legislación campesina vigente," accompanying Oficio 02177, 7 abril 1956, *Oficios* 10, 1956, 2001-2250.

20. Oficio 02177, 7 abril 1956, *Oficios* 10, 1956, 2001-2250.

21. See Oficio 5283, 27 mayo 1940, and accompanying documentation on this case, *Oficios* 16, 1940, 5051-5300.

22. Not until 1954 was the housing code actually made available, although general provisions were included in the Decree of 1953 (DFL 244), which established a minimum agricultural wage. The provisions of the Code as adopted are reproduced in Oficio-Circular 7883, Santiago, 7 octubre 1954, *Oficios* 32, 1954, 7651-7900.

23. Letter from SNA to Jefe del Departamento de Inspección de la Dirección General del Trabajo, 3 septiembre 1955, accompanying Oficio 06465, 30 septiembre 1955, *Oficios* 29, 1955, 6301-6500. The commission to which this letter referred was an informal arrangement through which the Labor Department brought together representatives of the agricultural interests and of rural labor to discuss the application of labor law in the countryside. This was the first time rural labor had been given this sort of institutional access to the department. Both ASICH and the Federación Nacional de Trabajadores Agrícolas were represented.

24. Oficio 06465, 30 septiembre 1955, *Oficios* 29, 1955, 6301-6500.

25. *Regalía* refers to an in-kind payment, service, or perquisite constituting part of the worker's wage. From the minimum agricultural wage in 1953 proprietors could legally subtract up to 75 percent for regalías provided to the workers, and pay, at a minimum, 25 percent in cash. The value of housing provided could not be legally deducted if it did not meet the provisions of the housing code.

26. Letter from SNA to Director General del Trabajo, 5 febrero 1958, signed by Recaredo Ossa, Presidente de la Sociedad Nacional de Agricultura, accompanying document No. 3890, 28 agosto 1958, *Providencias* 24, 1958.

27. Document 3890, ibid., "La modificación al inciso 2 artículo 9 del Decreto No. 243, ya fue solicitada al Ministerio del Trabajo."

28. "Notas de Actualidad," *El Campesino* 71 (julio 1939).

29. "El avaluó de las regalías de los obreros agrícolas no puede ser modificado por decisión exclusiva del Seguro Obrero," *El Campesino* (nov.-dic. 1947), p. 31.

30. Ibid.

31. Ibid.

32. Ibid.

33. The commission's first report dealt with the need for a minimally decent diet for rural labor. Compliance would have meant dedicating 40 percent of the minimum agricultural wage to food rations. See Oficio 732, 20 julio 1955, "Informa Oficio-Circular No. 41 de fecha 17 de junio pasado," *Oficios* 25, 1955, 5501-5700.

34. Formal interviews with various Labor Department officials and conver-

sations with Labor Department employees confirmed that compliance, not the application of sanctions, was of primary concern. Some Labor Department officials attributed this phenomenon to the influence of International Labor Organization ideology after World War I and its adoption as part of the socialization process of new inspectors.

35. Oficio 1848, Santiago, 29 abril 1933, "Transcribe oficio del inspector del trabajo de San Bernardo," *Providencias* 14, 1933, 3201-3450.

36. Oficio 268, San Fernando, 25 marzo 1936, "Informa sobre inspecciones agrícolas y reitera pedidos aperos que faltan," *Providencias* 1936, 1501-1700.

37. I have reviewed the *instrucciones* left by this labor inspector. Labor Code violations existed in every fundo visited, ranging from lack of labor contracts to failure to provide accident insurance. No fines were levied, and return visits to check for compliance (*revisitas*) were left to the local labor inspectors, who did not have access to an automobile as did Concha Vera ("El Huaso Vera," as his colleagues in the Labor Department called him).

38. Oficio 1495, 2 marzo 1953, "Sobre incumplimiento de leyes del trabajo en la agricultura y necesidad de organizar sección especial para su fiscalización permanente," *Oficios* 8, 1953, 1451-1650.

39. Oficio 325, Osorno, 7 mayo 1953, "Sobre problemas que atañen a los servicios del trabajo," *Providencias* 15, 1953, 3851-4100.

40. Oficio 4515, 8 junio 1954, "Se refiere a providencia No. 2216 de 14 del mes ppdo . . . ," *Oficios* 20, 1954, 4351-4600.

41. See Oficio 888, 24 febrero 1961, "Sobre medios de movilización que deben facilitarse a inspectores del trabajo," *Oficios* 4, 1961. See also Oficio 4326, 27 septiembre 1962, "Sobre visitación agrícola," *Oficios* 21, 1962, 4301-4530; Oficio 4647, 20 septiembre 1962, "Sobre visitación agrícola," *Oficios* 22, 1962, 4531-4800; and Oficio 4417, 9 septiembre 1962, "Sobre visitación agrícola," *Oficios* 21, 1962, 4301-4530. On the attempted purchase of vehicles see Oficio 5360, 12 septiembre 1964, "Solicita dictación de decreto autorizando a la Dirección del Trabajo la adquisión de seis camionetas," *Providencias* 28, 1967, 5701-5875. In December 1963 the Contraloría General had rejected such a decree (see Contraloría General de la República de Chile, No. 85823, 31 diciembre 1963). In 1954-1955 the Labor Department actually ordered inspectors to stop making rural visits because of lack of funds (see "Informa Prov. No. 5," Talca, 5 marzo 1955, accompanying Oficio 2141, Talca, 8 marzo 1955, "Informa Prov. No. 834," *Providencias* 9, 1955, 1401-1600).

42. See Oficio 1134, San Fernando, 23 septiembre 1961, "Informa diligencias dispuesta por la Dirección del Trabajo por telegrama No. 1158 de 2 de Septiembre de 1961, al Fundo Santa Julia del Dpto. de Santa Cruz," accompanying Oficio 4614, 3 octubre 1961, *Oficios* 20, 1967, 4618-4820.

43. See Oficio-Circular 4997, 4 octubre 1963, "Uso de taxi para visitas que se indican," *Oficios* 22, 1963, 4981-5185.

44. See Oficio 5360, 12 septiembre 1964, *Providencias* 28, 1967, 5701-5875.

45. Interview with Guillermo Videla Vial, Santiago, December 4, 1971.

46. Interview with Alejandro Chelén Rojas, Santiago, June 30, 1971.

47. According to the corresponding *Annual Reports* of the Labor Department, the following number of rural *visitas* were made in the years 1931-1963: 1931, no data; 1932, no data; 1933, no data; 1934, 1882; 1935, 1743; 1936, 2300; 1937, no data; 1938, no data; 1948, 1324; 1949, 2261; 1950, no data; 1951, no data; 1952, no data; 1953, 868; 1954, 1102; 1955, 993; 1956, 1037; 1957, 1169; 1958, 846; 1959, 1065; 1960, 863; 1961, 748; 1962, 1010; 1963, 1039. From January 1939 to October 1940, 2680 visitas were made. Visitas could range from a complete inspection of all labor legislation to the processing of a minor complaint for one worker. After 1964 the number of visitas increased greatly, as did the proportion of complete inspections.

48. See Oficio 1840, 1961, "Refiérese a despidos de obreros agrícolas y cumplimiento de la legislación de trabajo en la agricultura de la provincia de Colchagua," *Oficios* 8, 1961, 1741-1920.

49. For example, in 1941 landowners were using a contract which included the stipulation that the landowner could call to work "when he believes it necessary any member of the inquilino's family, including his woman and children." The Labor Department ruled that "It is obvious that this [clause] can degenerate into abuses that must be avoided. To this end the contract should stipulate which members of the inquilino's family are obligated to work for the hacienda or fundo" (Oficio 6317, 2 julio 1941, *Oficios* 22, 1941, 6201-6600). A similar case in 1940 in Rancagua concerned a labor contract which stipulated the obligations of the workers "to work every day at whatever task directly or indirectly related to the operation of the fundo in the manner ordered by the patrón or his agent" (Oficio 9687, 6 septiembre 1940, *Oficios* 31, 1940, 9501-9800).

50. Most other labor legislation could also be used as an example, with compliance varying from law to law but always far from universal. See for example the report by Eduardo Tobar Fuentes, Inspector del Trabajo, Rancagua, 20 diciembre 1952, "Informa sobre cumplimiento de una comisión y visitas agrícolas que indica," *Oficios* 1, 1953, 1-200.

51. Oficio 5520, 30 julio 1948, *Oficios* 22, 1948, 5401-5700. Application of these provisions of Law 8.811 gave rise to a great many legal opinions by the Legal Section of the Labor Department. See for example Oficio 10749, 24 noviembre 1948, *Oficios* 41, 1948, 10501-10750; Oficio 108, 5 enero 1948, *Oficios* 1, 1948, 1-300; Oficio 5898, 9 julio 1948, *Oficios* 23, 1948, 5701-6000; Oficio 5434, 9 julio 1948, *Oficios* 21, 1948, 5151-5400; Oficio 6557, 26 julio 1948, *Oficios* 25, 1948, 6301-6600.

52. Dirección General del Trabajo, Departamento Administrativo, Sección

Estadística, 30/5/53, "Sobre cumplimiento artículo 27, ley 8.811, sobre pago asignación familiar obreros agrícolas en el país—marzo—1953," *Providencias* 15, 1953, 3851-4100.

53. Ibid.

54. Ibid.

55. "Informa oficio 6874 y providencia 710 sobre visita a la Hacienda Chacabuco," 28 octubre 1936, *Providencias* 1936, 6701-6990.

56. "Informe sobre visita a la Hacienda La Dehesa," no. 1, Santiago, 28 febrero 1939, *Providencias* 9, 1939, 2001-2300.

57. Literally this was not true. The Labor Code did stipulate minimum housing conditions for rural workers in the vague terms "adequate and hygienic." In practice, a section of the National Health Service (Higiene Ambiental) was expected to enforce "health" provisions, including the housing provisions of the Labor Code. Sometimes, however, labor inspectors did issue administrative orders (*instrucciones*) requiring improved housing. Oficio 1039, San Felipe, 17 noviembre 1963, "Informa sobre visita a la Hacienda 'San José de Piguchén' del Señor Alegría Catán Dabike," *Oficios* 2, 1961, 231-510, accompanying Oficio 393.

58. But in 1961 the director of the Labor Department explicitly rejected this practice in reference to the labor inspector's report cited in the text and ordered inspectors to require compliance with the housing code. See Oficio 421, 25 enero 1961, "Refiérese a oficio No. 1039 de 17 de Noviembre de 1960," "Sobre fiscalización a la Hacienda 'San José de Piguchén'," *Oficios* 2, 1961, 231-510.

59. For example, in 1954 in Fundo Las Bandurrias in the Los Andes region of Aconcagua, a labor inspector found housing conditions unacceptable and turned the case over to the health inspector: "In regard to the repairs on the houses, these are being carried out under the permanent supervision of the director of the department of Higiene Ambiental del Centro de Salud, Sr. Belisario Lepe Montenegro" (Oficio 499, San Felipe, 7 septiembre 1954, *Providencias* 24, 1954, 4901-5200).

60. Oficio 335, La Calera, 16 abril 1953, "Devuelve Prov. No. 1007, sobre visita de inspección a la Hacienda Rabuco y Pachacama," *Providencias* 21, 1954, 4201-4400.

61. See Brian Loveman, "The Logic of Political Corruption," Workshop in Political Theory and Policy Analysis (Bloomington: Indiana University, Department of Political Science, 1973).

62. After almost a year of reviewing Labor Department documents and interviewing, formally and informally, retired and active Labor Department personnel, I found that the level of corruption was, in fact, relatively insignificant. No illustrative cases are presented in this section because I was asked by those who provided access to the department's archives to avoid discussion of *sumarios* (internal administrative hearings) in general—to guarantee the privacy of Labor Department personnel afforded them by

law. I am convinced, in any case, after serious consideration, that such discussion would have added little if anything to this study. Corruption did occur in the Labor Department; its impact was marginal. The *belief* by campesinos that corruption was widespread did, however, limit the department's credibility and the willingness of rural workers to make formal complaints.

63. The worst case I encountered involved a landowner who had made no social security payments for 14 years. One- to three-year lapses were common.

64. This was confirmed by Pedro Donoso, the jefe of the first special inspection team—Comisión Especial Para Fiscalización Agrícola (CEFA)—in an interview with the author (Santiago, December 6, 1971). In personal conversations with career Labor Department officials, the extent of corruption within the Social Security Administration frequently was pointed out to me.

65. Oficio confidencial 1463, Talca, 3 octubre 1932, "Sobre actuación inspector señor Menzel," *Providencias* 21, 1932, 6251-6500.

66. "Como dije a Ud. en carta anterior, la investigación encargada al Inspector Provincial de Talca, no dará resultado alguno, porque éste último es amigo del primero y encubre sus faltas" (letter from Alejandro Dussaillant to the director of the Labor Department, Lontué, 2 octubre 1932, *Providencias* 21, 1963, 6251-6500).

67. Orden del Servicio No. 74, Santiago, 17 octubre 1932, "Dispone amplie investigación por inspector visitador Alfredo Bañados," *Providencias* 21, 1932, 6251-6500.

68. Ibid.

69. Oficio 6328, Santiago, 12 diciembre 1932 (typographical error in document gives date as 1930—prior to the enactment of the Labor Code—which is impossible), *Providencias* 21, 1932, 6251-6500.

70. Naturally, this same insulation obtained when workers complained that Code enforcement was not vigorous enough. Knowledge of the formal rules of the game also sometimes made bureaucrats less vulnerable to the demands of their supposed clientele.

71. Oficio 80, Melipilla, 29 marzo 1939, "Informa su telegrama No. 668 sobre despido obreros campesinos de la Hacienda 'Huechun Alto'," *Providencias* 21, 1939, 5301-5420.

72. Oficio confidencial, sin número, Rancagua, 18 mayo 1938, "Informa sobre atropello en Pelequen al inspector provincial del trabajo en comisión de servicio," *Oficios* 20, 1938, 4201-4500.

73. I could find no record of the disposition of this case if it was, in fact, heard by the court.

74. Oficio 24, Curicó, 8 enero 1940, "Informa visita practicada al fundo Huañuñe. . . ," *Providencias* 17, 1940, 4901-5300.

75. Article 76 declared in part, "the labor of agricultural workers will be

regulated by the general provisions for labor contracts, insofar as these are not incompatible with agricultural work. . . ."

76. Oficio 6523, 1 septiembre 1934, "Sobre reglamentos internos para faenas agrícolas," *Oficios* 26, 1934, 6451-6693. This oficio instructed inspectors to adapt the model reglamentos already in existence for use in agriculture. Mariano Bustos and Hector Escríbar insisted on the Labor Code's application in the countryside, including the provisions requiring *Reglamentos Internos* (see Oficio 3511, 8 junio 1935, "Absuelve consulta sobre aplicabilidad a obreros agrícolas, del título III del libro I y del título III del libro II del Código del Trabajo," *Oficios* 8, 1935, 8901-9100).

77. Ministerio del Trabajo, "Modelo de Reglamento Interno para obreros agrícolas" 1936. Reproduced in Brian Loveman, *Struggle in the Countryside: A Documentary Supplement* (Bloomington, Ind.: International Development Research Center, 1976).

78. In reviewing the Labor Department Archive I did find one reglamento interno which antedates the approved Labor Department model by over three years. Interestingly it was adopted in Viña Conchalí, the property of Pedro Aguirre Cerda, the future Popular Front president of Chile (1938-1941). At this time a model reglamento existed for industrial and commercial establishments, but not for agriculture. For this reason the labor inspector in cooperation with management adapted the model reglamento instead of employing it integrally. (This procedure was recommended by the Labor Department in 1934 before development of the model reglamento for agriculture.)

79. Letter from Juan d'Etigny to Director General del Trabajo, Santiago, 17 julio 1940, accompanying Oficio 986[?], 10 septiembre 1940, *Oficios* 32, 1940, 9801-10100.

80. Oficio 986[?], 10 septiembre 1940, *Oficios* 32, 1940, 9801-10100.

81. "Informa comisión No. 1190," Santiago, 24 mayo 1962, *Providencias* 21, 1962, 6121-6360.

82. "Informa sobre antecedentes solución conflicto de obreros agrícolas del Fundo Rincomavida. . . ," Santiago, 10 diciembre 1965, accompanying Oficio 9299, 16 diciembre 1965, *Oficios* 53, 1965, 9051-9300.

83. See M. Mamalakis and C. Reynolds, *Essays on the Chilean Economy* (Homewood, Ill.: Irwin, 1965), pp. 117-48; and T. Schultz, *Economic Growth and Agriculture* (New York: McGraw Hill, 1968), pp. 184-91.

84. For a discussion of different sharecropping arrangements see Cristóbal Kay, "Comparative Development of the European Manorial System and the Latin American Hacienda System: An Approach to a Theory of Agrarian Change for Chile" (Ph.D. diss., University of Sussex [England], 1971), p. 123 and table A-24, p. 218.

85. Ibid., pp. 107, 132.

86. Between 1955 and 1965 the number of tractors on Chilean farms almost doubled, as did the number of mechanized seeders (ibid., p. 228).

87. Landlords Survey, ICIRA Fundo Project 1965-1966, cited in ibid., p. 208.

88. Alexander Schejtman Mishkin, *El inquilino de Chile central* (Santiago: ICIRA, 1971), p. 201, citing the agricultural census for each year.

89. Ibid., p. 202.

90. Kay, "Comparative Development," p. 113.

91. Schejtman Mishkin, *El inquilino*, p. 202.

Chapter 4

1. While the politico-legal context is considered separately in this chapter for analytical purposes, the legal and administrative maneuverings described here were a response to the active pressure by rural unions and "ligas" on the hacendados. Key periods in the legal story—1932, 1933, 1939, 1941-1944, 1947-1948—coincide with the concrete actions of rural labor in the countryside, a point elaborated further in the last section of this chapter and in chapter 5.

2. See for example Oficio 8327, "Informa sobre aplicación de la ley 8811 en las faenas ganaderas de la Provincia de Magallanes," 17 septiembre 1948, *Oficios* 32, 1948, 8251-8500, and accompanying documentation.

3. *Empleados* are distinguished from *obreros* in Chilean labor legislation by the predominance of intellectual work over manual work. Over the years pressure from different organized workers to be categorized as empleados instead of obreros has made this distinction more a measure of political organization than of intellectual-versus-manual labor. Higher welfare benefits and pension arrangements for empleados reinforce this tendency.

4. Zapata was founder and leader of the Liga Nacional de Defensa de Campesinos Pobres (1935). His role in the rural labor movement is discussed in chapters 5 and 6.

5. Oficio 986 and accompanying documents, *Oficios* 4, 1933, 751-1000.

6. Ibid.

7. Oficio 1444 and accompanying documents, *Oficios* 6, 1933, 1241-1500.

8. See Oficio 1444, 3 marzo 1933, "Sobre sindicalización en los campos," *Oficios* 6, 1933, 1241-1500.

9. Telegrama 460-461, *Oficios* 8, 1933, 18 marzo-1 abril, 1801-2100. (This document is also referred to as No. 4060-4061.)

10. The only deputy in the Congress who formally protested this measure was a Socialist, Carlos Alberto Martínez. See 31a Sesión Extraordinaria, 21 marzo 1933, Cámara de Diputados. Senator Cox presented the landowners' position by essentially reiterating the arguments that the SNA had made to the Labor Department (Sesión Ordinaria, 8 junio 1933).

11. Letter from SNA to the Labor Department, n.d., *Providencias* 28, 1933, 7001-7248.

12. Providencia 2348, 31 marzo 1933, *Providencias* 10, 1933, 2201-2450.

13. República de Chile, Consejo de Defensa Fiscal, no. 175, 15 mayo 1933.

14. Letter from the SNA to the Labor Department, 6 junio 1933, *Providencias* 28, 1933, 7001-7248.

15. República de Chile, Consejo de Defensa Fiscal, no. 260, 12 julio 1933.

16. In 1936 the Sindicato Profesional de Horticultores de Antofagasta was legally constituted. But this case was marginal and extremely atypical. See Brian Loveman, *Antecedentes para el estudio del movimiento campesino chileno: Pliegos de peticiones, huelgas y sindicatos agrícolas, 1932-1966*, vol. 1 (Santiago: ICIRA, 1971).

17. Ibid., p. 1.

18. This figure does not include the local and regional chapters of the Liga Nacional de Defensa de Campesinos Pobres. The leaders of this organization have lost the documentation which would have allowed quantitative evaluation of the extension of the Liga. Total membership estimates for the Liga Nacional varied from 10,000 to 30,000. (Interviews by the author with Emilio Zapata, Carlos Acuña, and Bernardo Yuras, the three principal leaders of the Liga.)

19. This letter is reproduced in *El Campesino* (March 1939).

20. Aguirre Cerda's formal reply is reproduced in *El Campesino* (April 1939), pp. 181-82.

21. This "bargain" is explicitly acknowledged in various CTCH documents. See for example the letter from the CTCH in Los Andes (21 marzo 1940) to President Aguirre Cerda, *Providencias* 12, 1940, 3501-3800, and from the CTCH in Limache (15 abril 1940), *Providencias* 26, 1940, 8101-8200. These letters are reproduced in full in Brian Loveman, "Property, Politics and Rural Labor: Agrarian Reform in Chile, 1919-1972" (Ph.D. diss., Indiana University, 1973), pp. 250-52.

22. On this see Alejandro Chelén Rojas, *Trayectoria del socialismo* (Argentina: Editorial Astral, 1967), especially pp. 94-96.

23. *Telegrama-Circular*, 655-656, 25 marzo 1939.

24. Diputado Emilio Zapata severely criticized the government-proposed legislation and presented a counterproposal in 42a Sesión Ordinaria, 14 agosto 1940, of the Cámara de Diputados. The text of this proposal is reproduced on pages 2163-2172 of the minutes of this session under the heading "Defensa del campesinado—contraproyecto de sindicalización campesina."

25. These deputies included Emilio Zapata, Carlos Rosales, Cesar Godoy, Jorge Dowling, and Natalio Berman.

26. See for example the letter sent by the CTCH leadership to President Aguirre Cerda, 9 marzo 1940, *Providencias* 14, 1940, 4201-4500.

27. Related letters came to the minister of labor from regional consejos of the CTCH and from farm unions formed prior to the ministerial order that suspended unionization in the countryside. For example, see the letter from the CTCH consejo in San Felipe (16 julio 1940) to the minister of labor, *Providencias* 2, 1941, 301-600.

28. Confederación de Trabajadores de Chile, Consejo Directivo Nacional, no. 3236, 30 octubre 1940.

29. República de Chile, Consejo Superior del Trabajo, Comisión de Agricultura, Acta 3, 20 mayo 1943, pp. 1-2.

30. Ibid., p. 4.

31. Ibid., pp. 2-3.

32. The text of Valenzuela's testimony can be found in Comisión de Agricultura, Acta 7, 29 julio 1943.

33. Ibid., pp. 1-2.

34. Ibid., p. 2.

35. For example, instead of requiring 10 workers in order to form a union, the legislation proposed by the Consejo eventually required 25 workers. The proposed legislation also maintained the prohibition on sindicatos profesionales in the countryside (that is, on unions which had members in more than one farm).

36. Comisión de Agricultura, Acta 22, 19 mayo 1944.

37. Comisión de Agricultura, Acta 27, 12 junio 1944, pp. 3-4.

38. Oficio Circular 12627, 22 noviembre 1946, *Oficios* 43, 1946, 12601-12900.

39. The Labor Department sent out the following provisional notification to its functionaries: "Santiago: noviembre 19 de 1946. Biensocial, no. 2508. Mientras enviase oficio circular correspondiente comunicole que por orden ministerial ciento seis de quince actual derogose orden ministerial treinta y cuatro de veintiocho de marzo año treinta y nueve sobre constitución sindicatos agricolas/trabajo."

40. In Chilean presidential elections when no absolute majority is gained by any candidate the Congress decides the election between the two candidates with the largest pluralities. In this election the Liberal party held the deciding votes in the Congress and was thus in a position to bargain with González Videla, who had the largest plurality, and set conditions for supporting his candidacy.

41. This deal is mentioned by Almino Affonso et al., *Movimiento campesino chileno*, vol. 1 (Santiago: ICIRA, 1970), pp. 44-45. It was confirmed by the then falanje diputado, Jorge Rogers S. (interview, February 1, 1971, Santiago).

42. Affonso et al., *Movimiento*, p. 47.

43. Loveman, *Antecedentes.*

44. *Boletín de sesiones extraordinarias*, Cámara de Diputados, Período 1946-1947, vol. 2, 1082-3.

45. Law 8.811 can be found in *Boletín de leyes y decretos del gobierno*, Libro 116, julio 1947, pp. 792-820.

46. Jorge Rogers Sotomayor, "Nueva Organización Social del Campo Chileno," Discurso pronunciado el 29-1-47 en la Cámara de Diputados de

Chile (Santiago: Imprenta Universitaria, 1947).

47. Ibid., pp. 20-21.

48. Thus, the landowner union, Sindicato Profesional de Agricultores de Caupolicán, Rengo, asked the Labor Department to dissolve a number of rural unions that the landowners claimed had been illegally formed shortly after the Campesino Unionization Law was passed. An account of these developments is given in *El Campesino* (August 1947), p. 7.

49. "Notas de actualidad," *El Campesino* (julio 1947).

50. Letter from José del Carmen Donoso and Audilio Bustamante to the Labor Department, accompanying Oficio 5282, 23 octubre 1963, *Oficios* 23, 1963, 5186-5357.

51. Oficio 5282, ibid.

52. Law 4.057 of 1924, eventually incorporated into the Labor Code as the section on unionization, contained no discriminatory provisions with respect to rural labor. The struggle won by the landowners in 1947 was waged precisely over the application of the Labor Code in the countryside. In this sense Law 8.811 represented a deterioration of conditions from the formal status quo.

53. Communist representatives in the Congress were also stripped of their nonparliamentary governmental positions. See Decreto No. 5275, 14 septiembre 1948, *Providencias* 25, 1948, 7401-7700.

54. Oficio Confidencial 1955, 15 junio 1949, *Providencias* 23, 1949, 6401-6700.

55. Oficio Confidencial 208, Parral, 23 mayo 1949, "Sobre tramitación pro-personalidad jurídica del sindicato oo. agrícolas del Fundo 'San Manuel' de Parral," *Oficios* 23, 1949, 5701-6000, accompanying Oficio 5797.

56. "El Presidente de la Sociedad Nacional de Agricultura Llama a Colaborar con S.E. en la Extirpación del Comunismo," *El Campesino* (October 1947), p. 9.

57. Loveman, *Antecedentes*, p. 24.

58. *Memoria Anual*, Dirección General del Trabajo, 1964.

59. Oficio 3955, 18 junio 1958, "Propone reformas al Libro III del Código del Trabajo de la Organización Sindical," *Oficios* 20, 1958, 3001-4100. In 1971 Juan Arrancibia was editor of the prestigious *Revista Jurídica del Trabajo*. There are those in the Labor Department who believe that he should have been named its director in 1964.

60. See the editorial in *El Campesino* (February 1959); and "La penetración del comunismo en los campos," *El Campesino* (April 1962).

61. After 1955 the Communist party adopted tactics in rural organizations which did not include, in the vast majority of cases, efforts to unionize. As Law 8.811 was too restrictive, the Communists opted for farm committees and "free unions." This was also true of the Catholic-oriented rural labor movement after 1958 and until 1964. Still, progressively more re-

strictive interpretation of existing legislation (for example, the case of labor petitions discussed above) was an important tool in de-legalizing the activity of these associations. Since the law allowed labor petitions where no unions existed, it became necessary not only to make it virtually impossible to form unions but also to preclude legal labor petitions. With unions, strikes, and labor petitions essentially precluded, at least legally, any collective resistance to the authority and rule of rural proprietors became "criminal."

Chapter 5

1. Editorial, *La Prensa* (5 septiembre 1971).

2. For a discussion of the "social question" in English see James O. Morris, *Elites, Intellectuals and Consensus: A Study of the Social Question and the Industrial Relations System in Chile* (New York: New York State School of Industrial and Labor Relations, Cornell University, 1966), especially pp. 78-118.

3. A recent study by Arnold Bauer contains valuable information about the rural sector in nineteenth-century Chile but does not deal with labor conflict. Arnold Bauer, "Chilean Rural Society in the Nineteenth Century" (Ph.D. diss., University of California, 1969).

4. Manuel José Balmaceda, "Manual del hacendado chileno," *Antología chilena de la tierra* (Santiago: ICIRA, 1970), pp. 54-80.

5. José Campusano, long-time Communist party militant and leader in rural labor organizations, suggested that an example of campesino struggle in the late nineteenth century was the conflict between the comuneros at Espíritu Santo and the police in 1896. The campesinos attempted to defend their land against usurpation by an hacendado (interview with José Campusano, Santiago, October 15, 1971). Serious historical research is needed to determine the quality and intensity of rural labor conflict in the nineteenth century.

6. The strike was recorded in Los Andes, February 3, 1911. The hacienda is not identified.

7. Labor Department statistics generally understate the extent of rural labor conflict and strikes. The data for 1919 to 1920, for example, does not include a strike which took place in Hacienda Colcura (Concepción) in 1920 in which the landowner wrote to the Labor Office. See letter from representative of Enrique Matthews, Lota, 7 febrero 1920, Oficina del Trabajo, *Comunicaciones Recibidas del Interior* 1, 1921. (The letter is dated 1920—apparently a typing error, since it makes reference to the Labor Office Oficio No. 124 of February 4, 1921. No. 124 is directed to Ladislao Munita Rispatrón, Administrador de la Hacienda Colcura, and asks for information concerning the strike by inquilinos in the hacienda. A copy can be found in Oficina del Trabajo, 1921, la Cuatrimestre, *Comunicaciones Enviadas*.) Likewise, a strike in Hacienda El Escuadrón or "Coronel" in March 1921 is ignored in the Labor Office's summary of

labor conflict. See Oficio 1391, Santiago, 20 diciembre 1921; Oficina del Trabajo, 3a Cuatrimestre, *Comunicaciones Enviadas;* Inspección de Concepción, oficio sin número, 20 mayo 1921, *Comunicaciones Recibidas,* 1921; Oficio 10, Concepción, 18 julio 1921, includes the terms of settlement, or *acta de avenimiento.*

8. (1) May 22 in Valparaíso, solved with arbitration, intervention of Labor Office; (2) August 8-22 in Limache, workers obtained higher salary and better food rations, solved with the intervention of police; (3) May 3 in Quillota, solved through arbitration, workers obtained higher wages; (4) May 22-30, Vichuquen, strike leaders dismissed, strike ended peacefully with intervention of the police; (5) April 25, Quillota, solved through arbitration, workers obtained higher salaries.

9. Consejo Federal no. 2, Inquilinos, Illapel, Los Hornos; Consejo Federal no. 1 de Agricultores, Illapel, Pintacura; Consejo Federal no. 1 de Agricultores, Illapel, Tunga; Consejo Federal no. 1 de Agricultores Los Vilos, Cabilolen; Consejo Federal no. 1 de Agricultores, La Ligua; Consejo Federal de Agricultores, Cocalán; Consejo no. 2 de Agricultores Puchacavi; Consejo Federal no. 2 de Agricultores, El Melón; Consejo Federal no. 1 de Agricultores, Nogales; Consejo Federal no. 1 de Agricultores, Colina; Consejo Federal no. 2 de Agricultores, Quilicura; Consejo Federal no. 1 de Agricultores, Talagante; Consejo Federal no. 1 de Agricultores i Oficios Varios, Peñaflor; Consejo Federal no. 1 de Inquilinos, Nos; Consejo Federal no. 1 de Campesinos, Ñipas (Concepción); Consejo Federal no. 3 de Campesinos, S. Pedro, Concepción; Consejo Federal no. 6 de Campesinos, Escuadrón, Coronel; Consejo Federal no. 8 de Campesinos, Calabozo, Coronel; Consejo Federal no. 4 de Campesinos, Colcura, Lota; Consejo Federal no. 6 de Campesinos, Curanilahue; Consejo Federal no. 1 de Oficios Varios e Inquilinos, Cherquenco (Cautín); Consejo Federal no. 1 de Agricultores La Unión (Valdivia).

10. For example, in 1924 members of the Consejo Federal de Oficios Varios in San Javier, Linares, were accused of setting fires to the harvest in this region. See Jorge Barría S., *Los movimientos sociales de Chile (1910-1926)* (Santiago: Editorial Universitaria, 1960), pp. 327-28.

11. The complete text of this letter can be found in *El Agricultor* (mayo 1921), pp. 88-91. Parts of the letter are reproduced in Affonso et al., *Movimiento campesino chileno,* vol. 1 (Santiago: ICIRA, 1970).

12. Text of the letter in *El Agricultor,* ibid., and Affonso et al., ibid., pp. 20-23. Robert Alexander (*Labor Relations in Argentina, Brazil and Chile* [New York: McGraw Hill, 1962], pp. 237-38) claims that "Alessandri was only allowed to come to office as a result of a tacit agreement that the landlords be left untouched. This meant that there would be no attempt at agrarian reform, and that the government would not allow the organization of agricultural workers into unions."

13. Affonso et al., ibid., p. 20.

14. Barría S. (*Los movimientos,* pp. 307, 310, 313-14, 324, 327, 336)

describes partial successes by campesinos in labor conflicts.

15. "El paro general de las provincias, obreros y campesinos ferrea-mente unidos," *La federación obrera* (9 febrero 1922).

16. By October 1921 the SNA reported (*El Agricultor* [octubre 1921, pp. 206-7]) that President Alessandri had constituted a commission with representatives of the SNA and of FOCH to study "the problems derived from the social question in agriculture" and to "attempt to harmonize the interests and aspiration of all to the benefit of the nation." Cited in Affonso et al., *Movimiento*, p. 304, n. 19.

17. Letter to Pedro Aguirre Cerda, Ministerio del Interior, 3 mayo 1921, *Comunicaciones recibidas del interior* 2, 1921.

18. For its part, the FOCH Junta Ejecutiva de Santiago added the follow-ing complaint: "For the same motives . . . in Fundo Lo Herrera, property of señor Eliodoro Yáñez, inquilinos Rosalindo Salinas (with 20 years of service), Juan B. López (with 27 years of service), and Rufino López, a voluntario who is imprisoned in the police post (Retén) in the fundo, have been dismissed. Awaiting justice and support for these humble workers. . . . Enrique Díaz Nera, Secretario."

19. For a collection of such letters to Chilean presidents from 1939 to 1970, see Brian Loveman, *El campesino chileno le escribe a su excelencia* (Santiago: ICIRA, 1971).

20. Moisés Poblete claims that, by 1924, 604 hacendados belonged to the Liga Agraria (Unión Agraria), a landowner association parallel to the SNA which dedicated itself to resistance of FOCH activity and labor organiza-tion in the countryside (cited in Morris, *Elites*, p. 202). For further mention of this landowner organization see chapter 2 of the present study.

21. Analysis for rural labor petitions from 1960 to 1966 can be found in Affonso et al., *Movimiento*, vol. 2, pp. 17-54. Conclusions of this study were that "The orientation of the petitions is markedly economic, with strong pressure relative to salaries, in-kind payments, and perquisites [*regalías*] . . . . Orientation toward representation is of least importance" (p. 53). While these conclusions are open to challenge in regard to the authors' interpretation of the meaning of particular kinds of petitions, it is clear that during the period 1960-1966 "recognition of union by the landowners" appeared in only about 5 percent of the labor petitions. In contrast, all FOCH-oriented labor petitions in the countryside demanded recognition of the local FOCH consejo. The legitimacy of rural labor or-ganizations was a principal issue in this first organized challenge to the authority of rural proprietors.

22. In two respects, however, the petition in El Melón was slightly dif-ferent from other rural labor petitions of this period. There was no clause asking for a guarantee against retaliation by the landowner. The workers did request, however, reinstatement of workers already dismissed (retalia-tion had already occurred). Second, the proprietor agreed to recognize the FOCH Consejo de Agricultores, a victory for the workers not generally

accomplished during this period.

23. This decree of 1917 called for voluntary submission of labor conflicts to arbitration. For the landowners' reaction to the decree, see the case of La Higuera in 1921, which is discussed in chapter 2.

24. Arbitral resolution in labor conflict, Hacienda El Melón, 20 mayo 1921, Inspección de Valparaíso, *Comunicaciones recibidas*, 1921.

25. Labor petition in Hacienda Huemul, 1924. Copy of the original can be found in Brian Loveman, *Struggle in the Countryside: A Documentary Supplement* (Bloomington, Ind.: International Development Research Center, 1976).

26. Barría S., *Los movimientos*, p. 153.

27. Jorge Barría Seron, *El movimiento obrero en Chile* (Santiago: Ediciones de la Universidad Técnica del Estado, 1971), p. 54.

28. A. Chelén Rojas, *Trayectoria del socialismo* (Buenos Aires: Editorial Astral, n.d.), pp. 48-49.

29. During this period the government sent a number of "subversives" to Isla Más Afuera. Among those so detained were Emilio Zapata, later to be the founder of the Liga Nacional de Defensa de Campesinos Pobres, and Juan Chacón Corona, life-long Communist rural labor organizer.

30. FOCH was never completely destroyed. Even in the rural areas some "vestigial" conflicts took place. For example, in the summer of 1928 strikes occurred in several vineyards in the Molina region of Talca. Previously in 1925, FOCH-oriented labor conflicts had occurred in Santa Rosa, Los Molinos, Viña Lontué, Viña Casa Blanca, Los Quillayes, Santa Ana, San Javier, Todos Santos, and Santa Trinidad, and inquilinos were evicted from the fundos. See Oficio 1026, 10 octubre 1925, Intendencia de Talca, "Sobre un conflicto entre la Viña Casa Blanca de Lontué i algunos operarios," Oficio 115, Molina, 23 abril 1925, *Varios*, 1925; Gobernación de Lontué, *Varios*; Oficio 71, Santiago, 16 enero 1928, Archivo 1-200, 13 diciembre 1927-16 enero 1928.

31. In 1929 a Sindicato Profesional Agrícola de Lonquimay was formed in the region where Chile's most infamous massacre of campesinos was later to take place—Ranquíl—but the union did not have legal personality in 1931.

32. Sindicato Industrial (S.I.) Viña Casa Blanca; S.I. Viña San Pedro; S.I. Jorge Broquaire; S.I. Viña Lontué. Also formed in the same year were Sindicato Profesional de Pequeños Agricultores, Olmué; S.I. El Vergel (Angol); S.I. Los Perales (Machalí).

33. See the letter from Alejandro Dussaillant to Sótero del Río, Ministro de Bienestar Social, 2 marzo 1932, *Providencias* 19, 1932, 5651-6000.

34. Alberto León was later to play an interesting role in the development of the Catholic rural labor movement in the region around Molina in the early 1950s. Always an avid anti-Communist, León supported ASICH and even became active in its efforts to unionize the campesinos in the vineyards. The role of ASICH is discussed later in this chapter. See also Henry

A. Landsberger and Fernando Canitrot M., *Iglesia, intelectuales y campesinos, la huelga campesino de Molina* (Santiago: Editorial del Pacífico, S.A., 1967).

35. Letter (manuscript) from Alberto León to the Inspección General del Trabajo, Molina, 12 octubre 1932, *Providencias* 21, 1932, 6251-6500.

36. The inspector provincial in Talca reported in October 1932 that "Opposition on the part of the patrones to the constitution of unions in this province has been recently intensified. With the pretext of their unconstitutionality, they allege that the instructions currently in effect have their origin in decree-laws of de facto governments and that, therefore, they lack any legal status" (Oficio 1519, Talca, 14 octubre 1932, *Providencias* 19, 1932, 5651-6000).

37. Oficio 834, Molina, 13 octubre 1932, "Da cuenta de ultrajes que ha debido de soportar el infrascrito e Inspector Provincial por razones que se expresan," *Providencias* 19, 1932, 5651-6000.

38. Oficio 6567, Santiago, 24 octubre 1932, "Contratos Fundo Casa Blanca de A. Dussaillant," *Oficios* 15, 1932, 6301-6600. See also Oficio 1455, Talca, 30 septiembre 1932, "Contrato de trabajo de la Viña Casa Blanca," accompanying Oficio 6321, *Oficios* 15, 1932, 6301-6600.

39. Letter to Fernando García Oldini, Ministro del Trabajo, from Domingo Muñoz P., president of the Sindicato Industrial Viña Casa Blanca, Lontué, 11 enero 1933, *Providencias* 12, 1933, 2701-2950.

40. For a concise summary of this incident see Affonso et al., *Movimiento*, vol. 1, pp. 26-30. For background on the conflicting legal claims see Consejo de Defensa Fiscal, no. 165, 4 mayo 1933.

41. Individual Communist and Socialist organizers were active in the rural sector but their efforts were not well financed and lacked organizational support. Not even the Communist party paid much attention in a systematic way to the countryside in this period.

42. The CIDA report on Chile (*Chile: Tenencia de la tierra y desarrollo socio-económico del sector agrícola*, 2d ed. [Santiago: CIDA, 1966], p. 50) reports for the pre-1955 period: "Una de las características ya destacadas del sistema de inquilinaje y de la mano de obra campesina en general, es su disvinculación con la marcha del predio. De allí la escasa iniciativa del inquilino derivada de la falta de incentivos. El precario funcionamiento de esta complicada e inerte estructura de trabajo descansa en el numeroso personal de vigilancia de que dispone cada predio. Ordinariamente, el personal de vigilancia es más numeroso que los obreros especializados."

43. To be noted is the important symbolic role of labor legislation in mobilizing rural labor. Landowners' noncompliance with legal norms provided concrete goals around which the campesinos could structure their demands.

44. Of course, where laws are not implemented, implementation may rep-

resent a dramatic, even revolutionary innovation. These concepts are meant to be descriptive rather than evaluative. Where the thrust of the movement is to obtain "what's coming to you" and not to alter existing (formal) arrangements, the label "reactive" is applied.

45. Oficio 970, Linares, 10 septiembre 1932, "Amplía detalles del conflicto colectivo del cual se dio cuenta en los telegramas Nos. 478 y 479," *Providencias* 14, 1932, 4001-4500.

46. This case also is an example of relatively smooth workings of the Labor Department-worker-landowner relationship, still quite rare in 1932.

47. "Informe Providencia 1485 y Tel." Peumo, 23 febrero 1933, *Providencias* 8, 1933, 1751-1950.

48. Oficio 81, Los Angeles, 29 enero 1935, "Sobre conflicto colectivo obreros inquilinos Hacienda Canteras," *Providencias*, 1935, 701-900.

49. At the end of the conflict, inquilinos received 2 pesos a day, payday every 15 days, ¼ cuadra of land of "clase regular," 4 galletas or "panes," and pasture rights for 2 animals. Forasteros received 2 pesos a day, 4 galletas or 8 panes, and a place to sleep in the houses of the fundo. Milkmaids obtained a rate of 15 centavos per "gas can" of milk and 20 centavos a can in July and August, plus a bonus of 5 pesos per month and 1 galleta per day. (Before the conflict they already earned 15 centavos a day and averaged 30-35 pesos a month in earnings.) Oficio 1055, 12 febrero 1934, "Sobre visita a fundos Santa Elvira y Lo Prado, Barrancas" and accompanying documents, *Oficios* 4, 1934, 851-1150.

50. Much of the following material on the incidents in Zapata's life is based on three interviews with Emilio Zapata Díaz in October 1971.

51. The police accused Zapata of being drunk. A medical certificate obtained by Zapata demonstrated that this was a fabrication. Like Carlos Alberto Martínez, Zapata had been active in the anti-alcoholic movement in Chile and, therefore, the charge was not even credible to the Rightist politicians in the Congress. In addition, Zapata went to the minister of interior to report the incident and demonstrate that he had not had any alcoholic beverages to drink.

52. Interview with Emilio Zapata Díaz, Santiago, October 22, 1971.

53. Ibid.

54. Ibid.

55. Ibid.

56. Ibid.

57. In an introduction to Atilano Oróstegui, *Como vive el campesino chileno*, Colección "Através de mi país" (Santiago: 1936), Zapata declared: "No deben olvidar los dirigentes de la clase obrera que la tarea de organizar al campesinado, es una tarea indispensable; esto deben comprenderlo especialmente los diversos sectores revolucionarios, puesto, que ningún hecho revolucionario que inicie el proletariado, podra alcanzar el éxito, si acaso no se acompaña con la acción del campesinado."

58. Oficio 4672, Santiago, 6 julio 1934, "Sobre informes solicitados por el Diputado Don Emilio Zapata," *Oficios* 1934, 4626-4900.

59. "La revolución proletaria y la tierra," *Izquierda* (6 febrero 1935).

60. The Liga Nacional de Defensa de Campesinos Pobres eventually used this date on its rubber stamps as the date of foundation of the Liga. In fact, the constitution of the first ligas in Santiago seems not to have occurred until mid-September 1935.

61. "La desidia del gobierno para solucionar la miseria de los pequeños agricultores. Se ha organizado la más poderoso colectividad del campesinado," *Izquierda* (15 octubre 1935), pp. 1, 4.

62. "Despertar de las masas campesinas. El gran congreso de los campesinos pobres," *Izquierda* (30 mayo 1936), p. 4.

63. Among these lawyers was Oscar Waiss. In 1971 Waiss was director of the government newspaper *La Nación*. On October 17, 1971, the Socialist party honored Zapata for his early leadership of the campesinos, and Waiss wrote an editorial tribute to accompany the news story "Sentido homenaje rindió el P.S. a luchador social Emilio Zapata" (*La Nación* [18 octubre 1971], p. 6).

64. The text of this law and discussion of the role of Zapata in the legislation can be found in "Préstamos para pequeños agricultores, medieros inquilinos y parceleros," *Boletín de la Liga Nacional de Defensa de Campesinos Pobres*, no. 3 (enero 1939), p. 2. See also the *Boletín*, no. 2 (diciembre 1938).

65. Interview with Emilio Zapata, Santiago, October 22, 1971. Zapata, Yuras, and Acuña did sometimes visit the local ligas to provide organizational assistance and to meet the local leaders. Use was made also of local Socialist party cadres.

66. The circular sent out by the Liga in order to raise money for the Primer Congreso Nacional del Campesinado Chileno is reproduced in Brian Loveman, "Property, Politics and Rural Labor: Agrarian Reform in Chile" (Ph.D. diss., Indiana University, 1973).

67. Interview with Emilio Zapata, Santiago, October 22, 1971.

68. *Boletín de la Liga* (diciembre 1938), p. 3.

69. Ibid., p. 4.

70. José Miguel Varas, *Chacón* (Santiago: Impresora Horizonte, 1968), p. 107.

71. Ibid., p. 108.

72. See Juan Chacón Corona, "El problema agrario y el partido comunista. Informe ante el XI Congreso Nacional del Partido Comunista de Chile, 1939" (Santiago: Ediciones del Comité Central del Partido Comunista de Chile, 1940), pp. 34-35, cited in Almino Affonso et al., *Movimiento*, p. 40; and Brian Loveman, *Antecedentes para el estudio del movimiento campesino chileno: Pliegos de peticiones, huelgas y sin-*

dicatos agrícolas, 1932-1966, vol. 1 (Santiago: ICIRA, 1971), pp. 2-10.

73. See Varas, *Chacón*, p. 40.

74. Interview with Emilio Zapata, Santiago, October 22, 1971.

75. Interview with Bernardo Yuras, Santiago, November 5, 1971.

76. "Discurso pronunciado por El Compañero Bernardo Yuras, en la concentración efectuada en San Bernardo—el día 2 abril de 1939—de la Liga de Campesinos Pobres" (copy provided the author by Bernardo Yuras).

77. *La Nación* (29 abril 1939), p. 12, cited in Almino Affonso et al., *Movimiento*, vol. 1, p. 38.

78. Interview with Emilio Zapata, Santiago, October 22, 1971.

79. *Boletín*, Año 1, Órgano Interno del C.C. del Partido Comunista, p. 6.

80. Arturo Olavarría, *Chile entre dos Alessandri*, vol. 1 (Santiago: Editorial Nascimento, 1962), pp. 452-53.

81. Zapata laughingly told me that he had to take special lessons to learn how to stay on a horse. Yuras provided him technical advice and had a sense of rural production patterns as well as of current cleavages in international Marxism. Acuña was an experienced labor leader within the plasterers' trade. Thus, the three main leaders of the Liga were all of blue-collar origin.

82. See Oficio 251, Gobernación de Lontué, Molina, 10 octubre 1939, "Inf. s/Centro Unión del Cap. y Trab. de la Viña Lontué" and the accompanying "Protocolización del acta constitutiva y estatutos de la Corporación Unión del Capital y El Trabajo de la Viña Lontué," *Providencias* 36, 1939, 8801-9000. In this case the landowner formed a parallel organization by providing benefits to workers who would leave the union already existing in the vineyard.

83. Letter from Agricultores de la Comuna de Pirque to President Pedro Aguirre Cerda, Pirque, 13 marzo 1939, *Providencias* 18, 1940, 5301-5600. The letter is signed by Hector Marchant, Carlos Vial Infante, Máximo Valdes Fontecilla, Oscar Dávila Izquierdo, José Julio Nieto E., Hernan Prieto Vial, Hernan Prieto Subercaseaux, Sergio Marambio Ruiz, Vicente Izquierdo P., Francisco Hunneuss G., and Máximo Valdes Vial.

84. For example, from the intendente of Linares in February came a telegram that read: "An organized movement to dismiss workers has been initiated by landowners. The situation is grave. Indispensable to solve" (Telegrama 388, Linares, 3 febrero 1940, *Providencias* 8, 1940, 2401-2650).

85. Intendencia de Curicó, Oficio 1053, Curicó, 11 abril 1939, *Providencias* 23, 1939, 5551-5700.

86. By March 1940, a year after the "temporary suspension" of rural unionization, the massiveness of landowner retaliation was so evident and

the plight of the campesinos so miserable that the Communist party could no longer publicly accept the continued suspension of unionization. See the letter from Juan Chacón Corona, leader of the "Comité Relacionador de Sindicatos Agrícolas de Chile," to President Pedro Aguirre Cerda, 27 marzo 1940, *Providencias* 12, 1940, 3501-3800.

87. The CTCH also provided support for inspectors attacked by proprietors for being too responsive to the workers, and attempted to avoid the transfer of inspectors who they felt were doing their best to insist on legal compliance. For example, see the letter from Bernardo Ibáñez, secretary general of the CTCH to the minister of labor in 1941, *Providencias* 15, 1941, 4401-4800, reproduced in Loveman, "Property, Politics," pp. 376-78.

88. See for example the letter from the technical secretary of the CTCH, Bruno Burgas Jamett, to the director of the Labor Department, 26 octubre 1939, *Oficios* 38, 1939, 10101-10500; letter from the CTCH to the director of the Labor Department on behalf of the union in Fundo El Guindo de Longotoma, 16 enero 1940, *Providencias* 5, 1940; and "Denuncia persecuciones contra sindicato y funcionarios del trabajo," 16 enero 1940, *Providencias* 5, 1940.

89. Oficio 202, 5 enero 1940, *Oficios* 1, 1940, 1-400. See also Oficio 7197, 12 julio 1940, "Sobre autorización para que dirigentes de la CTCH pueden asistir a los comparendos ante la inspección del trabajo," *Oficios* 23, 1940, 7101-7400.

90. See for example the request in a letter to President Aguirre Cerda in 1940, transcribed in Presidencia de la República, Secretaría, Oficio 3695, *Providencias* 20, 1940, 5701-5950.

91. An example from Curacaví (Fundo Santa Julia and Fundo Santa Margarita) is described in Oficio 9395, 24 septiembre 1941, *Oficios* 29a, 1941, 9301-9700.

92. See "Inspector del trabajo Sepúlveda Falcón provocó un grave escándalo callejero insultó y agredió de hecho a un dirigente de campesinos," *El Siglo* (25 noviembre 1941).

93. The department's feelings toward Luis Coray are expressed in Oficio 4319, 27 mayo 1942, *Oficios* 15, 1942, 4301-4600.

94. From 1939 to 1941 approximately 485 labor petitions were presented in the countryside and 71 strikes resulted. For more details see Loveman, *Antecedentes*, vol. 1, pp. 37-39; vol. 2, pp. 2-16.

95. Letter from the representatives of the owner of Fundo San Luis de Quilicura to the minister of interior, Santiago, 7 enero 1941, *Providencias* 7, 1941, 1651-1900.

96. Olavarría, *Chile*, p. 505.

97. Gobernación de Petorca, La Ligua, 12 enero 1943, transcribing Dirección General de Investigaciones e Identificación, Sub-Inspectoría, Ligua, no. 12, La Ligua, 7 agosto 1942.

98. Loveman, *Antecedentes*, vol. 1, p. 12.

99. See the letter from the union in Fundo San José de las Claras (Puente Alto, Santiago Province), 18 enero 1944, *Providencias* 44, 1944, 1001-1300. This letter is reproduced in Loveman, "Property, Politics," p. 373.

100. The year 1946 also saw the split of the CTCH into two (Socialist and Communist) factions. This division of the national labor movement persisted until the formation of the Central Única de Trabajadores de Chile (CUTCH) in 1953.

101. Letter from CTCH to minister of labor, Mariano Bustos Lagos, 11 enero 1946, signed by Bernardo Araya and Bernardo Ibáñez, CTCH Oficio 22, "ref. Sobre organización trabajadores agrícolas," *Providencias* 7, 1946, 1501-1800.

102. Loveman, *Antecedentes*, vol. 1, pp. 13-23.

103. This organization was variously called (in Labor Department documents) Federación Nacional De Obreros Agrícolas, Federación Nacional de Asalariados Agrícolas, Federación Industrial Nacional de Asalariados Agrícolas—as well as by its official name.

Juan Ahumada Trigo was among the foremost Communist rural labor leaders. He also served as a deputy in the Chilean Congress. In 1971 he worked in INDAP. For Ahumada's participation during the period under discussion, see for example Oficio 4129, marzo 1947, "Informa sobre reclamo por despedidos de obreros agrícolas Hacienda Chalaco Petorca" and accompanying documentation, *Oficios* 14, 1947, 3901-4200. On April 15, 1947, Ahumada Trigo was named workers' representative for the Junta Especial de Conciliación para la Agricultura, Departamento de Santiago.

104. See letter from Lorenzo Medina Díaz to minister of labor, Collipulli, marzo 1947, *Providencias* 35, 1947, 9100-9369.

105. *Acta*, 16 abril 1947, signed by Fernando Landaeta T., Inspector Provincial del Trabajo, Malleco, *Providencias* 35, 1947, 9100-9369.

106. See Oficio 55, Santiago, 14 abril 1947, "Informa sobre cumplimiento orden del servicio No. 10 y providencia No. 3129 Dirección General respecto numerosos despidos dirigentes sindicales y obreros agrícolas en diecinueve predios departamento de Maipo (Buin)," *Providencias* 20, 1947, 9100-9369. This document is reproduced in Brian Loveman, *El mito de la marginalidad: Participación y represión del campesinado chileno* (Santiago: ICIRA, 1971), pp. 34-35.

107. See for example, "Sobre desahucios de inquilinos en provincia de O'Higgins," Santiago, 17 marzo 1947, *Oficios* 9, 1947, 2401-2700, accompanied by a report of complaint by the CTCH of dismissals in 15 fundos, no. 303, 7 marzo 1947; Oficio Confidencial 1416, Rancagua, 29 abril 1947, "Sobre despido de inquilinos," *Providencias* 35, 1947, 9100-9369; Oficio 97, San Bernardo, 14 abril 1947, "Sobre despidos obreros agrícolas y dirigentes sindicales," *Providencias* 35, 1947, 9100-9369.

108. See for example Oficio 7303, 8 agosto 1947, "Refiérese reclamo de la Sociedad de Agricultores de Traiguen, por agitación en los campos," *Oficios* 25, 1947, 7201-7500.

109. Telegrama 22, La Serena, to González Videla from Pres. Sociedad Agrícola del Norte, accompanying Oficio 80, La Serena, 18 enero 1947, "Informa telegrama de reclamación de la Sociedad Agrícola del Norte por constitución de sindicatos agrícolas," *Oficios* 3, 1947, 601-900.

110. As suggested in chapter 4, the terms of Law 8.811 allowed landowners to break existing unions and require them, if they attempted to reconstitute themselves, to conform to the restrictive provisions of the new law. Legal labor petitions also became difficult to present given the law's prohibition on petitions during the harvest or planting season, which in some farms was always. See Oficio 9218, 29 septiembre 1947, *Oficios* 31, 1947, 9001-9300; and Oficio 5606, 27 junio 1949, "El pliego de peticiones presentado en época de cosecha es nulo y debe tenerse por no presentado para todos los efectos legales," *Oficios* 22, 1949, 5401-5700.

111. Loveman, *El mito*, p. 8.

112. Interview with José Campusano, Santiago, October 6, 1971.

113. For more detailed accounts of Catholic Action in the countryside and the activity of the Instituto de Educación Rural, see Oscar Domínguez, *El condicionamiento de la reforma agraria* (Estudio de los factores económicos, demográficos y sociales que determinan la promoción del campesino chileno) (Louvain: Université Catholique de Louvain, Collection de Ecole des Sciences Politiques et Sociales no. 173; *Surco y Semilla*, Revista de la Familia Campesina, editada por el Instituto de Educación Rural (from 1955); Landsberger and Canitrot, *Iglesia*, especially chapters 2, 6, and 8.

114. Oscar Larson and Carlos Valenzuela, Pbros., "Respuesta a Don Rosendo Vial y Carlos Aldunate E.," Apéndice (Santiago, 1940), p. 109, cited in Affonso et al., *Movimiento*, p. 40.

115. Ibid., p. 41.

116. Landsberger and Canitrot, *Iglesia*, p. 201.

117. Ibid., p. 157.

118. Oficio 2121, Buin, 23 julio 1941, "Informa Providencia 172-14-VII-41...," *Providencias* 24, 1941, 7501-8000.

119. Affonso et al., *Movimiento*, p. 41.

120. Ibid., p. 42.

121. FOCH activity in the zone of Molina had resulted in strikes in the vineyards in 1925 and 1928. In 1941, *El Mercurio* (April 4) headlined "Nuevos movimientos huelguísticos han provocado los comunistas." The story included reference to strikes in El Cóndor, Santa Lucía, Santa Elena, Parroncillo, Santa Adela, San Hilario, La Maravilla, Cerrillo Verde, Santa Rosa, Reims, Lontué, La Estancia, "y otras ocho propiedades más." These strikes were broken up using police to "contract" nonstriking workers from other farms.

122. Landsberger and Canitrot, *Iglesia*, p. 48.

123. This Congress reunified the national labor movement which had split in 1946 when Socialist and Communist factions divided the CTCH.

124. Landsberger and Canitrot, *Iglesia*, pp. 131-36.

125. Affonso et al., *Movimiento*, vol. 1, pp. 80-86.

126. See Landsberger and Canitrot, *Iglesia*, pp. 11-35.

127. These complaints are analyzed in ibid., pp. 126-30.

128. Oficio 2472, 19 abril 1955, "Sobre visita efectuada por El Ingeniero Agrónomo Zonal Del Servicio a Las Viñas de la Zona de Molina," *Oficios* 12, 1955, 2351-2600.

129. Landsberger and Canitrot (*Iglesia*) call this *"La Decadencia"* (see their chapter 5).

130. Ibid., p. 292.

131. Ibid., p. 293. (Actually Landsberger and Canitrot cite, to this effect, Solon Barraclough, "Lo que implica una reforma agraria," *Panorama económico*, no. 230 [mayo 1962], pp. 123-30.)

132. *Tierra y Libertad*, Segunda Quincena de marzo, 1954.

133. According to Affonso et al. (p. 82), seven of the ten national directors (*consejeros*) were of urban extraction.

134. Ibid., p. 94.

135. Ibid., p. 121.

136. Ibid., p. 165.

137. Ibid., p. 167.

138. Ibid., p. 168.

139. Ibid., p. 177.

140. Ibid., p. 179.

141. Ibid., p. 180.

142. Ibid.

143. Ibid., p. 195.

144. Ibid.

145. In one such letter reference is made to problems in the following farms: El Escorial, El Sauce, Viña Errázuriz and Las Bandurrias (Aconcagua); El Molino de Llay Llay (Valparaíso); San Vicente de Naltagua, Santa Laura de Viluco, San Miguel de Colina, Las Lilas and Cuarta Hijuela de Renca (Santiago); Totihue, Carlota, Las Palmas de Cocalán (O'Higgins); La Ramada, El Carmen, Nincullanta, El Medio, San Juan de la Sierra, El Paraíso (Colchagua); La Cantera (Bío Bío).

146. Juan Ahumada, *La cuestión agraria y el movimiento de liberación nacional*, Redacción Alexi Rumiantzev (Praga: Editorial Paz y Socialismo, 1964).

147. An example of the sort of letters written to the Labor Department on

behalf of campesinos by the Federación Nacional de Trabajadores Agrícolas is reproduced in Loveman, "Property, Politics," pp. 378-79.

148. See Oficio 03597, 2 junio 1955, "Sobre rechazo pliego peticiones de los obreros agrícolas de la Viña La Finca," *Oficios* 16, 1955, 3351-3600 and accompanying documents: Oficio 3350, 25 mayo 1955, "Sobre pliegos de peticiones de los obreros de la Viña La Finca"; Inspección Provincial del Trabajo, Oficio 61, Buin, 14 abril 1955, "Contesta providencia No. 362 de 12 de marzo Ppdo., sobre pliego de peticiones obreros agrícolas Viña La Finca"; República de Chile, Ministerio de Agricultura, Oficio 38, 14 mayo 1955, "Ref. Oficio 3022."

149. Interview with José Campusano, Santiago, October 6, 1971.

150. Those detained included Chacón, Luis Corvalán, and Volodia Teitelboim.

151. Oficio 41, 20 enero 1956, "Instrucciones sobre cumplimiento del Art. 36 de la Ley de Defensa Permanente de la Democracia," *Providencias* 19, 1956, 3641-3820.

152. See no. 726, Santiago, 26 septiembre 1956, "Crea Comisión Asesora Agrícola en la Dirección General del Trabajo," accompanying Resolución no. 134, 11 mayo 1957, "Designa integrantes de la Comisión Asesora del Trabajo Agrícola," *Resoluciones* 2, 1957, 86-188.

153. ASICH representatives to this comisión were Héctor Pizarro Acosta and Manuel Silva P. The SNA named Fernando Errázuriz Lastarria and Manuel Maldonado Brand.

154. For example, see Oficio 03727, 7 junio 1955, and accompanying documents on Fundo Las Lilas, *Oficios* 17, 1955, 3601-3850; Oficio 08264, "Contesta presentación de fecha 24 de agosto sobre incumplimiento D.F.L. No. 244 en fundos que se indican," *Oficios* 38, 1955, 8251-8500; Oficio 08265, 12 diciembre 1955, "Contesta presentación de fecha 24 de octubre sobre situación obreros fundo La Palma," *Oficios* 38, 1955, 8251-8500; Oficio 368, Santiago, 19 enero 1956, "Sobre dificultades existentes en el Fundo 'La Flor del Llano' de San Clemente," *Oficios* 2, 1956, 201-400; Oficio 467, 26 enero 1956, "Sobre situación existente fundos Los Cristales y Capellanía de Pencahue y La Estrella de S. Clemente," *Oficios* 3, 1956, 401-600.

155. Partido Comunista, Projecto de Reforma Agraria de la Asociación de Agricultores de Chile, Imprenta Lautauro, 1958.

156. Campusano was of campesino extraction. He first led rural labor movements in Hacienda Limarí in the period 1934-1936 and was a long-time Communist party member. He was employed by ICIRA and directed the section charged with *capacitación* ("training") during the Popular Unity government (1970-1973). For events leading up to the creation of FCI see Affonso et al., *Movimiento*, vol. 1, pp. 125-129.

157. U.S. policymakers also began to take great interest in the rural sector. AID and the International Development Foundation pumped in large sums of money to fund the Catholic rural labor organizations against their Marxist rivals. On this see Affonso et al., *Movimiento*, vol. 2, p. 92, and

Punto Final Suplemento de la edición no. 114, martes, 29 septiembre 1970, "Alerta! La CIA Opera en Chile."

158. This competition sometimes resulted in the Labor Department's being used as a scapegoat. In one case, in a mass meeting in the plaza of Buin, Communist Deputy Juan Acevedo Pavez and regidor Hugo Leiva J. insulted the labor inspector for the area, accusing her of being dishonest and corrupt—among the lesser of the insults. The inspector asked the Labor Department to initiate a libel suit against those who had offended her. See Oficio 3455, 16 julio 1964, "Devuelve antecedentes sobre injurias y calumnias de que ha sido objeto la Inspectora del Trabajo de Buin, y acompaña escrito de denuncia criminal," *Oficios* 17, 1964, 3601-3800.

Chapter 6

1. Urbanization of the countryside was varied in content and also geographically. Changes generally seem to have been most rapid in rural areas closest to large urban centers, mines, or rural-based agricultural industries. But as railroads and roads were constructed, the physical distance between towns and rural areas was less important, for example, in predicting rural labor conflicts, union organization, or migration patterns. Campesinos from relatively isolated rural zones could be found in the nitrate fields, copper mines, and urban enterprises. Migrant workers from Antofogasta or Coquimbo rode trains to Chillán or Valdivia and worked the wheat harvest. The urbanization of the countryside, including intersectoral labor mobility from 1919 onward, would thus be a most profitable field of study in Chile. Pascal's case study (Andrés Pascal, *Relaciones de poder en una localidad rural* [Santiago: ICIRA, 1968]) is an important step in this direction, but the need exists for more macro-studies on the national situation during these years, isolating regional and local differences and attempting to better explain the complex phenomenon that Pascal has labeled "urbanization of the countryside."

2. Only recently have these questions begun to be answered in the case of the Chilean railroads constructed in the nineteenth century. See for example John Whaley, "The Transportation Revolution in the Development of the Bío Bío Region, 1850-1915" (Ph.D. diss., Indiana University, 1974).

3. Hugo Zemelman, *El migrante rural* (Santiago: ICIRA, 1971), p. 25.

4. In the expanding literature on peasants and peasant movements there is a running controversy over the relative radicalness of different strata of rural labor—wage laborers, "poor" peasants, "middle" peasants, "kulaks," and so on. In Chile this controversy is represented in Zemelman, *El migrante;* Raúl Urzua, *La demanda campesina* (Santiago: Ediciones Nueva Universidad, 1969); and James Petras and Maurice Zeitlin, "Miners and Agrarian Radicalism," in Petras and Zeitlin, eds., *Latin America, Reform or Revolution* (Greenwich, Conn.: Fawcett, 1968), pp. 235-48.

5. See for example the letter from F.P. Cadet to the Labor Department, Santiago, 30 diciembre 1921, *Comunicaciones recibidas del interior* 3 (1921).

6. Oficio 341, Linares, 15 abril 1932, "Da cuenta de abandono de trabajo por cesantes ocupados en fundos de la localidad," *Oficios* 6, 1932, 2501-3000, accompanying Oficio 2610.

7. See for example Intendencia de Arauco, Oficio 189, Lebu, 18 noviembre 1926, *Comunicaciones recibidas* 1927, 1501-2000.

8. Intendencia de Curicó, Oficio 80, 15 enero 1926, "Manifiesta difícil situación agricultura por escasez brazos," *Comunicaciones recibidas* (enero 1926).

9. For data on mechanization from 1915 to 1965 see C. Kay, "Comparative Development of the European Manorial System and the Latin American Hacienda System: An Approach to a Theory of Agrarian Change for Chile" (Ph.D. diss., University of Sussex [England], 1971), p. 228.

10. For example, "Ruégole contestarme mayor brevedad si habría facilidad en esa para enganchar seiscientos trabajadores para trabajos de cosechas, para llevarlos a la zona de Collipulli y alrededores. Además indique que jornales se pagan actualmente para esta clase de trabajos y demás condiciones que exigen los obreros" (Oficio 32, 9 enero 1925, *Notas enviadas*, enero-abril 1925). In this case, the minister of agriculture intervened to obtain free passes for the workers so that the landowners need not pay for their transportation. Over 500 workers were eventually sent to the fundos of Mercedes Badilla, Celendo Muñoz, Alberto Seguel, Aníbal Isla, Clodomiro Cerda, Arnolfo Decher, T. Benavente, and Jorge Lavandero to work for wages between 2.5 and 3 pesos a day plus food and lodging (Oficio 56, Concepción, 4 febrero 1925, *Varios*, 1925).

11. Oficio 2296, 15 abril 1931, "Acusa Recibo Oficio 326 sobre autorización pasajes obreros agrícolas," *Oficios* 7, 1931, 2121-2490.

12. *El Campesino* (agosto 1934), p. 372.

13. Oficio-Confidencial, San Bernardo, 8 noviembre 1946, "Informa sobre obreros agrícolas despedidos en el fundo Cuatro Alamos," *Providencias* 38, 1946, 9791-9940.

14. See H. Landsberger and F. Canitrot, *Iglesia, intelectuales y campesinos* (Santiago: Editorial del Pacífico, 1965), *passim.*

15. Gobernación de Lontué, Oficio 63, Molina, 20 marzo 1939, *Providencias* 21, 1939, 5301-5420.

16. Intendencia de Curicó, Oficio-Confidencial no. 850, 18 mayo 1940, *Providencias* 29, 1940, 8551-8800.

17. William Thiesenhusen, "Profit Margins in Chilean Agriculture: A Reply" (University of Wisconsin, Land Tenure Center, Reprint no. 34), p. 246.

18. For a detailed consideration of the performance of the Chilean agricultural sector in this period see CIDA, *Chile: Tenencia de la tierra y desarrollo socio-económico del sector agrícola*, 2d ed. (Santiago: CIDA, 1966), chapters 3, 11, and 12.

19. Ibid., p. 145.

20. Ibid., pp. 146-47.

21. By 1950 agriculture contributed only 14 percent of domestic income and occupied approximately 31 percent of the active labor force. In 1963 these figures had shrunk to 9.4 percent and 26 percent, respectively (ibid., p. 17).

22. For some support of the landowner's position see James O. Bray, "Mechanization and the Chilean Inquilino System: The Case of Fundo 'B'," *Land Economics* 42 (February 1966): 125-29; and University of Wisconsin, Land Tenure Center, Reprint no. 34, with a reply by William Thiesenhusen and a rejoinder by Bray.

23. See chapter 5 of the present study; and Landsberger and Canitrot, *Iglesia,* especially chapters 2, 6, and 8.

24. See Landsberger and Canitrot, ibid., especially chapter 6.

25. Jorge Rogers, *Dos caminos para la reforma agraria 1945-1965* (Santiago: ORBE, 1966), pp. 66-67. The proposal is reproduced in Appendix 1-A, pp. 255-68.

26. Cited in Landsberger and Canitrot, *Iglesia*, pp. 211, 212.

27. Official English translation, cited in William C. Thiesenhusen, *Chile's Experiments in Agrarian Reform* (Madison: University of Wisconsin Press, 1966), p. 55.

28. These experiments, involving systems of private land or mixed private-collective systems of production and management, are the subject of ibid.

29. The Mexican case is an exception, but the extent to which a competitive party system has existed in Mexico during this period is debatable. Military intervention in Uruguay ended that country's traditional democratic regime prior to the Chilean coup in 1973.

30. For discussion of party activities in student organizations and trade unions see, respectively, Frank Bonilla, "The Student Federation of Chile: Fifty Years of Political Action," *Journal of Inter-American Studies* 2 (July 1960); and Robert Alexander, *Labor Relations in Argentina, Brazil and Chile* (New York: McGraw Hill, 1962) and *Communism in Latin America* (New Brunswick, N.J.: Rutgers University Press, 1957). On the scope of the Chilean party system, see Arturo Valenzuela, "The Scope of the Chilean Party System," *Comparative Politics* 4 (January 1972): 179-99.

31. See Frank Marshall Lewis, "The Political Effects of a Multi-Party System upon the Presidential Form of Government in Chile" (Ph.D. diss., University of Texas, 1955).

32. James Petras, *Politics and Social Forces in Chilean Development* (Berkeley and Los Angeles: University of California Press, 1969), p. 100.

33. Sergio Aranda and Alberto Martínez, *La industria y la agricultura en el desarrollo económico chileno* (Santiago: Universidad de Chile, Instituto de Economía y Planificación y Departamento de Sociología, Publicación

122, 1970), pp. 78-79.

34. The CIDA study on Chile *(Chile: Tenencia)* claims that from 1947 to 1964 agricultural prices maintained themselves with reference to other sectors; no relative deterioration of prices occurred. The report recognizes, however, subperiods of unfavorable changes in relative prices. The CIDA report, thus, rejects the landowners' contentions that price levels negatively affected agricultural production. Yet throughout this period the SNA argued that government price policy discriminated against agriculture. A more precise study of the price variable (R. Echeverría, "The Effect of Agricultural Price Policies on Intersectoral Income Transfers [Ph.D. diss., Cornell University, 1969], p. 107) concluded that "Although the price controls on farm products at the consumer level tended to depress farm profits, this was offset by large subsidies in the use of inputs and transportation, in addition to quasi-subsidies derived from credit and the privileged tax situation." It must be remembered, of course, that the quasi-subsidies of credit and privileged tax status did not benefit agriculture per se but, rather, landowners. Precisely because agriculture was not an attractive investment landowners utilized much of the credit they obtained in nonagricultural pursuits. Discrimination against agriculture could occur while large landowners did not necessarily suffer the consequences.

35. Jose Cademártori, *La economía chilena* (Santiago: Editorial Universitaria, 1968), p. 109, citing Oscar Domínguez in *La Nación* (7 julio 1965), further claimed that the aggregate loss to rural workers (1953-1964) exceeded the assessed value of Chile's 261,000 rural properties. M. Mamalakis and C.W. Reynolds *(Essays on the Chilean Economy* [Homewood, Ill.: Irwin, 1965], p. 144) estimate the decline in real income for unskilled rural labor at 20 percent between 1940 and 1952.

36. Letter from Bernardo Yuras to the Partido Socialista (page 2, of two-page letter; page 1 lost). Copy provided the author by Bernardo Yuras.

37. See A. Olavarría, *Chile entre dos Alessandri*, vol. 1 (Santiago: Editorial Nascimento, 1962), pp. 344-45.

38. See for example reports on rural labor unions and political activities in Fundo Cajón de Zapata and Fundos Miraflores, Cerrillos, San Joaquín, La Laguna, and Santa Inés, signed by Ezequial Sepúlveda, Luis González, and Moisés Muñoz, 16 agosto 1940, *Providencias* 33, 1940, 9501-9900.

39. Interview with José Campusano, Santiago, October 6, 1971.

40. For some case histories see Oficio 24123, 10 diciembre 1947, "Informa término comisión Hacienda la Tercera de Longaví," accompanying Oficio 254, 9 enero 1948, *Oficios* 1, 1948, 1-300; Oficio 486, Rengo, 16 junio 1947, "Informe sobre actividades del ciudadano a que se refieren los antecedentes que devuelve," *Providencias* 24, 1947, 6251-6600.

41. See for example the telegram from Deputy Hugo Arias et al. to the minister of labor, 9 marzo 1944, *Oficios* 11, 1944, 3001-3300; Oficio 54[??], 14 agosto 1940, "Sindicatos de campos y . . . ," *Providencias* 24, 1940, 7331-7700.

42. Oficio 702, San Felipe, 2 octubre 1939, "Sobre presencia de elementos extraños a los interesados en los reclamos y comparendos en esta Inspección," *Providencias* 1, 1940, 1-400.

43. For an exceptional case see the participation of a Radical deputy in cooperation with CTCH leaders in Linares in 1944, Oficio 3013, 20 marzo 1944, "Informa denuncio . . . ," *Oficios* 11, 1944, 3001-3300 and the telegram cited in note 40 above.

44. Cámara de Diputados, no. 112, 20 noviembre 1939.

45. "Instrucciones" left by Inspector Luis A. Bahamondes Cespedes, 25 enero 1940, *Providencias* 8, 1940, 2401-2650.

46. Intendencia de Colchagua, Oficio 532, San Fernando, 27 julio 1962.

47. Ibid.

48. Oficio 4416, 3 septiembre 1962, "Refiérese a falta de personal . . . ," *Oficios* 21, 1962, 4301-4530.

49. Interview with José Campusano, Santiago, October 6, 1971. It is possible, of course, that Campusano was not aware of the existence of some paid rural organizers. Since he had no hesitancy about confirming Party support for functionaries in the rural areas after 1938, there is little reason to suppose that he deliberately misinformed the author concerning the pre-1938 period.

50. See for example Oficio 5134, 19 junio 1940, *Providencias* 17, 1940.

51. Oficio 7585, 18 noviembre 1954, "Sobre reclamo formulado por el señor Manuel Muñoz Bahamondes . . . ," and accompanying documentation, *Oficios* 38, 1954, 8901-9100.

52. Pedro Correa, "Las tareas de los Socialistas en la dirección del Movimiento Campesino," *Arauco* (Tribuna del Pensamiento Socialista), no. 31 (agosto 1962): 10-11.

53. Ibid., p. 11.

54. The role of the United States in events leading to the anticommunist legislation in 1948 and the repression of the labor movement has been largely unexplored. I am indebted to Pat Peppe for pointing out to me that the United States' role was critical. U.S. State Department documents make clear that when labor activism and, finally, a coal strike in late 1947 brought the Chilean economy to the brink of disaster, González Videla turned to the United States for assistance in crushing the Communist threat. The United States agreed to send emergency coal shipments to Chile, allowing the government to move against the striking miners. Soon after, the Communist party was outlawed. See *Foreign Relations of the United States* 8 (1947): 497-518.

55. Letter from campesinos in Hacienda Trancura to minister of lands and colonization, 10 junio 1946, *Providencias* 27, 1946, 7201-7300.

56. Germán Urzua Valenzuela, *El partido radical*, pp. 128-29.

57. Federico Gil (*The Political System of Chile* [New York: Houghton

Mifflin, 1966], p. 233) suggests, "What was indeed a surprise, however, was the remarkable strength shown by the leftist candidate in the agricultural areas of the central valley—traditional oligarchical strongholds."

58. *Ercilla* (15 abril 1961): 17, cited in ibid., p. 237.

59. For a discussion of Alliance for Progress-induced land reform legislation in Latin America see Ernest Feder, "Counterreform," in Rodolfo Stavenhagen (ed.), *Agrarian Problems and Peasant Movements in Latin America* (Garden City, N.Y.: Anchor, 1970), pp. 173-233.

60. See Robert Kaufman, *The Chilean Right and Agrarian Reform: Resistance and Moderation* (Washington, D.C.: Institute for Comparative Study of Political Systems, 1967), p. i.

Chapter 7

1. P.T. Ellsworth, *Chile, An Economy in Transition* (New York: Macmillan, 1945), p. 104. Ellsworth later notes that "Since the properties offered for sale far exceed the amount the Institute has had the means to buy . . . a substantial increase in the funds made available to this functioning agency would permit a rapid acceleration of the rate at which large properties are being subdivided" (pp. 156-57).

2. CIDA, *Chile: Tenencia de la tierra y desarrollo socio-económico del sector agrícola* (Santiago: CIDA, 1966), p. 249.

3. Ibid.

4. In the 1961 congressional elections the Conservatives lost seats in Districts 4 (Coquimbo), 5 (San Felipe, Petorca, Los Andes), 6 (Valparaíso, Quillota), 9 (O'Higgins), 10 (Colchagua), 17 (Concepción), 18 (Arauco), and 19 (Laja, Mulchen, Nacimiento). The Liberals lost seats in Districts 3 (Copiapó, Chañaral, Huasco, Freirina), 11 (Curicó, Mataquito), and 17 (Concepción). At the same time, an "independent" lost his seat in District 14 (Linares) and another independent lost a seat in Concepción, while the Partido Nacional lost one seat in Linares and two in Cautín (District 21). The Conservatives gained a seat only in Santiago (District 1), and the Liberals picked up a seat in the far southern District 24 (Llanquihue-Aysén). For the most part, the beneficiaries of these losses by the traditional parties were either Marxists (Socialists and Communists) or Christian Democrats.

5. For a discussion of Alliance for Progress-induced land reform legislation in Latin America see Ernest Feder, "Counterreform," in Rodolfo Stavenhagen (ed.), *Agrarian Problems and Peasant Movements in Latin America* (Garden City, N.Y.: Anchor, 1970), pp. 173-223; and Robert Kaufman, *The Chilean Right and Agrarian Reform: Resistance and Moderation* (Washington, D.C.: Institute for Comparative Study of Political Systems, 1967), p. i.

6. Domingo Godoy Matte, *Diario illustrado* (Santiago: 12 diciembre 1961), p. 2.

7. All discussions of Law 15.020 refer to *Ley No. 15.020, Reforma Agra-*

ria y Sus Reglamentos (Santiago: Ediciones Gutenberg Actualizada, para 1966).

8. This phraseology represented adoption of a long-time Marxist political slogan, *"la tierra para él que la trabaja."*

9. If noncompliance were proved by the Dirección de Agricultura y Pesca, "it shall be communicated to CORA for the effects of expropriation [of the property] in accord with Article 15, letter *e* of Law 15.020. . . ."

10. The regulations of Law 15.020 in regard to expropriation can be found in R.R.A. 9, *Diario Oficial*, 6 marzo 1963.

11. This land was to be dedicated to national parks.

12. With minor exceptions contained in sections *i* and *j* of Article 15, which delegated this authority to the minister of lands and colonization.

13. See Kaufman, *The Chilean Right*, pp. 11-18, for a discussion of the internal debate within the rightist parties and the SNA over this amendment. For the SNA reaction to the amendment see "Informe sobre la reforma constitucional," *El Campesino* 94 (enero 1962): 9-19.

14. Article 29 listed the following agricultural societies as those with rights to designate members to the special agrarian courts: Asociación de Agricultores (Tarapacá); Sociedad Agrícola del Norte; Sociedad Agrícola e Industrial de Valparaíso; Sociedad Nacional de Agricultura; Asociación Agrícola Central; Sociedad Agrícola de Ñuble; Sociedad Agrícola del Sur; Sociedad de Fomento Agrícola de Temuco; Sociedad Agrícola y Ganadera de Valdivia; and the Asociación de Ganaderos de Magallanes.

15. Inflation made this option of dubious advantage to rural workers. In fact, maintenance or extension of regalías was generally a better defense against inflation than was a totally cash wage.

16. D.S. 1464, 20 julio 1960, Ministerio de Obras, Públicas, Reglamento de Viviendas Campesinas.

17. R.R.A. 23, 18 abril 1963, que fija el procedimiento para las reclamaciones de los trabajadores agrícolas por falta de pago de las asignaciones familiares.

18. Oficio-Circular 4205, 26 agosto 1963, "Transcribe Decreto R.R.A. No. 23 . . . ," *Oficios* 18, 1963, 4161-4340.

19. Ibid.

20. Decreto del Trabajo no. 410, 25 septiembre 1963; and Decreto no. 488, 2 octubre 1963.

21. Decreto Reglamentario no. 14, 1 marzo 1963, provided that in subdividing rural properties preference be given to settling empleados and workers already on the acquired property.

22. See Oficio 1126, 9 marzo 1963, "Eleva antecedentes de paralización y desahucio colectivo Hacienda Mariposas," *Oficios* 6, 1963, 1121-1340; Oficio 1257, 15 marzo 1961, "Informa providencia 247 relacionada con despido colectivo en Fundo Santa Elena del Servicio Nacional de Salud,"

Oficios 6, 1961, 1221-1490; Oficio 1939, 19 abril 1962, "Informa providencia No. 230 recaída en solicitud del Servicio de Seguro Social para desahuciar a obreros fundos Mariposas y Lipingue," *Oficios* 9, 1962, 1801-2000.

23. D.F.L. no. 49, 11 diciembre 1959, and artículo 1 transitorio de la ley no. 10.383.

24. The point system used by the Caja in designating land reform beneficiaries is reproduced in CIDA, *Chile*, pp. 252-53.

25. Labor Department authorization was required to dismiss more than ten workers at one time according to Decreto 98, 20 enero 1945.

26. Oficio 452, Rancagua, 2 marzo 1961, "Informa providencia No. 790; presentación hecha por Servicio Nacional de Salud, Gerencia Agrícola de S.S. . . . ," accompanying Oficio 1257, 15 marzo 1961, *Oficios* 6, 1961, 1221-1490.

27. Some resident workers did in fact receive *parcelas* or *huertos*, as, for example, in Hacienda Mariposas in the province of Talca. But in Santa Elena, Carlos Ayala Montenegro (*Principios* 112 [1966], pp. 36-48) claimed that only 55 percent of the recipients of land reform parcels were campesinos. He reported the names of local notables, merchants, and politicians who received land. Likewise, Elisabeth Reiman and Fernando Rivas (*La lucha por la tierra* [Santiago: Quimantu], p. 64) report that in one of the last properties subdivided by the Caja de Colonización, Hacienda Lautaro, "De los treinta y dos inquilinos de la hacienda, veinticuatro recibieron 'huertos familiares' de 1 a 4 hectáreas de rulo, que en total no sumaban 100 hectáreas. El resto del vasto predio se subdividió en parcelas de 70 a 647 hectáreas, que se repartieron entre cuarenta y seis santiaguinos y terratenientes vecinos. También recibieron parcelas los seis administradores y mayordomos del fundo. Los inquilinos restantes, al carecer de dinero para pagar el pie del 'huerto' debieron abandonar la hacienda con lo puesto."

28. CIDA, *Chile*, p. 250.

29. From 1962 until September 1964 the government established 1066 new properties, divided among 781 parcelas and 285 huertos. These figures do not include the 149 huertos in Hacienda Mariposas which had not yet been delivered to the campesinos (CIDA, *Chile*, p. 250).

30. Juan Carlos Collarte, Ph.D. diss. (draft), chapter 7.

31. Collarte (ibid.) described the colonias as follows: "They consist basically of family parcels complemented by *huertos*, that were minifundias ranging from .5 to 2 hectares. In addition the buildings (silos, warehouses, stables, etc.) were in the hands of a cooperative (compulsory) composed of *parceleros* and *huerteros*."

32. CIDA, *Chile*, p. 375.

33. Collarte, Ph.D. diss.

34. Ibid.

35. Ibid.

36. Richard L. Meyer, "Debt Repayment Capacity of the Chilean Agrarian Reform Beneficiaries" (Ph.D. diss., Cornell University, 1970), p. 34.

Chapter 8

1. There exists a large and still growing literature on the Christian Democratic party in Chile (see the bibliography). The present chapter is limited to certain aspects of the Christian Democratic agrarian program.

2. Jacques Chonchol, "La reforma agraria," *Mensaje*, no. 123 (octubre 1963): 571.

3. Ibid.

4. See reglamento de la ley 8.811 sobre organización sindical de los obreros agrícolas, 29 julio 1947, decreto 261, artículo 7; and Oficio 74, 26 febrero, 1965, "Modifica artículo 7 del decreto no. 261," *Providencias* 19, 1965, 2558-2700.

5. Oficio 2863, 6 abril 1966, *Oficios* 15, 1966, 2805-3000.

6. See Law 16.362, *Diario oficial*, 5 noviembre 1965; and Oficio-Circular 869, 2 febrero, *Oficios* 5, 1966, 801-1000.

7. For details see Oficio-Circular 1373, 4 marzo 1967, "Transcribe reglamento para la aplicación de la Ley No. 16.455 e imparte instrucciones," *Oficios* 4, 1967, 1201-1500.

8. Letter to the director of the Labor Department signed by eleven campesinos, *Providencias* 6, 1966, 793-1000.

9. In February 1967 the government also enacted a law providing that rural proprietors had to pay workers for days not worked because of climatic conditions. Workers in the provinces of Linares to Magallanes were entitled to 40 percent of the daily minimum cash wage in addition to regalías. From Maule to Tarapacá this provision increased to 50 percent.

10. Oficio 7905, 30 octubre 1965, "Sobre planes de fiscalización leyes sociales sector asalariado agrícola," accompanying Oficio 9168, 14 diciembre 1965, *Oficios* 53, 1965, 9051-9300.

11. Ibid.

12. Ibid.

13. Much of the discussion which follows relies on information obtained in an interview with Pedro Donoso in Santiago, December 6, 1971.

14. In order to eliminate the internal campesino enterprise, some landowners had introduced a system (*ración cosechada*) of delivering to the workers quantities of produce estimated to be equivalent to what their land allotments could have produced.

15. A reproduction of one of these forms as it was filled out in an inspection visit can be found in Brian Loveman, *Struggle in the Countryside: A Documentary Supplement* (Bloomington, Ind.: International Development Research Center, 1976).

16. Oficio-Circular 886, 3 febrero 1966, "Imparte instrucciones acerca

oportunidad en que debe aplicarse sanción administrativa por incumplimiento legislación social," *Oficios* 5, 1966, 801-1000; and Oficio-Circular 3074, 25 mayo 1967, "Sobre aplicación de multas en caso de infracciones a disposiciones legales . . . ," *Oficios* 13, 1967, 3001-3099.

17. For example, Sociedad Agrícola Sierra Nevada Limitada (Fundo Punta Negra, Curacautín) was fined E80,628.24 at a time when the land was assessed for tax purposes at E40,703. See the letter contesting this fine from Pedro García Saenz to the director of the Labor Department, accompanying Resolución No. 1, Curacautín, 21 julio 1966, "Aplicación de multa administrativa," *Providencias* 10, 1967, 1901-2113.

18. See for example Resolución No. 2, Victoria, 13 mayo 1966, "Aplicación de multa administrativa," accompanying Oficio 4936, 15 junio 1966, "Refiérese denuncia . . . ," *Oficios* 25, 1966, 4901-5100.

19. Indicative are the fines applied in Talca in 1967 in fundos La Peña de Duao, Parroncillo de Sagrada Familia, Carrizal de Sagrada Familia, Huertos de Maule, La Serena de Molina, Los Aromos de Río Claro and San Enrique de Río Claro. See Oficio 118, Talca, 7 febrero 1968, accompanying Minuta Postal Circular 65, 4 marzo 1968, *Minutas postales,* 1968.

20. Letter to the director of the Labor Department from campesinos in Pullally, received November 22, 1966, *Providencias* 19, 1967, 3601-3800.

21. Authorization depended upon quite severe conditions, including transfer of at least 40 percent of the farm to be subdivided to the heads of the campesino families living in the farm during three of the last four years.

22. Translation after Theron O'Connor, cited in Joseph R. Thome, "Expropriation in Chile under the Frei Agrarian Reform," LTC Reprint no. 73, University of Wisconsin, Land Tenure Center, pp. 499-500, n. 47.

23. The estimate of 495 farms is found in CORA, *Reforma agraria chilena, 1965-1970* (Santiago: CORA, 1970), p. 36. Other sources, citing earlier CORA documents, set this figure at 478 (see Jorge Echenique, "Las expropriaciones y la organización de asentamientos en el período 1965-1970," in ICIRA, *Reforma agraria chilena,* p. 96; and Thome, "Expropriation," p. 496, n. 38).

24. Cipriano Pontigo, "Los comités de asentamiento en el Valle de Choapa," *Principios* 27 (marzo-abril 1966): 51.

25. CORFO, Secretariado Técnico de Planeamiento y Vivienda Rural, "Informe referente recursos y equipamiento Hacienda Choapa en relación al plan de reforma agraria de CORA" (Santiago, febrero 1965), p. 112.

26. This resume is based on Pontigo, "Los comités," and José Campusano, "El papel de las organizaciones campesinas en la lucha por la Reforma Agraria," *Principios* 27 (marzo-abril 1966): 28-35.

27. An official reglamento for the SARA was not adopted by CORA until June 1966 (CORA, "Reglamento del Asentamiento." Aprobado por el Consejo de la Corporación de la Reforma Agraria por Acuerdo No.

235 Tomado en la 29a Sesión Ordinaria Celebrada el 2 de junio de 1966). The reglamento underwent several revisions from 1966 to 1968. In 1968 CORA functionaries were eliminated officially from the Consejo de Administración.

28. In this regard see the poem by a union leader reproduced in Almino Affonso et al., *Movimiento campesino chileno*, vol. 1, p. 153.

29. For studies of the performance of individual asentamientos see Jaime Gazmuri, *Asentamientos campesinos* (Buenos Aires: DESAL, 1970); Richard L. Meyer, *Debt Repayment Capacity of the Chilean Agrarian Reform Beneficiaries* (Cornell University, Dissertation Series Number 14, February, 1970); A.L. Jolly et al., "An Economic Evaluation of the Asentamientos of the Agrarian Reform" (preliminary draft [Santiago: ICIRA, 1968]); Rogelio Imable, "Asentamientos de Choapa: Cambios en la tenencia de la tierra y los ingresos de los campesinos," *Economía* (primer cuatrimestre, 1967): 3-13; United Nations, Food and Agricultural Organization and ICIRA, "Evaluación preliminar de los asentamientos de la reforma agraria en Chile" (Santiago, 1967); and Jeannine Swift, *Agrarian Reform in Chile* (Lexington, Mass.: D.C. Heath, 1971), chapters 4 and 5.

30. Gazmuri, *Asentamientos*, p. 144.

31. In visiting over fifty asentamientos in order to carry out interviews (1971) it became clear that the success of asentamientos, in addition to the natural resource endowment, depended critically on the availability of campesino leadership skills and organizational capabilities. Where these did not exist, CORA functionaries tended to dominate asentamiento decision making. When the transitional period ended the campesinos still lacked the necessary entrepreneurial skills and organizational strength to deal effectively with the outside world.

32. This period is treated in detail in Affonso et al., *Movimiento*, vols. 1, 2.

33. See Oficio 956, San Fernando, 7 abril 1966, transcribed in Oficio 3043, 14 abril 1966, "Da a conocer . . . ," *Oficios* 16, 3001-3214.

34. For an early insight into this mobilization see *Revista nacional de trabajadores* (mayo 1965): 14-15, 28. An interesting account of government personnel's engaging in labor agitation can be found in Arturo Olavarría, *Chile bajo la Democracia Cristiana*, Segundo Año (Santiago: Editorial Nascimento, 1966), p. 40.

35. From November 1964 to December 1966, 179 rural unions obtained legal recognition (*personalidad jurídica*).

36. See for example CORA, no. 1181, 19 abril 1965, "Situación producida debido incumplimiento leyes sociales . . . ," *Providencias* 20, 1966, 3255-3400; Oficio 5059, 27 julio 1965, "Informa presentación . . . ," *Oficios* 30, 1965, 4990-5150; CORA, Providencia no. 24, 22 febrero 1965, "Sobre reclamos de campesinos . . . ," *Oficios* 40, 1965, 6700-6879; INDAP, Oficio no. 5, 18 marzo 1966, accompanying Oficio 4521, 1 junio 1966, "Refiérese fiscalización predios agrícolas . . . ," *Oficios* 23, 1966, 4301-4600; Oficio

4879, 19 junio 1966, "Sobre petición de envío de un inspector para fisca-lización agrícola," *Oficios* 24, 1966, 4601-4900; Oficio 2538, 28 marzo 1965, "Informa oficio-confidencial . . . ," *Oficios* 13, 1966, 2401-2600.

37. Oficio 8914, 11 noviembre 1966, "Funcionarios de INDAP no pue-den . . . ," *Oficios* 45, 1966, 8801-9100.

38. Almino Affonso et al., *Movimiento*, vol. 2, p. 26.

39. José Campusano, "Enseñanzas de la huelga campesina de colchagua," *Principios* 28 (enero 1967): 27.

40. For the reaction of the landowners during this period see R. Kaufman, *The Politics of Land Reform in Chile, 1950-1970* (Cambridge, Mass.: Harvard University Press, 1972), especially chapter 5.

41. For example, in Los Cristales in Curicó (1965) and in the large strike organized by FCI in Colchagua (1966).

42. Like all Chilean legislation the unionization law is supplemented with an administrative reglamento. In discussing Law 16.625, features of the reglamento rather than the law itself are indicated by the notation "(Reg.)." In the case of Law 16.625, the reglamento is about twice as long as the law itself.

43. See for example Resolución no. 769, 20 septiembre 1968, "Autoriza constitución de sindicato de trabajadores de la Comuna de Vichuquén, con un número inferior a cien personas," *Oficios* 23, 1968, 6001-6200.

44. Reglamento para la aplicación de la ley número 16.625, Decreto 453, 21 septiembre 1967, in Juan Díaz Salas, *Código del Trabajo*, 13 (Santiago: Editorial Nascimento, 1968), pp. 243-78.

45. Enforcement of these provisions and collection of the employers' contribution to the unions was not altogether rigorous in the first two years of the law's application. Various unions complained about employer noncompliance. See for example the letter directed to President Frei from the sindicato de trabajadores agrícolas no. 1 de la comuna de Río Bueno, 22 febrero 1969, accompanying Oficio 6680, 23 septiembre 1969, "Sobre denuncia no pago de aportes sindicales . . . ," *Oficios* 30, 1969, 6501-6700.

46. Indications of the monthly income of existing federations and con-federations as of December 1968 can be found in Memorandum No. 123, 19 diciembre 1968. "Relación aportes financieros a confederaciones y federaciones de trabajadores agrícolas," *Oficios* 39, 1968, 9081-9250. According to this report income of the federations ranged from 1200 escudos to 12,000 escudos in December 1968.

47. In the United States, in Indiana, this authority was only revoked in 1972 by a court decision against the Morgan Packing Company. See "Migrants Win Victory over Morgan, Access to Workers' Camps Ordered," *Louisville Courier Journal*, August 2, 1972.

48. An important innovation in the Junta de Conciliación allowed the president of the Junta to break tie votes. Since the president of the Junta was always a Labor Department functionary, this gave the government

significant leverage in labor disputes handled through legal channels. The president of the Junta also had authority to determine the legality of labor petitions in cases of a tie vote.

49. Articles 166-175 of the reglamento detail the procedure for legal strikes.

50. The corporativist bias of some sectors of the Christian Democratic party lent ideological support for these provisions.

51. Gonzalo Arroyo and Sergio Gómez, "Una etapa conflictiva en la Reforma Agraria," ICIRA, Santiago, 30-8-1971, p. 11.

52. A copy of this labor petition can be found in Loveman, *Struggle in the Countryside: A Documentary Supplement.*

53. Oficio 222, Melipilla, 6 mayo 1967, "Informa presentación de pliego de peticiones de los obreros agrícolas de la comuna de Melipilla y solicita instrucciones al respeto," unbound, Archivo de la Dirección del Trabajo.

54. Telegrama-Circular 160, 24 mayo 1967, *Telegramas* 1, 1967.

55. Oficio-Circular 4078, 20 junio 1967, "Imparte instrucciones para la aplicación del Artículo 26 de la Ley 16.625 . . . ," *Oficios* 19, 1967, 3938-4121; Oficio 4179, 23 junio 1967, "Transcribe texto de instrucciones . . . ," *Oficios* 20, 1967, 4122-4273; Oficio-Circular 4453, 12 julio 1967, "Complementa instrucciones . . . ," *Oficios* 21, 1967, 4274-4457; Oficio-Circular 5226, 11 agosto 1967, "Instrucciones sobre constitución de sindicatos agrícolas . . . ," *Oficios* 26, 1967, 5101-5295; Oficio-Circular 6778, 14 octubre 1967, "Refiérese a constitución y otros aspectos de sindicatos agrícolas . . . ," *Oficios* 34, 1967, 6701-7000; Oficio-Circular 8059, 5 diciembre 1967, "Complementa y modifica oficio-circular No. 6778 . . . ," *Oficios* 40, 1967, 7951-8200.

56. Minuta Postal No. 231, 29 abril 1967, transcribed in Oficio 3787, 29 julio 1967, "Sobre constitución de sindicatos agrícolas," *Oficios* 18, 1967, 3774-3937.

57. Minuta Postal Circular 288, 1 junio 1967, *Minutas postales*, vol. 1, 1967, 1-534.

58. Oficio 3809, 9 junio 1967, "Sobre Reglamento Ley 16.625," *Oficios* 18, 1967, 3774-3937.

59. Minuta Postal Circular 304, 17 junio 1967, *Minutas postales*, vol. 1, 1967, 1-534.

60. CORA, *Reforma agraria chilena.*

61. INDAP sponsored *El Triunfo Campesino*. The independent Christian unions combined to form *Libertad*. Marxist unions formed the confederation *Ranquil.*

62. In 1968 in Aconcagua Province the government sent several hundred police equipped with armored vehicles (*tanquetas*) to dislodge FCI-affiliated campesinos from Fundo San Miguel. The campesinos occupied the farm in protest against government orders to go back to work after a long, unsolved strike.

63. Eventually Chonchol and other advocates of still more rapid and radical transformation of the countryside left the Christian Democratic party and formed a movement called MAPU. This group joined with the Marxist parties in the 1970 presidential elections, and Chonchol subsequently occupied the Ministry of Agriculture.

64. Ley de Reforma Agraria No. 16.640, Edición Oficial (Santiago: Editorial Jurídica, 1967). For a discussion of the legislative debates on this law see Terry McCoy, "Agrarian Reform in Chile, 1962-1968: A Study of Politics and the Development Process" (Ph.D. diss., University of Wisconsin, 1969), chapters 4, 6, and 7.

65. ICIRA, *Exposición metódica y coordinada de la Ley de Reforma Agraria de Chile* (Santiago: Editorial Jurídica, 1968).

66. Article 172 of the law established equivalents to 80 hectares of irrigated land in the central valley for other regions according to soil quality and other ecological factors.

67. Exceptions to this article were provided for farms of less than 80 hectares (BIH) meeting a number of other stiff requirements (Article 6).

68. The legal and administrative details of expropriation can be found in Articles 30-38.

69. Article 191 detailed the character of agrarian reform cooperatives, and Article 192, that of campesino cooperatives.

70. From the time of expropriation to the creation of the asentamiento there existed a lag for the *"toma de posesión."* The campesinos in these farms considered themselves in a "pre-asentamiento."

71. "Reglamento sobre la calificación de las condiciones de explotación de un predio rústico para que no se estime mal explotado," in *Recopilación de leyes y decretos con fuerza de ley, reglamentos y decretos agrarios* (Santiago: Editorial Nascimento, 1968), pp. 147-54.

72. ICIRA, *Reforma agraria*, p. 48.

73. Ibid., p. 45.

74. Ibid.

75. Micro studies of asentamiento performance are included in Meyer, *Debt Payment*; E. Broughton, "Chile, Land Reform and Agricultural Development" (Ph.D. diss., University of Liverpool, 1970); Jolly, "An Economic Evaluation"; Imable, "Asentamientos"; Guzmán, *Asentamientos*; and Swift, *Agrarian Reform*.

76. In some asentamientos I visited in 1971 CORA had not provided an economic balance to the campesinos since 1967. The asentados had no idea of the source and cost of inputs, marketing channels, or economic performance of the asentamiento.

77. Wayne Ringlein, "Economic Effects of Chilean National Expropriation Policy on the Private Farm Sector, 1964-1969" (Ph.D. diss., University of Maryland, 1971); Solon Barraclough, "Agrarian Reform in Chile" (draft,

1971); CORA, unpublished data cited in William C. Thiesenhusen, "Agrarian Reform in Chile," in Peter Dorner, ed., *Land Reform in Latin America*, Land Economics Monograph Series, no. 3, 1971, pp. 105-25.

78. Thiesenhusen, ibid., p. 121.

79. Ibid.

80. Olavarría, *Chile Bajo*, vol. 6, p. 84.

81. Ibid.

82. Plinio Sampaio, "Notas sobre la organización campesina," in ICIRA, *Reforma agraria chilena*, p. 45.

83. Jorge Echenique, "Las expropriaciones y la organización de asenta-mientos en el período 1965-1970," in ibid., pp. 105-6.

84. Ibid., p. 107.

85. Ibid., p. 106.

86. *INDAP, 1964-1970*, Gerencia General del Instituto de Desarrollo Agropecuario, 31 octubre 1970, n.p.

87. From 1965 to 1967 I worked with various INDAP promoters and assisted in the formation of cooperatives. The incentive to organize inevitably came from INDAP in the form of promised credit, seeds, or assistance in selling produce. In conversations with INDAP officials in 1971, estimates on the "failure" of these cooperatives ran from 80 to 99 percent. No economic studies generally preceded formation. Political criteria predominated.

88. Barraclough, "Agrarian Reform in Chile," p. 4.

89. In 1971 I visited some of these enterprises that specialized in hog and chicken production. For the most part they consisted of multiple partnerships in which individual campesinos provided small amounts of land and labor to a production unit subsidized by INDAP. In some cases these enterprises had been quite successful, but they remained isolated experiments benefiting a small number of campesino families.

Chapter 9

1. Solon Barraclough has pointed out that Oscar Lange generally predicted this sort of reaction to a program of socialization. Lange declared: "A Socialist government really intent upon socialism has to decide to carry out its socialization program at one stroke or to give it up altogether. The very coming into power of such a government must cause a financial panic and economic collapse. Therefore, the Socialist government must either guarantee the immunity of private property and private enterprise in order to enable the capitalist economy to function normally, in doing which it gives up its socialist aims, or it must go through resolutely with its socialization program at maximum speed. Any hesitation, any vacillation and indecision would provoke the inevitable economic catastrophe" (O. Lange and F.M. Taylor, *On the Economic Theory of Socialism* [Uni-

versity of Minnesota Press, 1938], cited in Solon Barraclough, "Agrarian Reform in Chile," draft, November 1970, p. 27).

2. The preliminary agrarian program of the Popular Unity government was spelled out in the "20 points," which are reproduced in *Avancemos* (Revista Sindical Campesina) 3, (FEES: Santiago, 1971) (Points 1-10 in no. 6 and 11-20 in no. 7).

3. See for example "Discurso de Miguel Enríquez, Secretario General del MIR," *El Mercurio* (3 noviembre 1971).

4. Newspapers headlined these events daily during the first year of the Allende government. Typical are "Movimiento revolucionario de campesinos ocupo seis fundos," *El Mercurio* (25 enero 1971); "Campesinos ocuparon Fundo San José de Quecherehua," *El Mercurio* (26 enero 1971); "Exproprian fundos tomados en Parral," *El Mercurio* (28 marzo 1971); "Refuerzos del MCR están llegando a zona conflictiva," *La Prensa* (25 abril 1971); "Las tácticas del movimiento campesino revolucionario retardan acción del gobierno," *El Siglo* (26 mayo 1971); "131 fundos permanecen ocupados ilegalmente," *El Mercurio* (13 noviembre 1971); "Entregan lista de fundos ocupados ilegalmente por extremistas de Izquierda," *La Prensa* (17 noviembre 1971).

5. MIR intervention in Cautín was also widely covered by the press. See for example "Veinticinco fundos tomados en Lautaro," *El Mercurio* (12 diciembre 1970); "Sobre un volcán de violencia vive la Provincia de Cautín," *La Prensa* (29 diciembre 1970); "Campesinos dispuestos a morir por la tierra," *Puro Chile* (31 diciembre 1970); "Armados para sedición latifundistas de Cautín," *El Siglo* (19 enero 1971); "50 fundos paralizados en Provincia de Cautín," *El Mercurio* (22 enero 1971).

6. "Murió agricultor baleado en toma de fundo," *La Prensa* (20 abril 1971); "Un muerto en incidente a tiros en Fundo de Cautín," *El Mercurio* (24 octubre 1971); "Un mapuche muerto y tres heridos en enfrentamiento en Cautín," *El Siglo* (23 noviembre 1971).

7. "Gobierno parte hoy a solucionar problemas de Cautín," *El Siglo* (4 enero 1971); "A Cautín se traslada hoy ministerio de agricultura," *La Prensa* (5 enero 1971).

8. "El gobierno actuará de acuerdo a resoluciones del poder judicial," *El Mercurio* (30 diciembre 1970); "El presidente de la república responde a la S.N.A.," *El Diario Austral* (Temuco) (20 enero 1971); "La alianza oficialista condenará públicamente las tomas de fundos," *La Prensa* (14 febrero 1971); "El gobierno no aceptará más tomas ilegales," *La Prensa* (30 julio 1971).

9. Chile, Cuerpo de Carabineros, Dirección General O.S. 3, "Relación de ocupaciones ilegales de fundos ocurridos desde el 1 de noviembre, 1970 al 5 de abril, 1972," *El Mercurio* (5 junio 1972), pp. 9-15, and *El Mercurio* (6 junio 1972), pp. 24-28, cited in Cristóbal Kay, "La participación campesina en el gobierno de la Unidad Popular," typed (sent to author directly by Kay).

10. "Movilización de agricultores ante ocupaciones ilegales," *El Mercurio* (17 febrero 1971); "Lucha a muerte por la tierra en San Carlos," *La Prensa* (26 febrero 1971); "Agricultores impidieron toma de Hijuela," *El Mercurio* (23 marzo 1971); "Violenta recaptura de fundos ocupados," *La Segunda* (26 marzo 1971); "Momios forman 'grupos de despeje' en Linares," *El Siglo* (27 julio 1971); "Empresarios agrícolas solicitan protección," *La Prensa* (21 febrero 1971); "Protección efectiva piden los propietarios agrícolas," *El Mercurio* (16 marzo 1971).

11. ICIRA, "Cartilla sobre intervención de predios agrícolas," n.d.

12. On this see "Abusiva actuación de interventores agrícolas," *El Mercurio* (editorial) (15 febrero 1971); "Consecuencias de intervención agrícola," *El Mercurio* (editorial) (16 febrero 1971); "Los interventores tienen orden de arruinar a los proprietarios," *Las ultimas noticias* (16 febrero 1971); "Cartilla sobre intervención en la agricultura," *El Mercurio* (editorial) (19 febrero 1971); "339 predios agrícolas intervenidos en un año," *El Mercurio* (28 noviembre 1971).

13. For example, "Constituyen asentamiento en Cautín," *El Siglo* (18 febrero 1971), describes the establishment of Asentamiento Santa Rosa in the first property expropriated by the Popular Unity government in Cautín.

14. As early as November 1970 Solon Barraclough, Chonchol's friend and colleague at ICIRA, described the outlines of such an enterprise. See Barraclough, "Agrarian Reform in Chile."

15. Partido Socialista, "Síntesis de la política agraria del partido socialista," mimeographed, 1971.

16. Jaime Lazo, "Informe preliminar de la comisión política del partido comunista," mimeographed, 1971.

17. MAPU, *El primer año del Gobierno Popular,* Documentos y Posiciones del MAPU, no. 1, n.d., cited in Cristóbal Kay and Peter Winn, "Reforma agraria y revolución rural en el Chile de Allende," (sent to author by Cristóbal Kay).

18. The government claimed that SOCORA increased its share in total agricultural exports from 5 percent in 1970 to 15 percent in 1971. For 1972 the government expected SOCORA to account for 40 percent of the value of agricultural exports (Centro de Estudios Agrarios, "Informe coyuntural del Agro" *Boletín* no. 3 (junio 1972), p. 30, citing *El Siglo* (8 junio 1972).

19. Chile, Ministerio de Agricultura, Decreto 481, "Que crea consejo nacional campesino." See also "Reglamento del consejo campesino."

20. *El Siglo* (27 noviembre 1970), p. 10.

21. "Funcionarios impiden constitución de consejos campesinos," *La Prensa* (18 febrero 1971); "INDAP e ICIRA forman consejos campesinos al margen de la ley," *La Prensa* (24 octubre 1971).

388 : NOTES TO PAGES 287-297

22. See for example, "Expropiación de 341 predios piden campesinos en Ñuble," *El Mercurio* (27 enero 1971).

23. See Emilio Klein and Sergio Gómez, "Informe sobre el estado actual de los consejos comunales campesinos," mimeographed, ICIRA, abril 1972, cited in Kay and Winn, "Reforma agraria," p. 21; and E. Maffei and P. Marchetti, "Algunos alcances teóricos sobre los consejos campesinos y el poder de los trabajadores" (draft), March 1972, cited in Kay, "La participación," p. 11.

24. "Pide ampliación de consejos comunales," *El Siglo* (7 octubre 1971).

25. "Campesinos rechazan mero cambio de patrón," *La Prensa* (5 septiembre 1971).

26. "Nueva forma de organización para sector reformado: Agro," *El Siglo* (20 agosto 1971).

27. Ibid.

28. ICIRA, "Los centros de reforma agraria," mimeographed, 19 agosto 1971.

29. ICIRA, "Centros de reforma agraria," 9 septiembre 1971.

30. "The previous government, instead of uniting the campesinos without creating proletarians, preferred to divide them, promising to make proprietors of some few [of them]. . . . The reasons for this problem can be found in the fact that the asentamiento transformed asentados into proprietors of land. The CERAs put an end to this problem and do not stimulate divisions" (cited in "La CORA no quiere que campesinos sean dueños de la tierra," *La Prensa* [22 septiembre 1971]).

31. "La CORA no quiere."

32. Centro de Estudios Agrarios, Boletín no. 3, p. 23, citing *La Prensa* (11 junio 1972).

33. *Vía Chilena*, Año 1, no. 2 (noviembre 1971), p. 11.

34. Ibid.

35. Cristóbal Kay reported that, at the end of 1972, 45 percent of all expropriated farms were organized as asentamientos, another 45 percent as "campesino committees," and 10 percent as CERA or centro de producción (state farm) ("The Development of the Chilean Hacienda System 1850's-1972," paper presented to Symposium on Landlord and Peasant in Latin America and the Caribbean [University of Cambridge, December 20-21, 1972], citing data from a study on the land reform process by N. Langand, typescript, ICIRA, 1972, chapter 2).

36. On September 25, 1972, *El Mercurio* ("Catastrófica será en 1973 la producción de trigo") reported that unavailability of needed inputs, and bureaucratic mismanagement, led in 1972 to the lowest wheat output in recent memory. Even if the SNA and *El Mercurio* exaggerated the magnitude of the problems, it is clear that the disarray of the agricultural sector notably affected production.

37. In carrying out survey research in the countryside in late 1971 I repeatedly heard views of this sort expressed by campesinos, especially those in asentamientos.

38. Cited in "A campesinos no les gusta el estado de patrón," *La Prensa* (23 enero 1971).

39. "Protesta campesina: Tomadas tres oficinas de la CORA," *La Prensa* (17 octubre 1971), p. 8.

40. Ibid.

41. "Gobierno se opone a las empresas de trabajadores," *El Mercurio* (18 noviembre 1971).

42. "Qué son las empresas de los trabajadores. Responde el Diputado Demócrata Cristiano Emilio Lorenzini," *La Prensa* (26 noviembre 1971).

43. See Pablo Ramírez, *Cambio en las formas de pago a la mano de obra agrícola* (Santiago: ICIRA, 1968).

44. See "La Izquierda Cristiana reclama por aceptación de renuncia de Chonchol," *El Mercurio* (4 noviembre 1972).

Chapter 10

1. For a discussion of agriculture in the Soviet Union, Eastern Europe, and China see Jerzy F. Karcz, "Comparative Study of Transformation of Agriculture in Centrally Planned Economies: The Soviet Union, Eastern Europe and Mainland China," in Erik Thorbecke, ed., *The Role of Agriculture in Economic Development* (New York: National Bureau of Economic Research, 1969), pp. 237-76; on Cuba see Sergio Aranda, *La revolución agraria en Cuba* (México D.F.: Siglo 21, 1968).

2. See William Thiesenhusen, *Chile's Experiments in Agrarian Reform* (Madison: University of Wisconsin Press, 1966), pp. 3-5.

3. "Jurisprudencia sobre usurpación," *El Mercurio* (2 agosto 1972), p. 3.

4. *El Mercurio* (24 diciembre 1973), p. 32.

5. *Latin America* (January 4, 1974), p. 6.

6. On the Stolypin reforms see William Henry Chamberlin, "The Ordeal of the Russian Peasantry," *Russian Review* 14 (October 1955): 297. For a description of the counterrevolution in Guatemala see Thomas and Marjorie Melville, *Guatemala: The Politics of Land Ownership* (New York: The Free Press, 1971).

7. For a discussion of counterreform see Ernest Feder, "Counterreform," in Rodolfo Stavenhagen, ed., *Agrarian Problems and Peasant Movements in Latin America* (Garden City, N.Y.: Anchor, 1970), pp. 173-223.

8. See, for example, "Estatuto tipo para comités de campesinos," Decreto Publicado en el "Diario Oficial" de 20 de abril de 1968; "Cooperativas campesinas; normas por las que se rigen," Decreto con Fuerza de Ley No. 13, de 18 enero de 1968; "Cooperativas de reforma agraria;

normas por las que se rigen," Decreto con Fuerza de Ley No. 12, 18 enero de 1968. All of these decrees are reproduced in *Recopilación de Leyes, Decretos con Fuerza de Ley, Reglamentos y Decretos Agrarios* (Santiago: Editorial Nascimento, 1968).

9. "340 mil campesinos en Huelga," *El Mercurio* (31 octubre 1972), p. 8. While the headline was an obvious exaggeration, the article cited campesino leaders and listed their demands on the government.

10. "Rechazo al estanco del trigo y a requisiciones," *El Mercurio* (1 febrero 1973), p. 25; "Total rechazo al estanco del trigo," *El Mercurio* (2 febrero 1973), p. 7.

11. "Reaccionario y retrogrado es el estanco del trigo," *El Mercurio* (27 enero 1973), p. 26.

12. "Alimentos y créditos quitarán a campesinos," *El Mercurio* (28 enero 1973), p. 39.

13. Ibid.

14. CORA, *Reforma agraria chilena, 1965-1970* (Santiago: CORA, 1970), p. 95.

15. Rafael Menjivar, *Reforma agraria chilena* (San Salvador: Editorial Universitaria de El Salvador, 1970), pp. 133-34.

16. Ibid., p. 134.

17. Solon Barraclough, "Reforma agraria: Historia y perspectivas," *Cuadernos de la realidad nacional* 7 (marzo 1971): 54-55.

18. Ibid., p. 55.

19. Cited in *Ercilla*, no. 1996 (31 octubre-6 noviembre 1973): 26.

20. Cristóbal Kay, "The Development of the Chilean Hacienda System 1850's-1972," paper presented to the Symposium on Landlord and Peasant in Latin America and the Caribbean, University of Cambridge, December 20-21, 1972, p. 29.

21. This study was under the direction of Marion Brown of the University of Wisconsin Land Tenure Center.

22. In 1965, 49 percent of all farms contained less than 5 hectares and in aggregate represented about 0.7 percent of land in farms. Another 36 percent of all farms (5 hectares, 49.9 hectares) included only 5 percent of all farmland. Except where wage labor was employed, the agrarian reform from 1965 to 1972 did not greatly affect the internal distribution of proprietary authority in these farms. Discussion in this section is essentially limited, therefore, to farms of more than 40 hectares (BIH) or to the commercial farm sector.

23. Wayne Ringlein, "Economic Effects of Chilean National Expropriation Policy on the Private Commercial Farm Sector, 1964-1969" (Ph.D. diss., University of Maryland, 1971), cited in William Thiesenhusen, "Agrarian Reform: Chile," in Peter Dorner, ed., *Land Reform in Latin America: Issues and Cases*, Land Economics Monograph no. 3 (Madison, Wis.: University

of Wisconsin Press, 1971), p. 113.

24. Kay, "The Development," p. 28.

25. Robert R. Kaufman, *The Politics of Land Reform in Chile, 1950-1970* (Cambridge, Mass.: Harvard University Press, 1972), p. 177.

26. Ibid.

27. A. Mattelart et al., *La ideología de la dominación en una sociedad dependiente* (Buenos Aires: Ediciones Signos, 1970), p. 157, n. 15.

28. Gonzalo Arroyo and Sergio Gómez, "Una etapa conflictiva en la reforma agraria" (Santiago: ICIRA, 1971), pp. 11-12.

29. "Miles de Campesinos en Huelga," *El Mercurio* (27 octubre 1972).

30. In 1965 there existed 120,000 properties of less than 5 hectares and another 92,000 units containing between 5 and 50 hectares. Even taking into account multiple holdings and multiple ownership of single properties, the approximately 90,000 campesinos organized in cooperatives and committees represented less than one-half of smallholders.

31. In 1972 some 190,000 farms contained less than 5 hectares (BIH).

32. Aníbal Correa, letter to *La Nación* (23 diciembre 1964), p. 3, cited in Kaufman, *The Politics*, p. 153.

33. See Dale L. Johnson, "The National Progressive Bourgeoisie in Chile," *Studies in Comparative International Development* 4 (1968-1969): 76.

34. Jorge Echenique, "La batalla contra el latifundio," *Revista Agraria* 1 (diciembre 1972), suplemento agrario, *Chile Hoy* (diciembre 1972): 8-9.

35. "Confederación campesina 'libertad' repudia el estanco del trigo," *El Mercurio* (4 febrero, 1973), p. 31.

36. Similarly, *El Mercurio* quoted representatives of the Federation of Small Farmers of Talca on February 2, 1973 ("Total rechazo al estanco del trigo," p. 7): "Since the government knows that all real farmers repudiate these measures, it has refused to allow us to attend the meeting at the UNCTAD building where agricultural problems were treated. We deny all validity to decisions made at that meeting."

37. Solon Barraclough and Almino Affonso, "Diagnóstico de la reforma agraria (noviembre 1970-junio 1972)," artículo para publicar en *Revista Agraria* 2, suplemento, *Chile Hoy* (enero 1973), p. 3 of draft.

38. "¿Justicia diferida?" ibid., p. 6.

BIBLIOGRAPHY

Documentary Sources

In this study all citations that refer to volumes of *Oficios, Providencias,* or *Telegramas* and do not make reference to another governmental source refer to the Labor Archive in Santiago, Chile. Since 1906 the Chilean Labor Department systematically retained and bound materials related to its internal administration and to its role in the Chilean political system. After 1930 materials were typically bound in volumes labeled *oficios, providencias,* or *telegramas* in addition to some more specialized volumes. The volumes labeled *oficios* usually contain documents that originated with the central headquarters of the Labor Department in Santiago. At times accompanying documents are copies of materials found also in the *providencias,* which generally contain materials that originated outside of the Labor Department's Santiago offices. These materials include telegrams, reports by labor inspectors, letters from private citizens or organizations, and communications from other governmental agencies or from the national Congress. The volumes labeled *telegramas* usually contain a numbered series of telegrams sent by Santiago personnel to officials in the provinces.

Books, Monographs, and Theses in English

Alexander, Robert J. *Agrarian Reform in Latin America.* New York: Macmillan, 1974.

_____. *Communism in Latin America.* New Brunswick: Rutgers University Press, 1957.

_____. *Labor Parties in Latin America.* New York: League for Industrial Democracy, 1942.

_____. *Labor Relations in Argentina, Brazil, and Chile.* New York: McGraw Hill, 1962.

_____. *Organized Labor in Latin America.* New York: Free Press of Glencoe, 1965.

Alroy, Gil Carl. *The Involvement of Peasants in Internal Wars.* Princeton University: Center for International Studies, 1966.

Angell, Alan. *Politics and the Labour Movement in Chile.* London: Oxford University Press, 1972.

Bannon, John Francis. *Indian Labor in the Spanish Indies.* Boston: Heath, 1966.

Bauer, Arnold J. "Chilean Rural Society in the Nineteenth Century." Ph.D. dissertation. University of California, Berkeley, 1969.

Birns, Laurence, ed. *The End of Chilean Democracy.* New York: Seabury Press, 1973.

Bloch, Marc. *Land and Work in Mediaeval Europe.* London: Routledge and Kegan Paul, 1967.

Broughton, F. "Chile: Land Reform and Agricultural Development." Ph.D. dissertation. University of Liverpool, 1970.

Burnett, Ben G. *Political Groups in Chile: The Dialogue Between Order and Change.* Austin: University of Texas Press, 1970.

Butland, Gilbert J. *Chile: An Outline of Its Geography, Economics, and Politics.* London: University of Oxford Press, 1956.

Chamberlain, Robert S. *Castilian Background of the Repartimiento Encomienda.* Washington, D.C.: Carnegie Institution of Washington, 1939.

Cheshire, G.C. *Chile: Under Military Rule.* New York: IDOC/North America, 1974.

———. *The Modern Law of Real Property.* London: Butterworth, 1958.

The Chilean Economy under the Popular Unity Government. Prepared by the Business School of Valparaíso, Adolfo Ibáñez Foundation, March 1974.

Cohen, Morris R. *Law and the Social Order: Essays in Legal Philosophy.* New York: Harcourt, Brace, 1933.

Coulanges, Fustel de. *The Origin of Property in Land.* London: Allen and Unwin, 1927.

Daugherty, Charles H., ed. *Chile: Election Factbook.* Washington, D.C.: Institute for the Comparative Study of Political Systems, 1963.

Dorner, Peter, ed. *Land Reform in Latin America: Issues and Cases.* Land Economics Monograph No. 3. Madison: University of Wisconsin Press, 1971.

Dovring, Folke. *Land and Labor in Europe in the Twentieth Century.* The Hague: Martinus Nijhoff, 1965.

———. *Land and Labor in Europe, 1900-1950: A Comparative Study of Recent Agrarian History.* The Hague: Martinus Nijhoff, 1956.

Duby, Georges. *Rural Economy and Country Life in the Medieval West.* Columbia: University of South Carolina Press, 1968.

Echeverria, Roberto P. "The Effect of Agricultural Price Policies on Intersectoral Income Transfers." Ph.D. dissertation. Cornell University, 1969.

Edleman, Murray. *The Symbolic Uses of Politics.* Chicago: University of Illinois Press, 1967.

Elliot, G.F. Scott. *Chile: Its History and Development, Natural Features, Products, Commerce and Present Conditions.* New York: Scribner, 1907.

Ellsworth, P.T. *Chile: An Economy in Transition.* New York: Macmillan, 1945.

Evans, Les, ed. *Disaster in Chile*. New York: Pathfinder Press, 1974.

Faron, L.C. *Mapuche Social Structure*. Urbana: University of Illinois Press, 1961.

Feinberg, Richard E. *The Triumph of Allende: Chile's Legal Revolution*. New York: Mentor Press, 1972.

Fetter, Frank W. *Monetary Inflation in Chile*. Princeton: Princeton University Press, 1931.

Finer, Herman. *The Chilean Development Corporation*. Montreal: International Labour Office, 1947.

Frank, Andrew Gunder. *Capitalism and Underdevelopment in Latin America: Historical Studies of Chile and Brazil*. New York: Monthly Review Press, 1967.

Fuentes, Carlos, et al. *Whither Latin America?* New York: Monthly Review Press, 1963.

Gadalla, S.M. *Land Reform in Relation to Social Development*. University of Missouri Studies. Vol. 29. Columbia: University of Missouri Press, 1962.

Galdames, Luis. *A History of Chile*. Chapel Hill: University of North Carolina Press, 1941.

Gil, Federico G. *Chile: Election Factbook*. Washington, D.C.: Institute for the Comparative Study of Political Systems, 1965.

––––––. *Genesis and Modernization of Political Parties in Chile*. Gainesville: University of Florida Press, 1962.

––––––. *The Political System of Chile*. Boston: Houghton Mifflin, 1966.

Gil, Federico, and Charles J. Parrish. *The Chilean Presidential Election of September 4, 1964*. Washington, D.C.: Institute for the Comparative Study of Political Systems, 1965.

Gill, Clark C. *Education and Social Change in Chile*. Washington, D.C.: U.S. Department of Health, Education, and Welfare, Office of Education, 1966.

Gómez, Sergio. "Class Organizations and Conflict in Rural Chile." Master's thesis. University of Essex, England, 1971.

Gregory, Peter. *Industrial Wages in Chile*. Ithaca: Cornell University Press, 1967.

Gross, Leonard. *The Last Best Hope: Eduardo Frei and Chilean Democracy*. New York: Random House, 1967.

Halperin, Ernst. *Nationalism and Communism in Chile*. Cambridge: M.I.T. Press, 1965.

Hanson, Earl Parker. *Chile: Land of Progress*. New York: Reynal and Hitchcock, 1941.

Herrick, Bruce H. *Urban Migration and Economic Development in Chile*. Cambridge: M.I.T. Press, 1965.

Hirschman, Albert O. *Journeys Toward Progress*. New York: Doubleday, 1965.

_____. *Latin American Issues: Essays and Comments*. New York: Twentieth Century Fund, 1961.

Huizer, Gerritt. *The Revolutionary Potential of Peasants in Latin America*. Lexington, Mass.: D.C. Heath, 1972.

Irvine, Helen Douglas. *The Making of Rural Europe*. London: Allen and Unwin, 1923.

Jefferson, Mark. *Recent Colonization in Chile*. New York: Oxford University Press, 1921.

Johnson, Dale L., ed. *The Chilean Road to Socialism*. Garden City, N.Y.: Anchor, 1973.

Kay, Cristóbal. "Comparative Development of the European Manorial System and the Latin American Hacienda System: An Approach to a Theory of Agrarian Change for Chile." Ph.D. dissertation. University of Sussex, England, 1971.

Kaufman, Robert R. *The Chilean Political Right and Agrarian Reform*. Washington, D.C.: Institute for the Comparative Study of Political Systems, 1967.

_____. *The Politics of Land Reform in Chile, 1950-1970*. Cambridge: Harvard University Press, 1972.

Kerridge, Eric. *Agrarian Problems in the Sixteenth Century and After*. London: Allen and Unwin, 1969.

Kautsky, John H., ed. *Political Change in Underdeveloped Countries: Nationalism and Communism*. New York: Wiley, 1962.

Lambert, Jacques. *Latin America: Social Structure and Political Institutions*. Berkeley and Los Angeles: University of California Press, 1969.

Landsberger, Henry A., ed. *Latin American Peasant Movements*. Ithaca: Cornell University Press, 1969.

Lewis, Frank Marshall. "The Political Effects of a Multi-Party System upon the Presidential Form of Government in Chile." Ph.D. dissertation. University of Texas, 1955.

Mazzella, Frank. "Party-Building in a Modernizing Society: A Study of the Intermediate Leaders of the Chilean Christian Democratic Party." 2 vols. Ph.D. dissertation. Indiana University, 1972.

McBride, George M. *Chile: Land and Society*. New York: American Geographical Society, 1936.

McCoy, Terry L. "Agrarian Reform in Chile, 1962-1968: A Study of Politics and the Development Process." Ph.D. dissertation. University of Wisconsin, 1969.

_____. "The Politics of Structural Change in Latin America: The Case of Agrarian Reform in Chile." University of Wisconsin, Land Tenure

Center, Reprint No. 37, 1969.

McDonald, Ronald H. *Party Systems and Elections in Latin America.* Chicago: Markham, 1971.

Maitland, Francis J. *Chile: Its Land and People.* London: F. Griffiths, 1914.

Mamalakis, Markos. *The Changing Structure and Roles of the Chilean Agricultural Sector.* New Haven: Yale University Press, 1967.

Mamalakis, Markos, and C.W. Reynolds. *Essays on the Chilean Economy.* Homewood, Ill.: Richard D. Irwin, 1965.

Martin, Gene Ellis. "Land Division in Central Chile." Ph.D. dissertation. Syracuse University, 1955.

Menges, Constantine. *Peasant Organizations and Politics in Chile: 1958-1964.* Santa Monica: Rand Corp., n.d.

Meyer, Richard L. "Debt Repayment Capacity of the Chilean Agrarian Reform Beneficiaries." Ph.D. dissertation. Cornell University, Latin American Studies Program Dissertation Series, 1970.

Mitrany, David. *Marx Against the Peasant: A Study in Social Pragmatism.* Chapel Hill: University of North Carolina Press, 1951.

Moore, Barrington, Jr. *Social Origins of Dictatorship and Democracy.* Boston: Beacon Press, 1966.

Moreno, Francisco Jose. *Legitimacy and Stability in Latin America: A Study of Chilean Political Culture.* New York: New York University Press, 1969.

Morris, David J. *We Must Make Haste—Slowly.* New York: Random House, 1973.

Moss, Robert. *Chile's Marxist Experiment.* Newton Abbot, England: David & Charles, 1973.

North, Liisa. *Civil-Military Relations in Argentina, Chile and Peru.* Berkeley: University of California, Institute of International Studies, 1966.

Nunn, Frederick M. *Chilean Politics 1920-1931: The Honorable Mission of the Armed Forces.* Albuquerque: University of New Mexico Press, 1970.

Parsons, Kenneth; R. Penn; and P. Raup. *Land Tenure. Proceedings of the Conference on World Land Tenure Problems.* Madison: University of Wisconsin Press, 1956.

Payne, James L. *Labor and Politics in Peru: The System of Political Bargaining.* New Haven: Yale University Press, 1965.

Petras, James L. *Chilean Christian Democracy: Politics and Social Forces.* Berkeley: University of California, Institute of International Studies, 1967.

——. *Politics and Social Forces in Chilean Development.* Berkeley and Los Angeles: University of California Press, 1969.

Petras, James L., and Robert LaPorte, Jr. *Cultivating Revolution: The*

United States and Agrarian Reform in Latin America. New York: Random House, 1971.

Petras, James L., and Maurice Zeitlin, eds. *Latin America: Reform or Revolution.* Greenwich, Conn.: Fawcett, 1968.

Petras, James, and Zemelman, Merino, Hugo. *Peasants in Revolt.* Austin and London: University of Texas Press, 1972.

Philips, W.A. *Labor, Land, and Law: A Search for the Missing Wealth of the Working Poor.* New York: Scribner, 1886.

Pike, Frederick B. *Chile and the United States, 1880-1962.* Notre Dame: University of Notre Dame Press, 1963.

Poblete Troncoso, Moises, and Ben G. Burnett. *The Rise of the Latin American Movement.* New York: Bookman, 1960.

Proudhon, P.J. *What Is Property? An Inquiry into the Principle of Right and of Government.* New York: Dover, 1970.

Ralston, Jackson H. *Confronting the Land Question.* New York: Comet Press, 1945.

Rhodes, Leonard A. "Some Economic Aspects of Chilean Agriculture." Mimeographed. Santiago: Advisor on Agricultural Economics, USAID/Chile, 1962.

Ringlein, Wayne. "Economic Effects of Chilean National Expropriation Policy on the Private Commercial Farm Sector, 1964-69." Ph.D. dissertation. University of Maryland, 1971.

Sachs, Ignacy, ed. *Agriculture, Land Reforms and Economic Development.* Warsaw: Polish Scientific Publishers, 1964.

Schultz, Theodore W. *Economic Growth and Agriculture.* New York: McGraw Hill, 1968.

Senior, Clarence O. *Land Reform and Democracy.* Gainesville: University of Florida Press, 1958.

Shaw, Paul V. *The Early Constitutions of Chile, 1810-1833.* New York: F. Mayans, 1930.

Silvert, Kalman H. *Chile: Yesterday and Today.* New York: Holt, Rinehart & Winston, 1965.

_____. *The Conflict Society: Reaction and Revolution in Latin America.* New Orleans: Hauser Press, 1961.

Simpson, Lesley Byrd. *The Encomienda in New Spain: The Beginning of Spanish Mexico.* Berkeley and Los Angeles: University of California Press, 1950.

Smith, T. Lynn, ed. *Agrarian Reform in Latin America.* New York: Knopf, 1965.

St. Lewinski, Jan. *The Origin of Property, and the Formation of the Village Community.* London: Constable, 1913.

Stavenhagen, Rodolfo, ed. *Agrarian Problems and Peasant Movements in Latin America.* New York: Anchor, 1970.

Sternberg, Marvin. "Chilean Land Tenure and Land Reform." Ph.D. dissertation. University of California, 1962.

Stevenson, John R. *The Chilean Popular Front.* Philadelphia: University of Pennsylvania Press, 1942.

Subercaseaux, Benjamin. *Chile: A Geographic Extravaganza.* New York: Macmillan, 1943.

Swift, Jeannine. *Agrarian Reform in Chile: An Economic Study.* Lexington, Mass.: Lexington Books, 1971.

Tai, Hung-Chao. *Land Reform and Politics: A Comparative Analysis.* Berkeley, Los Angeles, and London: University of California Press, 1974.

Tawney, R.H. *The Agrarian Problem in the Sixteenth Century.* London: Longmans, Green, 1912.

Thiesenhusen, William C. *Chile's Experiments in Agrarian Reform.* Madison: University of Wisconsin Press, 1966.

Thorbecke, Erik, ed. *The Role of Agriculture in Economic Development.* New York: National Bureau of Economic Research, 1969.

Tomasek, Robert, ed. *Latin American Politics: Studies of the Contemporary Scene.* New York: Doubleday, 1966.

Tuma, Elias H. *Twenty-Six Centuries of Agrarian Reform: A Comparative Analysis.* Berkeley and Los Angeles: University of California Press, 1965.

Warriner, Doreen. *Land Reform and Development in the Middle East.* London: Royal Institute of International Affairs, 1957.

———. *Land Reform and Economic Development.* Cairo: National Bank of Egypt, 1955.

———. *Land Reform in Principle and Practice.* Oxford: Clarendon Press, 1969.

Wayland-Smith, F.G. "The Christian Democratic Party in Chile: A Study of Political Organization and Activity with Primary Emphasis on the Local Level." Ph.D. dissertation. Syracuse University, 1968.

Weaver, Frederick Stirton, Jr. *Regional Patterns of Economic Change in Chile, 1950-1964.* New York: Cornell University Press, 1968.

Whaley, John. "The Transportation Revolution in the Development of the Bío Bío Region, 1850-1915." Ph.D. dissertation. Indiana University, 1974.

Winter, Nevin O. *Chile and Her People of Today: An Account of the Customs, Characteristics, Amusements, History and Advancement of the Chileans, and the Development and Resources of Their Country.* Boston: L.D. Page, 1912.

Williams, Edward. *Latin American Christian Democratic Parties.* Knoxville: University of Tennessee Press, 1967.

Wolf, Eric. *Peasants.* Englewood Cliffs, N.J.: Prentice Hall, 1966.

Young, Jordan Marten. "Chilean Parliamentary Government 1891-1924." Ph.D. dissertation. Princeton University, 1953.

Zammit, J. Ann, ed. *The Chilean Road to Socialism*. Austin and Sussex, England: University of Texas Press and Institute of Development Studies, University of Sussex, 1973.

Books, Monographs, and Theses in Spanish

Acción Sindical Chilena (ASICH). *Tierra y libertad. Por la reforma agraria*. Santiago: ASICH, 1961.

Affonso, Almino. *Reforma agraria y participación campesino*. Documento No. 70. Santiago: ICIRA, 1970.

Affonso, Almino; Sergio Gómez; Emilio Klein; and Pablo Ramírez. *Movimiento campesino chileno*. 2 vols. Santiago: ICIRA, 1970.

Aguilera, Ángel. *Las tierras fiscales de Chile*. Santiago: ICIRA, 1966.

Aguirre Cerda, Pedro. *El problema agrario*. Paris: n.p., 1929.

Ahumada, Jorge. *En vez de la miseria*. Santiago: Editorial del Pacífico, 1958.

_____. *La crisis integral de Chile*. Santiago: Editorial Universitaria, 1966.

Almeyda Arroyo, Elías. *Geografía agrícola de Chile*. Santiago: Imprenta San Francisco, 1957.

Álvarez Andrews, Oscar. *Chile, monografía sociológica*. México, D.F.: Instituto de Investigaciones Sociales, Universidad Nacional, 1965.

Ampuero Díaz, Raúl. *1964, año de prueba para la revolución chilena*. Santiago: Prensa Latinoamericana, 1964.

Amunátegui Solar, Domingo. *La democracia en Chile: Teatro político, 1810-1918*. Santiago: Universidad de Chile, 1946.

_____. *Las encomiendas indígenas*. Santiago: Cervantes, 1909.

_____. *Historia social de Chile*. Santiago: Nascimento, 1932.

Andrade Geywitz, Carlos. *Elementos de derecho constitucional chileno*. Santiago: Editorial Jurídica de Chile, 1963.

Aranda, Sergio, and Alberto Martínez. *La industria y la agricultura en el desarrollo económico chileno*. Santiago: Universidad de Chile, 1970.

Arcos, Juan. *El sindicalismo en América Latina*. Santiago: Centro de Investigaciones y Acción Social, 1964.

Arroyo, Gonzalo, and Sergio Gómez. *Una etapa conflictiva en la reforma agraria: campesinos y patrones*. Santiago: ICIRA, 1971.

Baraona, Rafael; Ximena Aranda; and Roberto Santana. *Valle de Putaendo: Estudio de estructura agraria*. Santiago: Editorial Universitaria, 1961.

Barraclough, Solon. *Notas sobre tenencia de la tierra en América Latina*. Santiago: ICIRA, 1968.

Barría Soto, Francisco. *El Partido Radical: Su historia y sus obras*. Santiago: Editorial Universitaria, 1957.

Barría Serón, Jorge. *El movimiento obrero en Chile*. Santiago: Ediciones de la Universidad Técnica del Estado, 1971.

———. *Trayectoria y estructura del movimiento sindical chileno, 1946-1962*. Santiago: Universidad de Chile, Instituto de Organización y Administración, 1963.

Barros Arana, Diego. *Historia general de Chile*. Santiago: Rafael Jover, 1886.

———. *Riquezas de los antiguos jesuitas en Chile*. Santiago: Ercilla, 1932.

Besa García, José. *Tenencia de la tierra y reforma agraria, bibliografía*. Buenos Aires: Ediciones Troquel, 1968.

Birou, Alain. *Fuerzas campesinas y políticas agrarias en América Latina*. Madrid: IEPAL, 1971.

Boizard B., Ricardo. *La democracia cristiana en Chile*. Santiago: Editorial Orbe, 1963.

Borde, Jean, and Mario Góngora. *Evolución de la propiedad rural en el Valle de Puangue*. Santiago: Editorial Universitaria, 1956.

Breve descripción de la república de Chile. Leipzig: Imprenta de F.A. Brockhaus, 1903.

Cademartori, José. *La economia Chilena*. Santiago: Editorial Universitaria, 1968.

Campos Harriet, Fernando. *Desarrollo educacional, 1810-1960*. Santiago: Editorial Andrés Bello, 1960.

———. *Historia constitucional de Chile*. Santiago: Editorial Jurídica de Chile, 1956.

Castillo, Jaime. *Las fuentes de la democracia cristiana*. Santiago: Editorial del Pacífico, 1955.

Castro, José Luis. *El sistema electoral chileno*. Santiago: Editorial Nascimento, 1941.

Chaparro, Leoncio. *Anotaciones críticas sobre el trabajo de la tierra en Chile*. Santiago: Imprenta Universo, 1939.

Chelén Rojas, Alejandro. *Trayectoria del socialismo*. Buenos Aires: Editorial Astral, 1967.

Chonchol, Jacques. *El desarrollo de América Latina y la reforma agraria*. Santiago: Editorial del Pacífico, 1964.

———. *Informe sobre las posibilidades de incorporar más plenamente las Provincias de Aysén y Chiloé continental a la economía nacional*. Santiago: 1952.

———. *Perspectivas comunitarias para una reforma de nuestra actual estructura agraria*. Santiago: Galrol, 1948.

Chonchol, Jacques, et al. *Proposiciones para una acción política en el período 1967-70 de una vía no capitalista de desarrollo.* Santiago: Separata Especial de *PEC*, 1967.

Collarte, Juan Carlos. "Análisis de una alternativa de los sistemas de tenencia de tierras en Chile." Tesis, Universidad de Chile, Facultad de Agronomía, 1964.

_____. *El minifundio en una política de desarrollo agrícola.* Santiago: ICIRA-INDAP, 1971.

Comité Interamericano de Desarrollo Agrícola (CIDA). *Chile, tenencia de la tierra y desarrollo socio-económico del sector agrícola.* Santiago: 1966.

Contreras Labarca, Carlos. *Adelante en la lucha por el programa del frente popular.* Santiago: Ediciones del Comité Central del Partido Comunista, 1940.

CORFO (Fundación Aguirre Cerda). *Geografía económica de Chile.* Tomo III. Santiago: 1962.

Correa Vergara, Luis. *Agricultura chilena.* 2 vols. Santiago: Imprenta Nascimento, 1938.

Corvalán, Antonio, ed. *Antología chilena de la tierra.* Santiago: ICIRA, 1970.

Corvalán L., Luis. *Camino de victoria.* Santiago: Sociedad Impresora Horizonte, 1971.

_____. *Chile hoy: La lucha de los comunistas chilenos en las condiciones del gobierno de Frei.* Buenos Aires: Editorial Anteo, 1965.

Cruz-Coke, Ricardo. *Geografía electoral de Chile.* Santiago: Editorial del Pacífico, 1952.

Delgado, Oscar, ed. *Reformas agrarias en la América Latina.* México and Buenos Aires: Fondo de Cultura Económica, 1965.

Domínguez C., Óscar. *Aspiraciones de los inquilinos de la provincia de Santiago.* Santiago: ICIRA, 1966.

_____. *El campesino chileno y la acción católica rural.* Madrid: FERES, 1961.

_____. *El campesino de San Clemente.* Mimeographed. Santiago: 1964.

_____. *El condicionamiento de la reforma agraria.* Louvain: Université catholique de Louvain, Collection de l'Ecole des Sciences Politiques et Sociales No. 173, 1963.

_____. *La tierra es la esperanza.* Santiago: Instituto de Educación Rural, 1961.

Domínguez, Óscar, and Cristina Osorio. *Recursos humanos calificados.* Santiago: ICIRA-ODEPA, 1971.

Donoso, Ricardo. *Alessandri, agitador y demoledor.* Ciudad de Méjico: Fondo de Cultura Económica, 1953.

———. *Desarrollo político y social de Chile.* Santiago: Imprenta Universitaria, 1943.

———. *Las ideas políticas en Chile.* Ciudad de Méjico: Fondo de Cultura Económica, 1946.

Donoso, Ricardo, and Flanor Velasco. *La propiedad austral.* Santiago: ICIRA, 1970.

Durán Bernales, Florencio. *El Partido Radical.* Santiago: Editorial Nascimento, 1958.

———. *Población, alimentos y reforma agraria.* Santiago: Editorial Universitaria, 1966.

Echeverría, Roberto, and Jorge Soto. *Respuesta de los productores agrícolas ante cambios en los precios.* Santiago: ICIRA, 1968.

Edwards Vives, Alberto. *La fronda aristocrática en Chile.* Santiago: Editorial del Pacífico, 1952.

Edwards Vives, Alberto, and Eduardo Frei. *Historia de los partidos políticos chilenos.* Santiago: Editorial del Pacífico, 1949.

Encina, Francisco Antonio. *Historia de Chile.* Redacción, iconografía y apéndices de Leopoldo Castedo. 3 vols. Santiago: Editorial Nascimento, 1954.

———. *Nuestra inferioridad económica.* Santiago: Editorial Universitaria, 1955.

Espinoza, Enrique. *Geografía descriptiva de la república de Chile.* Quinta edición. Santiago: Imprenta, Litografia I Encuadernación Barcelona, 1903.

Eyzaguirre, Jaime. *Historia constitucional de Chile.* Santiago: Editorial Universitaria, 1965.

Feder, Ernest. *El crédito agrícola en Chile.* Santiago: Universidad de Chile, Publicación No. 29, 1960.

Fernández C., Juan. *Pedro Aguirre Cerda y el frente popular chileno.* Santiago: Ediciones Ercilla, 1938.

Fichter, Joseph H. *Cambio social en Chile: Un estudio de actitudes.* Santiago: Editorial Universitaria Católica, 1962.

Frei Montalva, Eduardo. *Chile desconocido.* Santiago: Ediciones Ercilla, 1937.

———. *Chile, 1964-1970.* Santiago: Editorial del Pacífico, 1964.

———. *Pensamiento y acción.* Santiago: Editorial del Pacífico, 1958.

———. *La política y el espíritu.* Santiago: Ediciones Ercilla, 1940.

———. *El social cristianismo.* Santiago: Editorial del Pacífico, 1951.

Fuenzalida Villegas, Humberto, et al. *Desarrollo de Chile en la primera mitad del siglo XX.* Santiago: Universidad de Chile, 1951.

Galdames, Luis. *Estudio de la historia de Chile.* Santiago: Nascimento, 1938.

Garcés, Joan. *1970. La pugna política por la presidencia en Chile.* Santiago: Editorial Universitaria, 1971.

García, Antonio. *Dominación y reforma agraria en América Latina.* Lima: Francisco Moncloa Editores, Campodonico Ediciones, 1970.

——. *Reforma agraria y economía empresarial en América Latina.* Santiago: Editorial Universitaria, 1967.

García Rival, Osvaldo. *Panorama agrario chileno, reforma agraria integral, solución del problema agrario.* Santiago: 1971.

Gay, Claudio. *Historia física y política de Chile, agricultura.* Tomo I. Santiago: Museo de Historia Natural de Santiago, 1862.

Gazmuri, Jaime. *Asentamientos campesinos, una evaluación de los primeros resultados de la reforma agraria en Chile.* Buenos Aires: Ediciones Troquel, 1970.

Gitahy, C.; Leda Manuel; Donoso D.; and Francisco Encina M. *La Organización sindical del sector afuerino.* Santiago: Fondo de Educación y Extensión Sindical, 1971.

Goldenberg, Gregorio. *¿Después de Frei Quien?* Santiago: Editorial Orbe, 1966.

Gómez, Sergio. *Empresarios agrícolas.* Santiago: ICIRA, 1972.

Góngora, Mario. *Origen de los inquilinos de Chile central.* Santiago: Editorial Universitaria, 1960.

Guerra, José Guillermo. *La constitución de 1925.* Santiago: Establecimientos Gráficos, Balcells y Co., 1929.

Guzmán Dinator, Jorge. *Nueva sociedad, vieja constitución.* Santiago: Editorial Orbe, 1964.

Guilisasti Tagle, Sergio, ed. *Partidos políticos chilenos.* Santiago: Editorial Nascimento, 1964.

Hamuy, Eduardo et al. *El problema del pueblo de Chile.* Santiago: Editorial del Pacífico, 1961.

Heise González, Julio. *La constitución de 1925 y las nuevas tendencias político-sociales.* Santiago: Editorial Universitaria, 1951.

——. *Historia constitucional de Chile.* Santiago: Editorial Jurídica de Chile, 1954.

Herring, Hubert. *Chile en la presidencia de don Pedro Aguirre Cerda.* Santiago: Editorial Francisco de Aguirre, 1971.

Hidalgo, Pedro; Emilio Robles; and Arnoldo Rosenfeld. *Evaluación institucional y de la acción socio-económica del Instituto de Desarrollo Agropecuario* (INDAP). Santiago: ICIRA, 1970.

ICIRA. *Cinco años de ICIRA: Noviembre de 1964-Noviembre de 1969.* Santiago: ICIRA, 1969.

——. *Exposición metódica y coordinada de la ley de reforma agraria de Chile.* Santiago: Editorial Jurídica de Chile, 1968.

_____. *Reforma agraria chilena: Seis ensayos de interpretación*. Santiago: ICIRA, 1970.

Imable D., Rogelio. *Cambios en los ingresos de campesinos chilenos participantes en reforma agraria: Casos de asentamiento y parcelación*. Memoria: Universidad de Chile, 1967.

Izquierdo F., Gonzalo. *Un estudio de las ideologías chilenas: la Sociedad de Agricultura en el siglo XIX*. Santiago: Centro de Estudios Socio-Económicos, Imprenta Técnica LTDA, 1968.

Jiles Pizarro, Jorge. *Partido Comunista de Chile*. Santiago: Academia de Ciencias Políticas, 1957.

Jobet, Julio Cesar. *Ensayo crítico del desarrollo económico-social de Chile*. Santiago: Editorial Universitaria, 1955.

_____. *El Partido Socialista de Chile*. Santiago: Ediciones Prensa Latino-americana, 1971.

_____. *Recabarren: Los orígenes del movimiento obrero y del socialismo chileno*. Santiago: Prensa Latinoamericana, 1955.

_____. *Socialismo y comunismo*. Santiago: Editorial Espartaco, 1952.

Joxe, Alain. *Las fuerzas armadas en el sistema político de Chile*. Santiago: Editorial Universitaria, 1970.

Keller, Carlos R. *Minifundio y latifundio, Chile: Su futura alimentación*. Santiago: Editorial Nascimento, 1963.

_____. *Un país al garete*. Santiago: Editorial Nascimento, 1937.

_____. *Revolución en la agricultura*. Santiago: Editorial Zig-Zag, 1956.

Lagos Escobar, Ricardo. *La concentración del poder económico. Su teoría. La realidad chilena*. Santiago: Editorial del Pacífico, 1960.

Lagos, V., Julio. *Bosquejo histórico del movimiento obrero chileno*. Santiago: El Esfuerzo, 1941.

Landsberger, Henry A., and Fernando Canitrot M. *Iglesia, intelectuales, y campesinos*. Santiago: Editorial del Pacífico, 1967.

Landsberger, Henry; Manuel Barrera; and Abel Toro. *El pensamiento del dirigente sindical chileno*. Santiago: Instituto de Organización y Administración, Universidad de Chile, 1963.

León Echaiz, René. *Evolución histórica de los partidos políticos chilenos*. Santiago: Editorial Francisco de Aguirre, 1939.

Lira Urquieta, Pedro. *Código Civil de Chile*. Madrid: Instituto de Cultura Hispánica, 1961.

Lechner, Norbert. *La democracia en Chile*. Santiago: Ediciones Signos, 1970.

Legislación social y sindicatos legales de Chile. Santiago: Editorial Ginebra, n.d.

Leighton, Bernardo. *Propiedad rústica y gremios agrarios*. Santiago: El Esfuerzo, 1933.

Lizama Cornejo, Carlos. *La sindicalización campesina.* Memoria. Santiago: 1939.

Loveman, Brian. *Antecedentes para el estudio del movimiento campesino chileno: Pliegos de peticiones, huelgas y sindicatos agrícolas, 1932-1966.* Santiago: ICIRA, 1971.

_____. *El campesino chileno le escribe a su excelencia.* Santiago: ICIRA, 1971.

_____. *El mito de la marginalidad: Participación y represión del campesinado chileno.* Santiago: ICIRA, 1971.

McBride, George. *Chile, su tierra y su gente.* Santiago: ICIRA, 1970.

Macciavello Varas, Santiago. *Política económica nacional.* Santiago: Balcells, 1931.

Madrid Cerda, Emilio. *Antecedentes políticos y sociales de la reforma agraria en Chile.* Santiago: ESCOLATINA, 1962.

Mann, W. *Chile, luchando por neuvas formas de vida.* Tomo I. Santiago: Prensas de la Editorial Ercilla, 1935.

Marin Molina, Ricardo. *Condiciones económico-sociales del campesinado chileno.* Santiago: La Hora, 1947.

Martner, Daniel. *Historia de Chile.* Vol. 1. Santiago: Balcells y Co., 1929.

Mattelart, Armand; Carmen Castillo; and Leonardo Castillo. *La ideología de la dominación en una sociedad dependiente, la respuesta ideológica de la clase dominante chilena al reformismo.* Santiago: Ediciones Signos, 1970.

Matthei, Adolfo. *La agricultura en Chile y la política agraria chilena.* Santiago: Nascimento, 1939.

_____. *Política agraria chilena.* Santiago: Editorial San Francisco, Padre Las Casas, 1935.

Maureira Lagos, Jorge. *Ideología sindical cristiana para América Latina.* Santiago: Editorial Jurídica, 1968.

Maza, José. *Sistemas de sufragio i cuestión electoral.* Santiago: Imprenta "La Illustración," 1913.

Menjivar, Rafael. *Reforma agraria chilena.* Editorial Universitaria de El Salvador, 1970.

Mercier Vega, Luis. *Mecanismos del poder en América Latina.* Buenos Aires: Sur, 1967.

Millas, Orlando. *Los comunistas, los católicos y la libertad.* Santiago: Editorial Austral, 1964.

Moral López, Pedro. *Temas jurídicos de la reforma agraria y del desarrollo.* Santiago: ICIRA, 1968.

Morris, James O. et al. *Afiliación y finanzas sindicales en Chile, 1932-1959.* Santiago: Universidad de Chile, Instituto de Organización y Administración, 1962.

Olavarría Bravo, Arturo. *Chile bajo la democracia cristiana.* 6 vols. Santiago: Editorial Nascimento, 1966-1971.

_____. *Chile entre dos Alessandri.* Santiago: Editorial Nascimento, 1962.

Olivares, José. *Las políticas de tierra de la corona española en América Latina durante la conquista y la colonia.* Santiago: ESCOLATINA, 1962.

Pascal, Andrés. *Relaciones de poder en una localidad rural.* Santiago: ICIRA, 1968.

Pellegrini, Vicente. *Teoría y realidad de la reforma agraria.* Buenos Aires: Editorial Universitaria, 1959.

Pinto Santa Cruz, Aníbal. *Chile, una economía difícil.* Buenos Aires: Fondo de Cultura Económica, 1964.

_____. *Chile: Un caso de desarrollo frustrado.* Santiago: Editorial Universitaria, 1959.

_____. *Cuestiones principales de la economía.* Santiago: Editorial del Pacífico, 1955.

_____. *La estructura de nuestra economía.* Santiago: Editorial del Pacífico. 1947.

_____. *Hacia nuestra independencia económica.* Santiago: Editorial del Pacífico, 1953.

Poblete Troncoso, Moisés. *El movimiento obrero latinoamericano.* Méjico: Fondo de Cultura Económica, 1946.

_____. *La organización sindical en Chile.* Santiago: R. Brias, 1926.

Partido Demócrata Cristiano. *Antecedentes sobre la agricultura chilena y proyecto de ley sobre reforma agraria.* Mimeographed. Santiago: 1962.

_____. *Programa de reforma agraria del Partido Demócrata Cristiano.* Mimeographed. Santiago: 1962.

Partido Liberal. *Informe de la comisión de agricultura.* Santiago: 1961.

Partido Radical. *Programa de fomento agrícola y de reforma agraria aprobado en la XXI convención nacional, el 24 de junio.* Santiago: 1961.

Ramírez Necochea, Hernán. *Antecedentes económicos de la independencia de Chile.* Santiago: Editorial Universitaria, 1959.

_____. *Historia del imperialismo en Chile.* 2d ed. Santiago: Editorial Austral, 1970.

_____. *Historia del movimiento obrero en Chile—antecedentes—siglo XIX.* Santiago: Talleres Gráficos Lautaro, 1956.

_____. *Origen y formación del Partido Comunista de Chile.* Santiago: Editorial Austral, 1965.

_____. *El Partido Comunista y la universidad.* Santiago: Editorial Aurora, 1964.

Ramírez, Pablo. *Cambio en las formas de pago a la mano de obra agrícola.* Santiago: ICIRA, 1968.

Recabarren, Luis Emilio. *Obras escogidas.* Tomo I. Santiago: Editorial Recabarren, 1965.

La reforma constitucional 1970. Santiago: Editorial Jurídica de Chile, 1970.

Ríos Ladrón de Guevara, Ivan. *La dirección general de trabajo.* Santiago: Memoria de Prueba, Universidad de Chile, 1960.

Rivas Vicuña, Manuel. *Historia política y parlamentaria de Chile.* Santiago: Ediciones de La Biblioteca Nacional, 1964.

Rodríguez Mendoza, Emilio. *El golpe de estado de 1924.* Santiago: Editorial Ercilla, 1938.

Rogers Sotomayor, Jorge. *Dos caminos para la reforma agraria en Chile, 1945-1965.* Santiago: Editorial Orbe, 1966.

_____. *Nueva organización social del campo: Discurso pronunciado el 29 de enero, 1947, en la Cámara de Diputados de Chile.* Santiago: Imprenta Universitaria.

Rumiantsev, Alexi, ed. *La cuestión agraria y el movimiento de liberación nacional.* Praga: Editorial Paz y Socialismo, 1964.

Saavedra, Alejandro. *La cuestión mapuche.* Santiago: ICIRA, 1971.

Sampaio, Plinio et al. *Organización, planificación y coordinación de las instituciones del sector pública agrícola de Chile, a nivel de terreno.* Santiago: ICIRA, 1966.

Santa Cruz, E. Gonzalo. *El mejoramiento de los trabajadores agrícolas y la sindicalización campesina.* Memoria. Santiago: 1941.

Schejtman Mishkin, Alexander. *El inquilino de Chile central.* Santiago: ICIRA, 1971.

Secretariado General del Episcopado de Chile. *La iglesia y el problema del campesinado chileno.* Santiago: 1962.

Sierra, Enrique. *Tres ensayos de estabilización en Chile.* Santiago: Editorial Universitaria, 1970.

Silva Solar, Julio. *El régimen comunitario y la propiedad.* Ediciones del departamento nacional de capacitación doctrinaria del Partido Demócrata Cristiana. Santiago: 1964.

Silva Solar, Julio, and Jacques Chonchol. *El desarrollo de la nueva sociedad en América Latina. (Hacia un mundo comunitario).* Santiago: Editorial Universitaria, 1965.

Sociedad Nacional de Agricultura (SNA). *Memoria de la Sociedad Nacional de Agricultura.* Santiago: Departamento de Relaciones Públicas, 1962.

_____. *Reforma Agraria, Documento presentado por la Sociedad Nacional de Agricultura de Chile a la II Convención de Asociaciones Agrope-*

cuarias Americanas Amigas. Mimeographed. Santiago: 1962.

———. *Situación económica y social de la agricultura chilena.* Santiago: Editorial Universitaria, 1955.

Solari, Aldo E. *Sociología rural Latinoamericana.* Buenos Aires: Editorial Paidos, 1968.

Tarres B., Adela. *Conflictos sociales en el sector agrario en 1969.* Santiago: Fondo de Educación y Extensión Sindical, 1972.

Tenencia de la tierra y campesinado en Chile. Buenos Aires: Ediciones Troquel, 1968.

Thayer, William. *Trabajo, empresa, y revolución.* Santiago: Zig-Zag, 1968.

La tierra para quien la trabaja, Documentos del XIII Congreso Nacional del Partido Comunista de Chile. Folleto No. 4. Santiago: 1965.

Tratado práctico sobre organización sindical y conflictos colectivos del trabajo. Tomo II. Santiago: Ediciones Revista Técnica del Trabajo y Previsión Social, 1970.

La tributación agrícola en Chile, 1940-1958, algunas implicaciones económicas del sistema tributario agrícola chileno. Santiago: Universidad de Chile, 1960.

Ulrich B., Kurt. *Algunos aspectos del control de comercio en la agricultura chilena, 1950-1958.* Santiago: Ministerio de Agricultura, Consejo Superior de Fomento Agropecuario, 1964.

Urzua, Raúl. *La demanda campesina.* Santiago: Ediciones Nueva Universidad, Universidad Católica de Chile, 1969.

Urzua Valenzuela, Germán. *El partido radical, su evolución política.* Santiago: Academia de Ciencias Políticas y Administrativas, 1961.

———. *Los partidos políticos chilenos.* Santiago: Editorial Jurídica de Chile, 1968.

Varas, José Miguel. *Chacón.* Santiago: Impresora Horizonte, 1968.

Vitale, Luis. *Los discursos de Clotario Blest y la revolución chilena.* Santiago: Imprenta Victoria, 1961.

———. *Y después del 4, ¿qué? Perspectivas de Chile después de las elecciones presidenciales.* Santiago: Ediciones Prensa Latinoamericana, 1970.

Vodanovic H., Antonio. *Recopilación de leyes, decretos con fuerza de ley, reglamentos y decretos agrarios posteriores a la ley No. 16.640, sobre reforma agraria.* Santiago: Editorial Nascimento, 1968.

Volski, Yu, Onúfrien; A. Volkov; I. Sheremétiev; E. Kovaliov; B. Koval; P. Ananiev; A. Sivolóbov; and S. Semiónov. *La cuestión agraria y los problemas del movimiento de liberación en la América Latina.* Editorial de la Agencia de Prensa Nóvosti, n.d.

Vuskovic, Sergio, and Osvaldo Fernández. *Teoría de la ambigüedad: Bases ideológicas de la democracia cristiana.* Santiago: Editorial Austral, 1964.

Waiss, Oscar. *Presencia del socialismo en Chile.* Santiago: Ediciones Ex-
partaco, 1952.

Walker Linares, Francisco. *Nociones elementales de derecho del trabajo.*
Santiago: Editorial Nascimento, 1957.

Wolpin, Miles D. *La intervención extranjera en las elecciones chilenas.*
Buenos Aires: Ediciones Kikiyon, 1969.

Wosconboinik B., Betty. "Inquilinaje en el medio rural de Puente Alto."
Tesis de la Escuela de Servicio Social, Universidad de Chile, 1953.

Zemelman, Hugo. *El migrante rural.* Santiago: ICIRA, 1971.

Zenteno, Escobar. *Compendio de la legislación social y desarrollo del
movimiento obrero en Chile.* Santiago: 1940.

Articles in English

Adams, Richard N. "Rural Labor." In John J. Johnson (ed.), *Continuity
and Change in Latin America.* Stanford: Stanford University Press,
1964.

Agor, Weston. "The Decisional Role of the Senate in the Chilean Political
System." University of Wisconsin, Land Tenure Center, Research
Paper 66 (August 1969).

_____. "The Senate in the Chilean Political System." In A. Kornberg and
M. Lloyd (eds.), *Legislatures in Developmental Perspective.* Durham:
Duke University Press, 1970.

_____. "Senate vs Cora: An Attempt to Evaluate Chile's Agrarian Reform
to Date." *Inter-American Economic Affairs* 22 (Autumn 1968):
47-53.

Angell, Alan. "Chile: The Christian Democrats at Mid-Term." *The World
Today* 23 (October 1967): 434-43.

_____. "Chile: The Difficulties of Democratic Reform." *International
Journal* 24 (1969): 515-28.

_____. "Christian Democracy in Chile." *Current History* 58 (1970): 79-84.

_____. "Counterrevolution in Chile." *Current History* 66 (January 1974):
6-9.

Ayres, Robert L. "Economic Stagnation and the Emergence of the Political Ideology of Chilean Underdevelopment." *World Politics* (October
1972): 34-61.

_____. "Political History, Institutional Structure, and Prospects for Social-
ism in Chile." *Comparative Politics* 5 (July 1973): 497-523.

Ballesteros, M., and Tom E. Davis. "The Growth of Output and Employment in Basic Sectors of the Chilean Economy, 1908-1957." *Economic Development and Cultural Change* 11, Part 1 (January 1963):
152-76.

Barlowe, R. "Land Reform and Economic Development." *Journal of
Farm Economics* 35 (1953): 173-87.

Barraclough, Solon. "Agrarian Reform in Chile." Draft. Santiago: ICIRA, 1970.

------. "Agricultural Policy and Land Reform." *The Journal of Political Economy* 78, Part 2 (July-August 1970): 906-47.

------. "Alternate Land Tenure Systems Resulting from Agrarian Reform in Latin America." *Land Economics* 46 (August 1970): 215-28.

------. "Employment Problems Affecting Latin American Agricultural Development." *Monthly Bulletin of Agricultural Economics and Statistics* 18 (July-August 1969).

------. "Institutional Coverage and Strategies for Integrated Rural Development." Paper prepared for the FAO/SIDA Symposium on Agricultural Institutions for Integrated Rural Development, Rome, Italy, June 1971.

------. "The Latin American Agrarian Problem." Papers on Agrarian Reform No. 2. Santiago: ICIRA, n.d.

------. "Why Land Reform." *CERES* 2 (November-December 1969): 21-24.

Barraclough, Solon, and L. Domike. "Agrarian Structure in Seven Latin American Countries." *Land Economics* 42 (1966): 391-424.

Barrera R., Manuel J. "Participation by Occupational Organizations in Economic and Social Planning in Chile." *International Labor Review* 96 (August 1963): 151-76.

Becket, James. "Land Reform in Chile." *Journal of Inter-American Studies* 5 (April 1963): 177-211.

------. "Tempest in a Copper Pot: Chile's Mini-Revolution." *Commonweal* (December 29, 1967): 406-8.

Biehl del Rio, J., and Gonzalo Fernandez R. "The Political Pre-requisites for a Chilean Way." *Government and Opposition* 7 (Summer 1972): 305-26.

Bicheno, H.E. "Anti-Parliamentary Themes in Chilean History: 1920-70." *Government and Opposition* 7 (Summer 1972): 351-88.

Bloch, Marc. "Toward a Comparative History of European Societies." In Frederic C. Lane and J.C. Riemersma (eds.), *Enterprise and Secular Change: Readings in Economic History*. Homewood, Ill.: Richard D. Irwin, 1953.

"Blood on the Peaceful Road." *Latin American Perspectives*. Special Issue on Chile. Vol. 1 (Summer 1974).

Bonilla, Frank. "The Student Federation of Chile: 50 Years of Political Action." *Journal of Inter-American Studies* 2 (July 1960): 311-34.

Borricaud, Francois. "Chile: Why Allende Fell." *Dissent* (Summer 1974): 402-14.

Bray, Donald W. "Latin American Political Parties and Ideologies: An Overview." *The Review of Politics* 29 (January 1967): 76-84.

_____. "Chile: The Dark Side of Stability." *Studies on the Left* 4 (Fall 1964): 85-96.

Bray, James, and W. Thiesenhusen. "Mechanization and the Chilean Inquilino System: The Case of Fundo B." University of Wisconsin, Land Tenure Center, Reprint No. 34.

Breckenridge, J.C. "Landownership in Its Relation to National Stability." *Annals of American Academy of Political and Social Science* 134 (1927): 207-19.

Brown, Marion. "Agricultural 'Extension' in Chile: A Study of Institutional Transplantation." University of Wisconsin, Land Tenure Center, Reprint No. 64.

Carroll, Thomas. "The Concept of Land Reform." Mimeographed. Prepared for the Center on Land Problems in Asia and the Far East, Bangkok, Thailand, 1954. Rome, Italy: FAO, 1955.

_____. "The Land Reform Issue in Latin America." In Albert O. Hirschman (ed.), *Latin American Issues, Essays and Comments.* New York: Twentieth Century Fund, 1961.

Cheyney, E.P. "Recent Tendencies in the Reform of Land Tenure." *Annals of the American Academy of Political and Social Science* 2 (July 1891-June 1892).

"Chile, France and Italy: A Discussion." *Government and Opposition* 7 (Summer 1972): 389-408.

Cohen, Morris R. "Property and Sovereignty." In *Law and the Social Order: Essays in Legal Philosophy.* New York: Harcourt, Brace, 1933.

Conacher, H.M. "The Relations of Land Tenure and Agriculture." Presidential Address in *Journal of Proceedings of the Agricultural Economic Society* 4 (November 1939): 167-85.

Cope, Orville G. "The 1964 Presidential Election in Chile: The Politics of Change and Access." *Inter-American Economic Affairs* 19 (Spring 1966): 3-29.

Cook, Walter W., "Ownership and Possession." *Encyclopedia of the Social Sciences* 11 (1948): 521-25.

Davenport, P.M. "Land Tenure in Chile." *Foreign Agriculture* 16 (May 1952): 87-91.

Davis, Tom. "Changing Conceptions of the Development Problem: The Chilean Example." *Economic Development and Cultural Change* 14 (October 1965): 20-32.

Dorner, Peter, and Juan Carlos Collarte. "Land Reform in Chile: Proposal for an Institutional Innovation." *Inter-American Economic Affairs* 19 (Summer 1965): 3-22.

Douglas-Irvine, H. "The Landholding System of Colonial Chile." *Hispanic American Historical Review* 8 (November 1928): 449-95.

Duncan, W. Raymond. "Chilean Christian Democracy." *Current History* 53 (November 1967): 263-309.

Eramus, Charles J. "Agrarian Reform vs Land Reform: Three Latin American Countries." In Philip K. Bock (ed.), *Peasants in the Modern World*. Albuquerque: University of New Mexico Press, 1969.

Feder, Ernest. "Feudalism and Agricultural Development: The Role of Controlled Credit in Chile's Agriculture." *Land Economics* 36 (February 1960): 92-108.

Felix, David. "An Alternative View of the 'Monetarist-Structuralist' Contorversy." In A. Hirschman (ed.), *Latin American Issues: Essays and Comments*. New York: Twentieth Century Fund, 1961.

_____. "Structural Imbalance, Social Conflict and Inflation: An Appraisal of Chile's Recent Anti-inflationary Policy." *Economic Development and Cultural Change* 8 (January 1960): 113-47.

Fennel, Richard. "Chile." In John C. Honey, *Toward Strategies for Public Administration Development in Latin America*. Syracuse: Syracuse University Press, 1968.

Fleet, Michael. "Chile's Democratic Road to Socialism." *Western Political Quarterly* 26 (December 1973): 766-86.

Frei, Eduardo. "Paternalism, Pluralism, and Christian Democratic Reform Movements in Latin America." In William V. D'Antonio and F.B. Pike (eds.), *Religion, Revolution and Reform*. New York: Praeger, 1964.

_____. "Christian Democracy in Theory and Practice." In Paul E. Sigmund (ed.), *The Ideologies of the Developing Nations*. New York: Praeger, 1964.

Gall, Norman. "The Agrarian Revolt in Cautín. Part II: Land Reform and the MIR." American Universities Field Staff, West Coast South America Series 14, No. 5. Chile, September 1972.

Garces, Joan. "Chile 1971: A Revolutionary Government within a Welfare State." *Government and Opposition* 7 (Summer 1972): 281-304.

Gil, Frederico. "Chile, Society in Transition." In Martin C. Needler (ed.), *Political Systems of Latin America*. New York: Van Nostrand, 1964.

_____. "Chile: 'Revolution in Liberty'." *Current History* 51 (November 1966): 291-95.

Goldrich, Daniel; Raymond B. Pratt; and C.R. Schuller. "The Political Integration of Lower Class Urban Settlements in Chile and Peru." *Studies in Comparative International Development* 3, No. 1 (1967/1968): 1-22.

Goncalves de Souza, Joao. "Aspects of Land Tenure Problems in Latin America." *Rural Sociology* 25 (March 1960): 26-37.

Gray, Richard B., and F.R. Kerwin. "Presidential Succession in Chile:

1817-1966." *Journal of Inter-American Studies* 2 (January 1969): 144-59.

Grayson, George W., Jr. "Christian Democrats in Chile." *SAIS Review* 9 (Winter 1965): 12-20.

———. "Chile's Christian Democratic Party: Power, Factions and Ideology." *Review of Politics* 31 (April 1969): 145-69.

———. "Significance of the Frei Administration for Latin America." *Orbis* 9 (Fall 1965): 760-79.

Hammer, Conrad. "The Land Tenure Ideal." *Journal of Land and Public Utility Economics* 19 (1943): 69-84.

Harris, Marshall. "Legal Aspects of Land Tenure." *Journal of Farm Economics* 23 (1941): 173-84.

Hassinger, Edward. "Social Relations between Centralized and Local Social Systems." *Rural Sociology* 26 (1961): 354-64.

Hirschman, Albert. "Inflation in Chile." In A. Hirschman, *Journeys Toward Progress.* New York: Twentieth Century Fund, 1963.

Hobsbawm, Eric J. "Peasants and Rural Migrants in Politics." In C. Veliz (ed.), *The Politics of Conformity in Latin America.* London: Oxford University Press, 1967.

Johnson, V.W. "Significance of Land Ownership in Land Reform." *Land Economics* 42 (1966): 391-424.

Johnson, V.W., and B.H. Kristjanson. "Programming for Land Reform in the Developing Agricultural Countries of Latin America." *Land Economics* 40 (1964): 353-60.

Johnston, Bruce F., and John W. Mellor. "The Role of Agriculture in Economic Development." *American Economic Review* 51 (September 1961): 566-93.

Karcz, Jerzy F. "Comparative Study of Transformation of Agriculture in Centrally Planned Economies: The Soviet Union, Eastern Europe and Mainland China." In Erik Thorbecke (ed.), *The Role of Agriculture in Economic Development.* New York: Columbia University Press, 1969.

Karst, Kenneth L. "Latin American Land Reform: The Uses of Confiscation." University of Wisconsin, Land Tenure Center, Reprint No. 20.

Kelso, M.M. "A Critique of Land Tenure Research." *Journal of Land and Public Utility Economics* 10 (1934): 393-402.

Kay, Cristóbal. "The Development of the Chilean Hacienda System 1850's-1972." Paper presented at the Symposium on Landlord and Peasant in Latin America and the Caribbean, University of Cambridge, December 20-21, 1972.

Laclau, Ernesto. "Feudalism and Capitalism in Latin America." *New Left Review* 67 (May-June 1971): 19-38.

Lehman, D. "Political Incorporation vs Political Stability: The Case of the Chilean Agrarian Reform 1965-1970." *Journal of Development Studies* 7 (July 1971): 365-95.

_____. "Social Structure and Agrarian Reform in Chile: Preliminary Findings." Mimeographed. Santiago: ICIRA, 1970.

Lens, Sidney. "Chile's 'Revolution in Liberty'." *Progressive* 30 (October 1966): 32-35.

Long, Erven J. "Land Reform in Underdeveloped Economies." *Land Economics* 37 (May 1961): 113-23.

McCoy, Terry L. "The Seizure of 'Los Cristales': A Case Study of the Marxist Left in Chile." *Inter-American Economic Affairs* 21 (Summer 1967): 73-93.

Martz, John. "Democratic Political Campaigning in Latin America: A Typological Approach to Cross-Cultural Research." *The Journal of Politics* 33 (May 1971): 370-98.

Medhurst, K. "Why Chile?" *Government and Opposition* 7 (Summer 1972): 273-80.

Menges, Constantine. "Public Policy and Organized Business in Chile: A Preliminary Analysis." *Journal of International Affairs* 20 (1966): 343-65.

Millas, Orlando. "Economic Chaos in Chile." *World Marxist Review* 17 (September 1974): 113-22.

Nisbet, Charles. "Interest Rates and Imperfect Competition in the Informal Credit Market of Rural Chile." *Economic Development and Cultural Change* 16 (October 1967): 73-90.

_____. "Supervised Credit Programs for Small Farmers in Chile." *Inter-American Economic Affairs* 21 (Autumn 1967): 37-54.

North, Douglas C., and R.P. Thomas. "The Rise and Fall of the Manorial System, A Theoretical Model." *Journal of Economic History* 31 (December 1971): 777-803.

Nuñez, Lucio Mendieta. "The Balance of Agrarian Reform." *Annals of the American Academy of Political and Social Sciences* 208 (March 1940): 111-31.

Nunn, Frederick. "Chile's Government in Perspective: Political Change or More of the Same?" *Inter-American Economic Affairs* 20 (Spring 1967): 73-89.

"Organization of Rural Workers in Chile." *International Labour Review* 96 (October 1967): 420-21.

Parrish, Charles J.; Arpad von Lazar; and Jorge Tapia Videla. "The Chilean Congressional Election of March 7, 1965: An Analysis." Institute for the Comparative Study of Political Systems, Washington, D.C., 1967.

_____. "Electoral Procedures and Political Parties in Chile." *Studies in Comparative International Development* 6, No. 12 (1970-1971).

Parsons, Kenneth H. "John R. Commons' Point of View." *Journal of Land and Public Utility Economics* 18 (1942): 245-66.

_____. "Institutional Aspects of Agricultural Development Policy." University of Wisconsin, Land Tenure Center, Reprint No. 28.

_____. "Land Reform in the Postwar Era." *Land Economics* 33 (1957): 213-27.

Paz, Octavio. "The Centurions of Santiago." *Dissent* 21 (Spring 1974): 354-56.

Pearse, Andrew. "Agrarian Change Trends in Latin America." *Latin American Research Review* 1 (Summer 1966): 45-69.

Penn, R.J. "Public Interest in Private Property (Land)." *Land Economics* 37 (May 1961): 99-104.

Petras, James. "After the Chilean Presidential Election: Reform or Stagnation?" *Journal of Inter-American Studies* 7 (July 1965): 375-84.

Petras, James, and M. Zeitlin. "Miners and Agrarian Radicalism." *American Sociological Review* 32 (August 1967): 578-86.

_____. "The Working Class Vote in Chile: Christian Democracy versus Marxism." *The British Journal of Sociology* 21 (March 1970): 16-29.

Pike, Frederick. "Aspects of Class Relations in Chile, 1850-1960." In J. Petras and M. Zeitlin (eds.), *Latin America: Reform or Revolution?* Greenwich, Conn.: Fawcett, 1968.

_____. "The Catholic Church and Modernization in Peru and Chile." *Journal of International Affairs* 20, No. 2 (1966): 272-88.

Pike, Frederick, and Donald W. Bray. "A Vista of Catastrophe: The Future of United States-Chilean Relations." *Review of Politics* 22 (July 1960): 393-418.

Plastrik, Stanley. "A First Word on the Chilean Tragedy." *Dissent* 21 (Winter 1974): 7-12.

Plotke, David. "Coup in Chile." *Socialist Revolution* 3 (July-August 1973): 99-123.

Portes, A. "Leftist Radicalism in Chile." *Comparative Politics* 2 (January 1970): 251-74.

Powell, John D. "Peasant Society and Clientelistic Politics." *American Political Science Review* 64 (June 1970): 411-25.

Powell, S. "Political Change in the Chilean Electorate." *Western Political Quarterly* 22 (June 1970): 365-79.

Prothro, James W., and Patricio E. Chaparro. "Public Opinion and the Movement of Chilean Government to the Left, 1952-1972." *Journal of Politics* 36 (February 1974): 2-41.

Quijano Obregon, Anibal. "Contemporary Peasant Movements." In

S. Lipset and A. Solari (eds.), *Elites in Latin America.* London: Oxford University Press, 1967.

Reinsch, Paul S. "Parliamentary Government in Chile." *American Political Science Review* 3 (November 1909): 507-38.

Rosenstein-Rodan, Paul N. "Why Allende Failed." *Challenge* 17 (May-June 1974): 7-13.

Rowntree, B.S. "Rural Land Reform." *Contemporary Review* 104 (1913): 609-23.

Sanders, T. "A Note on Chilean Politics." American Universities Field Staff Reports (April 1968).

Sartori, Giovanni. "European Political Parties: The Case of Polarized Pluralism." In J. LaPalombara and M. Weiner (eds.), *Political Parties and Political Development.* Princeton: Princeton University Press, 1966.

Schickele, R. "Theories Concerning Land Tenure." *Journal of Farm Economics* 34 (1952): 743-44.

Schulman, Sam. "The Colono System in Latin America." *Rural Sociology* 20 (March 1955): 34-40.

Sigmund, Paul E. "Allende in Retrospect." *Problems of Communism* 23 (May-June 1974): 45-62.

_____. "Christian Democracy in Chile." *Journal of International Affairs* 20, No. 2 (1966): 332-42.

Silvert, K.H. "Elections, Parties and the Law." American Universities Field Staff Reports (March 10, 1957).

Sinding, Steven W. "The Evolution of Chilean Voting Patterns: A Reexamination of Some Old Assumptions." *Journal of Politics* 34 (August 1972): 774-96.

Snow, Peter. "The Political Party System in Chile." *South Atlantic Quarterly* 62 (Autumn 1963): 474-87.

Soares, Glaucio, and Robert Hamblin. "Socio-economic Variables and Voting for the Radical Left: Chile 1952." *American Political Science Review* 61 (December 1967): 1053-65.

Steenland, Kyle. "Chile: Two Years of the Unidad Popular." *Socialist Revolution* 3 (May-June 1973): 71-111.

Stewart, C.T., Jr. "Land and Income Distribution in Peasant Economies." *Land Economics* 37 (November 1961): 337-46.

Sunkel, Osvaldo. "Big Business and 'dependencia'." *Foreign Affairs* 50 (April 1972): 517-31.

_____. "Change and Frustration in Chile." In C. Veliz (ed.), *Obstacles to Change in Latin America.* London: Oxford University Press, 1969.

"Terror in Chile." *New York Review of Books* 21 (May 30, 1974): 38-44.

Thayer, A.S. "Possession and Ownership." *Law Quarterly Review* 23 (1907): 175-94, 314-30.

Thiesenhusen, William. "Agrarian Reform: Chile." In Peter Dorner (ed.), *Land Reform in Latin America Issues and Cases.* Monograph. Land Economics, Madison, Wisconsin, 1971, pp. 105-25.

_____. "Agrarian Reform and Economic Development in Chile: Some Cases of Colonization." *Land Economics* 42 (August 1966): 282-92.

_____. "Chilean Agrarian Reform: The Possibility of Gradualistic Turnover of Land." *Inter-American Economic Affairs* 20 (Summer 1966): 3-22.

_____. "Grassroots Economic Pressures in Chile: An Enigma for Development Planners." *Economic Development and Cultural Change* 16 (April 1968): 412-29.

_____. "Latin American Land Reform: Enemies of Promise." *Nation* 202 (January 24, 1966): 90-94.

Thome, J. "Agrarian Reform Legislation: Chile." In Peter Dorner (ed.), *Land Reform in Latin America Issues and Cases.* Monograph. Land Economics, Madison, Wisconsin, 1971, pp. 81-101.

_____. "Expropriations in Chile Under the Frei Agrarian Reform." *The American Journal of Comparative Law* 19 (Summer 1971): 489-513.

Tuma, Elias H. "The Agrarian-Based Development Policy in Land Reform." *Land Economics* 39 (1963): 265-74.

Valenzuela, Arturo. "The Scope of the Chilean Party System." *Comparative Politics* 4 (January 1972): 179-99.

Von Lazar, Arpad, and Luis Quiros Videla. "Chilean Christian Democracy: Lessons in the Politics of Reform Management." *Inter-American Economic Affairs* 21 (Spring 1968): 51-72.

Weekly, James K. "Christian Democracy in Chile—Ideology and Economic Development." *South Atlantic Quarterly* 66 (Autumn 1967): 520-33.

Weeks, David. "European Antecedents of Land Tenure and Agrarian Organization of Hispanic America." *Journal of Land and Public Utility Economics* 23 (February 1947): 60-75.

_____. "The Agrarian System of the Spanish American Colonies." *Journal of Land and Public Utility Economics* 23 (May 1947): 151-68.

Winnie, W.F., Jr. "Communal Land Tenure in Chile." *Annals of the Association of American Geographers* 55 (March 1965): 67-86.

Wolf, Eric. "Types of Latin American Peasantry: A Preliminary Discussion." *American Anthropologist* 57 (June 1955): 452-71.

Zemelman, H., and Patricio Leon. "Political Opposition to the Government of Allende." *Government and Opposition* 7 (Summer 1972): 327-50.

Zimbalist, Andy, and Barbara Stallings. "Showdown in Chile." *Monthly Review* 25 (October 1973): 1-23.

Articles in Spanish

Affonso, Almino. "Sindicato campesino, agente de cambio." *Cuadernos de la realidad nacional* 5 (septiembre 1970): 118-39.

_____. "Trayectoria del movimiento campesino chileno." *Cuadernos de la realidad nacional* 1 (septiembre 1969): 15-31.

Allende, Salvador. "Significado de la conquista de un gobierno popular para Chile." *Cuadernos Americanos* 5 (septiembre-octubre 1964): 7-24.

Almeyda, Aniceto. "La constitución de la propiedad según un jurista Indiano." *Revista chilena de historia y geografía* 89 (1940): 96-132.

Araya, Bernardo. "Una verdadera reforma agraria." *Principios* 136 (octubre-diciembre 1970): 25-30.

Arroyo, Gonzalo. "Reforma agraria en Chile." *Mensaje* 146 (enero-febrero 1966): 2-15.

Astudillo, Oscar. "El latifundio, freno del progreso." *Principios* 112 (marzo-abril 1966): 15-23.

Ayala Montenegro, Carlos. "Resultados negativos de la 'reforma agraria' de Alessandri." *Principios* 112 (marzo-abril 1966): 63-73.

Barraclough, Solon. "Elementos para una teoría del cambio agrario." In Oscar Delgado (ed.), *Reformas agrarias en América Latina, Mexico, fondo de cultura económica* (1965).

_____. "Lo que implica un reforma agraria." *Panorama económico* 230 (mayo 1962): 123-30.

_____. "¿Qué es una reforma agraria?" In Oscar Delagdo (ed.), *Reformas agrarias en América Latina*. Mexico: Fondo de Cultura Económica, 1965.

_____. "Reforma agraria: historia y perspectivas." *Cuadernos de la realidad nacional* 7 (March 1971): 51-83.

_____. "Situación actual y problemas de la reforma agraria en América Latina." Mimeographed. 1969.

Barraclough, Solon, and Edmundo Flores. "Estructura agraria de América Latina." In *Curso de capacitación de profesionales en reforma agraria*. Vol. 1. Santiago: ICIRA.

_____. "Tipos de tenencia de la tierra." In Oscar Delgado (ed.), *Reformas agrarias en América Latina*. Mexico: Fondo de Cultura Económica, 1965.

Barraclough, Solon, and Jacobo Schatan. "Política tecnológica y desarrollo agrícola." *Cuadernos de la realidad nacional* 5 (septiembre 1970): 91-117.

Baytelman, David, and Rolando Chateauneuf. "Interpretación del censo agrícola y ganadero de 1955." *Panorama Económico* 1 (septiembre 1960): 165-66, 184, 273-74; 2 (noviembre 1960): 349-51; 3 (marzo

1961): 62-65; 4 (agosto 1961): 222-24.

Cabieses Donoso, Manuel. "La ley mordaza." *Aurora* 1 (enero-marzo 1964): 96-99.

Campusano, José. "El papel de las organizaciones campesinas en la lucha por la reforma agraria." *Principios* 112 (marzo-abril 1966): 28-35.

Campusano, José, and Miguel González. "El Valle de Choapa y la reforma agraria." *Principios* 106 (marzo-abril 1965): 85-92.

Carvallo, Gastón. "Leyes en relación con la reforma agraria en Chile." *Panorama económico* 10 (junio 1956): 311-17.

Carroll, Thomas F. "La estructura agraria." In Oscar Delgado (ed.), *Reformas agrarias en América Latina*. Mexico: Fondo de Cultura Económica, 1965.

Centro Agronómico y Veterinario de Coquimbo. "Contribución al estudio de una reforma agraria para Chile." *Simiente* (1961): 1-4.

Cerda, César, and Juan Ahumada. "Acerca de la reforma agraria del gobierno." *Principios* 89 (marzo-abril 1962): 11-20.

Chonchol, Jacques. "Desarrollo económico y sus consecuencias para la agricultura." In R. Vekemans (ed.), *La tierra y el hombre*. Actas del IV Congreso Internacional Católico de la Vida Rural, Santiago (16 abril 1957). Santiago: Gráfico del Atlántico, 1958.

_____. "Elementos para una discusión sobre el camino chileno hacia el socialismo." *Cuadernos de la realidad nacional* 7 (marzo 1971): 165-84.

_____. "Los factores de acceleración revolucionaria." *Mensaje*. Número especial 115 (1962): 82-86.

_____. "Participación de las organizaciones campesinas en el proceso de reforma agraria," *Boletín Informativo* 31 Plandes (enero-febrero, 1969): 58-68.

_____. "Poder y reforma agraria en la experiencia chilena." *Cuadernos de la realidad nacional* 4 (junio 1970): 50-87.

_____. "Razones económicas, sociales y políticas de la reforma agraria." In Oscar Delgado (ed.), *Reformas agrarias en América Latina*. Mexico: Fondo de Cultura Económica, 1965.

Cumplido, Francisco. "Constitución política de 1925: Hoy, crisis de las instituciones políticas chilenas." *Cuadernos de la realidad nacional* 5 (septiembre 1970): 25-40.

Delgado, Oscar. "Las elites de poder versus la reforma agraria." In Oscar Delgado (ed.), *Reformas agrarias en América Latina*. Mexico: Fondo de Cultura Económica, 1965.

Domínguez Correa, Oscar. "Las críticas al informe CIDA." *Política y espíritu* 20 (octubre 1966): 24-85.

_____. Sub-empleo de mano de obra y reforma agraria." In Thomas F.

Carroll (ed.), *Seminario sobre reforma agraria y desarrollo económico*. Santiago: ESCOLATINA, 1961.

Dorner, Peter. "Carta abierta a los agricultores chilenos." *La nación* (21 junio 1965).

Echenique, Jorge. "La batalla contra el latifundio." *Revista agraria*, Vol. 1. Suplemento agraria de *Chile Hoy* (diciembre 1972): 8-9.

Garreton, Oscar G. "Concentración monopólica en Chile: Participación del estado y de los trabajadores en la gestión económica." *Cuadernos de la realidad nacional* 7 (marzo 1971): 143-64.

González, José. "Hacia un verdadera reforma agraria." *Principios* 100 (marzo-abril 1964): 21-30.

Graf Marín, Alberto. "Conceptos de la unidad económica y de minifundio." *Simiente* 1-4 (1961).

Hernández Parker, Luis. "Polémica sobre reforma agraria." *Panorama económico* 225 (octubre-noviembre 1961): 273-78.

Hoselitz, Bert F. "El desarrollo económico de la América Latina." *Desarrollo económico* 2 (octubre-diciembre 1962): 49-65.

Jiles, Jorge. "La reforma agraria y el derecho de propiedad." *Principios* 27 (marzo-abril 1966): 36-48.

Jobet, Julio César. "Acción e historia del socialismo chileno." *Combate* 12 (septiembre-octubre 1960): 32-45.

––––––. "Balance de la política popular desde Aguirre Cerda a González Videla." *Espartaco* 4 (1948): 17-32.

––––––. "Teoría y programa del partido socialista de Chile." *Arauco* 3 (abril 1962): 9-24.

Kaldor, Nicholas. "Problemas económicos de Chile." *El trimestre económico* 26 (abril-junio 1959): 170-221.

Kay, Cristóbal. "La participación campesina en el gobierno de la Unidad Popular." Unpublished. Santiago, 1972.

Kay, Cristóbal, and Peter Winn. "Reforma agraria y revolución rural en el Chile de Allende." Unpublished. Santiago, 1972.

Kirkpatrick, F.C. "La encomienda sin tierra." *Revista chilena de historia y geografía* 102 (1943): 363-74.

Laclau, Ernesto. "Modos de producción, sistemas económicos y población excedente, aproximación histórica a los casos argentinos y chilenos." *Revista Latinoamericana de sociología* 5 (1969): 276-316.

Lehmann, David. "Hacia un análisis de la conciencia de los campesinos." *Cuadernos de la realidad nacional* 2 (enero 1970): 31-59.

Leiva, Joaquín. "Proceso de colonización y reforma agraria." Mimeographed. Santiago: ICIRA, 1964.

Luksic S., Zarko. "La política económica demócratacristiana." *Política y espíritu* 21 (enero-marzo 1967): 108-23.

Maldonado, Carlos. "Experiencias agrarias en América Latina." *Principios* 27 (marzo-abril 1966): 74-88.

Marín, Juan Carlos. "Asalariados rurales en Chile." *Revista Latinoamericana de sociología* 5 (1969): 317-43.

Moreno, Rafael. "Resultado de los asentamientos." *Política y espíritu* 21 (junio 1967): 81-85.

Oyarce, José. "Importancia de la acción común en las luchas campesinas." *Principios* 28 (septiembre-octubre 1967): 64-68.

Peña H., Rubén. "El tipo de tenencia y administración en relación a la utilización de la tierra." *Economía* 18, 2d trimestre (1960): 34-35.

Pinto Santa Cruz, Aníbal. "Desarrollo económico y relaciones sociales en Chile." *El trimestre económico* 30 (octubre-diciembre 1963): 641-58.

Pontigo, Cipriano. "Los comités de asentamiento en el Valle de Choapa." *Principios* 27 (marzo-abril 1966): 49-62.

Robles, Emilio. "La reforma agraria de la D.C." *Principios* 102 (julio-agosto 1964): 66-74.

Saavedra, Alejandro. "La cuestión mapuche." *Cuadernos de la realidad nacional* 5 (septiembre 1970): 70-90.

Sepúlveda Andrade, Hugo. "El cuerpo electoral chileno." *Revista de derecho y ciencias sociales* No. 139 (enero-marzo 1967): 151-64.

Serrano L., Julio. "Como han votado los chilenos 1937-1961." *Política y espíritu* 278 (febrero-marzo 1963): 24-36.

Sociedad Agronómica de Chile. "Un enfoque técnico de la reforma agraria en Chile." *Panorama económico* 14 (septiembre 1960): 269-71, 278.

Sternberg, Marvin. "Distribución de los ingresos en la agricultura chilena." *Panorama económico* 15 (diciembre 1961): 324-28.

Sunkel, Osvaldo. "Cambios estructurales, estrategias de desarrollo y planificación en Chile 1938-1969." *Cuadernos de la realidad nacional* 4 (junio 1970): 31-49.

Trellez, Amarildo. "En los caminos de la reforma agraria." *Política y espíritu* 21 (octubre 1966): 79-87.

Urzuá, Raúl. "Poder, autoridad y reforma agraria." *Cuaderno de sociología* No. 1 (1969).

Varela Carmona, Helio. "Distribución del ingreso nacional en Chile a través de las diversas clases sociales." *Panorama económico* 199 (febrero 1959): 61-70.

Vargas, Manuel. "Reforma agraria y lucha por el agua." *Principios* 27 (mayo-junio 1966): 102-9.

Vuscovic, Pedro. "Distribución del ingreso y opciones de desarrollo." *Cuadernos de la realidad nacional* 5 (septiembre 1970): 41-60.

Zeitlin, Maurice. "Determinantes sociales de la democracia política en Chile." *Revista Latinoamericana de sociología* 2 (julio 1966): 223-36.

Zemelman, Hugo. "Factores determinantes en el surgimiento de una clase campesina." *Cuadernos de la realidad nacional* 7 (marzo 1971): 84-115.

INDEX

Acción Católica Rural. *See* ACR
Acción Sindical Chilena. *See*
ASICH
ACR (Acción Católica Rural), 180
Acuña, Carlos, 120, 156, 163
Afuerinos: Popular Unity agrarian
policy, 284, 288; rural labor
conflicts, 191
Agrarian Labor party, 182, 207,
211, 219
Agrarian question, xxv, 3, 187,
220: Alliance for Progress, 220,
225
Agrarian reform: definition of,
xxix, xxxiii
Agrarian tribunals, 269-70
Agricultural cooperatives: CORA,
233-34
Agricultural credit, 51: Banco del
Estado, 227; CORFO, 227;
nationalized by Popular Unity,
284
Agricultural prices: urban labor,
202-203
Agriculture: government economic
policy, 110-11; low productivity of, 197-98; modernization of, 57-58; national economy, 304; reformed sector
(1973), 317-19
Aguirre Cerda, Pedro, 120, 122,
124, 223: Liga Nacional de Defensa de Campesinos Pobres,
158; as minister of interior, 136;
rural legislation of, 124; rural
policy of, 162, 169; suspension
of rural unionization, 118-19;
veto of anticommunist legislation, 217
Ahumado Trigo, Juan, 172, 183-
86, 189, 217-18, 365n

Alessandri, Arturo, 61, 115, 138,
144: rural policy of, 135-36;
SNA, 135-36; suspension of
rural unionization, 115
Alessandri, Jorge, 131, 187: land
reform program of, 235-39, 253;
Law 15.020, 223, 225-26; rural
policy of, 231-32
Allende, Salvador: election of 1958
(FRAP), 187; government of,
chapter 9 *passim*; as minister of
health, 174, 215, 252
Alliance for Progress: agrarian
question, 220, 225
Amigables componedores, 42
ANOC (Asociación Nacional de
Organizaciones Campesinos),
328: denied recognition by
CUT, 181-82; formation of,
181; mobilization of rural labor,
257; rural unionization, 263;
training programs of, 182
Anticipos: in asentamientos, 254
Apadrinamiento, 184
Araya Zuleta, Bernardo, 217
Arrancibia, Juan, 131
Asentamientos, 234, 243, 289-90,
306: anticipos, 254; conservative critiques of, 274; CORA,
271-72; dependence upon
CORA of, 255-56; described,
252; economic performance of,
272-75; evolution of, 252-56;
Law 16.640, 270; leftist critiques of, 274-75; Marxist criticism of, 256; military government (1973), 314; Popular
Unity government, 283-84,
288-91, 299-300, 314; production problems of, 299-300
ASICH (Acción Sindical Chilena),

425

thority, 206, 213; CEFA, 247-
50; congressional veto power of,
202-205, 220; electoral reform,
219; employers' unions, 261-62;
FOCH, 138, 140; IER, 180-81;
Labor Department, 326-27; manipulation of rural elections,
202, 203-204; nitrate workers,
191-92; obligations to rural labor of, 311-12; obligations under Law 16.625, 260-61; pressures on (1964-1967), 258; reaction to Law 15.020, 239; resistance to ASICH, 176-80; resistance to labor inspectors, 103-
105; resistance to labor legislation by, 105-12, 245-46, chapter
3 *passim*; resistance to land occupations by, 281; resistance to
rural education, 193-94; resistance to rural unions, 112, 137-
40, 141-44, 164-69, 173, 185,
203-204; social security taxes,
111; subdivision of rural property, 250. *See also* Hacendados;
Hacienda system; Proprietary
authority
Land reform, xxviii: Catholic church,
198-200; costs of (1964-1970),
313; definition of, xxix-xxxiii
Land reform agencies, 300: Consejo Nacional Campesino, 287;
labor conflicts, 257; Labor Department, 257; lack of campesino participation in, 299; Law
15.020, 232-35; paternalism of,
298; personnel of, 235-36, 325-
26; Popular Unity government,
328. *See also* CONSFA; CORA;
INDAP
Land reform legislation, 223-25:
Catholic political groups, 199-
200; colonization, 224; Labor
Department enforcement of,
311; landowner veto power,
202-203; Law 4.174, 27; proprietary authority, 307; Radical

party, 220; rationale for, 223;
summary of, 307-34. *See also*
Law 4.496; Law 5.604; Law
7.747; Law 15.020; Law 16.640
La Prensa, 293
Larraín, Bishop Manuel, 199, 223
Larson, Oscar, 175-76
Law 4.053 (Law of Labor Con-
tracts), 42, 56, 113
Law 4.054 (Social Security Law),
44, 45: Caja de Seguro Obliga-
torio, 86-87
Law 4.057, 113
Law 4.174: described, 27
Law 4.496, 28: creation of Caja de
Colonización Agrícola by, 224
Law 5.558: Liga Nacional de Defensa de Campesinos Pobres,
154-56
Law 5.604, 224
Law 6.290, 157
Law 7.747, 78, 224
Law 8.811 (Campesino Unionization Law), 131, 177, 183, 185,
230, 257: effect on labor petitions of, 126-31; enforcement
of, 93; Labor Code, 124-28;
provisions of, 124-28; replaced
by Law 16.625, 259; rural
unions, 173; strikes outlawed
by, 126-28
Law 8.837, 128, 131
Law 8.987 (Law for the Permanent Defense of Democracy),
174, 178, 209: repealed by Ibáñez, 219; repression of Communist party, 128-29, 185-86; repression of rural unions, 128-31,
173
Law 15.020, 220, 251: application
under Christian Democrats, 250-
56; assessment of regalías, 230;
campesino family allowances,
230; CONSFA, 232-33; CORA,
233-34; and definition of rural
property, 226; expropriation of
rural land, 227-30, 252; imple-

BRIAN LOVEMAN is the author of numerous articles on Latin American politics and development. In 1975, he was a Research Consultant for the International Development Research Center and the Department of Agriculture. Since 1973 he has been Assistant Professor of Political Science at California State University, San Diego.

Struggle in the Countryside

DESIGNED BY CLANCEY MALONEY
COMPOSED BY THE INTERNATIONAL DEVELOPMENT
RESEARCH CENTER IN COLD TYPE BASKERVILLE
WITH DISPLAY LINES IN PALATINO